William

C0-AOE-182

October, 1953

RARE MASTERPIECES
OF PHILOSOPHY AND SCIENCE
EDITED BY DR. W. STARK

ARISTOTLE'S

DE ANIMA

IN THE VERSION OF WILLIAM OF MOERBEKE

AND THE COMMENTARY OF

ST. THOMAS AQUINAS

ARISTOTLE'S
DE ANIMA

IN THE VERSION
OF WILLIAM OF MOERBEKE
AND
THE COMMENTARY
OF
ST. THOMAS AQUINAS

TRANSLATED
BY KENELM FOSTER, O.P., M.A.
AND SILVESTER HUMPHRIES, O.P., M.A.
WITH AN INTRODUCTION
BY IVO THOMAS, O.P., M.A.

ROUTLEDGE AND KEGAN PAUL LTD

*This edition first published in 1951
by Routledge & Kegan Paul Limited
68–74 Carter Lane London E.C.4*

*Printed in Great Britain
by Butler & Tanner Limited
Frome and London*

Typography by Seán Jennett

CUM PERMISSU SUPERIORUM ORDINIS

B
415
.A5
F6
1951

TRANSLATORS' NOTE

Our intention, at first, was to translate only St. Thomas's Commentary on the *ΠΕΡΙ ΨΥΧΗΣ* of Aristotle, though it was obvious from the beginning that the Commentary, being a step-by-step exposition of its text, would demand a continual reference to the latter. And clearly it would only make difficulties if we were to print, along with the Commentary, a modern translation of the Greek text known to St. Thomas in the contemporary Latin version of his fellow Dominican, William of Moerbeke. Eventually therefore it seemed best to put this version itself into English, dividing its three books according to the *lectiones* of the Commentary, and the latter into the conveniently numbered paragraphs of Pirotta's edition (*Sancti Thomae Aquinatis in Aristotelis Librum de Anima Commentarium*, cura ac studio Angeli M. Pirotta, O.P., S.T.L., Ph.D.; Turin, 1925).

The text, both of version and Commentary, printed by Pirotta, is also in the main the one translated. But Pirotta's is not a critical edition, and we have occasionally altered his text: where this is done a footnote mentions, and sometimes justifies, the alteration.

Without aiming, in the notes, at an exhaustive discussion of textual difficulties, we have not overlooked them. We have tried to help, if not always entirely to satisfy, the curious reader; noting for instance (with a translation in inverted commas of Aristotle's text) whenever Moerbeke seems to depart from the Greek text as we have it now. Throughout the Commentary Bekker references are given for all quotations from Aristotle.

Square brackets [ ] in the translation of Moerbeke's version indicate an addition by the translator for the sake of clarity, where such addition is more than merely grammatical, e.g. a noun added to the adjective which presupposes it.

The version has been rendered more literally than the Commentary. The latter could, it seemed, be made congenial to the modern reader only by dint of much excision and compression; in particular we have abbreviated those minutely analytical divisions with which St. Thomas introduces each of his *lectiones* and sometimes also a portion of a *lectio*. We have tried to avoid latinisms. Whether our effort to be readable has cost us anything in point of accuracy is for the experts to decide.

Our thanks are due to the Very Rev. Dr. D. Callus, O.P., for his help with textual difficulties; and, for help with the translation, to many other fellow-Dominicans, in particular to Frs. Drostan Maclaren, Sebastian Bullough, John Dominic Cheales, Columba Ryan and Henri de Riedmatten.

K. F.
S. H.

CONTENTS

BOOK ONE

CONTENTS

BOOK TWO

CONTENTS

CONTENTS

BOOK THREE

CONTENTS

II

CONTENTS

INTRODUCTION

I. GENERAL CHARACTER OF THE COMMENTARY

THE procedure adopted in this Commentary is apt to be a puzzling one for the modern reader. In the works of Aristotle himself, however difficult or unfamiliar his concepts and cast of thought may seem, we are always aware of a spirit of inquiry. Sometimes he cuts short his investigations at a point which may nowadays seem extremely naïve and elementary; sometimes his conclusions raise new problems; sometimes they mark a permanent advance in understanding; but the approach is always predominantly inductive. In the *de Anima* as elsewhere he discusses his method of procedure, examines opinions advanced by previous thinkers, and, in feeling his way forward by very gradual stages, does not hesitate to state his difficulties and uncertainties. When we turn to St. Thomas's Commentary, we are aware of a great difference of approach. In the first place the run of Aristotle's text, jerky, pithy, even haphazard in appearance, is expounded as a minutely linked sequence of thought. Each *lectio* begins by shewing the place within the whole work of the passage immediately under consideration; this passage is then logically divided and subdivided down to its atomic phrases. Only after this formal analysis of the text has been made does the commentator go on to explain the material embodied in it.

Furthermore, in the subsequent material exposition, the body of the Commentary, we find a far more authoritative tone than in the original. A definite body of doctrine is being inculcated, presented in a predominantly deductive form. There are several points to be noticed about this procedure.

(1) It cannot be too clearly emphasised that the Commentary is only what it calls itself, an exposition of a text. It is that even before being an exposition of what is said in the text; that perhaps more

than an exhaustive assertion of what in detail the commentator held to be the truth.

(2) Medieval Aristotelians considered that in the works of Aristotle his ideal of science, as developed in the Posterior Analytics, was in a fair way to being attained. It is by no means clear that Aristotle would have agreed with them. He modestly calls his *de Anima* an ἱστορία just as he calls his Nicomachean Ethics a μέθοδος; an 'inquiry' in both cases.[1] In his inquiries, so close in spirit to those of Socrates and Plato for all the differences in style, the medievals found a fully planned and largely developed scientific system, based on copious experiential data, harmonising these under indemonstrable self-evident principles of reason by means of achieved definitions and deductive chains of argument. It is evident that Aristotelianism had by then emerged from the chrysalis of Aristotle. The scholastics were the heirs to a tradition.

(3) Nevertheless, the concept of authority, the prestige of an *Auctor* regarded as classical, did hold for the medievals a value which moderns find it hard to grasp. *Auctores*, e.g. the Bible and the Fathers of the Church in theology, Priscian in Grammar, Aristotle in the faculty of Arts, were considered so deserving of respect that they were never rejected, but only 'interpreted' where not consistent with truth. With the exception of the Bible, however, they were not deemed infallible—there would then have been no place for such interpretation—and St. Thomas is clear that authority as a *locus* or *sedes argumenti*, while most proper to theology which is based on revealed principles, yet holds the lowest place in philosophy.[2] The very close adherence to the text in such a philosophical commentary as the one before us must therefore be explained on the analogy of a modern edition with notes, rather than by means of an *a priori* judgment about the medieval attitude to Aristotle.

(4) A strongly synthetic speculative tendency is undoubtedly shewn in the demonstrative form in which the exposition is cast. There was a common 'medieval practice of throwing merely probable arguments into strictly demonstrative form', and while in many places in his works St. Thomas clearly marks the considered status of his arguments by such phrases as *Ad huius evidentiam* or

---

[1] *de Anima*, 402ᵃ 4; *Nic. Eth.*, 1094ᵃ 1.   [2] *Summa Theol.*, I., 1, 8 ad 2.

magis videtur verum, there are others which commentators have generally agreed to qualify as probable, though the author gives no explicit guidance.[1]

We should, then, read the Commentary as an exposition of an inquiry composed within a living tradition still vitally active in speculation. The advantages which a commentator, working thus in communion with the author of his text, has over even the most scholarly annotator for whom the text is a piece of dead history, are very great. Marcel de Corte[2] has repeated occasion to notice the superior sureness of St. Thomas's interpretation over that of many more recent commentators, and where this is verified it must be in part ascribed to this cause.

II. DATE OF THE COMMENTARY

The version of the text of Aristotle upon which the Commentary is based, and which is here given an English rendering, is that of William of Moerbeke (1215–86).[3] A Dominican like St. Thomas, he translated many works of Greek philosophy at the latter's instigation and was thus a genuine collaborator of the Saint. His method was that of a word for word translation, in general so closely following the original that there is usually little difficulty in seeing what was the state of the text upon which he worked. As regards the *de Anima*, a Latin version had been made in the twelfth century, but in this, as in many similar cases, William set out to better his predecessor, as in the fifteenth century, Leonardo Bruni of Arezzo[4] would endeavour to improve on *him*. As we shall see, the dating of the Commentary is linked with that of the work of the translator.

Two recent studies do much to supersede all earlier investigations into the date when the Commentary was composed. These

---

[1] Cf. P. Rousselot, S.J., *The Intellectualism of St. Thomas* (London, 1935), pp. 11 and 151 n. 9; J. Collins, *The Thomistic Philosophy of the Angels* (Washington, D.C., 1947), pp. 38 ff.

[2] Marcel de Corte, *La Doctrine de l'Intelligence chez Aristote* (Paris, 1934).

[3] Cf. M. Grabmann, *Guglielmo di Moerbeke, O.P., Il Traduttore delle Opere di Aristotele* (Rome, 1946).

[4] E. Gilson, *La Philosophie au Moyen Age* (2nd edn., Paris, 1944), p. 736.

are G. Verbeke's *Les Sources et la Chronologie du Commentaire de S. Thomas au de Anima d'Aristote* in the *Revue Philosophique de Louvain*, LV (1947), pp. 214–348, and A. Mansion's *Date de Quelques Commentaires de saint Thomas sur Aristote* in *Studia Mediaevalia in honorem A. R. P. R. J. Martin, O.P.* (Bruges, 1948). The latter summarises all the attempts at dating the Commentary up to and including Verbeke's work.

The two standard methods of teaching in the medieval university were the *lectio* and the *disputatio*. In the *lectio* a text from the author under consideration was read and expounded; in the *disputatio* a thesis was proposed and debated. It is an example of a series of *lectiones* that we have in St. Thomas's Commentary on the *de Anima* of Aristotle, his *Quaestiones Disputatae de Anima* representing the alternative method. The earliest catalogue of the Saint's works, which P. Mandonnet calls the 'Official Catalogue', records that only the last two books present St. Thomas's own text, the first being a *reportatio* by his companion Reginald of Piperno.[1] Reginald was the recipient of the dedication of several of the *Opuscula* of St. Thomas, inherited his manuscripts, and succeeded him in the chair of Theology at Naples when he died. Mandonnet considers that the Official Catalogue was Reginald's own compilation.

It has been questioned whether the *reportatio* and the remainder of the Commentary belong to the same series of lectures. In 1933 M. de Corte[2] showed that in writing the first book of the Commentary St. Thomas evidently had before him Themistius' paraphrase of the text, probably as translated by William of Moerbeke. Still, he did not, it seemed, use Themistius in writing the last two books: hence it appeared that the first book belonged to a later series of lectures. But this opinion is no longer tenable, and the work in this field which either preceded it or depended upon it, though by no means without methodological interest, is in great part irrelevant. For in 1942 there was published by M. J. M. Millás Vallicrosa a catalogue of manuscripts in the library of Toledo Cathedral, including one of the fourteenth century in which is found *Themistii paraphrasis eorum que de anima Aristotelis*. This para-

---

[1] P. Mandonnet, O.P., *Des Ecrits Authentiques de S. Thomas d'Aquin* (Fribourg, 1910), pp. 18 ff.

[2] M. de Corte, *Themistius et S. Thomas d'Aquin* (Paris, 1932).

phrase closes with the words: *Expleta fuit translatio huius operis anno Domini MCCLXVII decimo Klas decembris Viterbii; fuit autem Themistius tempore Juliani Apostate apud eum plurimum honoratus.* The translation is in the manner of William of Moerbeke who is moreover known to have been at work in Viterbo in 1267-8. On the basis of this work G. Verbeke[1] has detected that the second and third books of the Commentary do after all show evidences of reference to Themistius, not so explicit and numerous indeed as those of the first book, but none the less unmistakable. There is therefore no longer any ground for supposing the work as we have it to be in reality a conflation of two works. And the date on which Moerbeke is said to have finished his translation of the paraphrase—22nd November 1267—gives us a point before which the Commentary could not have been written. Further, the work is known to have been completed before St. Thomas left Paris in 1272. Is it possible to bring in any further precision? Here the work of F. Pelster, S.J., is important.[2] He notes that in this work St. Thomas refers to the books of Aristotle's *Metaphysics* according to the method of numeration which omits *K* and so allows for only twelve books. The *Nova Translatio* of the *Metaphysics* by William of Moerbeke, being the first to include Book *K*, abandoned that method, and St. Thomas began to refer to the last book but one as '*XII*' about 1271-2, viz. between writing the *Prima Secundae* and *Secunda Secundae* of the *Summa Theologica*. Another indication may be gathered from § 695: *Sunt autem plura alia quae contra hanc positionem dici possunt; quae alibi diligentius pertractavimus.* The reference is on the one hand to the Averroist assignation of a unique *intellectus possibilis* to all men, and on the other to some work of St. Thomas which it might be possible to identify and date with certainty. The candidates are the *Summa Contra Gentiles*, where this question is dealt with at length, in Bk. II, cc.59 ff., and the *Opusculum De Unitate Intellectus contra Averroistas.* The former was composed between 1258 and 1264; the latter would seem to be not later than 10th December 1270, the date of the Averroist condemnation at Paris. That St. Thomas was referring to the *Contra Gentiles* is a clear

---

[1] *loc. cit.*

[2] F. Pelster, S.J., *Die Uebersetzungen der aristotelischen Metaphysik in den Werken des hl. Thomas von Aquin* (Gregorianum XVII, 1936).

possibility; is there anything in favour of the *Opusculum*? The latter cites Themistius, but that reason for taking it to be later than the second and third books of the *de Anima* no longer has validity. Failing reasons to the contrary, the words in § 695 may therefore refer to the *Opusculum*, in that case but recently published; and since this treatment of one of the most important questions of the day would be far fresher in the memory of the auditors than the earlier *Summa contra Gentiles*, we have, on this hypothesis, a reason that goes far to account for the really surprising restraint of St. Thomas when he comes to the passages in the *de Anima* which he certainly knew to be crucial to the controversy.

Moreover, on 10th December 1270, Stephen Tempier, Bishop of Paris, published a condemnation of fifteen philosophical errors, of which the first was the Averroist thesis of the unicity of the intellect.[1] While St. Thomas's silence about this event in the *Opusculum* is, in the circumstances of the time and place (the Bishop's See), the strongest indication that it had not yet taken place, we may also think that, once the condemnation had been made, there would not have been much urgency to deal with the subject in a work which was primarily expository, especially if the strictly polemical *Opusculum* had only recently appeared. We may therefore conclude that there is considerable probability in favour of dating the Commentary as late as 1271.

III. THE AVERROIST ISSUE

We have already referred to the Averroist interpretation of the *de Anima* and the slight explicit attention which St. Thomas pays to it in this Commentary. Without some knowledge of the elements of the question, and of St. Thomas's attitude towards it, the importance in history of this aspect of his work would be very incompletely understood.

Speaking of the 'agent intellect' in 430ª 17 Aristotle says that it is (in Moerbeke's words) *separabilis et impassibilis et immixtus*. That the ontological status, whether in truth or in Aristotle's theory, of

---

[1] For the background of this condemnation see P. Mandonnet, O.P., *Siger de Brabant et l'Averroisme Latin au XIIIᵉ Siècle* (Louvain, 1911), and F. van Steenberghen, *Siger de Brabant d'après ses Oeuvres Inédites*, II, pp. 704 ff. (Louvain, 1942).

the intellect so described is by no means generally agreed on by modern commentators will be evident to anyone who consults, for example, the introduction and notes of R. D. Hicks,[1] or J. Maritain's appendix on the subject in *La Philosophie Bergsonienne*.[2] The word translated *separabilis* is χωριστός, which might also be translated 'separate'; and the sense in which it is to be taken, whether in truth or simply in Aristotle, is the kernel of one of the most long-standing disputes in the history of philosophy.[3]

In earlier times Alexander of Aphrodisias (c. A.D. 200) interpreted χωριστός as 'separate' and identified the agent intellect with God. Among the Arabs Ibn Sina (Avicenna, 980–1037) considered it to be unique for all men and the lowest of the series of intelligences emanating from God. Ibn Roschd (Averroes, 1126–98) held a similar view, with an addition which the scholastics understood as the affirmation of a unique 'possible' intellect as well as a unique 'agent intellect' for all men. This way of understanding the Arabian philosopher provided common terminological ground between St. Thomas and his Averroist opponents; but it is liable to mislead us nowadays into thinking that a *second* 'separated substance' is in dispute. This is not correct. Averroes posited on the one side the separated agent intellect, on the other a 'passive intellect' in each individual. This last is an aptitude to receive the influence of the agent intellect, and, being perishable, is not properly an intellect at all. From the conjunction of the two arises a potency of knowledge called the 'material' intellect, incorporeal indeed, but rather the uniform influence of the agent intellect than a power belonging to each individual. It is this 'material' intellect which the scholastics discuss under the name of the 'possible intellect'.[4]

The Averroists followed their master in identifying philosophic truth with what Aristotle had said on any subject; thus providing what is perhaps the only authentic justification for the oft-repeated charge that the Middle Ages were completely dominated by Aristotle. Opinions may always be divided as to which side had the right of the matter in Aristotelianism. St. Thomas, indeed, was

[1] *Aristotle, de Anima* (Cambridge, 1907).
[2] 3rd edn. (Paris, 1948), Gloses sur Aristote, pp. 331 ff.
[3] Cf. D. J. B. Hawkins, *A Sketch of Medieval Philosophy* (London, 1946), p. 51.
[4] Cf. E. Gilson, *loc. cit.*, p. 366.

convinced that the Averroists were misinterpreting their source; but this was for him only an *argumentum ad hominem*. In the *De Caelo et Mundo* (Bk. I, lectio 22) he says: *Studium philosophiae non est ad hoc quod sciatur quid homines senserint, sed qualiter se habeat veritas rerum*: 'the purpose of philosophy is not to know what men have thought, but what is the truth of things'. His aim was to confute the Averroists on philosophical grounds; since no claim was made that their doctrine of the unity of the intellect was in accord with Christian teaching. (It is obvious enough of course that if the only incorruptible and immortal part of the soul is not part of the soul at all, but one and the same for all men, then there is no possibility of personal immortality or of individuals receiving in an after-life the rewards and punishments which are their due.) So in the *De Unitate Intellectus* he says: 'We mean to shew that the aforesaid position is no less contrary to philosophical principles than to the teachings of Faith.' Moreover, 'because some are not content with what the Latins say about this matter, but proclaim themselves followers of the Peripatetics, none of whose books on the subject they have ever seen except those of Aristotle who founded the Peripatetic school, we shall shew the aforesaid position to be altogether at variance with his [Aristotle's] words and his thought'. The exegesis which then follows in the *Opusculum* is so indispensable a complement to the Commentary on the *de Anima* that we proceed to trace its development in full.[1]

Beginning with the definition of the soul in *de Anima* II, as the 'first actuality of an organic physical body' St. Thomas insists that this is intended by Aristotle to apply to all souls whatsoever. The subsequent passage (412^b 10) is adduced in proof: 'It has been said universally what the soul is, etc.' Nor is the intellective part excluded, for 'From this it indubitably follows that the soul is inseparable from its body, or at any rate that certain parts of it are (if it has parts), for the actuality of some of them is nothing but the actuality of their bodily parts. Yet some may be separable, not being the actualities of any body at all' (413^a 3-9), i.e. the intellectual parts are not organic powers, but are nevertheless allowed to be parts of the soul. This passage introduces the crucial word

---

[1] S. *Thomae Aquinatis Opuscula Omnia*, I, ed. P. Mandonnet, O.P. (Paris, 1927).

χωριστός. The whole dispute may be summed up in the question: In what sense is the soul or any part of it separable from the body? St. Thomas's full conclusion is that the intellectual soul *can* exist without the body, retaining its sense powers only radically; that in its state of union with the body, it is the latter's substantial form; and that whereas the sense powers actually 'inform' their organs, the intellectual powers 'inform' no corresponding material part. Whatever Aristotle's opinion, he certainly reaches no conclusion that is so precisely stateable; and in the *Opusculum* St. Thomas is only concerned to show that the Philosopher held the intellectual powers to be genuinely parts of the soul. So he continues by emphasising the universal applicability of the definition of soul. Aristotle, seeking to determine more clearly whether the soul is the form of the body or merely its 'motor', examines the activities of living things and enumerates 'thinking or perception or local movement and rest, or movement in the sense of nutrition, decay and growth'. Some of these can exist without the others but, whatever the explanation of that, 'the soul is the source of these phenomena and is characterised by them, namely by the powers of self-nutrition, sensation, thinking and motivity' (413^b 13).

Aristotle's next question, 'Is each of these a soul or a part of a soul?', St. Thomas assigns to his wishing to consider Plato's view that different vital operations pertain to different souls in the living thing. Aristotle goes on: 'In the case of certain of these powers, the answers to these questions are easy, in the case of others we are puzzled what to say', viz. 'we have no evidence as yet about mind or the power to think' (413^b 15). These statements, says St. Thomas, refer to the questions asked, and mean that it is not clear whether the intellect is soul, or part of soul, and, if the latter, whether 'merely distinguishable by definition or a part distinct in local situation as well'. Averroes and his followers 'perversely expound' the statements as though they indicated that Aristotle wished to shew that the intellect is not part of soul. 'It seems to be a different kind of soul,' says Aristotle (413^b 25), thus occasioning another 'perverse exposition' from the Averroists—as though a 'soul' could only be called intellectual equivocally, or the definition could not be adapted to a soul of this sort, i.e. an intellectual one.

Aristotle continues: 'It seems to be a widely different kind of soul, differing as what is eternal from what is perishable'; and so 'it alone is capable of existence in isolation from all other psychic powers'. This last translation[1] goes, however, beyond the text, and in St. Thomas's sense. The Averroists said 'in isolation from the body', but that, as St. Thomas points out, is not under discussion. The immediate question for Aristotle is whether the various powers are distinct from the soul and each other, and in what way. St. Thomas summarises the passage thus: 'It was asked above whether one part of the soul is separated from another in concept only or in place. Here he leaves the question so far as intellect is concerned, and comes to no conclusion about that; but of the other parts of the soul he says that they are evidently not separable, viz. in place, though they differ in concept. Having then established that soul is vegetative, sensitive, intellective and motive, he wants to shew that the soul with all these parts is united to the body, not as a sailor to a ship, but as form to matter. And so the general definition of soul, outlined above, will have been confirmed.'

This confirmation follows when it is said that the soul is 'the primary principle', not only of our living, sensing and moving, but also of our understanding; and concludes with the statement that 'it follows that the soul must be a *ratio* or formulable essence, not matter or subject' (414^a 14)—the process of argument clearly implying that the intellective soul, as well as other forms of soul, is envisaged throughout.

St. Thomas's review of the second Book concludes with the argument that when Aristotle speaks of the intellective part or power of soul (*intellectivum*) he means intellect itself (*intellectus*); for in explaining his division of the powers of the soul he says: 'still another order of animate beings, viz. man . . . (possesses) the power of thinking, i.e. mind' (414^b 19). That the two are the same, and also that the definition of soul covers all the aforesaid 'parts' of it, Aristotle makes still clearer with the following: 'It is now evident that a single definition can be given of soul only in the same sense as one can be given of figure. For, as in that case there is no figure distinguishable and apart from triangle etc., so here there is no soul apart from the forms of soul just enumerated' (414^b 22ss).

With a reference to the second Book's final statement on the intellect—'Lastly, certain living beings, a small minority, possess calculation and thought'—St. Thomas ends his consideration of the

[1] Oxford transl. of the Works of Aristotle, Vol. III.

matter so far as this part of the *de Anima* is concerned. We would
point out the thoroughness of his examination and the minutely
consequential treatment of the text, the same style of treatment,
in fact, as we have noted in the Commentary. The method will
perhaps be sought in vain in any modern commentary, though it is
particularly needed and helpful in reading so disjointed a style as
Aristotle's. St. Thomas's interest in the matter appears in his brief
digression at this point, remarkable in so purposeful a work as the
Opusculum, on 'the wonderful order and carefulness of Aristotle's
treatment'. In particular he refers to the fact that the philosopher
begins his third Book with just those questions on the intellect
which had been left undecided in the second.

At the close of Book II, 3, Aristotle reserves his detailed treatment of the speculative intellect to a later stage. This comes in III,
4–8. The phrase of reservation is (415ᵃ 11): 'περὶ δὲ τοῦ θεωρητικοῦ
νοῦ ἕτερος λόγος'—'but we reserve discussion about the speculative
intellect'. Now Averroes took this as excluding intellect from psy-
chological treatment, perhaps understanding 'λόγος', *ratio*, in the
sense of 'definition'. That, in St. Thomas's view, is another 'perverse exposition'; as though intellect was 'neither soul nor part of
soul'. But the subject is clearly being postponed, and is resumed
with the words (429ᵃ 10), 'Turning now to the part of the soul
with which the soul knows and thinks', another point against the
Averroist interpretation. St. Thomas continues, 'Nor ought we to
say that this refers to the distinction between the possible and agent
intellects, as some people imagine (*sicut aliqui somniant*)'. For that
distinction had not yet been put forward.

So far two questions about intellect have been left unsolved.
The first is whether it is separated from the other parts of the soul
by definition only or also spatially. This doubt is resumed at the
opening of III, 4, but Aristotle at once proceeds to examine the
altera ratio with mention of which he had closed the discussion of
intellect in Book II,—the question, namely, of the nature of the
latter's difference from 'the other parts': 'we have to enquire what
differentiates this part.' He intends therefore, says St. Thomas, to
assign a difference compatible with either alternative of the preceding doubt. Hence it is clear that he does not mean to assign as
a difference that intellect is a separate substance from the body, for
this would not be compatible with both alternatives; but that it

differs in its mode of operation; which is why, continues St. Thomas, Aristotle adds 'and how thinking can take place'. 'So then', he concludes, 'from what we have been able to gather from Aristotle's words up to now, it is clear that he meant the intellect to be a part of that soul which is the actuality of a physical body.'

IV. ARISTOTLE'S METHOD IN DEFINITION

The importance of the establishment of the definition of soul at the opening of the second Book will be readily appreciated when we recall the Aristotelian ideal of scientific knowledge. Moreover the difficulties that in principle surround the establishment of definitions give this passage value as a typical example worked out in a detailed way. St. Thomas's analysis of the passage is an exquisite piece of ordered exposition. For all these reasons we offer some comments on it.

At the opening of the *Posterior Analytics* Aristotle asserts that 'All instruction given or received by way of argument proceeds from pre-existent knowledge' (71^a). This pre-existent knowledge may be 'admission of the fact' which is being investigated, or 'comprehension of the meaning of the term used'. There is a clear instance of the latter assumption in our Commentary (§ 220): *Per animam enim intelligimus id quo habens vitam vivit.*—'By soul we understand that by which a living thing is alive.' There is a certain elementary understanding of the terms used, and so of the nature of the facts to which they are referred, which must be shared by any who will conduct an inquiry in common, or even dispute together. It is by no means clear from Aristotle's always very concise text whether he makes the other assumption or not. Certainly it takes St. Thomas's minute dissection to bring to light any suggestion that Aristotle actually argues for the *fact* of soul. This occurs in § 219, referring to 412^a 14–15, which the Latin version renders: *physicorum autem alia quidem habent vitam, alia autem non habent. Vitam autem habere dicimus id quod per seipsum alimentum et augmentum et decrementum habet.* This explanation, as St. Thomas says, is given rather by way of example than definition, but the point is that unless the distinction between living and non-living things is given in reality, it would be useless to pursue the inquiry.

In the *Posterior Analytics* Aristotle continues by analysing the

most genuinely scientific knowledge into undemonstrated knowledge of ultimate premisses and the syllogisms based on them,
which show in their middle terms the cause of their conclusions.
Of the undemonstrated premisses some will be metaphysical
truths applicable in all sciences, others will be definitions proper
to the subject-matter under consideration. Of the former class we
have several instances in this part of the Commentary, notably in
the preliminary distinctions from which the search for the soul's
definition must begin, *quasdam divisiones ex quibus habetur via ad
investigandum definitionem animae* (§ 212)—as, for instance, that
'being is divided into the ten categories' and that 'some substances
are bodies, others not'. There is also an example of a definition
proper to psychology: 'life is essentially that by which anything
has the power to move of itself' (§ 219). This definition is here undemonstrated. But the most interesting question for the epistemo-
logist or logician is to what extent such definitions are in principle
demonstrable, and how they come to be apprehended. Plato's con-
stant recurrence to this theme was of course familiar to Aristotle,
and while his own theory of syllogistic demonstration enabled him
to build a more complete and systematic picture of the various
aspects of scientific knowledge, he did not neglect an attempt to
deal with this fundamental one. The difficulties he experienced in
doing so can be seen in the second Book of the *Posterior Analytics*,
a great part of which is precisely concerned with the manner of
our acquiring definitions. At the outset comes the distinction we
have already noted between questions of fact—i.e. of existence,
and of nature—i.e. of definition. The former must be answered
affirmatively before the latter can be significantly asked; if we do
not think there is such a thing as soul, we cannot ask what soul is.
The soul can only be defined if it exists in some appropriate sense.
What that appropriate sense is, has considerable relevance to the
case in question. It is of course no individual soul that is being defined—only universals are susceptible of definition—but it would
be a mistake to read the Commentary with some specific kind of
soul predominantly in mind. As Marcel de Corte says:[1] 'From the
outset of the *de Anima* he [Aristotle] carefully points out that the
human soul is not the basis of his study, and that the explanation at

[1] *L'Intelligence etc.*, p. 25.

which he aims is to include in a general way every kind of soul' (cf. *de Anima*, 402^b 3). As the same writer remarks, the exclusively analogical standpoint is adopted by Aristotle for this purpose. There is no univocal genus, soul, for intellective, sensitive non-intellective, vegetative non-sensitive souls. We are prepared for this attitude by the important passage, 402^b 1 ff: 'We must also consider whether soul is divisible or not, and whether all souls are specifically the same or not; and in the latter case, whether it is in species that they differ or merely in genus. For the current statements and inquiries about soul seem to bear only on the human soul. Again, we must be careful not to pass over the question whether soul has, like "animal", only one definition, or a different one for each kind of soul, e.g., that of horse or dog or man or god. Now "animal" as a universal is either nothing at all or posterior; and the same is true of every general predicate.' The sense of this passage from the first Book, which dominates the opening proceedings of the second, has not been better given than by Alexander of Aphrodisias.[1] 'Aristotle means to say that if horse, dog, man and god were not of the same genus, each of them would have its own definition, in which case the term "animal" which is affirmed of them all in common would either signify no particular nature and be a mere homonym, or, if significant, would be so in the way that terms with different meanings are applicable to things subordinated one to another as prior and posterior. For the term universally affirmed of things of this kind doubtless designates a certain nature, but one which is not the same in each of its possessors. That is why it is "posterior" to them. What is affirmed of a number of subjects as a genus cannot be suppressed without at the same time suppressing all the subsumed subjects, but not conversely. And therefore the genus is naturally prior. But a common predication made of things related as prior and posterior disappears if the first of the subjects is suppressed, and hence it is not previous to but consequent on them. Now Aristotle shows that the soul is a form of this kind.' Soul in fact is diversely realised in plants, brutes and men; what in plants is a vegetative soul, in brutes is a vegetative-sensitive one, and in men a vegetative-sensitive-intellective

---

[1] Ἀπορίαι καὶ Λύσεις, I, XI^a, 22, 23–26, 20. Cited by G. Rodier, *Aristote, Traité de l'Ame*, II (Paris, 1901).

one. In each higher nature the defining characteristic of the lower soul is present, but subordinated to the defining characteristic of its own soul. Suppress plants, there will still be animate bodies; brutes and men are species of animate body. But suppress vegetative soul, there will be no souls; the three kinds of soul are not species of a common genus. They are all called 'soul' because of an analogy of function, diversely effected in the various cases. Hence, since a definition is properly constructed by assigning specific differences to a genus, soul, in general, cannot, strictly speaking, be defined. That is not to say that a formula cannot be devised which will be accurately descriptive of the common, but not univocal, nature which is diversely realised in different types of soul.[1] And it is such a formula for which Aristotle searches, and by methods which do not differ in principle from those governing the quest of definitions in the strict sense.

St. Thomas signalises three stages in the process: *investigatio, manifestatio, demonstratio. Investigatio*, 'tracking down', is referred to in §§ 212, 214, 217, 220, and consonant with the metaphor is *venatio (venatur)* in §§ 227 and 230. This use of the metaphor goes back to Plato who frequently speaks of the definitions, of which his characters are in search, as an elusive prey. The image is sometimes momentary, sometimes developed with considerable circumstance, as in *Republic* 432[b] ff. where the disputants surround a thicket where Justice has hidden and offer prayer to the gods before launching their attack.[2] Aristotle, who uses the metaphor less frequently, does so once where just this matter of finding the elements of definitions is under discussion (*Anal. Post.*, 96[a] 22). A dialectical rather than a demonstrative process is clearly suggested, and in the *de Anima* we find the *investigatio* preceded by certain divisions or distinctions such as it was one function of the Platonic dialectic to bring to light: *Praemittit quasdam divisiones, ex quibus habetur via ad investigandum definitionem animae* (§ 212, cf. *supra*). The gaining of definitions by means of divisions which reveal into which of their members the *definiendum* falls is recommended in *Topics*, VII, 3 ff., and the relation of this method to demonstration is considered in *An. Pr.*, I, 31, and *Anal. Post.*, II, 5, in the latter of

---

[1] Cf. G. Rodier, *loc. cit.*, notes on 402[b] 5, 414[b] 20.

[2] Cf. P. Louis, *Les Métaphores de Platon* (Paris, 1945), pp. 53 ff.

which we have: 'Division demonstrates as little as does induction. For in a genuine demonstration the conclusion must not be put as a question nor depend on a concession, but must follow necessarily from its premisses, even if the respondent deny it. The definer asks "Is man animal or inanimate?" and then assumes—he has not inferred—that man is animal.'

Though there is indeed a process of reasoning implicit in division (cf. *Topics*, *loc. cit.*), sheer insight plays the greatest part and the process does not measure up to the Aristotelian ideal of demonstration. The divisions preparatory to the definition of soul and the fundamental insights gained by their means may be tabulated in accordance with St. Thomas's minute analysis.

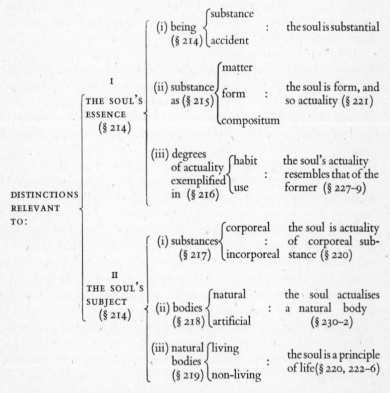

In § 233 the elements of the definition that have emerged in the light of these divisions are collected, the statement of the definition being prefaced with the hesitant: *Si aliqua definitio communis debeat assignari*—'If any general definition is to be given'. This reservation should be read in the light of what we have previously said about the possibility of defining soul. The only passage in these sections that is likely to give any real difficulty is § 222, in which the qualification of the subject assigned to the soul, that it is 'that which has life potentially', is explained. The need for that qualification and its explanation is occasioned by the difficulty of abstracting the notion of a body, which is the proper subject of soul, from the total body-soul entity. For the precise kind of body which soul informs is animated, i.e. besouled body. Yet if we posit that in the definition, we commit the logical error of defining *idem per idem*. That is the point of the maxim *Compositum non ponitur in definitione formae*. Yet it is clearly impossible to assign soul its proper subject without some reference to soul itself. The difficulty is at least partly overcome by saying that the body which is proper to be 'informed' by soul is that which is potentially alive. By saying 'potentially', the soul as in act, and therefore the *compositum*, is kept out of the definition; yet by saying 'potentially' a reference to soul is also retained, since potentiality is essentially relative to its proportionate act. The difficulty is not exclusive to this subject. S. Alexander met it in his account of the inter-relationships of space and time, and interestingly uses this very example of soul and body to explain his meaning. 'So understood, not only are they [Absolute Space and Absolute Time] useful and valid conceptions, but they are real, in the same sense as the material body of an organism can be said to be real and the life of it also real, though the life does not exist without a body of a certain sort, and the body, to be the kind of body that it is, depends on life. In other words, the reality of Space-Time may be resolved into the elements total Space and total Time, provided only it be remembered that in their combination Space is always variously occupied by Time and Time spread variously over Space.'[1] So too the reality of animated body may be resolved into the elements soul and body, provided only it be remembered that in their combination soul is the substantial form of body and body the matter organised by soul. Sections 224 and 234 are further explanatory of the relationships, as also is much

[1] S. Alexander, *Space, Time and Deity* (Gifford Lectures, London, 1920), I, pp. 82–3.

of the following *lectio* which contains the *manifestatio*, or further explanation, of the definition.

The definition given in § 233 is, says St. Thomas, '*quasi demonstrationis conclusio*' (§ 212), and in the same place he promises one which will be *quasi demonstrationis principium*. The distinction in this place belongs wholly to the Commentary. It is not till the beginning of the second chapter, 413ᵃ 11, that Aristotle, conformably with his teaching in the *Posterior Analytics*, distinguishes between definitions which are like conclusions and state bare fact, from those which state a reason for the fact; and there he does not point the application of this general teaching, so recalled, to the case in question. It is our purpose to see how far St. Thomas's ascription of a logical process to his text is justified.

To explain the distinction mentioned, the commentator takes (§ 212) an example from the *Posterior Analytics*. Thunder is supposed to be defined as a noise in the clouds caused by the extinction of fire. This definition can be embodied in a syllogism in which the material element appears as the major term, and the formal, most explanatory element as the middle term; thus:

The extinction of fire in the clouds is a noise in the clouds;
Thunder is the extinction of fire in the clouds:
Therefore, thunder is a noise in the clouds.

In the *de Anima* another instance is taken. What is squaring? By definition squaring is the finding of a mean proportional between two unequal sides of an oblong, which mean is the side of an equilateral figure equal in area to the oblong. Cast in syllogistic form this becomes:

To find a mean is to find an equilateral orthogon equal to an oblong;
Squaring is to find a mean:
Therefore, squaring is to find an equilateral orthogon equal to an oblong.

Here again the middle term gives the reason for the conclusion. If the latter is taken as a definition, it has, says Aristotle in 413ᵃ 18, the nature of a conclusion, whereas the minor premiss gives the cause of the fact.

In adducing this distinction St. Thomas therefore leads us to anticipate two definitions differing as the conclusion and minor premiss of the last stated syllogism. First we are to have one like the conclusion, then one like the premiss. Now in the first *lectio* a definition is obtained, as we have seen, by means of division, which method, we learn in the *Posterior Analytics*, is not demonstration; for it leads one to the fact only, not to the reason for the fact. We may say then that on this score the definition in § 221 has the nature of a conclusion. It is more difficult to see how the other member of the distinction is verified in the third and fourth *lectiones*, where two definitions make their appearance without St. Thomas saying that either of them is like a principle of demonstration. In § 252, however, he says that one of them, identical with that already gained in the first *lectio*, will be demonstrated, but that the demonstration, unlike that in the examples of the thunder and squaring, will be *a posteriori, ab effectu*; and therefore will not give the reason for the conclusion (cf. §§ 245–6, 253). The middle term in fact is comparable to the major term in the foregoing instances, and the major term to their middle. Instead of the more formal definition appearing in the premisses, and the more material one in the conclusion, the positions are reversed. In the syllogism,

The prime principle of life is the form of a living body;
The soul is the prime principle of life:
Therefore, the soul is the form of a living body,

the minor premiss and conclusion are both definitions (§ 271 fin.), but that in the latter is the cause and explanation of that in the former. It has accordingly the nature of a principle of demonstration, notwithstanding the fact that it here has the place of a conclusion of an (*a posteriori*) demonstration.

V. SOME DIFFICULT PASSAGES IN THE COMMENTARY

We now notice a few passages in the Commentary which may cause the reader especial difficulty.[1] The first four appear in the first Book, of which the text, as explained above, is due originally to Reginald of Piperno, not to St. Thomas.

(1) Bk. I, lectio 3 (404ᵃ 25 ff.); §§ 40–1. It is not at first sight clear

---

[1] Our thanks are due to the translator, Fr. K. Foster, O.P., for bringing these passages to our attention.

how the exposition and criticism of the view of Anaxagoras given in the Commentary can be co-ordinated with that given by Aristotle. At 404^b 1 the Latin version signalises a doubt about the position of Anaxagoras—*minus certificat de ipsis*; namely about the unity or diversity of soul and intellect. There follows a reason for our thinking that Anaxagoras did in fact identify them, and a reason for his doing so. Then at 404^b 5—*non videtur autem*—a reason is given for their not being identical, but it is not evident whether this reason is attributed to Anaxagoras or is Aristotle's objection to the identification. The form of words might favour the latter interpretation, but then the fact of Anaxagoras' doubt will not have been substantiated, and the passage precisely claims to be doing this. St. Thomas conflates the two interpretations. In § 40 he states the doubt of Anaxagoras, but also argues for his having identified soul and intellect. We may note that the argument is based on an undistributed middle term:

Anaxagoras says: 'There is soul in all animals';
Anaxagoras says: 'There is intellect in all animals';

therefore it is clear that Anaxagoras identifies soul and intellect. In § 41, corresponding to 404^b 5, the words '*non videtur autem etc.*' appear to be taken as Aristotle's, convicting his predecessor Anaxagoras of holding contradictory views. Now, as we have seen, this can only be done if 404^b 5 continues the exposition of Anaxagoras. When therefore St. Thomas says *Ostendit contrarietatem etc.* he can only mean that in stating the two views of Anaxagoras, Aristotle is implicitly declaring their contradiction; he is not attributing the second of them to Aristotle at all. It should be noted, in connection with the faulty argument embedded in § 40, that the version translates a text different from that given in the Teubner edition which scarcely gives rise to any of these difficulties. There 404^b 1-3 reads: πολλαχοῦ μὲν γὰρ τὸ αἴτιον τοῦ καλῶς καὶ ὀρθῶς τὸν νοῦν λέγει, ἑτέρωθι δὲ τοῦτον εἶναι τὴν ψυχήν which is clearly a statement of the twofold view of Anaxagoras. 404^b 5 then becomes Aristotle's own objection to the identification of soul and intellect.

(2) Bk. I, lectio 9 (407^b 30); § 133. The version has *et in iis qui in communi fiunt sermonibus*: this phrase turns the Greek accurately enough. The *sermones qui in communi fiunt*, 'public discussions', are variously interpreted as works published either by Plato or by

Aristotle or by both—since the former's *Phaedo* and the latter's *Euthedemus* both deal with this subject—and current verbal disputations. But in place of this phrase the Commentary quotes *quantum ad id quod est in communi*, indicating either a different text, or a complete misunderstanding, or perhaps a mis-reporting by Reginald.

(3) Bk. I, lectio 10 (408^b 18 ff.); § 163. The Commentary has: *Dicit ergo, quod videtur praedictis philosophis quod intellectus sit quaedam substantia, quae est in fieri et nondum completa, et quod non corrumpitur.* The version has: '*Intellectus autem videtur innasci substantia quaedam existens et non corrumpi*', and the Greek: ὁ δὲ νοῦς ἔοικεν ἐγγίνεσθαι οὐσία τις οὖσα, καὶ οὐ φθείρεσθαι. *Innasci* turns ἐγγίνεσθαι well enough; we may render the words as 'to be born in', 'to be in from birth'. There seems no good reason for the Commentator's introduction of and emphasis upon the notion of evolutionary process. The misunderstanding is the more curious when we remember that St. Thomas shows himself very familiar with a connection between *nascor* and *natura* (cf. *Summa Theol.*, III, 2, 12). The *videtur* (ἔοικεν) would in any case seem to mark the introduction of Aristotle's own views, and it is not easy to see why St. Thomas should have taken the subsequent passage as an argument *ad hominem*. Though this subject is not here in question, the opening sentence recalls the well-known passage in the *de Generatione Animalium*, 736^b ss., about the origination of intellect.

(4) Bk. I, lectio 13 (411^a 23); § 197. In interpreting the *existet* of the version by *id est, immortalis est secundum eos*, St. Thomas seems to have been over-ingenious in finding his way through a somewhat elliptical passage. *Existet* turns ὑπάρξει and there is no reference, even implicit, to immortality. We may expand the last five lines of this section of the version thus:

'If then the air that is thus divided off (so as to be the soul of a living thing) be homogeneous, but the soul be composed of heterogeneous parts, something of the soul will pertain to the air and something not. So either the soul must be composed of homogeneous parts (which it manifestly is not), or, it cannot be in any and every part of the whole (air).'

The general process of the argument of § 197 is not seriously affected by this point.

(5) Bk. II, lectio 3 (413^a 15); § 251. The term *tetragonismus* of the

version means 'squaring' not 'a square'. St. Thomas's equation of it with the latter—*id est quadratum*—makes the argument appear more difficult than it really is: the second definition—*quadratum est inventio mediae*—thus becoming perforce a genetic definition instead of the essential definition intended by Aristotle.

(6) Bk. III, lectio 10 (430ª 20–25); §§ 740–5. The text here has given rise, on various counts, to much perplexity. For reference in discussion it will be well to have before us the Greek text and Latin version:

Τὸ δ' αὐτό ἐστιν ἡ κατ' ἐνέργειαν ἐπιστήμη τῷ πράγματι · ἡ δὲ κατὰ δύναμιν χρόνῳ προτέρα ἐν τῷ ἑνί, ὅλως δ' οὐ χρόνῳ · ἀλλ' οὐχ ὁτὲ μὲν νοεῖ, ὁτὲ δ' οὐ νοεῖ. Χωρισθεὶς δ' ἐστὶ μόνον τοῦθ' ὅπερ ἐστί, καὶ τοῦτο μόνον ἀθάνατον καὶ ἀΐδιον. Οὐ μνημονεύομεν δέ ὅτι τοῦτο μὲν ἀπαθές, ὁ δὲ παθητικὸς νοῦς φθαρτός, καὶ ἄνευ τούτου οὐδὲν νοεῖ.

'Idem autem est secundum actum scientia rei; quae vero secundum potentiam, tempore prior in uno est. Omnino autem neque tempore. Sed non aliquando quidem intelligit, aliquando autem non intelligit. Separatus autem est solum hoc, quod vere est. Et hoc solum immortale et perpetuum est. Non reminiscitur autem, quia hoc quidem impassibile est; passivus vero intellectus, est corruptibilis, et sine hoc nihil intelligit anima.'

The English translation given below (p. 425) follows the version more closely than the latter follows the Greek. The main problems are (1) to find the antecedent of *intelligit* in the third sentence, (2) to find what *separatus* agrees with, and (3) to discover what Aristotle means by 'the passive intellect'.

(i) This question was already familiar to St. Thomas. The alternatives can be seen in *Summa Theologica*, I, 79, 4, obj. 2 and ad. 2m. The objection runs: 'The Philosopher (*de Anima*, III) says of the active (i.e. agent) intellect, *that it does not sometimes understand and sometimes not understand*. But our soul does not always understand: sometimes it understands, and sometimes it does not understand. Therefore the active (agent) intellect is not something in our soul.' To which St. Thomas replies: 'The Philosopher says those words not of the active (agent) intellect, but of the intellect in act: of which he had already said: *Knowledge in act is the same as the thing*. Or, if we refer those words to the active (agent) intellect, then

34

they are said because it is not owing to the active (agent) intellect that sometimes we do, and sometimes we do not understand, but to the intellect which is in potentiality.'[1] The conclusion of the objection shows the importance of the question for the Averroist thesis of the separated intellect. St. Thomas clearly shows his preference for taking *intelligit* to refer right back to 'knowledge in act', though finding the Averroist conclusion not necessitated by the alternative of taking it to refer to the agent intellect. Curiously, though the version does not give any help in deciding this point, the Greek seems fully to justify St. Thomas's preference. The ἀλλά is the strongest particle in its sentence and would seem absolutely to demand that its antecedent should be all of the sentence which precedes it. Commentators have not always seen this, but de Corte is surely right in making it one of his main arguments for taking the passage in the sense preferred by St. Thomas in the *Summa* and adopted by him in the Commentary.[2]

It is matter of less moment but worthy of remark, that St. Thomas shows his penetration in overcoming, correctly, a further obscurity which is absent from the Greek but introduced by the author of the version by his writing *omnino* for ὅλως. An early variant is ἁπλῶς which comes to the same thing. The contrast is between knowledge in potency considered in the individual and the same considered absolutely or universally, without qualification. *Omnino* does not give this sense unmistakably, but St. Thomas does so understand it in the Commentary.

(ii) *Separatus* is commonly taken as referring only to the agent intellect, the last aspect of the intellective soul to have been considered. St. Thomas, with at least as much probability in his favour, argues for its reference to the intellective soul without qualification, on the ground that the 'possible' as well as the 'agent' intellect has been characterised as 'separate' in the *foregoing* passage. De Corte insists that the same interpretation is imposed by the whole theory of the soul and its parts which Aristotle presents.

We may note that the version's *vere* is one of its rare verbal additions to the text, admirably, however, bringing out the emphasis

[1] Translation by Fathers of the English Dominican Province (Burns, Oates & Washbourne, Ltd.).

[2] For detailed exegesis of the whole of this passage see de Corte, *L'Intelligence* etc., pp. 64–91.

of the Greek. Its presence renders less objectionable St. Thomas's transference of the adverb *solum* into an adjective; the transference is to be explained by his taking *solum* with *separatus* rather than with *est hoc quod vere est*. But the presence of *vere* does much to retain the emphasis on the clause in which it occurs. It would be possible, consonantly with St. Thomas's principles, to translate: 'By itself, the intellect, when separated, is that which it truly is', the general sense being, in any case, that, in the state of separation from the body, intellective soul is purely intellective, the organic powers being necessarily in abeyance.

(iii) The Version turns *μνημονεύομεν* by *reminiscitur*, but without serious consequences. With what previously mentioned period is the verb co-ordinated? It can only be with that indicated by *χωρισθείς*. In a state of separation from the body, the intellective soul no longer remembers. Memory has already been mentioned in 408^b 24–29 as perishing with the *compositum* of body and soul; St. Thomas refers to that passage in § 744, *supra dixit in primo quod intelligere corrumpitur, quodam interius corrupto*. We have already seen that the commentary on that passage (§ 163ss.) presents certain difficulties. This is the place to suggest that they may in part be caused by St. Thomas's awareness that Aristotle could not possibly be saying, in accordance with his own principles, that *intelligere* in the normal sense of that word is an act of the *compositum* as such and perishable with it. Yet the version gave him the statement, to which he here refers, *Intelligere igitur et considerare marcescunt alio quodam interius corrupto*. This genuine difficulty may have been the reason for the commentator's interpreting the passage as an *argumentum ad hominem*. But now in Book III, at the end of lectio 10 (§ 745) he has his finger on the solution: . . . *destructo corpore non remanet in anima separata scientia rerum secundum eundem modum quo modo intelligit. Sed quomodo tunc intelligat, non est praesentis intentionis discutere*. The word turned by *intelligere* is *διάνοια* and its association in these two passages with memory and other acts of the *compositum* suggests that this term could be applied to other than distinctively spiritual acts of the mind. Indeed its being coupled with *θεωρεῖν* in 408^b 24 is sufficient warrant for finding such another use, since *θεωρεῖν* is often used by Aristotle both for an act of sense and an act of mind. De Corte suggests that the preposition *διά* in composition with the verb may here, as in other cases, have the sense of 'penetration'. The act signified would then be intermediate between sense perception and understanding proper: that collaboration of intellect and sense which is inescapably necessary to intellectual activity, so long as the soul is united to the body. The total aptitude for such collaboration is the 'passive' intellect of which Aristotle here alone makes mention. It is certainly impossible to equate this with the 'possible', or knowing, intellect properly so called.

We may close our discussion of this difficult passage by expanding the translation in the sense which seems to be appropriate.

'Knowledge in act is the same as the thing (actually known). But (knowledge) that is potential is, in the individual, prior in time. Absolutely, however, not even in time. Whereas (knowledge in act) does not sometimes know and sometimes not know. When mind is separated (from the body) it is simply what it truly is. It does not (then) remember, because (mind) indeed is impassible; but the passive intellect is corruptible, and without it (in this life) the soul understands nothing.'

IVO THOMAS, O.P.

BOOK ONE

BOOK I, CHAPTER I

INTRODUCTORY. THE IMPORTANCE AND DIFFICULTY OF THE STUDY OF THE SOUL

HOLDING AS WE DO THAT KNOWLEDGE IS A GOOD and honourable thing, yet that some kinds of knowledge are more so than others, either because they are more certain or because they deal with subjects more excellent and wonderful, we naturally give a primary place, for both these reasons, to an enquiry about the soul. §§ 1–6

Indeed an acquaintance with the soul would seem to help much in acquiring all truth, especially about the natural world; for it is, as it were, the principle of living things. § 7

We seek then to consider and understand, first, its nature and essence, then whatever qualities belong to it. Of these, some seem to be proper to the soul alone, others to be shared in common[1] and to exist in animate beings on account of it. § 8

To ascertain, however, anything reliable about it is one of the most difficult of undertakings. Such an enquiry being common to many topics—I mean, an enquiry into the essence, and what each thing *is*—it might seem to some that one definite procedure were available for all things of which we wished to know the essence; as there is demonstration for the

---

[1] 'shared in common' is unsupported by most Greek manuscripts.

accidental properties of things. So we should have to discover what is this one method. But if there is no one method for determining what an essence is, our enquiry becomes decidedly more difficult, and we shall have to find a procedure for each case in particular. If, on the other hand, it is clear that either demonstration, or division, or some such process is to be employed, there are still many queries and uncertainties to which answers must be found. For the *principles* in different subject-matters are different, for instance in the case of numbers and surfaces. Perhaps the first thing needed is to divide off the genus of the subject and to say what sort of thing it is,—I mean, whether it be a particular thing or substance, or a quality, or quantity, or any other of the different categories. Further, whether it is among things in potency or is an actuality—no insignificant distinction. Again, whether it is divisible or indivisible, and whether every soul is of the same sort or no: and if not, whether they differ specifically or generically. Indeed those who at present talk of and discuss the soul seem to deal only with the human soul. One must be careful not to leave unexplored the question whether there is a single definition of it, as of 'animal' in general, or a different one for each [of its kinds]: as, say, for horse, dog, man or god. Now 'animal' as a universal is nothing real, or is secondary; and we must say the same of any other general predicate.   §§ 9–13

Further, if there are not many souls, but only many parts of a single one, we must ask whether one ought to look first at the whole or the parts. It is difficult to see what parts are by nature diverse from one another, and whether one ought to look first at the parts or their functions, for instance at the act of understanding or at the intellective power, at the act of sensing or at the sensitive faculty; and likewise in other instances. But if one is to examine first the operations, it might be asked whether one should not first enquire about their objects, as, in the sensitive function, the thing sensed; and in the intellectual, the thing intelligible.   § 14

Now, it seems that not only does knowledge of the essence help one to understand the causes of the accidents of any substance (as in Mathematics to know what is the straight and the curved[1] and what is a line and what a plane enables one to discover the number of right angles to which those of a triangle are equal)[2] but, conversely, accidental qualities contribute much to knowing what a thing essentially is. When we can give an account of such qualities (some or all) according to appearances, then we shall have material for dealing as well as possible with the essence. The principle of every demonstration is *what* a thing is. Hence, whatsoever definitions do not afford us a knowledge of accidents, or even a fair conjecture about them, are obviously vain and sophistical.

§ 15

[1] *Obliquum,* τὸ καμπύλον (402ᵇ 19); *curvum* in *Commentary.*
[2] Correcting *quod rectis* of Pirotta's text to *quot rectis,* πόσαις ὀρθαῖς.

ST. THOMAS'S COMMENTARY
LECTIO ONE

§ 1. In studying any class of things, it is first of all necessary, as the Philosopher says in the *De Animalibus*,[1] to consider separately what is common to the class as a whole, and afterwards what is proper to particular members of the class. Such is Aristotle's method in First Philosophy; for at the beginning of the *Metaphysics* he investigates the common properties of being as such, and only then does he go on to the particular kinds of being. The reason for this procedure is that it saves frequent repetition.

Now living beings taken all together form a certain class of being; hence in studying them the first thing to do is to consider what living things have in common, and afterwards what each has peculiar to itself. What they have in common is a life-principle or soul;[2] in this they are all alike. In conveying knowledge, therefore, about living things one must first convey it about the soul as that which is common to them all. Thus when Aristotle sets out to treat of living things, he begins with the soul; after which, in subsequent books, he defines the properties of particular living beings.

§ 2. In the present treatise on the soul we find, first, an Introduction: in which the author does the three things that should be done in any Introduction. For in writing an Introduction one has three objects in view: first, to gain the reader's good will; secondly, to dispose him to learn; thirdly, to win his attention. The first object one achieves by showing the reader the value of the knowledge in question; the second by explaining the plan and divisions of the treatise; the third by warning him of its difficulties. And all this Aristotle does here. First, he points out the high value of the science

[1] *De Partibus Animalium*, I, c.5; 645ᵇ 1–10.
[2] *Anima*: henceforth rendered 'soul'.

44

he is introducing. Secondly, at 'We seek then . . .'[1] he explains the plan of the treatise. Thirdly, at 'To ascertain anything reliable . . .'[2] he warns of its difficulty. Under the first point he explains, first the dignity of this science, and then, at 'Indeed, an acquaintance . . .'[3] its utility.

§ 3. As regards, then, the said dignity we should note that, while all knowledge is good and even honourable, one science can surpass another in this respect. All knowledge is obviously good because the good of anything is that which belongs to the fulness of being which all things seek after and desire; and man as man reaches fulness of being through knowledge. Now of good things some are just valuable, namely, those which are useful in view of some end —as we value a good horse because it runs well; whilst other good things are also honourable: namely, those that exist for their own sake; for we give honour to ends, not means. Of the sciences some are practical, others speculative; the difference being that the former are for the sake of some work to be done, while the latter are for their own sake. The speculative sciences are therefore honourable as well as good, but the practical are only valuable. Every speculative science is both good and honourable.

§ 4. Yet even among the speculative sciences there are degrees of goodness and honourableness. Every science is valued first of all as a kind of activity, and the worth of any activity is reckoned in two ways: from its object and from its mode or quality. Thus building is a better activity than bed-making because its object is better. But where the activities are the same in kind, and result in the same thing, the quality alone makes a difference; if a building is better built it will be a better building. Considering then science, or its activity, from the point of view of the object, that science is nobler which is concerned with better and nobler things; but from the point of view of mode or quality, the nobler science is that which is more certain. One science, then, is reckoned nobler than another, either because it concerns better and nobler objects or because it is more certain.

§ 5. Now there is this difference between sciences, that some excel in certainty and yet are concerned with inferior objects, while others with higher and better objects are nevertheless less certain. All the same, that science is the better which is about

[1] 402ª 7.   [2] 402ª 10.   [3] 402ª 4.

better and nobler things; because, as the Philosopher observes in Book XI of the *De Animalibus*,[1] we have a greater desire for even a little knowledge of noble and exalted things—even for a conjectural and probable sort of knowledge—than for a great and certain knowledge of inferior things. For the former is noble in itself and essentially, but the latter only through its quality or mode.

§ 6. Now this science of the soul has both merits. It has certainty; for everyone knows by experience that he has a soul which is his life-principle. Also it has a high degree of nobility; for among lower things the soul has a special nobility. This is what Aristotle means here when he says,[2] 'Holding as we do that knowledge', i.e. speculative science, 'is good and honourable.' And one science is better and nobler than another in two ways: either, as we have seen, because it is more certain—hence he says 'more certain',—or because it is about 'more excellent' things, i.e. things that are good in themselves, and 'more wonderful things', i.e. things whose cause is unknown. 'For both these reasons', he goes on to say, 'we give a primary place to an enquiry about the soul'. He uses the term 'enquiry'[3] because he is going to discuss the soul in a general way, without attempting, in this treatise, a thorough examination of all its properties. As to the words 'a primary place', if they are taken as applying to the whole of Natural Science, then they refer to superiority in dignity and not to priority in order; but if they refer to the science of living things only, they mean priority of order.

§ 7. Then, with 'Indeed an acquaintance etc.',[4] he gains the reader's good will by showing the utility of this science. Some knowledge of the soul, he says, would seem to be very useful in all the other sciences. It can be of considerable service to philosophy in general. In First Philosophy it is impossible to attain knowledge of the divine and highest causes except through what we can acquire by actualising our intellectual power; and if we knew nothing about the nature of this power we should know nothing about the immaterial substances, as the Commentator remarks *à propos* of Book XI of the *Metaphysics*. Again, as regards Moral Philosophy. We cannot master the science of morals unless we know the powers of the soul; thus in the Ethics[5] the Philosopher assigns the virtues to the different powers. So, too, it is use-

---

[1] *De Partibus Animal.*, I, c.5; 644ᵇ 20ss.   [2] 402ᵃ 1.   [3] *historia*, ἱστορία.
[4] 402ᵃ 4–5.   [5] E.N., I, 13, 1102ᵃ 5ss.

ful for the Natural Scientist, because many of the things he studies
are animate things, all of whose movements originate in the
soul: 'for it is,' says Aristotle, 'as it were, the principle of living
things': the phrase 'as it were' does not express a comparison; it is
descriptive.

§ 8. Next, at 'We seek then',[1] he states the plan of his treatise,
saying that we are 'to consider', i.e. by way of outward symp-
toms, and 'to understand', i.e. by way of demonstration, what the
soul really is in its nature and essence; 'and then whatever qualities
belong to it' or affect it. But in the latter a diversity appears: for
while some of the soul's modifications, such as understanding and
speculative knowledge, seem to belong to the soul of and in itself,
others, such as pleasure and pain, the senses and imagination,
though they depend on some soul or other, seem to be common
to all animals.

§ 9. Then at 'To ascertain',[2] he introduces the difficulty of this
study; and this from two points of view. It is hard, first, to know
the essence[3] of the soul, and secondly to know its accidents or
characteristic qualities.[4] As to the essence, there is a double difficulty: first, as to how it ought to be defined, and then as to the
elements of the definition (this point comes at 'Perhaps the first
thing needed').[5]

He remarks, therefore, that while knowledge of the soul would
be valuable, it is not easy to know just what the soul is. Now this
is a difficulty in studying anything; for the question about substance and essence[6] is common to the study of soul and of many
other things; the first difficulty being that we do not know what
method to use; for some say we should use deductive demonstration, others the method of elimination, others one of comparison.
Aristotle himself preferred the method of comparison.

§ 10. The second difficulty concerns the elements of the definition. A definition manifests a thing's essence;[7] and this cannot be
grasped apart from the principles on which it depends. But different
things have different principles, and it is hard to see which principle is involved in any particular thing. Hence, in formulating
or seeking for a definition of soul we encounter three main

---

[1] 402ª 5.   [2] 402ª 10.   [3] ...substantiam animae.
[4] ...accidentia seu proprias passiones.   [5] 402ª 22.
[6] circa substantiam . . . et circa quod quid est.   [7] essentiam rei.

difficulties: (*a*) concerning its essence; (*b*) concerning its parts; (*c*) concerning that necessary contribution to a definition which comes from knowing the soul's accidental qualities.

§ 11. As regards the essence of soul there is a doubt about that which is the first thing to be looked for in defining anything, i.e. the genus to which it belongs. What is the genus of soul? Is it a substance or a quantity or a quality? And not only must we decide upon the ultimate genus, but also on the proximate one; thus we do not define man as a substance, but as an animal. And if soul is found to belong to the genus of substance we shall still have to decide whether it is actual or potential substance, since every genus can be regarded both as potential and as actual. Also, since substances are either composite or simple, we shall have to ask whether soul is one or the other, and whether it is divisible or indivisible. There is also the question whether all souls are of the same species or not; and if they are not, whether they are generically different or not. Again there is uncertainty as to what is to be included in the definition, some things being defined in terms of genus, some as species; hence the question whether we should define soul in terms of genus or as the specification of a species.[1]

§ 12. For some enquirers seem to have in view only the human soul.[2] Among the earlier philosophers there were two opinions about soul. The Platonists, holding that universals existed separately as the Forms or Ideas that caused knowledge and being in individual things, maintained that there was a Soul-in-Itself which was the cause and 'idea' of particular souls and from which all that we find in these drew its origin. On the other hand were the Natural Philosophers who maintained that no universal substances existed in the real world, that the only real things were individuals. And this raises the question for us, whether we, like the Platonists, ought to look for one common idea of Soul; or rather, as the Natural Philosophers said, study this or that particular soul, e.g. of horse or man, or god. He says 'or god' because at that time men believed that the heavenly bodies were gods, and that they were alive.

§ 13. However, Aristotle chose to seek a definition of both—of Soul in general and of each kind of soul. But when he says, on this point, that 'animal as universal is nothing real, or is secondary',[3]

---

[1] *species specialissima.*   [2] This should be placed in § 11.   [3] 402[b] 8.

we must understand that one can speak of a 'universal animal' in two ways: either as *universal*, i.e. as one nature existing in, or predicated of, many individuals; or as *animal*. And both these aspects can be regarded either in relation to existence in the real world or as existing in the mind. As regards existence in the real world, Plato held that the universal animal did so exist and existed prior to particular animals; because, as has been said, he thought that there were universals and ideas with an independent existence. Aristotle, however, said that the universal as such had no real existence, and that if it was anything at all it came after the individual thing. But if we regard the nature of animals from a different point of view, i.e. not as a universal, then it is indeed something real, and it precedes the individual animal as the potential precedes the actual.

§ 14. Then, at 'Further, if there are not many',[1] Aristotle touches on the difficulties that arise concerning the soul's potentialities. For in the soul are 'parts' that exist as potencies: the intellectual and sensitive and vegetative 'parts'. The question is whether these are different souls, as the Platonists liked to think (and even maintained), or are only potencies in the soul. And if they are potencies, we must further decide whether to enquire first into the potencies themselves, and then into their acts, or into the acts first and then the potencies—e.g. into the act of understanding before the intellect. And if we take the acts first, there is still the question whether the *objects* of these acts should be studied before the faculties, e.g. the sense-object before the sense-faculty or the thing understood before the understanding.

§ 15. Next, at 'Now it seems',[2] he states the difficulties that arise with regard to those accidental qualities which contribute to a definition of the soul. These are relevant here because a definition ought to reveal a thing's accidental qualities, as well as its essential principles. If indeed the latter could be known and correctly defined there would be no need to define the former; but since the essential principles of things are hidden from us we are compelled to make use of accidental differences as indications of what is essential. Thus to be two-footed is not of the essence of anything, yet it helps to indicate an essence. By such accidental differences we are led towards knowledge of the essential ones. It would indeed be

[1] 402[b] 9.   [2] 402[b] 16.

easier to grasp even what is accidental to the soul if we could only first understand its essence, just, as in mathematics, it is a great help towards understanding that the angles of a triangle are equal to (two)[1] right angles to know first what is meant by straight, curved and plane. Hence the difficulty of our present position. On the other hand a prior examination of the accidental factors is a considerable help towards knowing the essence, as has been said. If, therefore, one were to propose a definition from which no knowledge of the accidental attributes of the defined thing could be derived, such a definition would not be real, but abstract and hypothetical. But one from which a knowledge of the accidents flows is a real definition, based on what is proper and essential to the thing.

[1] 'Two' is lacking in Pirotta; see note 2, p. 43.

BOOK I, CHAPTER I, CONTINUED

INTRODUCTION CONTINUED
QUESTIONS OF METHOD

THE MODIFICATIONS OF THE SOUL PRESENT A PROB-
lem: are they all shared by what has soul, or are some
proper to the soul alone?   § 16

It is necessary indeed, but not easy, to deal with this problem. For in most cases there is, apparently, no action or being
acted on without the body; as in anger, desire, confidence,
and sensation in general. Understanding however would
seem especially proper to the soul. Yet if this too is a sort of
imagination, or never occurs without it, not even this exists,
in fact, apart from the body.   §§ 17–20

But if the soul has some operation or affection exclusive to
itself, then it could exist as a separate entity. If, however, there
is nothing thus proper to it, then it is not separable, but is like
a straight line, which has, as such, many properties—such as
being able to touch a bronze sphere at a given point; but
straightness separated does not touch it; not being in fact
separable, since it is always with a bodily subject.   § 21

Now all the soul's modifications do seem to involve the
body—anger, meekness, fear, compassion, and joy and love
and hate. For along with these the body also is to some
degree affected. An indication of this is that sometimes

violent and unmistakable occurrences arouse no excitement or alarm; while at other times one is moved by slight and trifling matters, when the physical system is stimulated to the condition appropriate to anger. This is still more evident when, nothing fearful being present, feelings occur as in one who is frightened.[1] If this is the case, it is evident that the passions are material principles; hence such terms as 'becoming angry' mean a motion of such and such a body, or of a part or power proceeding from and existing for the body.   § 22

For this reason, therefore, the natural scientist ought to examine the soul, either all kinds, or this kind.   § 23

The natural scientist and the dialectician will define each of those modifications differently. Take the question, what is anger? The latter will say, a desire for retaliation, or something similar; the former, an effervescence of blood or heat about the heart. Of these, the natural scientist designates the matter, the dialectician, the form or idea. For this 'idea' is the thing's form. This however must have existence in material of the sort in question; if it is a house, one formula will be, 'a covering to prevent destruction from wind and rain and excessive heat'; the other, 'stones and beams[2] and timber'; another, 'the form; in these materials; for those reasons'. Which is the physical definition?[3] That which states the matter and ignores the idea? Or that which states the idea only?

---

[1] '... people have the same feelings as a person in fright', 403ᵃ 23–4 (E. Wallace's rendering). The translation given here of M. agrees with St. Thomas's commentary. M.: *in passionibus fiunt, his inquam quibus timens*; St. Thomas: *fiunt in aliquibus passiones similes*, etc. The subject implied by *fiunt* (γίνονται) is really 'men' in general, not 'passions'. It is not impossible that M. knew this. Incidentally, St. Thomas's quotations of his text here depart slightly from the (Pirotta) text of M. He says *adhuc fit magis manifestum* where M. has *adhuc autem magis hoc manifestum*; and *sunt rationes in materia* where M. says *rationes in materia sunt*.

[2] 'bricks', 403ᵇ 6.

[3] 'Physical' renders *naturalis*. 'Definition' is implicit here, corresponding to 'idea' (ratio); cf. St. Thomas, § 27.

Or rather, the compound of both? What then of the other two? Now there is no one who deals with inseparable qualities of matter, precisely as inseparable from it; but he who is concerned with the affections and activities of the special matter of this or that body is the natural scientist; whereas whatever things are not specifically such, another considers; in certain matters it may perchance be a technical expert, a carpenter or physician. Concerning however what is inseparable from matter, and yet as *not* involved in the specific qualities of this or that body, but abstracted from any, the mathematician; and concerning what is separable, the 'first philosopher'.

§§ 24–9

To return from our digression. We were saying that the passions of the soul are not separable from the physical material of animals (anger and fear having this kind of existence), and yet also that they differ, in this, from the line and the surface.

CHAPTER II

Investigating the soul, it is necessary, while suspending judgment on matters which should be held uncertain, that we study the opinions of certain thinkers who have dealt with the subject, so as to take note of anything they said pertinently, whilst avoiding their mistakes.   § 30

ST. THOMAS'S COMMENTARY
LECTIO TWO

§ 16. Having stated the difficulty of this science in respect of the problem of the soul's substance and essence, the Philosopher proceeds to the problem of its modifications and accidental qualities. And here he does two things: he states, first, and solves a difficulty concerning the soul's modifications;[1] and then, using this solution, he shows that knowledge of the soul pertains to natural science or 'physics', where he says, 'For this reason, therefore, the natural scientist . . .'.[2] As to the first point, he says it is a problem whether the soul's modifications and activities belong to it independently of the body, as Plato thought, or are none of them peculiar to the soul, being all shared by soul and body together.

§ 17. Going on at 'It is necessary',[3] he again does two things. First he shows the difficulty of the question, and then, at 'But if the soul . . .',[4] the necessity of putting it. He begins then by observing that we cannot avoid the question whether the soul's modes and activities are proper to it or shared by the body, and that this is not an easy question but a very difficult one. The difficulty, as he explains, arises from the fact that many activities *seem* to be common to soul and body and to require the body, for instance, getting angry and having sensations and so on; which all involve body as well as soul. If there is anything peculiar to the soul it would appear to be the intellectual activity or understanding; this seems to belong to the soul in a special way.

§ 18. And yet, on closer consideration, even understanding would not seem to pertain to the soul alone. For either it is the same as imagination, as the Platonists thought, or it does not occur without the use of imagination (for there used to be men, such as the early natural philosophers, who said that intellect in no way

[1] 403ᵃ 2 ff.   [2] 403ᵃ 27.   [3] 403ᵃ 5.   [4] 403ᵃ 10.

differed from the senses, which would imply that it does not differ from the imagination; as indeed the Platonists were led to say). As, then, imagination presupposes the body and depends on it, they said that understanding was common to soul and body together, rather than the work of the soul alone. And even granted that intellect and imagination are not identical, still the one cannot function without the other. It would follow that understanding is not of the soul alone, since imagining presupposes the body. Understanding then, it seems, does not occur where there is no body.

§ 19. Now although Aristotle clears up this problem in Book III,[1] we shall say something about it here. Understanding, then, is in one sense, proper to the soul alone, and in another sense common to both soul and body. For it should be realised that certain activities or modifications of the soul depend on the body both as an instrument and as an object. Sight, for instance, needs a body as object—because its object is colour, which is only found in bodies; —and also as an instrument—because, while the act of seeing involves the soul, it cannot occur except through the instrumentality of a visual organ, the pupil of the eye. Sight then is the act of the organ as well as of the soul. But there is one activity which only depends on the body to provide its object, not its instrument; for understanding is not accomplished with a bodily organ, though it does bear on a bodily object; because, as will be shown later, in Book III,[2] the phantasms in the imagination are to the intellect as colours to sight: as colours provide sight with its object, so do the phantasms serve the intellect. Since then there cannot be phantasms without a body, it seems that understanding presupposes a body—not, however, as its instrument, but simply as its object.

§ 20. Two things follow from this. (1) Understanding is an act proper to the soul alone, needing the body, as was said above, only to provide its object; whereas seeing and various other functions involve the compound of soul and body together. (2) Whatever operates of itself independently, has also an independent being and subsistence of its own; which is not the case where the operation is not independent. Intellect then is a self-subsistent actuality, whereas the other faculties are actualities existing in matter. And the difficulty in dealing with this type of question arises simply from

[1] §§ 765–86.   [2] §§ 770, 772, 791, 854.

the fact that all functions of the soul seem at first sight to be also functions of the body.

§ 21. After this, when Aristotle says 'But if the soul'[1] he states a reason for putting this question, namely, that on its answer depends the answer to a question that everyone asks very eagerly about the soul: whether it can be separated from the body. So he says that if the soul has any function proper to itself it can certainly be separated, because, as was pointed out above, whatever can operate on its own can exist on its own. Conversely, if the soul had no such proper function it would not be separable from the body; it would be in the same case as a straight line—for though many things can happen to a straight line *qua* straight line, such as touching a brass sphere at a certain point, still they can only come about in a material way: a straight line cannot touch a brass sphere at any point except materially. So also with the soul; if it has no activity proper to itself, then, however many things affect it, they will do so only in a material way.

§ 22. Next, when he says 'Now all the soul's'[2] he draws out what had been presupposed above, namely that certain modifications affect soul and body together, not the soul alone. And this he shows by one argument in two parts; which runs as follows. Whenever the physical constitution of the body contributes to a vital activity, the latter pertains to the body as well as the soul; but this happens in the case of all the 'modifications' of the soul, such as anger, meekness, fear, confidence, pity and so on; hence all these 'modifications' would seem to belong partly to the body. And to show that the physical constitution plays a part in them he uses two arguments. (1) We sometimes see a man beset by obvious and severe afflictions without being provoked or frightened, whereas when he is already excited by violent passions arising from his bodily disposition, he is disturbed by mere trifles and behaves as though he were really angry. (2) At 'This is still more evident:'[3] what makes this point even clearer is that we see in some people, even when there is no danger present, passions arising that resemble one such 'modification' of the soul; for instance melancholy people, simply as a result of their physical state, are often timid when there is no real cause to be. Obviously then, if the bodily constitution has this effect on the passions, the latter must be 'material principles',

[1] 403[a] 10.   [2] 403[a] 16.   [3] 403[a] 23.

i.e. must exist in matter. This is why 'such terms', i.e. the definitions of these passions, are not to be predicated without reference to matter; so that if anger is being defined, let it be called a movement 'of some body' such as the heart, or 'of some part or power' of the body. Saying this he refers to the subject or material cause of the passion; whereas 'proceeding from' refers to the efficient cause; and 'existing for' to the final cause.

§ 23. Then at 'For this reason',[1] he concludes from the foregoing that the study of the soul pertains to natural science—a conclusion following from the way the soul is defined. So he does two things here: (1) he proves his statement; (2) he pursues his discussion of definitions, where he says 'the natural scientist and the dialectician'.[2] The proof of his statement runs thus. Activities and dispositions of the soul are also activities and dispositions of the body, as has been shown. But the definition of any disposition must include that which is disposed; for its subject always falls within the definition of a disposition. If, then, dispositions of this kind are in the body as well as in the soul, the former must be included in their definition. And since everything bodily or material falls within the scope of natural science, so also must the dispositions of which we speak. Moreover, since the subject of any dispositions enters into the study of them, it must be the task of the natural scientist to study the soul,—either absolutely 'all' souls, or 'of this kind', i.e. the soul that is joined to a body. He adds this because he has left it uncertain whether intellect is joined to the body.

§ 24. Where he says 'The natural scientist and the dialectician'[3] he continues his discussion of definitions. Explaining that, while some definitions of the dispositions of the soul include matter and the body, others exclude matter and refer only to the form, he shows that the latter kind of definition is inadequate. This leads him to go into the difference between these types of definition. Sometimes the body is omitted, as when anger is defined as a desire of revenge; and sometimes the bodily or material factor is included, as when anger is called a heating of blood round the heart. The former is a logical definition, but the latter is physical, since it includes a material factor, and so pertains to the natural scientist. The natural scientist points to the material factor when he says that anger is a heating of blood round the heart; whereas the

[1] 403ᵃ 27.   [2] 403ᵃ 29.   [3] 403ᵃ 29.

dialectician points to the species or formal principle; since to call anger a desire of revenge is to state its formal principle.

§ 25. Now the first type of definition is obviously inadequate. The definition of any form existing in a particular matter must take account of the matter. This form, 'the desire for retaliation', exists in a definite matter, and if the matter is not included, the definition is clearly inadequate. The definition, then, must state that this thing, i.e. the form, has being in this particular sort of matter.

§ 26. Thus we have three kinds of definition.[1] The first states the species and specific principle of a thing, and is purely formal,—as if one were to define a house as a shelter from wind, rain and heat. The second kind indicates the matter, as when a house is called a shelter made of stones and beams and wood. But the third kind includes in the definition 'both', namely matter and form, calling a house a particular kind of shelter, built of particular materials, for a particular purpose—to keep out the wind, etc. So he says that 'another' definition has three elements: the material, 'in these', i.e. beams and stones; the formal, 'the form'; and the final, 'for those reasons', i.e. to keep out the wind. So matter is included when he says 'in these', form when he says 'form', and the final cause when he says 'for those reasons'. All three are needed for a perfect definition.

§ 27. To the question which of these types of definition pertains to the natural scientist, I answer that the purely formal one is not physical but logical. That which includes matter but omits the form pertains to no one but the natural scientist, because only he is concerned with matter. Yet that which includes both factors is also in a special way the natural scientist's. Thus two of these definitions pertain to natural science, but of the two the merely material one is imperfect, while the other, that includes the form also, is perfect. For only the natural scientist studies the *inseparable* dispositions of matter.

§ 28. But there are various ways of studying the dispositions of matter, as Aristotle now proceeds to show. He divides the students of these dispositions into three classes. One class consists of those who, while they study material dispositions, differ from the natural scientist in their point of view; thus the craftsman differs from the

[1] 403^b 3–16.

scientist in that he starts from the point of view of art, but the natural scientist from that of real nature. Another class consists of those who, though they consider forms that exist in sense-perceptible matter, do not include such matter in their definitions. The forms referred to are such as curved, straight, and so on, which, though they exist in matter and are, in fact, inseparable from it, are not, by the mathematician, regarded under their sense-perceptible aspect. The reason is that if it is through its *quality* that a thing is sense-perceptible, quality *presupposes* quantity; hence the mathematician abstracts from this or that particular material factor in order to attend exclusively to the purely quantitative. Finally, the third class studies things whose existence is either completely independent of matter or can be found without matter. This is First Philosophy.

§ 29. Note that this division of Philosophy is entirely based on definition and the method of defining. The reason is that definition is the principle of demonstration. Since things are defined by their essential principles, diverse definitions reveal a diversity of essential principles; and this implies a diversity of sciences.

§ 30. Then at 'To return . . .'[1] he comes back to the matter in hand after the apparent digression about definitions. The point under discussion was that such modifications of the soul as love, fear and so forth are inseparable from physical animal matter inasmuch as they have this sort of existence, i.e. as passions in the body; in which they differ from lines, plane-surfaces and so on, which can be considered by the mind apart from the matter that they naturally imply. If this is the case then the study of such dispositions, and even of the soul itself, becomes, as has been said, the affair of the natural scientist.

And 'concerning this',[2] i.e. the soul, we must, at our present stage, take account of the opinions of the ancients no matter who they were, provided they had anything to say about it. This will be useful in two ways. First, we shall profit by what is sound in their views. Secondly, we shall be put on our guard against their errors.

[1] 403^b 16.
[2] The quotation marks are in Pirotta, but this is not a direct quotation.

BOOK I, CHAPTER II, CONTINUED

PREVIOUS THEORIES
DEMOCRITUS, THE PYTHAGOREANS,
ANAXAGORAS

OUR ENQUIRY MUST BEGIN WITH A STATEMENT OF what seems most to belong by nature to the soul. The animated being would appear to differ from the inanimate in two primary respects: by motion and by sense-perception. And these two notions are roughly what our predecessors have handed down to us concerning the soul.

§§ 31–2

For some say that the soul is principally and primarily what moves. Holding that what does not itself move moves no other moving thing, they thought that the soul too was thus.

§ 33

Hence Democritus said it was a kind of fire or heat. There exist an infinite number of shapes and atoms, and those of the spherical kind are, he said, fire and soul: like the dust-motes in the air called 'atomies'[1] seen in the rays of the sun in door-ways; and of all the seeds of these,[2] he said, are the elements of all Nature. Leucippus had a similar opinion. Those round in shape make the soul, because they are most able to penetrate everywhere, and since they move of themselves, they have also the power to move everything else. The soul, they

---

[1] *Decisiones*: in Greek, ξύσματα, 'filings'.

[2] *quarum omne semen*, ὧν τήν . . . πανσπερμίαν: 'the seed aggregate of which', 404ᵃ 4.

maintained, is what causes movement in living things: and accordingly breathing is coterminous with living. That which envelops all bodies expels by compression the atoms [within], thus causing movement in animals, for these [atoms] are never at rest. A reinforcement must come therefore [he said] from without; in that other atoms enter by respiration, preventing from dispersal those that are within the animate body, and which simultaneously resist the constraining and compressing environment; and that animals live so long as they can do this.   §§ 34–5

The teaching of the Pythagoreans seems to have had much the same purport. Some of these said the soul consisted of atoms in the air; others, that it was what sets these in motion. And these atoms are mentioned because they seem to be always moving, even if the soul be quite tranquil.[1]   § 36

All who say that the soul is a thing that moves itself tend in the same direction; all seem to hold that movement is what is most proper to the soul, and accordingly that all things are in motion on account of the soul, but the soul itself on its own account; because one sees nothing moving other things that is not itself moving.   § 37

Anaxagoras likewise said that the soul is a mover, as also did anyone else who held that a Mind moves all things. But his view is not exactly Democritus'.   § 38

He [Democritus], asserts that intellect and soul are absolutely identical; and that what appears is the truth. And therefore that Homer aptly says of Hector that he lay 'otherminded'.[2] He does not use the term intellect to denote a

---

[1] 'Even when there is a perfect calm.' 'Soul' is not in the Greek; the phrase refers to the atmosphere (404[a] 20), and this is how St. Thomas understands it.

[2] 'Otherminded' means 'dazed'; *Iliad*, xxiii, 698; but the phrase does not apply to Hector.

definite faculty concerned with truth, but identifies soul and
intellect.   § 39

Anaxagoras is less definite about these matters. He often
says that the cause of being right or good is intellect, and that
this is the soul.[1] For it is, he says, in all animals, great and small,
noble and base.   § 40

It does not seem, however, that there exists mind, in the
sense of prudence, alike in all animals: nor even in all men.
                                                                § 41

All those therefore who have regarded life from the point
of view of movement have held soul to be pre-eminently a
moving force.   § 42

[1] 'but elsewhere he says that this is the soul', 404^{b}2. See Introduction, pp. 31-2.

ST. THOMAS'S COMMENTARY
LECTIO THREE

§ 31. So much by way of Introduction. The Philosopher has stated his aim in general and the difficulty of the undertaking; which he now proceeds to carry out in the order already indicated. The whole treatise divides into two parts. In the first the soul's nature is discussed as other philosophers have regarded it; but in the second as it is in reality. The latter section begins at Book II. The first part itself has two parts. The former simply relates the opinions of other philosophers; the second, beginning at 'The first thing to be considered',[1] examines them. The former part itself divides into two parts, in the first of which Aristotle distinguishes between the starting points of the other philosophers, while in the second, starting at 'For some say',[2] he shows how they severally came to hold their different opinions.

§ 32. First of all then he says that one ought to start by gathering together everything that would seem to belong to the soul by nature.[3] As to this, we should note that when we find things differing both by clear and understandable differences and by differences that are still obscure, we must assuredly take the former as a means to arrive at knowledge of the latter. This was the method used by the philosophers in their study of the soul. Living things differ from non-living in having 'souls'; but because the nature of the soul was not evident and could not be investigated except by way of certain more obvious notes which differentiate animate from inanimate things, the philosophers first took these more evident characteristics and tried, through them, to come to knowledge of the soul's nature. These evident notes are two: sensation and movement. Animate things seem to be characterised chiefly by movement, in that they move themselves, and by having sense-

---

[1] Lectio 6, § 68.   [2] § 33, 403[b] 28.   [3] 403[b] 20.

awareness or perception. So the ancients thought that if they could discover the principle of these two factors they would know the soul; hence their efforts to discern the cause of movement and sensation. They all agreed in identifying the soul with the cause of movement and sense-perception. But just at this point also their differences began; for some tried to arrive at the soul by way of movement, and others by way of sense-perception.

§ 33. Hence at 'For some say' he states these differences: taking those of his predecessors first who started their enquiry from movement; and then, at 'All who have considered',[1] those who started from knowledge; and thirdly, at 'But since the soul',[2] those who started from both.

With regard to the first group we should note that it had one principle in common, namely, that if living things are moving things, the soul must be both moving and moved. They assumed this because they thought that one thing could only move another if it were itself already moved; that is, only what is moved moves. So if living things are moved by the soul, then clearly the soul itself, and pre-eminently, must be moved. It was this that led the early students of Nature to class the soul among things that are moved. But about this also different opinions arose.

§ 34. When therefore he says, 'Hence Democritus',[3] Aristotle states first of all the view of Democritus, one of the early philosophers, who, thinking that the soul by nature was in a state of maximum movement, which state seems natural to fire, maintained that the soul 'was a kind of fire or heat'. Such was his view. For he did not admit the existence of anything in Nature except what is sense-perceptible and corporeal; and the first principles, he said, of all things are indivisible bodies, infinite in number, which he called atoms. These atoms, he said, are all the same by nature, differing from each other only in shape, position and arrangement (though here only the difference of shape is alluded to, as being the only necessary one. This consists in some being round, some square, some pyramids, and so on). He also maintained that the atoms were mobile and never ceased moving, and that the world had come into being through their fortuitous coming together. And to illustrate the mobility of these bodies he took the example of the particles that move in the air even when no wind blows, as

[1] Lectio 4, § 43, 404^b 7.   [2] § 52. 404^b 27.   [3] 403^b 31.

we can see when a sunbeam shines through a doorway. Since the atoms, being indivisible, are much smaller than such particles, they must obviously be extremely mobile. And because the spherical is, of all shapes, the one best suited for movement—having no angles to impede it,—and since the soul, as the cause of movement in living things, was thought to have maximum mobility, Democritus concluded that among these infinitely numerous bodies the spherical ones were the soul.[1]

§ 35. Leucippus, a companion of Democritus, held the same opinion. And Democritus thought the following was a sign of its truth. He maintained that 'coterminous with', or essential to, life is respiration (a short-sighted view since not all living things breathe), and that respiration is necessary because the body is full of small ever-moving spherical particles (the cause, as he thought, of all movement in animal bodies) and that the surrounding air compresses what it 'envelops', i.e. our bodies, and 'expels', i.e. thrusts out of them, those particles which are so shaped as to impart movement to animals, being never at rest themselves. Lest, therefore, our bodies should decay with the loss of all these particles, he said that respiration is necessary whereby fresh particles may be brought in, and those already within prevented from leaving by those that inhaling brings in. And he said that animals can live as long as they can do this, i.e. as long as they can breathe. The point of the argument is that if breathing is called the cause of life because it keeps the spherical particles inside the animal body, and also introduces fresh ones lest the body should decay through loss of particles by movement, then it is clearly implied that the particles are the soul itself. They are indeed the same particles that Democritus said were fiery by nature and the cause of heat.

§ 36. Next, at 'The teaching of the Pythagoreans . . .'[2] Aristotle mentions a view of certain Pythagoreans which resembles that of Democritus; for their statement and his seem to mean the same, although the Pythagoreans themselves do not all agree. Some of them, agreeing with Democritus, said that motes in the air, i.e. indivisible, infinitely numerous particles, were the soul. Others, however, of the same school, said that the soul was rather the force that moved those particles. Of this opinion was a certain Archelaus, the master of Socrates, as Augustine remarks in the *De Civitate Dei*.[3]

[1] Or 'souls'. [2] 404ᵃ 16. [3] *De Civ. Dei*, VIII, 2 (P.L., vol. XLI, col. 226).

The reason why the soul has been thus identified with these particles has been already given[1]—namely, that as the soul was regarded as being especially mobile, and as those particles seem to be always moving (even when the air is calm) they identified the one with the other.

§ 37. Then, at 'All who say . . .'[2] he summarises the views of a number of philosophers, saying that all who have defined the soul in terms of movement and called it that which moves itself, 'tend in the same direction', i.e. the same as those mentioned already. All these, it seems, agreed in thinking that the soul's first and chief characteristic was movement; all things being moved by soul, and soul by itself. The reason for this was, as has been noted, that they all thought that only what was itself in motion could move other things. Since the soul moves other things, they thought the soul especially and principally was in motion.

§ 38. In the third place, at 'Anaxagoras likewise',[3] he states the view of Anaxagoras. He first shows how this philosopher agrees with those already mentioned, saying that he, and anyone else who held that Intellect moved all things, really agreed with them that the source of all movement was a soul. Anaxagoras, however, differed in this that he denied that every mover was itself in motion, and maintained the existence of a pure and transcendent Intellect which, motionless itself, moved all other things; and that the soul was of this nature too. (This view led some into the error of divinising the soul.) Thus Anaxagoras agreed with the other philosophers in calling the soul a principle of movement, but disagreed with them in saying that it was not itself moved (for they said the contrary). And he also differed from Democritus in what he understood by intellect.

§ 39. When Aristotle therefore says 'He (i.e. Democritus) asserts,'[4] he states this last difference, first stating Democritus' opinion that intellect and soul were 'absolutely', i.e. everywhere and in all respects, the same. Democritus said this because he held that only sense-perceptible things existed in the real world, and that no cognitive faculty existed in the soul except sensitivity. From this he inferred that no definite truth about things was attainable, that nothing could be definitely known with certainty: truth being simply what appears to be true; and what one man

[1] §§ 32–3.   [2] 404ᵃ 20.   [3] 404ᵃ 25.   [4] 404ᵃ 27.

thought about anything being never any nearer the truth than what another man thought about the same thing at the same time. In consequence he maintained that contradictories were both true at the same time; and this because, as we have said, he took intellect to be, not the faculty for knowing truth and understanding intelligible objects, but a mere sense-faculty. Only the sensible, he thought, could be known, since only the sensible existed. And because the latter is continually changing there could be no certain truth about anything. Never attaining to an understanding of the intellect as the supreme faculty 'concerned with truth', i.e. which bears on true being, and admitting only the faculties of sense, he completely 'identifies soul and intellect'. The intellect changed, he said, as the whole man changed. Hence his approval of Homer's phrase 'Hector lies other-minded', i.e. Hector's mind was altered by Hector's condition; for he thought one thing as conqueror, another as conquered.

§ 40. Next, at 'Anaxagoras is less definite',[1] he shows how Anaxagoras differed from Democritus, first stating the former's opinion and then, at 'It does not seem',[2] criticising it. First then he observes that Anaxagoras spoke with less certainty and less conclusively about the soul. He often said that intelligence was the cause of right actions, whilst elsewhere he also identifies intelligence with the soul; for it is agreed that a soul is found in all animals, the lower as well as the higher, the smaller as well as the larger; and Anaxagoras said that intelligence was in all of them. Clearly then he identifies soul and intelligence.[3]

§ 41. Secondly, at 'It does not seem',[4] he shows the inconsistency of Anaxagoras' use of the term intellect. For sometimes Anaxagoras distinguishes between soul and intellect, but sometimes also he identifies them. These are contradictory statements which cannot both be true; as Aristotle proceeds to show. Right action, he says, admittedly derives from intellect perfected by prudence. If then the intellect that causes right action is the same thing as the soul, it follows that intellect perfected by prudence is the same as the soul. But this is false; because, while all animals have souls, not all—not even all men—are prudent. Therefore the soul is something else.

[1] 404^b 1.   [2] 404^b 5.   [3] See Introduction, pp. 31–2.   [4] 404^b 5.

§ 42. Lastly, at 'All those therefore . . .'[1] he states that all who have regarded animate beings from the standpoint of movement, i.e. as self-movers, thought that the chief mover in them was the soul, as the above-mentioned opinions show.

[1] 404^b 7.

BOOK I, CHAPTER II, CONTINUED

PREVIOUS THEORIES. EMPEDOCLES, PLATO, SOUL AS SELF-MOVING NUMBER

ALL WHO HAVE CONSIDERED IT AS KNOWING AND perceiving realities identify the soul with the [elemental] principles,—some making several principles, others one. §§ 43–4

Empedocles, for instance, says that it is composed of all elements, and that each of these is a soul, saying,

'*As by earth we know earth, by ether divine ether,*
By water water, by fire, it is clear, fire mysterious and hidden;[1]
Love by love, hate by sad hate.' §45

In the same way Plato in the *Timaeus* constitutes the soul from the elements. For like [he says] is known by like; and things are made up of elements. §§46–7

In the lectures 'On Philosophy' he likewise lays it down that the animate itself is compounded of the idea of the One, together with the primary Length and Depth and Breadth; other things existing in the same manner. §§ 48–50

Again, rather differently, that intellect is the One, knowledge the Two (for [this proceeds] as one to one), and the number of the Plane belongs to opinion, and that of the Solid to sensation. For he said that numbers are the specific forms and

---

[1] Or 'destructive', ἀίδηλος.

principles of beings, and are themselves constituted from elements. Some things are discerned by understanding, some by science, some by opinion, some by sensation. But these same numbers are the specific forms of things. § 51

But since the soul seems to be both a moving and a knowing principle, some have made it out to be a combination of these two, stating that it is a self-moving number. § 52

ST. THOMAS'S COMMENTARY
LECTIO FOUR

§ 43. Having shown how some have approached a knowledge of soul through movement, the Philosopher now turns to those who came to it by way of sensation or knowledge. He does this in two stages. First he shows where the latter were in agreement;[1] and secondly, at 'Empedocles, for instance,'[2] where they disagreed.

He begins then by saying that all who studied the soul in or through its knowing and sensing agreed in holding that the soul was composed of the principles of things; but some 'made', i.e. posited, many such principles, while others posited only one. Even the earliest philosophers assumed these principles to be in the soul, as though compelled by the force of truth itself; they dreamed, as it were, of the truth. The truth, in fact, is that knowledge is caused by the knower containing a likeness of the thing known; for the latter must be in the knower somehow. The early philosophers, however, thought that it existed in the knower in its own natural being, i.e. with the being that it has in itself. Like, they said, must be known by like. If then the soul is to know all things it must contain a likeness of all things according to their natural mode of being. They could not distinguish between the mode of existence that a thing has in the mind or the eye or the imagination from that which it has in itself. Therefore, since whatever is of a thing's essence is a constituent principle of the thing, and to know its constituent principles is to know the thing itself, these philosophers maintained that the reason why the soul can know all things is that it is made up of the principles of all things. This theory was common to them all.

§ 44. But they differed about these principles. They did not all admit the same; one admitted many, another only one, and one

[1] 404^b 8.   [2] 404^b 11.

this and another that. Hence they disagreed also about the constituents of the soul.

§ 45. So, at 'Empedocles, for instance,'[1] Aristotle states these differences. He gives first the opinion of Empedocles, saying that the early philosophers who studied the soul by way of its sense-perceptions thought it was composed of the elements. Those who admitted only one principle said that this precisely was the soul; and those who admitted many said that the soul was made up of many; thus Empedocles held that the soul was constituted by all the elements, and that each of these was itself a soul. Note that Empedocles admitted six principles: four material, namely earth, water, fire and air; and two active and passive principles, namely strife and friendship. And since he assumed that the soul knew all things, he said it was composed of all these principles. Thus as earthy we know earth; as ethereal or airy we know air; as aequous we know water; and as fiery, of course, we know fire. Through love we know love, and through 'sad hate' we know hatred. 'Sad' comes in here because Empedocles wrote in verse.

§ 46. Next, when he says 'In the same way Plato',[2] Aristotle states the opinion of Plato who also, he says, made the soul consist of elements, i.e. be constituted by the principles of things. And as evidence for this statement he takes three passages from Plato. The first is from the *Timaeus*,[3] where Plato says that there are two elements or first principles, Identity and Difference. For there is a certain kind of nature that is simple and unchanging, as are immaterial things; and this nature he calls Identity. And there is another kind which does not stay the same, but undergoes change and division, as do material things; and this nature he calls Difference. And it is of these two principles, of Identity and Difference, that the soul, he says, is composed; not that the two are in the soul as its parts; but rather as in the mean between extremes; for the rational soul is by nature lower and less noble than the higher and purely immaterial substances, but it is higher and nobler than inferior material things.

§ 47. Now this opinion rests on the principle already mentioned, that like is known by like. For it seemed to Plato that if the soul knew all things, and if Identity and Difference were fundamental principles, then the soul itself must be constituted of Identity and Difference; in so far as it participated in 'Identity' the soul, he

[1] 404[b] 11.   [2] 404[b] 16.   [3] 35A ss.

thought, knew the 'identical', while so far as it participated in 'Difference' it knew the 'different', i.e. material things. Hence the actual process of the soul in knowing things. For when it gathers things together under genera and species, then, said Plato, it manifests Sameness or Identity, but when it attends to accidents and differentiations he finds in it Difference. That is how Plato in the *Timaeus* understood the soul as made up of principles.

§ 48. The second passage, showing that this was Plato's theory, Aristotle refers to when he says 'In the lectures "On Philosophy".'[1] Here too the soul is represented as constituted from principles. Note, in this connection, that Plato took the objects known by the intellect to be things in themselves, existing apart from matter in perpetual actuality, and the causes of knowledge and of being in things of sense. For Aristotle this view involved so many difficulties that he was compelled to excogitate the theory of the 'agent intellect'.[2] But from Plato's position it followed that to what could be thought of in the abstract corresponded subsistent and actual realities. We can, however, form abstractions in two ways: one is by proceeding from particulars to universals; and the other is that by which mathematical objects are abstracted from objects of sense. So Plato found himself obliged to posit three types of subsistent being: the objects of sense-perception; mathematical objects; and universal ideas—these last being the cause, by participation, of the other two types.

§ 49. Plato also held that numbers were causes of real things, being unaware of the distinction between unity as identical with being, and unity as the principle of the number that is a kind of quantity. Hence he inferred that universals were of the nature of number; for the universal existing separately is the cause of things whose substance is numerical. He said indeed that the constituent principles of all beings were 'species' and 'specific number', which he called specific in the sense of being constituted from 'species'. And he reduced number itself to unity and duality as to its fundamental elements; for, as nothing can proceed from one alone, there must, he thought, be some nature, subordinate to unity, whence multiplicity might proceed; and this nature he called duality.

§ 50. Thus Plato envisaged three classes of beings, graded according to their connection with matter. As sensible objects are more

<hr />

[1] 404ᵇ 18.   [2] *intellectus agens*; cf. Bk. III, lectio 10, § 728ss.

material than the objects considered in mathematics, and the latter more so than the universal ideas, he placed sense-objects[1] on the lowest level, and above them mathematical objects, and above these the separately existing universals and ideas. Universals differ from mathematical objects in this that the latter include numerical differences within the same species, whereas ideas and separated substances exhibit no numerical differences in the one species; there is but one idea for each species. These ideas, he said, are numerical in nature, and from them are derived such numerical qualities of sensible things as length, breadth and depth. Hence he said that the idea of length was the primary duality, for length is from unit to unit, from point to point; and that of breadth was the first trinity, for the triangle is the first of plane figures; and that of depth, which includes both length and breadth, was the first quaternity, for the first solid figure is the pyramid which is constructed of four angles. So too the sensitive soul, in Plato's system, implied a Soul existing separately as its cause, and constituted, like the other 'separate' things and ideas, by number, that is, by the unity and duality which for him were fundamental in things.

§ 51. Then at 'Again, rather differently, . . .'[2] Aristotle alludes to the third text adduced to show that for Plato the soul was made up of elements or principles. As we have said,[3] it was Plato's view that the specific forms and principles of things were numbers; so when he came to treat of the soul he based its knowledge of things on its fundamentally numerical composition; all of its activities, he maintained, sprang from this source. Take for instance the diverse apprehensive functionings of the soul: simple understanding, science, opinion and sensation.[4] Simple understanding Plato connected with the idea of One; it has[5] the nature of Unity; for in one act it apprehends a unity. Again, science for him relates to Duality since it proceeds from one to one, i.e. from principles to conclusions. And opinion relates to the first Trinity, proceeding from one to two, i.e. from principles to a conclusion which is accompanied by the fear that a different conclusion may be true; so forming a triad out of one principle and one admitted and one

---

[1] *sensibilia.*   [2] 404[b] 21.   [3] §§ 48–50.

[4] *intellectum, scientiam, opinionem, sensum.*

[5] Reading, with Pirotta (in footnote), *in ea,* not *in una.*

feared conclusion. Finally, sensation derives from the first Quaternity, i.e. from the notion of a solid body constructed (as we have
said) from four angles; for bodies are the object of sensation. Since
then all knowing is contained in these four, i.e. in simple understanding, science, opinion and sensation, all of which, said Plato,
are in the soul in virtue of its participating in the nature of Unity,
Duality, Trinity and Quaternity, it obviously follows that for
Plato the separated Soul, the 'idea', as he called it, of particular
souls, was constituted by numbers, which are the elements or
principles of reality. So much to show that Plato regarded the soul
as made up of principles.

§ 52. Next at 'But since the soul seems . . .',[1] Aristotle observes
that some philosophers defined the soul, and came to know something about it, through both movement and sensation or knowledge. He says that, as the soul seemed to them to be both self-
moving and cognitive, they joined the two aspects in their definition and called it a 'self-moving number'. 'Number' refers to the
cognitive power because they thought, in accordance with what
has been said already, that the soul was able to know in virtue of
its participating in the nature of specific number (Plato's opinion).
'Self-moving' refers to the soul's motive power.

[1] 404^b 27.

BOOK I, CHAPTER II, CONTINUED

PREVIOUS THEORIES
SOUL AS IDENTIFIED WITH THE ELEMENTS

OPINIONS DIFFER HOWEVER AS TO THE ELEMENTAL principles—what they are, how many they are; and the difference is greatest between those who make these corporeal and those who make them incorporeal. But some, making a mixture, have defined the principles in terms of both. They differ also as to the number, some positing one, others several. And they assign a soul to these [principles] accordingly.[1] (For they not unreasonably assumed that what by nature causes movement was primary.)

§§ 53–4

Hence some have held it to be fire; for this is the most subtle, and much the least corporeal of the elements; moreover, it moves itself, being the first cause of movement in other things. Democritus said something which rather neatly gives the reason for either fact. He said that soul is the same as mind, and that this originates in primary indivisible particles and that it causes motion by its fineness and shape. He says that the sphere is the most light and mobile of shapes, and that fire and mind must both be of such a nature.   §§ 55–6

Anaxagoras, however (as we said above), seems to speak of soul and mind as diverse, yet he employs both terms as for a single essence. Nevertheless, he posits Intellect as the principle

---

[1] 'There is a consequent diversity in what they say of the soul', 405^a 2.

par excellence of the Universe, saying that this alone among beings is simple, unmixed and pure. He attributes, indeed, to the same principle both knowing and moving; saying that Intellect moves all things.   § 57

It seems that Thales, from what they recollect of him, was also of opinion that the soul was a cause of motion,—if it is a fact that he said that the magnet had a 'soul' because it attracts iron.   § 58

Now Diogenes, like certain others, held that air is the most subtle of all things and is their principle; and is the cause of the soul's knowing and moving. As primary, it is cognitive of all else: and as the most subtle thing, it is the motive force.
                                                                    § 59

· Heraclitus, however, says that soul, as a principle, is some vapour of which it is constituted,[1] since this is the least corporeal of substances and is always flowing; and that any moving object is known by a moving object—he and many others holding that all realities are in movement.   § 60

Alcmaeon seems to have held opinions on the soul similar to these. For he said it was immortal because it bore a resemblance to immortal beings. And this he attributed to it because it always moves; all heavenly things seem to be in motion continually—the sun, the moon, the stars, all heaven.   § 61

Some cruder thinkers, like Hippo, thought it was water. They seem to have been persuaded of this because semen is liquid in all animals. For he confutes those who say the soul is the blood, on the ground that semen, which is the inchoate soul, is not blood.   § 62

Others, such as Critias, held it was blood; that sensation was most distinctive of the soul; and that it was due to the nature of blood that this power was in it.   § 63

[1] 'from which other things are constituted', 405ᵃ 26,

For opinions have been given in favour of every element excepting earth: which no one has proposed, unless whosoever may have said it was derived from all the elements, or was identical with them, did so.   § 64

All, taken together, define soul, we may say, by three things: by movement, by sensation, and by immateriality. And each of these is reduced to elemental principles. Hence, in defining it as cognitive, they make it either an element or consist of several elements, one saying much the same as another (with a single exception). For they say that anything is known by what resembles it, and as the soul knows all things, so they constitute it of all principles: some saying that there is one cause and one element, and that the soul is a single thing—fire or water, for example; others that there are several principles, and that the soul is multiple.   § 65

But Anaxagoras, standing alone, says that mind is beyond the reach of influence and has nothing in common with other things. But, granted that this be true, he did not explain how it acquires knowledge, in virtue of what cause; nor is this made clear by anything else he said.   § 66

Those who posit contraries as first principles also maintain that the soul consists of such contraries, while those who favour some one among contraries (hot or cold, or some other like these) make the soul, accordingly, one of these. Whence also some follow names, as those who allege that it is heat, because life is due to heat and is named from it. But those who identify the soul with cold say that it is named from respiration and breathing.[1]

Such then are the opinions that have been transmitted to us about the soul, together with the reasons given for them.   § 67

---

[1] ζεῖν, to boil, ζῆν, to live; ψυχή, soul, ψυχρός, cold, 405ᵇ 26, 27.

ST. THOMAS'S COMMENTARY

LECTIO FIVE

§ 53. In the preceding chapters Aristotle has shown the old philosophers agreeing in their analysis of the soul, in that they all regarded it as the origin of movement and knowledge. In the section beginning now he shows how they variously interpreted that common presupposition. This section falls into three parts: in the first he shows the root of the divergence of these philosophers in their teaching on the soul;[1] the second enumerates the various points of difference (beginning at 'Hence some');[2] the third summarises all that we have to consider in these differences (at 'All, taken together').[3] The root of the divergence of the philosophers in their teaching on the soul is to be looked for in the way they analysed it into its ultimate elements; as they disagreed about these elements so did they differ about the soul. They all agreed that the soul was made up of ultimate elements, but they could not agree that it was made up of the same elements; and, differing as to the elements, they differed in their theories of the soul.

§ 54. They differ in two ways about the ultimate elements: first, as to their essential nature, i.e. 'what' they are; secondly, as to their number, 'how many' they are. As regards their essential nature, some said these principles were corporeal (fire or water or air) while others said they were incorporeal and immaterial, such as those who spoke of numbers and ideas; and there were others, like the Platonists, who blended both views and allowed that there existed both sensibly perceptible and separate immaterial principles. As to their number or multiplication, there were some who admitted only one principle. Heraclitus, for instance, said it was air; and someone else, fire; while others said there were many principles—Empedocles for instance, who maintained the theory

[1] 404^b 30–405^a 5.   [2] 405^a 5.   [3] 405^b 10.

of the four elements. And their theories of the soul in respect of the elements followed these various hypotheses concerning ultimate elements. Those who held to a theory of material first principles, like Empedocles, said the soul was composed of such; and those, like Plato, who held to immaterial principles, said that the soul was composed of these. But one and all considered the soul to be the chief source of movement.

§ 55. Next, at 'Hence some',[1] he proceeds to run through the more particular differences between the philosophers. It should be noted that of those who thought that a corporeal thing was the first principle, not one deigned to identify this with mere earth. Some said it was fire, others air, others water, but nobody said it was earth, except those who thought that all the four elements together were the first principle. (The reason being that, with its density, earth seemed always to presuppose some more ultimate principle). Aristotle, then, does three things here. He gives first the views of those who identified the first principle and the soul itself with fire;[2] secondly, of those who held that they were air (at 'Now Diogenes');[3] and thirdly, the opinion of those who held that water was both the first principle and the soul (beginning at: 'Some cruder thinkers').[4]

§ 56. As to the first of these groups, we should note that since movement and knowledge were ascribed to the soul, it appeared to some that the soul possessed these properties in the highest degree; and as movement and knowledge seemed to connote what is lightest and most rarified, they concluded that the soul was fire, which is the lightest and most rarified of bodies. And while many were of this opinion and thought the soul was fire, Democritus more subtly and rationally explained 'the reason for either fact', that is, he expressed more clearly the nature of movement and of knowledge. He held, as we have seen,[5] that all things are made of atoms; and though for him these atoms were primary he maintained, nevertheless, that the round ones were of the nature of fire, so that the soul, he said, was composed of spherical atoms. Considered as first principles, these atoms were by nature cognitive, but considered as spherical they were mobile; hence he said that the soul knows and moves all things precisely because it is made up of these round, indivisible bodies. And in assuming that

[1] 405[a] 5.   [2] 405[a] 5–20.   [3] 405[a] 21.   [4] 405[b] 1.   [5] § 34.

they were of the nature of fire, he agreed with those who thought that everything was fiery.

§ 57. Then at 'Anaxagoras, however',[1] Aristotle gives the view of Anaxagoras who agreed with the others already mentioned in ascribing knowledge and motion to the soul. Anaxagoras, as we saw, sometimes appears to distinguish between soul and intellect, but sometimes he uses both terms as though they meant the same thing. He ascribes to the soul motive power and knowledge, but he also says that intellect knows and moves all things, thus identifying the soul and the intellect. But he differed from the others in this, that whereas Democritus held that the soul was corporeal by nature, being composed of material elements, Anaxagoras said that intellect was 'simple', excluding intrinsic division from its essence, and 'unmixed', excluding composition with anything else, and 'pure', excluding any addition to it from outside. But he ascribed movement and knowledge to one and the same principle, i.e. the intellect; for intellect of its nature knows; and movement pertains to it, so he said, because it moves everything else.[2]

§ 58. Next, at 'It seems that Thales',[3] he states the opinion of a philosopher called Thales who had only this in common with the others mentioned above, that he identified soul with a motive force. This Thales was one of the Seven Wise Men; but while the others studied moral questions, Thales devoted himself to the world of nature and was the first natural philosopher. Hence Aristotle remarks 'from what they recollect etc.', referring to those who said that water was the basic principle of things. For Thales thought that the way to find the principle of all things was by searching into the principle of living things, and since all the principles or seeds of living things are moist, he thought that the absolutely first principle must be the most moist of things; and this being water, he said water was that principle. Yet he did not follow his theory to the point of saying that soul was water; rather, he defined it as that which has motive force. Hence he asserted that a certain stone, the magnet, had a soul because it moved iron. Anaxagoras and Thales, then, are included in the present list; not for identifying the soul with fire, but because the former said that the soul was the source of knowledge and sensation, and the latter that it was at the origin of movement.

[1] 405ᵃ 13.   [2] § 38.   [3] 405ᵃ 19.

§ 59. Where he says, 'Now Diogenes . . .'[1] Aristotle alludes to those who thought that air was the first principle and the soul. There were three of these. First there was Diogenes who held that air was the first principle and also the finest-grained of all bodies, and that the soul therefore was air,—hence its power to know and move. The knowing power was due to the fact that air was (as he said) the first principle; for as knowledge is through likeness, as we have seen,[2] the soul could not know all things unless it included the principles of all. And the moving power was due, he said, to the fact that air was the finest-grained of bodies and therefore the most mobile.

§ 60. Then at 'Heraclitus, however'[3] he states the second opinion, that of Heraclitus who thought that not mere air but vapour, the blend of air and water, was the first principle. He could not allow that this was either water by itself, or fire, or air; it had to be something betwixt and between, because, being a materialist, he was concerned to find a principle midway between the opposite extremes of material quality. Thinking that vapour answered this requirement most precisely, he said that the soul was vapour; which explained its extraordinary capacity to know and to move. His view was, indeed, that everything was in continual flux, that nothing stayed the same even for one hour, and that no definite statement could be made about anything. And it was just because vapour is so unstable that he identified it with the first principle of all things; which, he said, was a soul. As the first principle, soul has the power to know, whilst as the least material and most fluid of things it has movement.

§ 61. Thirdly, at 'Alcmaeon seems . . .'[4] he gives the third opinion, Alcmaeon's, which agrees with the others only as regards movement. This man said that the soul was pre-eminently a thing in motion, resembling in this the immortal heavenly bodies with their heavenly and divine nature. For he thought that the perpetual movement of the sun and moon and the rest, was the cause of their being immortal; and that the same inference was valid in the case of the soul.

§ 62. Then at 'Some cruder thinkers',[5] Aristotle states an opinion of some who made water the first principle. For there were certain

---

[1] 405[a] 21.　　　[2] § 43.　　　[3] 405[a] 25.　　　[4] 405[a] 29.　　　[5] 405[b] 1.

rather crude followers of Thales who tried to make the principle
of one particular thing an analogy of the first principle of Nature
as a whole. Observing that moisture was fundamental to living
things they concluded that it must be the first principle of all
things; in short, that the latter was water. So far indeed they followed their master, Thales; but whereas he, though admitting
water to be the first principle, would not, as we have seen, allow
that the soul was water, but rather a motive force,[1] his cruder dis-
ciples (such as Hippo) asserted that it was water. Hippo tried to
refute those who said the soul was blood with the argument that
blood is not the generating seed (which they called 'the inchoate
soul') of animate things. He identified this with water on account
of its humidity.

§ 63. Next, at 'Others, such as Critias',[2] he alludes to a philosopher who was more interested in the soul's knowledge. He was
still cruder in his expressions, saying that the soul itself was blood.
His reason was that sense-perception only takes place in animals
through the medium of blood: for the bloodless organs, such as
bones, nails and teeth are without sensation (he forgot the nerves
which are extremely sensitive and yet bloodless). If then, he said,
the soul is the root of knowledge, the soul must be blood. It was
Critias who said this.

§ 64. In case anyone should wonder why he has not mentioned
earth along with the other elements, Aristotle, at 'Opinions have
etc.',[3] explains that his predecessors' views on the soul followed on
what they thought about the first principles; and as nobody judged
earth to be a first principle, nobody said it was the soul; unless we
count those—such as Democritus and Empedocles—who said that
soul was, or was composed of, *all* the principles.

§ 65. Then, at 'All, taken together',[4] he summarises, concluding
this part of the enquiry; and first with reference to the elements or
principles themselves, and then with regard to the contrarieties
that are found in them.

First, then, he notes that the soul has been described by all in
terms of these three notes: fineness of grain or texture (incorpore-
ality); knowledge; movement; and that each of these notes has
been also traced back to a first principle. For that is called a principle which is simple. Also a 'principle', it is said, is essentially

[1] 405[a] 20; cf. § 58.   [2] 405[b] 5.   [3] 405[b] 8.   [4] 405[b] 10.

cognitive (for, to recall what was said above,[1] since like is known by like, they said that the soul was composed of, or even was, the elements of all things. Anaxagoras, to be sure, is an exception with his pure unmixed Intellect). Again, they identified the chief motive-force in things with a 'principle' since a principle is what is least corporeal. And the soul's knowledge of all things proves, they said, that it was composed of all the principles or elements. All their theories turn on this correspondence between the soul and the first principles. Whoever posited some one cause or principle or element, such as fire, air or water, identified just that one with the soul. So, too, whoever upheld many principles either identified them with the soul or with its component elements.

§ 66. Having excepted Anaxagoras, touching the theory of the soul's composition, he goes on, at 'But Anaxagoras',[2] to show how this man differed from the others. He alone, says Aristotle, denied the passivity of the intellect, its share in the nature of the things that it knows. But *how* intellect knows, Anaxagoras does not say; nor can one infer anything certain from what he does say.

§ 67. To end this section, Aristotle summarises[3] what he has to say touching the contrariety of the above-mentioned principles to one another. Some, he says, arrange the first principles of things in pairs of opposites; and the soul also they regard as a synthesis of contraries. Thus Empedocles thought that the heat and cold, the moisture and dryness which he found in the elements were intrinsic to the soul also. As earthy, he said, we know earth, as watery water, and so on. Others found their first principle in only one element, whose particular quality they then attributed to the soul. If it was fire, then the soul, they said, was hot; if water, then the soul was cold. According to the principle assumed so was the quality attributed to the soul, as though it shared in the nature of heat or cold etc. This is clear from the names they gave to the soul. Those who said it was hot gave it names derived from *zaein* or *zooein*, meaning to live, which itself comes from *zeein*, meaning to boil; while others who said it was cold called it *psychron*, meaning cold, whence comes *psyche*, a term applied to the soul because the coolness caused by breathing preserves animal life.[4] Those who thought

[1] §§ 43; 59.　　　　　[2] 405[b] 19–20.
[3] 405[b] 23.　　　　　[4] cf. *De Respir.*, cc.21–2; 478[a] 10ss.

84

the soul by nature hot, named it from life; those who thought it by nature cold, from respiration. And Aristotle concludes by saying that the foregoing are the opinions handed down about the soul, together with the grounds on which they are maintained.

BOOK I, CHAPTER III

PREVIOUS THEORIES
SOUL AS A SELF-MOVING ESSENCE

THE FIRST THING TO BE CONSIDERED IS MOVEMENT. For perhaps it is not only false to say that this is the essence of the soul, as some mean when they say the soul is self-moving, or is able to move itself; but that there should be movement in it at all is an impossibility. It has already been stated that it is not necessary that everything that causes motion be itself moving. For everything moves in one of two ways: either by another, or of itself. We say, 'by another', of anything that moves through being in that which moves, like sailors; for these are not in motion in the same way as the ship. The latter moves of itself, but they through being in what moves. This is evident if we consider their parts. Walking is the proper motion of the feet—and also of men—; but for the time being the sailors do not walk. Movement being thus predicated in two ways, we now turn to the soul, asking whether it moves of itself and participates in motion.   §§ 68–74

Since there are four kinds of movement (local, by alteration, by increase, by decrease) its motion must be one of these, or some, or all. But if its movement is not incidental, then motion will be in it by nature: and if so, it will be [in] place; for all the aforesaid movements are in place. If it is the essence of the soul to move itself, to be in motion will not

86

be in it incidentally, as in what is white or three cubits long; for these also participate in movement, but incidentally. For what moves is the body in which these inhere; hence of themselves they have no place; but the soul has it, if indeed it naturally participates in motion. §§ 75-7

Further, if it moves by nature, so it will move by force; and if by force, then, by nature. And its rest will be in the same way. Whithersoever it moves by nature, there it will come to rest by nature; and likewise wheresoever it is moved by force, there it will come to rest by force. But what kind of enforced motions and rests will there be in the soul? To find an answer is not easy,—nor, even to imagine one! §§ 78-9

Again, if it moves upwards, it will be fire; and if downwards, earth; for such are the movements of these bodies; and the same holds of the intermediate [elements].[1] § 80

Since it seems to move the body, it would seem reasonable [to say] that it does so by the same motions as those by which it moves itself. If so, then it is true to say, conversely, that just as the body moves, the soul also moves. Now the body moves by change of place; hence the soul too will move in accordance with the body, either the whole or the parts being transposed. If this is so, then it might happen that after leaving the body it could return to it. (But it is utterly impossible that the dead rise again.)[2] And it would follow that dead animals could rise again. §§ 81-3

If it does move, however, by something else, its motion will be incidental; for certainly an animal can be driven by force. But what has self-movement as of its essence cannot be moved by another, save incidentally; as that which is

[1] *de mediis*, περὶ τῶν μεταξύ. St. Thomas seems to understand 'elements', § 80.
[2] Not in the Greek.

good in itself or for its own sake cannot exist for the sake of another, or on account of another.

One might certainly say that, if the soul is moved at all, it is moved by the objects of sensation.   §§ 84–5

But if it moves itself it also is in motion. Hence if all motion is a displacement of the moved as such, then the soul must be displaced from its own essence by itself, unless its movement be incidental; but [in fact] this is a self-movement of its essence.   § 86

§ 68. The Philosopher now begins to criticise the theories he has
been recounting. These theories amount to three statements about
the soul: that it is the source of *movement* and of *knowledge*, and that
it is in a special way *incorporeal*. The two former attributions, the
principal ones, have been predicated of the soul in an absolute
sense, as referring directly to its essence. The third is, however,
true in one sense and false in another. For if immateriality[1] is taken
as predicated simply and absolutely of the soul, then the statement
is true; for soul is certainly the least material and most rarified of
things. But if it is predicated only in relation to the body, as if to
say that soul is the least material of bodies, then the statement is
not true. Hence the Philosopher sets to work only with the two
former attributions, of movement and of knowledge.

§ 69. This part of the treatise falls into three divisions. Aristotle
first argues against the philosophers who had made the soul the
source of movement; then at 'There are then three ways'[2] against
those who regarded it as the seat of knowledge; and thirdly, at
'Since knowledge pertains',[3] he raises the question whether movement, feeling and knowing ought to be attributed to the soul as to
one principle or several. The first of these divisions is again divided.
He first adduces objections against simply identifying the soul itself
with a source of movement; and then against an opinion, proceeding from this identification, according to which the soul was also
a self-moving number. (This comes at 'Much the most unreasonable'.)[4] The former argument again subdivides into, first a criticism of the way in which these philosophers had predicated move-

---

[1] *sc. quod sit subtilissimum.*   [2] Lectio 12, § 178s; 409[b] 19.
[3] Lectio 14, § 199s; 411[a] 26.   [4] Lectio 11, § 168s; 408[b] 32.

ment of the soul, and secondly, at 'One might with more reason
. . .',[1] a query whether this predication might have been made
differently. Then the criticism is divided into, first, a general argument against all who said that the soul was the source of movement; and secondly, at 'Some say that a soul moves',[2] a series of
particular discussions of special points. Finally, the general argument is subdivided. First, he says what he intends to do; secondly,
he argues in support of his own opinion. The latter begins at 'Since
there are four kinds of movement'.[3]

§ 70. He begins then by remarking that philosophers have
studied the soul from two points of view, from motion and from
knowledge. This is clear from what has been said. And Aristotle
says that he will start from motion. Now all the others who started
from this point of view had one notion in common, that everything that produces movement is itself moving. They thought
therefore that if soul is by nature a cause of movement, it must be
by its nature a moving essence. So they put movement into its
definition, calling it something that moves itself.

§ 71. Now here there are two disputable points; the theory itself
is disputable, and so is the principle upon which it rests. The principle presupposed as a self-evident truth, namely that every active
mover is itself in movement, is in fact not true, as is clearly enough
shown in Book VIII of the *Physics*,[4] where Aristotle proves the
existence of an unmoved mover. And as to this, we may give here
a short proof that if a thing produces movement it does not have
to be in movement itself. It is clear that in so far as a thing produces
movement it is in act, and in so far as it is caused to move, it is in
potency. (If then *as* causing movement it were moved), the same
thing would be in act and potency in the same respect; which
hardly makes sense.[5]

§ 72. But even setting this difficulty aside, the theory that the
soul is in movement is disputable. Its upholders indeed added the
further proposition, that movement was of the soul's essence; but
Aristotle denies both parts of this theory where he says, 'For perhaps', etc.[6] He puts it like this because he has not yet proved his

---

[1] Lectio 10, § 146s; 408ᵃ 34.   [2] Lectio 7, § 87s; 406ᵇ 15.
[3] § 75 *infra*; 406ᵃ 12.   [4] *Phys*., VIII, 5; 257ᵃ 31s.
[5] The context requires the parenthesis, which is lacking in Pirotta.
[6] 405ᵇ 31.

assertion, namely that not only is it false to say that movement is
of the essence of the soul (which is what they imply when they
define the soul as an actual or potential self-mover) but that it is
also quite impossible that the soul should move at all.

§ 73. That not everything which causes movement need itself be
moved was shown in an earlier work, Book VIII of the *Physics*.[1]
Now in any self-mover there are two things to be considered, the
thing moving and the thing moved; and the former cannot as such
be the same as the latter. In living things, however, though the
moving part is not moved in itself, absolutely speaking, yet it is
moved indirectly. For there are two kinds of movement, direct
and indirect: direct, when a thing itself is moving, e.g. a ship; indirect when a thing itself is at rest, but moved with the movement
of something else which contains it, as the sailor on board ship
moves with the ship's movement, not his own. So the ship moves
directly and in itself, but the sailor only in an accidental way or
relatively. This is clear if we consider that when anything moves
in itself, its parts are moving, as in walking the feet make the first
movement; but once the sailor is on board this does not happen.
Movement then can be taken in either of these two senses; but
since the philosophers we are discussing said that the soul moved
in itself, directly, we can forgo at present the question whether
it is moved indirectly, and consider only whether it is directly
affected by movement, as they maintained.

§ 74. To show that the soul does not move in itself, Aristotle
uses six arguments, with regard to which we should note that,
while they may not appear very cogent, still they are effective in
relation to the theory he is criticising. For it is one thing to argue
out the simple truth of a question, and another to reason against a
particular theory; in the former case you have to make sure that
your premises are true, but in the latter you proceed from what
your adversary concedes or asserts. Hence it is that when Aristotle
criticises the views of others, he often seems to use rather weak
arguments. In each case he is, in fact, destroying his adversary's
position by drawing out its logical consequences.

§ 75. The first argument begins at 'Since there are four kinds',[2]
and may be stated as follows. If the soul moves, its movement is
either direct (in the sense explained) or indirect. If indirect, then it

[1] *loc. cit.*   [2] 406a 12.

is not of the essence of the soul (which is against their opinion), and the soul moves in the same way as whiteness or 3 inches[1] which are accidental qualities moving only with the thing that is white or 3 inches long, and not themselves, as such, requiring a position in space. But if the soul moves in itself, it moves in one of the four kinds of movement: change of place, growth, decrease or alteration. Coming-to-be and passing-away are not movements, strictly speaking, but changes, because they are instantaneous, whilst movements are successive. Hence the soul will have to move in one of these four ways—from place to place; by increase or decrease in size; or by qualitative alteration. But if all these movements involve position in space, the soul will then be localised in space.

§ 76. There seem to be two doubtful points in this argument. The first is that, while it is clear enough as regards locomotion, growth and decrease, it suggests a difficulty about alteration. Some meet this difficulty by saying that as only bodies are subject to alteration, and all bodies are in place, alteration itself may be *said* to occur in place. But this does not keep to the letter of the argument: Aristotle says that this kind of movement is *in* place and not merely *according* to place. Movement in place is quite different from movement according to place; and, following Aristotle, I maintain that alteration certainly occurs *in* place. Of itself, and not simply because of its localised subject, it is in place; for, when any alteration occurs, the agent producing it must draw near to the thing altered; otherwise nothing would ever be altered. And since drawing near is a local movement, it follows that here and now the cause of a given alteration is a change in place.

§ 77. The second difficulty is that these philosophers do not in fact see anything unreasonable in the soul's being in place, since they maintain that it moves in itself, absolutely. So Aristotle's objection seems to misfire. To this two answers might be given, (*a*) that the objection to the soul's being in place will become clearer as we proceed, and (*b*) that if the soul were in place, it would have to be assigned a definite position in the body and thus would not be the form of the whole body. This reinforces the objection to the soul's being in place.

§ 78. The second argument, at 'Further, if it moves',[2] is this. If

---

[1] Literally, '3 cubits'.   [2] 406ᵃ 22.

the soul moves 'absolutely' from place to place, the movement must be natural to it. But anything that can be moved naturally can be moved violently.[1] Now its natural movement implies a natural ceasing to move; and therefore also its enforced, violent movement implies an enforced ceasing to move. Hence the soul may both move and stop moving under compulsion; which is impossible if by nature both its movement and ceasing to move are spontaneous.

§ 79. A difficulty here seems to be that[2] what moves naturally does not in fact move under compulsion. I answer that what Aristotle says is false absolutely speaking, but true relative to the theory under discussion. For these philosophers maintained that the only bodies that moved with a natural movement were the four elements; in which we do observe both natural and enforced movement and ceasing to move. This opinion is presupposed by the argument.

§ 80. The third argument, at 'Again, if',[3] runs as follows: these men who ascribe movement primarily to the soul, and to the body only as derived from the soul, also say that this movement is due to one or other of the elements, fire or earth or one of the others. But if the soul moved with the nature of fire it would only rise; if with the nature of earth it would only sink; whereas in fact it moves in all directions. This argument also is *ad hominem*.

§ 81. The fourth argument comes at 'Since it seems'.[4] It is this. You say that it is in moving the body that the soul moves. Logically, then, it follows that it moves the body by its own movements; and conversely that it is moved by the same movements which move the body. But the body moves by changing position in space; so also then the soul. But if the soul's local movements affect the body, the soul might, after leaving the body, enter it once more. And since it is the soul's presence that gives life to the body, it follows that dead animals might, even naturally, come back to life: which is impossible.

§ 82. Against this argument some have objected that it ignores the difference between the movements which affect the soul itself and those by which it moves other things, including the body. The former are movements of desire and will; not so the latter.

[1] i.e. against its nature. [2] Reading *quod*, not Pirotta's suggestion *quoad*,
[3] 406ᵃ 27. [4] *ibid.*, 30.

But in reply one may say that desires and volitions and so on are not properly 'movements' of the soul but 'operations'. 'Movements' and 'operations' are different: a movement is an act of something that is incomplete,[1] whereas an operation is an act of a subject already possessing full actuality.[2] Still, what Aristotle says is true relative to the theory under discussion; for this had identified all the movements of the soul with those by which it moved the body.

§ 83. But is it true that if the soul had local movement dead animals would come to life again? Well, some philosophers have maintained that the soul pervades the whole body, forming a unity with it through some kind of proportion, and that the two cannot be separated without this proportion being destroyed; so that, so far as *this* view is concerned, the conclusion would not follow. But it does follow from—and is a valid objection against—the opinion of those who say the soul is located in the body as in a vessel which it sometimes enters and sometimes leaves.

§ 84. The fifth argument comes at 'If it does move',[3] and runs as follows. It is clear that when anything is of the essence of a given subject its presence in the latter does not need, except incidentally, to be explained by anything else. If then the soul is essentially moving, it is mobile of its own nature; it does not need to be moved through or by anything else. But we know that it is in fact moved by sensible objects when it senses, and by things desirable when it desires; therefore it does not move of itself.

§ 85. The Platonists meet this argument by denying that the soul is moved by sensible objects; these, they say, are merely involved in the soul's own movement when it passes from one object to another. But this is untrue. As Aristotle has proved, the intellectual potency is brought into act precisely by means of the sensible objects as apprehended; so that it is moved by them in this way.

§ 86. The sixth argument begins at 'But if it moves itself'.[4] Clearly, if the soul is self-moving, its own essence governs its movement. But in every movement the moving thing comes away or proceeds from that which moves it and governs its movement; for instance, if anything is moved by a quantity, it departs and proceeds from the latter. If then the soul is moved by its own

[1] *motus est actus imperfecti.*

[2] *operatio . . . est actus perfecti.*

[3] 406^b 6.

[4] 406^b 11.

essence (as they say) it must depart or proceed from its own essence; which is as much as to say that it causes its own destruction. How then could it be through movement that the soul becomes god-like and immortal, as some philosophers whom we have mentioned supposed?[1] This argument bears against those who did not distinguish between movement proper and operation. For movement implies that what is moved comes away from the cause of movement; but operation is a perfection intrinsic to the operating agent itself.

[1] cf. § 61.

BOOK I, CHAPTER III, CONTINUED

SOUL AS A MOVER OF THE BODY
DEMOCRITUS AND PLATO

SOME SAY THAT A SOUL MOVES THE BODY IN WHICH it dwells just as it moves itself; as did Democritus, who spoke like Philip the comic poet; for the latter relates that Daedalus made a wooden Venus mobile by pouring quicksilver into it. Democritus, then, spoke in like manner, saying that there are in movement indivisible globules of which the nature is to be never at rest, and which therefore draw together and move the whole body. §§ 87–8

Now, what we would ask is, whether this is also the cause of coming to rest? How it could be, on this hypothesis, is difficult to see, indeed impossible. § 89

The soul seems, in general, not to move the animate being in this way, but rather by a sort of choice and understanding. § 90

In the same way, the *Timaeus* sets out a physical theory as to how the soul moves the body. For, from the fact that the soul moves itself, it moves the body, as a result of its connection with the body. § 91

'Being compounded of the elements and divided according to harmonic numbers, so that it have a connatural sense of

harmony, and the whole be borne along with well attuned
motions,   §§ 92–8

[God] bent the straight line into a circle, and, dividing it,
made out of one two circles, adjusted at two points; and,
again, he divided one of these into seven circles, as though
the heavenly motions were the soul's motions.'[1] §§ 99–106

[1] Paraphrasing the *Timaeus*, 35A ff.

§ 87. Having argued in a general way against the view that movement pertains essentially to the soul, the Philosopher now brings forward arguments against particular philosophers whose theories of the movement of the soul seem to give rise to some special difficulty.[1] These arguments fall into three groups. First, he opposes an opinion of Democritus;[2] then, at 'In the same way', one of Plato;[3] and thirdly, at 'There is another opinion',[4] another theory.

He begins, then, by stating the view of Democritus on the soul's movement; and then brings objections against it.

§ 88. This theory has already been referred to by Aristotle in his fourth objection to the view that the soul moves in itself and by this movement makes the body move. If the soul moves the body, he has said, it must do so in virtue of its own movement. This was admitted by those who said that each soul moved its own body in a manner corresponding to the movement in itself; among whom was Democritus who made use of the following illustration. There was a certain comic dramatist called Philip who tells somewhere of one Daedalus, that he made a wooden statue of the goddess Venus, and that this statue, being filled with quicksilver, was able to move. It moved as the quicksilver moved. And what Democritus said of the soul's movement was rather similar. The soul, he said, (as has been noted above)[5] was composed of indivisible spheres or atoms which, being round in shape, were always moving about, and by their incessant movement made the whole body cohere and move accordingly.

---

[1] The literal sense of Pirotta's text is doubtful here.   [2] 406^b 15.

[3] § 91; and Lectio 8, §§ 107–31; 406^b 25–30.   [4] Lectio 9, § 132; 407^b 25–30.

[5] §§ 34, 56.

§ 89. Then, at 'Now, what we, etc.',[1] Aristotle puts two objections to this. First, it is agreed that in animals the soul is the cause of resting as well as the cause of movement. But according to Democritus the soul is never the cause of rest, though it is the cause of animal movements. For he could hardly maintain that those spherical atoms ever rested if they never cease to move.

§ 90. Again, at 'The soul seems',[2] he puts a second objection. The movement caused by quicksilver in the statue is obviously not spontaneous; it is a compelled movement. On the contrary, that of the soul is spontaneous, proceeding from mind and will. Hence the view of Democritus seems worthless.

§ 91. Then at 'In the same way'[3] he first states the opinion of Plato, which, at 'Now in the first place,'[4] he will reject. But before explaining what Plato said about the soul he shows its similarity to the theory of Democritus. As Democritus had supposed that the soul's movements moved the body to which it was joined, so also did Timaeus, a speaker introduced by Plato. For he said that soul moves body in so far as soul itself moves; because the two are, as it were, bound up together.

§ 92. With 'Being compounded, etc.',[5] Aristotle makes Plato's view explicit; first as to what constitutes the essence of the soul, and then, at 'God bent, etc.',[6] as to how movement proceeds from it. Regarding the former question, note that the words quoted here are used by Plato in the *Timaeus*[7] and refer to the Soul of the world which, according to him, is imitated by inferior souls. So when he touches, as here, on the nature of the World-Soul, he refers also, in a way, to any soul. Now Plato, for the reason already given,[8] maintained that the essence of all things was numerical; and that in number the formal element, so to say, was one and the material element two—all numbers being made up of one and two. And as odd numbers retain something of the indivision of one, he laid down two elements of number, the even and the odd, attributing to the odd identity and finitude, but to the even difference and infinity.

§ 93. Some explanation of this theory may be found in the

[1] 406^{b} 22.   [2] 406^{b} 24.   [3] 406^{b} 25.
[4] Lectio 8, § 107; 407^{a} 2.   [5] 406^{b} 28.   [6] 406^{b} 31; cf. § 99.
[7] 35A ff.   [8] §§ 46–51.

Physics, Book III.[1] If odd numbers are added to unity in sequence the same type of number[2] always results; e.g. if 3, the first odd number, is added to 1, you get the square number 4; if to 4 you add the second odd number, 5, you get 9, which is also a square number; and so on to infinity. But with even numbers the result is always a different type of number. Add 2, the first even number, to 1, the result is the 'triangular' number 3; to which if you add 4, the second even number, you get 7 which is 'septangular'; and so on to infinity. Hence Plato made Identity and Difference the first elements of all things, attributing the former to odd numbers, the latter to even.

§ 94. And because he placed the soul mid-way between the higher substances, which never change, and corporeal substances, which change and move, he thought that the soul was constituted of the elements of Identity and Difference, and so of odd and even numbers. For the mean must participate in both extremes. This is why Aristotle says that Plato held the soul to be constituted by these elements.

§ 95. Again, we should note that in numbers there are different proportions and infinities, of which some are harmonic, i.e. the cause of harmony. The double proportion causes the harmony called a whole octave;[3] that of 3 to 2 causes the harmony called a fifth;[4] (that of 4 to 3 causes the harmony called a fourth); that of 9 to 8 causes a tone; and the other harmonies are caused by other proportions: for example, the harmony composed of an octave and a fifth is caused by the triple proportion; that of the double octave[5] is caused by the quadruple proportion which was discovered by Pythagoras, as Boethius[6] relates, from the striking of four hammers which sounded in harmony according to the aforesaid proportions. Thus if one hammer weighed twelve ounces, one nine, one eight and one six, the one that weighed twelve ounces would be in the proportion of two to one to the one weighing six, and the two together would render the harmony of the octave. Again,

---

[1] *Phys.*, III, c.4; 203ᵃ 10–15.   [2] *figura numeralis.*   [3] *diapason.*

[4] Pirotta has *diatesseron*, i.e. 'a fourth'; the mistake is due, as manuscript evidence shows, to his having left out the phrase in brackets (Balliol MSS. 278, fol. 9ᵛᵇ; 311, fol. 6ᵛᵇ; 313, fol. 92ᵛᵃ).

[5] Altering *quae sub diapason* to *quae est bis diapason.*

[6] *De Musica*, I, c.10 (P.L., vol. LXIII, col. 1176–7).

the one weighing twelve ounces would be as three to two to the one that weighed eight, and the harmony produced would be that of a fifth; similarly in the case of those that weighed nine ounces and six ounces. Again, the one weighing twelve ounces is in the proportion of from four to three to the one weighing nine, and makes with it the harmony of a fourth; so also does the one that weighs eight with that weighing six; while the one weighing nine is proportioned to the one that weighs eight, and produces with it the harmony called a tone.

§ 96. But if Plato reduced everything to numbers, these were not harmonic numbers, except in the case of the soul. Hence Aristotle gives it as Plato's view that the soul was 'divided' or, as it were, weighed out, 'according to harmonic numbers', i.e. to numbers related to each other in musical proportions. He said that the soul was constituted of the numbers 1, 2, 3, 4, 8, 9 and 27; in which these harmonic proportions are found.

§ 97. And he had two reasons for thinking this. One was the fact that similarity and connaturality are always a cause of pleasure. We find the soul taking pleasure in all harmonies and disliking whatever is unharmonious in sounds and colours and indeed in any sensible quality. So harmony seems to be natural to the soul. This is what he means by saying that the soul has 'a connatural sense (i.e. knowledge) of harmony'.

§ 98. The second reason is that the Pythagoreans and Platonists thought that beautifully harmonious sounds resulted from the movements of the heavenly bodies; and since they supposed these movements to be caused by the World-Soul they naturally concluded that the soul was made up of harmonic numbers. Hence Aristotle says 'that the whole (i.e. Universe) be borne along with well-attuned motions'.[1]

§ 99. Next, when he says 'God bent, etc.',[2] Aristotle explains how the World-Soul[3] is the cause of heavenly movements. Taking all numbers in their natural order, we must think of them as laid in a straight line, each one adding to the preceding one. Now the natural numerical series can give rise to several other series; for example, one might take the geometrical series whose common ratios are 2 or 3 or 4, and so on for other ratios. As then man, by thought, can manipulate numbers, so does God in building up the

[1] 406[b] 31. [2] 406[b] 31. [3] *anima mundi*.

substances of things from numbers. In constructing the soul's substance out of the aforesaid numbers, namely all those placed in a
straight line series according to their natural order, he divides
them into two series: one, the geometrical series whose common
ratio is 2; the other, the geometrical series whose common ratio is
3; because these two embrace all the harmonic proportions. For
the double proportion is divided into the ratios 3:2 and 4:3; the
triple into 2:1 and 3:2.[1] Therefore the above-mentioned numbers
are taken, in the geometrical series with common ratio 2, up to the
first cube number, e.g. 1,2,4 up to 8; so also with the series with
common ratio 3, e.g., 1,3,9,27. These two series meet at unity like
two straight lines containing an angle.

§ 100. Moreover, if the numbers in the series whose common
ratio is three are joined to unity we get as a result the numbers of
the series whose common ratio is 2; e.g. if to 1 is added 3 the result
is 4. Conversely, if to 1 is added 2 the result is 3. Thus it is as if two
lines were drawn intersecting each other like the Greek letter X.

§ 101. If we proceed further we return to the same numbers. For
from 4 we go on to 8 and from 3 to 27; both series concluding with
the same type of number, as though we were going round in a
circle.

§ 102. We must realise that for Plato the more complex things
found in nature are composed of simpler natures, just as the harmonies of sounds arise from the proportions between numbers.
He put the essence of the soul mid-way between numbers, which
are eminently abstract, and sensible substances; and so deduced the
soul's properties from the said numbers. Thus in the soul we find,
first, a direct knowing, in that it looks directly at its object; and
then the circular return by which the intellect reflects upon itself.
So too the intellectual soul moves in a sort of circle with respect to
the even and the odd in knowing things both like and unlike itself.
And this principle is extended to the substance of the visible
heavens moved by the World-Soul.

§ 103. For in the heavens we find two circular movements. One
is simple and uniform by which the heavens move or revolve daily
from east to west according to the equinoctial circle. The other is

[1] $\frac{3}{2}$ and $\frac{4}{3}$ are the arithmetic and harmonic means between 2 and 1; $\frac{2}{1}$ and $\frac{3}{2}$
are the same between 3 and 1.

that of the planets, which is from west to east according to the circle of the zodiac, intersecting the equinoctial circle at the two points of solstice, i.e. at the beginning of Cancer and of Capricorn.

§ 104. And since the former motion is uniform, it is not divided into several motions; and in this it resembles the circle of the odd numbers; which is also why it is the greatest circle; for the odd numbers referred to are greater than the even.

§ 105. The second motion, however, is very much diversified, and seems therefore to answer to the circle of even numbers. It divides into seven circles according to the intervals between the numbers in the two series of multiples of 2 and of 3, as is said in the *Timaeus*. Where there are six points of division there must be seven parts divided off. Hence these circles are smaller and are contained by the highest circle which is that of the odd numbers. So the text is to be interpreted thus: 'As the whole', i.e. the Universe, is 'borne along with well-attuned motions', that is to say, as the harmonised movements of the heavens are due to the harmony of the World-Soul, God 'bent the straight line into a circle' in the manner described, according to the properties of number and of the soul; and dividing this one circle—one by the unity of the natural series of numbers, or by that of the intellectual power of the soul—into two, he forms the pair of numerical circles, the odd and the even, and the pair of circles in the soul, the understanding of moving and of motionless objects, and the pair of heavenly circles, the equinoctial and zodiacal motions.

§ 106. He adds, however, 'adjusted at two points',[1] because any two intersecting circles touch each other at two points. And 'again one', i.e. the inferior one, 'he divided into seven circles', as if of the planets, 'as though the heavenly motions were the soul's motions', i.e. as if the heavens moved by the movement of the World-Soul.

[1] 406^{b} 34.

BOOK I, CHAPTER III, CONTINUED

SOUL AS A SPATIAL MAGNITUDE
CRITIQUE OF PLATO

NOW IN THE FIRST PLACE IT IS NOT CORRECT TO say that the soul is a magnitude. For that of the Whole he (Plato) regards as of the same nature as what is sometimes called mind, not as the sensitive or the appetitive soul; for the movement of these is not circular. Now mind is one and continuous, as is the act of understanding, which in turn consists of thoughts. But these have unity by succession, like number, not like extension. Therefore neither is mind thus continuous; but it is either indivisible, or not continuous in the way that anything extended is.

§§ 107–11

How would it understand, if it were an extended quantity? As a whole, or by each of its parts? If by its parts, then by an extended part or by a point, if one may call a point a part. If by a point (of which there is an infinite number) it is evident that it will never complete the process. If by an extended part, it will understand the same thing many times over, even to infinity. Yet it seems to do so once for all. But if it is sufficient that it make contact with any one of its parts, why should it move in a circle or have any magnitude at all? But if it is necessary that it understand by contact with the whole of its circumference, what is the contact it makes by its parts?

§§ 112–16

Again, how can the divisible be understood by the indivisible, or the indivisible by the divisible?   § 117

It is necessary that intellect be this circle; for as the movement of the intellect is to understand, and that of the circle is to revolve, if, then, understanding *is* a revolving, the intellect must be a circle whose revolving is thinking.[1] But then it will always think something—since revolving goes on for ever. Practical thoughts, however, have limits, each being for the sake of something else; while speculative thinking likewise is limited by ideas and every idea is either a definition or a demonstration. But demonstrations begin from principles, and have as their term a conclusion or an inference. Even if they do not reach a conclusion, they do not come round again to their starting-point; they always take a new middle term and conclusion, and proceed straight forward. But revolving returns again to the beginning. Definitions too are all finite.   §§ 118–21

Further, if the same revolving occurs many times over, there will be a multiple understanding of the same thing.
                    §§ 122–4
Moreover, intelligence is better compared with stillness and rest than with motion,—and the same holds of logical deduction.   §§ 125–6

Again, that will not be content which is not at ease but in a state of strain. But if movement is not of the essence of the soul, it will only move unnaturally.   § 127

It must be burdensome for the soul to be entangled with the body without possibility of release; and indeed this should be shunned if it is better for the mind not to dwell in the body, as is commonly said, and as seems true to many.   § 128

[1] St. Thomas reverses this argument, § 118.

It is not clear why the Heavens move by circular movement; for the essence of the soul is not the cause of the soul
moving in a circle, for such movement is only incidental to
soul. Still less is the body the cause, but rather the soul a
cause for the body. Nor is this alleged as for the best; yet the
reason why God made the soul revolve must have been
because it is more worthy for it to move than to remain
stationary, and to move in this way rather than in any other.
But this speculation is better suited to other contexts, so let us
now dismiss it. § 129

Another absurdity arises in this argument and in many
others dealing with the soul. They conjoin body and soul,
placing the soul in the body without stating anything definite
as to the cause of this, or how the body is disposed. Yet this
explanation is surely necessary, for it is in virtue of something
in common that one is an agent, the other acted upon, one
moves and the other is moved. No such correlations are to
be found at random. These thinkers only endeavour to state
what the soul is, without determining anything about the
body which receives it, as if it happened that any soul entered
any body, as in the fables of the Pythagoreans. For each body
seems to have its own proper form and species. It is like saying that carpentry enters into flutes; for each art must use its
tools, and the soul its body. §§ 130–1

ST. THOMAS'S COMMENTARY
LECTIO EIGHT

§ 107. Having stated Plato's opinion, Aristotle now proceeds to its refutation. Here we should note that often, in criticising Plato, it is not precisely Plato's own meaning that Aristotle criticises, but the obvious sense of his words. He has to do this because Plato's method of teaching was faulty; he constantly used figures of speech, teaching by symbols and giving his words a meaning quite other than their literal sense; as when he calls the soul a circle. So lest anyone should be led astray by this literal sense, Aristotle sometimes argues precisely against it, in criticising Plato.

§ 108. Against the above-mentioned opinion, then, he brings ten arguments, some of which bear on Plato's own view, and some on the literal sense of his words. Plato did not really mean that the intellect was anything quantitative or circular; he was talking metaphorically. Still, lest there should be any mistake about this, Aristotle argues on a literal interpretation of the words.

§ 109. In the first argument,[1] then, he explains what 'soul' Plato had in mind, that it was the Soul of the Universe, and that 'that' (soul) which is 'of the whole', i.e. of the Universe, is exclusively intellectual, according to Plato. It is not vegetative, since it needs no nourishment; nor sensitive since it has no organs of sense; nor appetitive since appetite follows sensitivity. Indeed it could not in any sense be sensitive or appetitive, granted that the movement of the Universal Soul is circular; because neither sense nor appetite moves in a circle (for sense does not reflect upon itself) but only the intellect (which does reflect upon itself, as when a man knows that he knows). So Plato concluded that the World-Soul was only intellectual, and said that intellect itself was a sort of spatial magnitude and a circle.

[1] 407ª 1.

§ 110. Aristotle denies this, saying that Plato was wrong in representing the soul as a spatial magnitude circular in shape, and in dividing it into two circles.

§ 111. And he points out where Plato went astray. In this matter of the nature of the soul we have to base our judgement concerning any of its faculties upon the act or operation of that faculty, and our judgement concerning the act or operation upon the object of this act or operation; for faculties are known by their acts, and acts by their objects. Thus in the definition of a faculty is included its act, and in the definition of an act its object. Now it is clear that a thing gets its unity from whatever gives it being and specific nature. If then the intellect gets its being and specific nature from the intelligible which is its object (I speak of the intellect in act, which as such is nothing before the act of understanding occurs)[1] it is clear that if it is one and continuous, as Plato held, it will be so in the same way as intelligible objects are one and continuous. For the intellect is one only in the same way as its operation (understanding) is one; and its operation is one only in the same way as its object is one; since acts are differentiated according to their objects. Since then the intellect's object is intelligibles, and intelligibles compose a unity, not like a magnitude or a continuum, but like numbers which follow in a series, it is clear that the intellect is not, as Plato thought, a magnitude. It is either indivisible, as it is the nature of first principles to be, or, if it is continuous, it is so not as a magnitude but as number is; for as one number leads to another, so do we understand one object after another. And frequently several numbers terminate in one, as the premises in a syllogism terminate in one conclusion.

§ 112. The second argument comes at 'How would it understand'.[2] For it might be answered that Plato's reason for attributing magnitude to the intellect was not that there are many intelligibles, but that each intelligible by itself shows it to be a magnitude.

§ 113. But this will not do. For Plato maintained that the act of understanding was not a reception of intelligible forms into the mind, but a sort of contact (as of a circle, we have seen) due to the mind's going out to meet intelligible forms. But I ask you, how

---

[1] cf. Bk. III, lectio 7, § 682, and lectio 9, § 722. Also *Contra Gent.* II, 78, under *Deinde subjungit 'idem autem etc.'.*

[2] 407ª 10.

precisely does the mind understand by contact, if it is a magnitude?
It must touch its object either with the whole of itself or with a
part. But if with the whole of itself, then its *parts* are not needed
and there is no necessity for supposing that the intellect is a magnitude or a circle. If, on the other hand, it touches with some of its
parts, and thus understands in part, then either several of its parts
are involved or only one. If only one, then again the other parts
are superfluous and we need not suppose that the intellect has
parts. But if it understands by touching with all its parts, these
must be either points or quantities; and if points, then, since the
number of points in any magnitude is infinite, the intellect would
have to touch its object an infinity of times before it understood
the latter at all; and thus it never would understand, since infinity
cannot be traversed.

§ 114. Aristotle says 'points' not because he thought that a magnitude could be partitioned into points, but as disputing with Plato
who regarded bodies as composed of planes, planes of lines, and
lines of points; an opinion refuted by Aristotle in the *Physics*,
Book VI, where it is shown that a point added to a point makes
no difference.[1]

§ 115. But if the mind understands by touching with quantitative parts, then, as each part is divisible into many, it must understand the same object many times over. Again, since any quantity
is infinitely divisible into parts that are proportionately, not quantitatively, the same, it would follow that the mind understands the
same thing an infinite number of times,—which raises difficulties.
It would seem then that it touches its object once only, and that it
cannot be called a magnitude, either with respect to many intelligibles or to only one.

§ 116. Notice that Aristotle is implying here that intellect is indivisible of its nature. What is intelligible in any thing is its essence
or nature; which is present wholly in every part of it, as the specific
nature is wholly present in each individual of the species; the whole
nature of man in each individual man; and the individual as such is
indivisible. Hence what is intelligible in anything is indivisible;
and therefore so is the intellect.

§ 117. The third argument comes at 'Again, how'.[2] Granted that
the mind is indivisible, we can easily see how it can understand

[1] *Phys.*, VI, c.1; 231ᵃ 20–5.   [2] 407ᵃ 18.

both the indivisible and the divisible. It understands the indivisible in virtue of its own nature which is indivisible; and the divisible by abstracting from divisibility. But once allow, with Plato, that mind is divisible, it becomes impossible to understand how it can think of the indivisible. Hence the difficulty of admitting Plato's theory.

§ 118. The fourth argument begins at 'It is necessary'.[1] It runs thus. You say that intellect is circular and in movement. Now the movement of circles is a circling and that of the intellect is understanding; hence if intellect is a circle, understanding must be a circling. But this is false; for, since circular movement has no *actual* beginning or end, as is shown in the *Physics*, Book VIII,[2] it would follow that understanding, the proper act of the intellect, never reached a term. But understanding has an actual beginning and end: hence it is not the same as circular movement, and therefore the intellect is not a circle.

§ 119. That understanding has an actual beginning and end can be proved in this way. All thinking is either practical or speculative. Clearly all practical thinking reaches a term or end; for it is all for the sake of something else, namely a work to be done, and in this work it terminates. And speculative thinking too has its proper end, namely ideas; for it always comes to rest in some idea: either in a definition, when the mind simply apprehends something, or in demonstrations, when it combines and distinguishes things. But the first demonstrations begin from absolute first principles and terminate, in their turn, in the conclusions of syllogisms.

§ 120. If it be objected that one conclusion follows another, and thus there is no definite end, I answer that conclusions are nevertheless not circular. For, as is shown in the *Posterior Analytics*, Book I,[3] demonstration cannot go in a circle; it always goes in a straight line; and an infinite movement or progression in a straight line is impossible.

§ 121. Definitions too have a beginning and an end, for you cannot go on to infinity in the enumeration of genera; the most general genus has to be taken as the first one. Similarly in enumerating species; you cannot particularise to infinity, but must stop at the most particular species. Hence the most general genus is the beginning, and the most particular species is the term or end, in

---

[1] 407ᵃ 18.   [2] *Phys.*, VIII, c.8; 264ᵇ 8ss.   [3] *Anal. Post.*, I, c.3; 72ᵇ 5–73ᵃ 20.

definitions. Clearly, then, every act of the mind has an actual starting point and term.

§ 122. The fifth argument begins at 'Further, if'.[1] In a sense this argument depends on the previous one and is a part of it. It has been shown that if the intellect were a circle, as Plato thought, understanding would be a circling; and in the preceding argument Aristotle has shown that understanding is not a circling; which he now proves once more in the following way. The difference between a circular motion and any other motion lies in this, that the latter can never be repeated on the same quantity.[2] This becomes clear if we think of the different kinds of movement in particular. Thus the movement of 'alteration' cannot be repeated in the same subject in the same respect; for the same thing is not in the same respect changed from white to black and black to white. So too in the movement of growth, the same thing cannot in the same respect both increase and diminish. So also in local movement; if this goes in a straight line it must have two actual terms; and if it is to be repeated, the term at the end of the movement must be used twice, once as end and once as beginning, and, since there must intervene a moment of rest at that term, it is not exactly the same movement. In circular motion alone can one and the same movement be many times repeated according to the same quantity; the reason being that in circular motion there are no *actual* terms; hence, no matter how often it is repeated, no interval of rest intervenes nor does the motion vary in any way.

§ 123. This being granted, Aristotle argues as follows. If you say that the intellect is a circle, then the act of thinking must be a circular motion. But this consequence is not admissible; therefore neither is the premiss.

§ 124. He then shows that the consequence is not admissible. Granted, he says, that the same circular movement is multiplied, that is, repeated, in the same respect. If thinking, then, is a circular movement, as you say, it will be repeated again and again as one and the same movement bearing upon one and the same object; and so the mind will think the same thing many times over. For the mind, in moving, touches and by this touching it thinks, as

[1] 407ᵃ 30.

[2] *super eamdem quantitatem:* which might be rendered, 'over the same area'; the movement itself remaining the same, or continuous.

they say. If then its motion is circular it touches and thinks the same thing over and over again; which gives rise to difficulties.

§ 125. The sixth argument, at 'Moreover, intelligence'[1] is as follows. If thinking is, as you say, a circular motion, it should be associated with movement, but in fact the contrary is true; thinking is associated rather with repose. This Aristotle himself teaches in Book VII of the *Physics*,[2] where he says that if a man is to become wise he must first achieve an inward tranquillity; which is why the young and the restless are not, as a rule, wise. Wisdom and prudence are acquired, says Aristotle, by one who is content to sit down and be quiet.

§ 126. But lest it be said that, while this is true of simple apprehension, it is not true of syllogistic reasoning, he adds that reasoning also is more like a repose than a movement. Because, of course, before the syllogism is complete the mind and intellect are swaying from one conclusion to another and resting in neither; but when it is finished the mind holds on to one conclusion and rests in it.

§ 127. The seventh argument, at 'Again, that, etc.',[3] runs as follows. Let us agree that thinking makes the soul happy. Now happiness cannot reside in anything violent or coercive, since it is the soul's perfection and last end. As then movement is not of the soul's essential nature, but is indeed alien to it, that operation in which the soul finds its happiness, namely understanding, cannot be a movement, as Plato maintained. But that movement is not of the soul's nature is implied by Plato's own theory,[4] for he said that the soul was first constituted by numbers, and then that it divided into two circles and was reflected into seven,[5] from which followed movement. According to this view, then, movement is in the soul not naturally but accidentally.[6]

§ 128. The eighth argument, at 'It must be burdensome',[7] goes as follows. It seems to have been Plato's view that it was not of the nature of the soul to be joined to the body; for he said that it was first constituted of the elements and then compacted with the body, so that it cannot leave the body at will. Well then; whenever one thing is united against its nature to another, and cannot

---

[1] 407[a] 32.　　[2] *Phys.*, VII, c.3, 247[b] 10.　　[3] 407[a] 34.　　[4] §§ 46-51; 92-8.
[5] Pirotta: *et reflexit in septimo*. In a footnote: *forte 'reflecti'*.　　[6] *per accidens*.
[7] 407[b] 1.

leave it at will, the resulting state is painful; and whenever a thing deteriorates through its union with another thing the union is harmful and to be avoided. But *ex hypothesi* the union of soul and body is contrary to the soul's nature; nor can the soul break away at will; and the result is bad for the soul, as the Platonists are always saying. Apparently, then, union with the body is a painful and fearful thing for the soul; which hardly squares with Plato's own theory that the soul is composed of elements and compacted with its body from the beginning.

§ 129. The ninth argument, at 'It is not clear',[1] is as follows. Plato speaks of the Soul of the Universe and says it moves round in a circle. But this provides no explanation of the circular movement of the heavens; that is to say, it does not define the cause of it. For if the heavens move in a circle, this must be due either to intrinsic principles or to some extrinsic purpose. If intrinsic principles are the cause, the 'nature' in question will be either that of the soul or of the heavenly bodies. But it cannot be the soul's nature, for circular movement is not of the essence of the soul, but is accidental to it; for, as we have said,[2] the nature of the soul is to 'move in a straight line' which is then 'bent into circles'. Nor can the cause be the nature of the heavenly bodies, for body as such is not the cause of the soul's movements, but rather the soul of the body's. But, if the cause is an extrinsic purpose, one cannot, on Plato's principles, point to any definite end in answer to the question why the heavens move in a circle rather than in any other way; unless one brings in the will of God. God has indeed, for some reason, chosen to move the heavens rather than leave them motionless, and to move them in a circular way. But why he does this Plato cannot tell. However, as this matter belongs rather to 'other contexts', i.e. to another treatise (the *De Coelo*),[3] we can leave it aside for the present.

§ 130. The tenth argument starts at 'Another absurdity'.[4] It is effective not only against Plato, but against many others also. It runs thus. It is clear that there must always be some proportion between mover and moved, agent and patient, form and matter. Not every form suits every body in the same way, nor does every agent act upon every patient. Nor, again, does every principle of movement move everything capable of receiving movement.

[1] 407^b 5.   [2] §§ 118–21.   [3] *De Coelo*, II, c.5. 287^b 22ss.   [4] 407^b 13.

There must be some correlation and proportion between them by which the one is naturally the mover, the other the moved in each case. Now obviously these philosophers admitted that the soul was in the body and moved it. Since then they spoke of the nature of the soul, it seems that they should also have had something to say about the nature of the body; about why the soul is joined to the body and how the body is related to and contrasts with the soul. Their study of the soul was inadequate so long as they discussed it alone and neglected to explain the nature of the body that receives it.

§ 131. Indeed, we may associate their thesis (Aristotle goes on to say)[1] with the Pythagorean fable that any soul can enter any body; the soul of a fly for instance might perchance enter the body of an elephant. This cannot in fact happen; for the body of each particular thing, and especially of living things, has its own form and species and type of movement: hence there are great differences between the bodies of a worm, a dog, an elephant and a gnat. When they say that any soul can enter any body, it is as if one were to say that the art of weaving[2] could enter flutes, or that the art of the coppersmith could enter a weaver's loom. If it was in the power of these arts to enter bodies or instruments they would not do so indiscriminately, but the art of playing the flute would enter flutes, and not lyres, while the art of playing stringed instruments would enter stringed instruments and not flutes. In the same way, if there is a body for every soul, *any* soul does not enter *any* body; rather the soul shapes the body fit for itself; it does not enter a ready-made body. Plato and the others who speak only about the soul are too superficial; they fail to define which body answers to which soul, and the precise mode of existence of each in union with the other.

[1] 407[b] 22.   [2] *ars textrina*; M. has *tectonica*, 'carpentry'.

BOOK I, CHAPTER IV

THEORY OF SOUL AS HARMONY

THERE IS ANOTHER OPINION HANDED DOWN ABOUT the soul, acceptable to many, and in no way inferior to the theories already discussed, yet chastised, as it were, and condemned[1] even in public discussions. For some call the soul a kind of harmony. §§ 132–3

And they say that harmony is a composition or tempering of opposites, and that the body is compounded of opposites.
§ 134

Yet a harmony is either a proportion in the components [of a compound] or the composition itself; and the soul cannot be either of these. § 135

Further [active] movement, which all attribute to the soul, does not pertain to harmony. § 136

It would be more appropriate to call health a harmony, and in general the powers of the body, rather than of the soul. This is evident if one tries to explain the passions and operations of the soul by some harmony: it is difficult indeed to correlate these! § 137

Further, we speak of harmony with two considerations in mind. Primarily as a correctly proportioned measurement, in

---

[1] 'and has rendered an account of itself in public discussions', St. Thomas seems to follow another version; see Introd., p. 32.

what has motion and position, of component parts, so that nothing is missing that is becoming to them. Secondly, the ratio of this composition. In neither way is this [predication of harmony to the soul] reasonable. The composition of the parts of the body is very easy to examine[1] for there are many and various such compositions. Of what and how can one suppose the mind to be a composition? Or sensation? Or appetite? It is no less absurd to account the soul the ratio of a composition. The synthesis of elements for bone is not the same as that for flesh. There would have to be many souls [in one body]; and indeed [a soul] for every body, if each is a mixture of elements, and the ratio of the mixture a harmony and a soul.[2]   §§ 138–40

One might at this point question Empedocles. He says that each of these exists in virtue of a proportion. Is this proportion then the soul; or is soul some other thing, thus inborn in the members?   § 141

Or further: is concord the cause of any chance combination, or only of one based on some ratio?   § 142

And whether this concord is the ratio of the composition or something else? These are the kinds of problem involved in this hypothesis.   § 143

But if the soul is other than the composition, why does it perish together with the essence of flesh and of other parts of the body? Moreover, granted that each of these parts has a soul,[3] if the soul is not the ratio of the whole composition, what is it that is corrupted when the soul departs?   § 144

---

[1] Oxford transl.: 'easily refutable' (i.e. that soul is a harmony as the composition, etc.); with which Hicks and Tricot substantially agree, but not Wallace. St. Thomas (§ 139) follows M. as rendered here.

[2] A possible rendering of M., though not of the Greek. It is fixed for us by the Commentary, § 140.   [3] 'has not a soul', 408ª 27.

It is evident, then, from what has been said, that the soul cannot be a harmony, or move by revolving. It can, however, be moved and move itself, incidentally, in so far as what it dwells in moves and is moved by the soul. In no other way can it move in place.   § 145

§ 132. After rejecting Plato's theory the Philosopher goes on to dispose of another opinion rather similar to Plato's. For certain philosophers thought the soul was a harmony; agreeing so far with Plato's view that the soul was composed of harmonic numbers; yet differing from him in that, while he spoke only of a numerical harmony, they extended the principle to include harmonies of compounds, mixtures and contrary qualities.

§ 133. First then he tells us[1] of a tradition handed down from the early philosophers concerning the soul, which seemed to contain some truth, not only about the soul, but about something common to all the principles of things. He says 'something common'[2] because the early philosophers said nothing about formal causes, treating only of material causes. Democritus and Empedocles were the two who seem to have come nearest to treating of the formal cause. The latter reduced everything to six principles, of which four—the elements—were material and two were formal, namely the part-active and part-passive principles, Concord and Strife. And the material elements were, they said, linked together by a certain proportion, whence they had a certain unity without which they could not exist together. And this proportion they called the form and harmony of things; whence it followed that the soul was a harmony like other forms.

§ 134. Then, at 'And they say that harmony',[3] he states the ground of this opinion: harmony is the combination and mixing in due proportion of contraries in compounds and mixtures. The

[1] 407b 27.

[2] *Et dicit 'quantum ad id quod commune est'*. But M. has simply *in communi*, ἐν κοινῷ, which has a different sense, 407b 30. *See* Introd., p. 32.

[3] 407b 30.

proportion itself is called harmony and is the form of the compound; and because the soul is a kind of form it was reckoned a harmony. Such was apparently the view of Dynarchus, Simiates and Empedocles.

§ 135. Next, at 'Yet a harmony',[1] he begins to criticise it: first in a general way, and then, at 'One might, etc.'[2] with particular reference to Empedocles who formulated it.

The general theory is attacked with four arguments. The first is as follows. Harmony, strictly speaking, pertains to sounds, but is transferred by these philosophers to mean any due proportion, whether in things composed of different parts or in mixtures of contrary elements. On this view, then, harmony is one of two things: either the compound or mixture itself, or the proportion existing in it. But the soul is clearly neither of these; therefore it is not a harmony. The reason why the soul cannot be, for these philosophers, either a compound or the proportion in a compound is that these are both accidental factors, whilst the soul, according to them, is a substance.

§ 136. The second argument begins at 'Further, movement'.[3] All philosophers agree that the soul moves something. But harmony does not move anything; rather it is a result and trace of movement, just as in music the movement of strings leaves its trace in harmonious sound. Similarly, the putting together and coadaptation of parts by some composing agent results in a certain proportional composition. If then the soul were a harmony resulting from some producer of harmony, we should have to posit another soul in the producer.

§ 137. The third argument comes at 'It would be more appropriate'.[4] In the *Physics*, Book IV,[5] Aristotle had said that, if the definition of anything is to be adequate, it must answer to all that the given thing can do of itself or receive from other things; for the best definition states not only the substance and nature of a thing, but also its accidental qualities and capacities. If then the soul were a harmony, we ought to be able to work out its capacities and accidental qualities from our knowledge of this harmony. But this is extremely difficult; if, for example, we want to derive the

[1] 407[b] 32.   [2] § 141; 408[a] 18.   [3] 407[b] 34.
[4] 408[a] 1.   [5] *Phys.*, IV, c.4; 211[a] 5ss.

operations of the soul from harmony, to what harmony does feeling or love, hating or understanding belong? It would be easier indeed to know the *body* through harmony. Thus we certainly can define good health as the duly proportioned and equally balanced commingling of the body's humours; and likewise with other bodily qualities. Thus harmony belongs apparently to the body rather than to the soul.

§ 138. The fourth argument starts at 'Further, we speak'.[1] Harmony is sometimes found in things composed together and moving, when, that is, such things are so coapted and arranged that 'nothing becoming to them is missing', i.e. no defect occurs within the nature of the thing in question. The parts then are said to be well harmonised and the whole composition is called a harmony, e.g. of wood or stones or other natural bodies. In the same way when stringed instruments or flutes are well-tuned, so that agreeable sounds result, they are said to be well harmonised. This is the proper meaning of the word. Sometimes, again, 'harmony' is found in mixtures of contraries; as, when contrary elements are so combined and mixed that no incompatibility remains, nor any excess of any one of them, e.g. of heat or cold or moisture or dryness; then they are said to be harmonised well and their ratio or proportion is called a harmony. So, if the soul is called a harmony it must be in one of these ways. But in fact it cannot rationally be so called in either of these ways. Those philosophers therefore spoke amiss.

§ 139. Clearly, the soul should not be called a harmony precisely in the sense in which compounds and compositions are harmonious. For in the body the interrelation of the various parts is quite evident; we can easily tell how the bones or the nerves are interrelated, what the arm is to the hand and the flesh to the bone. On the other hand the principle according to which the parts of the soul are interrelated is obscure; nor does the correlation of parts in the body reveal to us how the parts of the soul, the understanding, and the senses, and desire, and so forth, are related to each other.[2]

§ 140. Nor can the soul be called a harmony in the same way as the proportion in bodies compounded of a mixture of contrary qualities; and this for two reasons. One reason is that a different

---

[1] 408ᵃ 5.

[2] The rendering is a little uncertain. It takes *non enim per hoc possumus scire* as referring back to the 'order' in the body.

proportion is to be found in different parts of the living body; for the elements do not mix in the same ratio or proportion to form flesh as to form bone; and consequently there would be different souls for the different parts of the same living body, according to the proportional diversity and multiplication of its parts. The other reason is that all bodies are compounded of elements and contrary qualities; hence if the proportion of each compound is a harmony, and each harmony is a soul, there will be no body without a soul; which is an awkward thesis to maintain. It is not therefore of much use to call the soul a harmony.

§ 141. Next, at 'One might at this point',[1] Aristotle attacks Empedocles by drawing three unforeseen consequences from his account of the matter. The first is this. If you maintain that every body has a certain ratio or proportion, which you call harmony and identify with the soul, I put the question to you whether the soul itself is this ratio or proportion, or something else. If you answer that it is the proportion itself, then, since in the same body there are different proportions for the different parts, two difficulties arise; there will be many souls in the same body; and there will be a soul for every compound. But if you answer that the soul is not the proportion itself, then, since harmony is proportion, the soul will not be a harmony.

§ 142. The second argument begins at 'Or further'.[2] Empedocles had asserted that the cause of union in things was Concord and the cause of disunion was Strife. Now union implies a certain proportion. I ask you, then, whether Concord is the cause of any and every union or only of such unions as are harmonious. If you answer 'of every union', then you must find some cause other than Concord for the harmony and proportion proper to harmonious unions—unless you say that the latter occur by chance. But if you say that Concord is the cause of harmonious unions, then it is not the cause of all unions.

§ 143. The third argument, at 'And whether this',[3] runs as follows. Empedocles says that Concord is what unites things. I ask: is Concord the same as the actual union in harmony, or is it not? If it is the same, then, since nothing causes itself, love cannot be the cause of the union as Empedocles asserted. But suppose it is not the same. Still, harmonious union as such is only a kind of agreement,

[1] 408ᵃ 18.   [2] 408ᵃ 21.   [3] 408ᵃ 22.

which seems to be precisely what Concord is too. So they *are* the same after all; and the preceding argument applies as before.

§ 144. Proceeding, Aristotle shows how plausible is the theory in question.[1] Its plausibility, he says, relies on the argument that if you grant one thing another must follow, and if you remove one thing another is removed. Thus when a body loses its harmony it loses its soul, and while its harmony remains the soul too remains. Yet the conclusion does not follow; for this kind of proportion is not, as those philosophers thought, the form itself, but only a disposition of the matter in view of the form. And if the harmony of a composite being is taken in this its proper sense, i.e. to mean a disposition, then the consequence is quite correct, that, so long as the matter's disposition to the form remains, the form itself remains, and when the disposition goes, the form also goes. Not that the harmony is the form, but that it is a disposition of the matter in view of the form.

§ 145. Finally, where he says 'It is evident, then'[2] Aristotle, concluding, summarises his rejection both of Plato's view that the soul moves in a circle and of Empedocles' that it is a harmony. The soul, as has been said,[3] is moved indirectly,[4] and it moves itself. That it is moved indirectly is clear, for it moves when its body moves; but the body itself receives movement from the soul. Only indirectly, and in no other way, does the soul move from place to place.

[1] 408ª 24.   [2] 408ª 29.   [3] §§ 75-86.   [4] *secundum accidens.*

BOOK I, CHAPTER IV, CONTINUED

THEORY OF SOUL AS A SELF-MOVER
RECONSIDERED

ONE MIGHT WITH MORE REASON ENQUIRE ABOUT the soul as in movement by considering such facts as these: that it is, as we say, sad, pleased, confident, frightened; or again, that it is angry, feels and understands. All these seem to be movements; from which one might suppose that the soul moves.   § 146

This, however, is not a necessary conclusion. Even if feeling pain or being glad or understanding are in the fullest sense movements, and each of these is a 'being moved' (e.g. being angry or fearful occurs by some movement of the heart), this being moved is from the soul. But as for understanding, it is either of such a nature or perhaps something other.

§§ 147–50

Of these, however, some occur with a change of place in that which moves; others with an alteration,—of what sort or how is another question. To say that the *soul* is angry is like saying it builds or weaves. For it is perhaps better to say, not that the *soul* is compassionate, or learns, or understands, but a man by his soul. These modifications occur by movements not so much in the soul as, in some cases, proceeding to it, and in others, proceeding from it: as sensation proceeds from things, whilst remembering proceeds from the soul to the motions or rests which occur in the sensitive organs.

§§ 151–62

But intellect would seem to be a subsisting essence implanted in the soul, and not to corrupt.[1] For it would corrupt [if it did], principally through the debility accompanying old age. But in fact what happens is similar to the case of the sensitive powers. If an old man could acquire the eye of a young man,[2] he would see as a young man; hence, senility is not an affliction of the soul, but of that which it inhabits, like drunkenness or disease. Understanding and thinking, then, decay with the decay of something else within. Understanding itself cannot be affected. But reasoning and loving and hating are not affections of the intellect, but of that which has it, precisely in so far as it has it. Wherefore, when this decays, the soul ceases to remember or love. For these proceeded, not from it, but from what was common, which has disintegrated. But perhaps intellect is something more godlike and unalterable.

Therefore, that the soul cannot be moved is manifest from these arguments. But if it cannot be moved, it is evident that it cannot be self-moving.   §§ 163–7

[1] *See* Introd., p. 33.   [2] 'of the sort (needed).' 408[b] 21.

§ 146. After stating and criticising the arguments of those who thought that, because the soul moves the body, it must itself be in movement, the Philosopher is next concerned to show that a stronger support for the assertion that the soul was in movement might be drawn from considering the activities proper to it. Dividing his treatment into two parts, he first states the hypothesis that the soul's activities are evidence of its movement;[1] and then settles the problem so far as his present purpose requires, this part beginning at 'This, however, . . . '.[2]

First, then, he says that whereas the philosophers, of whom he has been speaking, thought that the soul might be in movement from considering the fact that it moved the body, a more rational, i.e. a more plausible, argument might be drawn 'by considering such facts as these', i.e. as the activities of the soul itself. For from these one might build up a very plausible argument in favour of the soul's being in movement. For we say that the soul 'is sad, pleased, confident (i.e. daring) and frightened'; and we say that it gets angry and senses and understands. And since all these are activities of the soul, and also types of movement, it would seem that the soul moves. And this is a more plausible suggestion than the one already discussed. For the latter argued the soul's movement from the body's, according to the principle that every mover is itself moved; so that if soul moves body the soul itself is moved. But the theory now to be considered regards the movement of the soul from the standpoint of the soul's own activities.

§ 147. Next, at 'This, however,' he clears up the difficulty. Here we should note that when Aristotle is searching for truth by a process of stating and answering objections, he will sometimes employ

[1] 408ᵃ 34–408ᵇ 4.   [2] 408ᵇ 5.

this method after having already demonstrated the truth in question; and then his objections and solutions are governed by the opinion he has already formed for himself. But sometimes he does all this *before* demonstrating the truth, and then he bases his objections and solutions on the views of others and not on his own opinion or on what he believes to be the truth. For example, in Book III of the *Physics*,[1] where he argues against those who maintained the existence of an infinite, he employs a number of principles false in themselves but considered true by his opponents, e.g. that every body is both light and heavy. For he had not yet decided about the lightness and heaviness of bodies; this he did later on in the *De Coelo*,[2] where, in consequence, he reopens the question of the infinite. And such is his method here. His criticism rests upon presupposing as true the views of his opponents.

§ 148. These latter, especially the Platonists, thought that sorrow, joy, anger, sensation and thought, and so forth, were movements in the soul, and that each of these activities, not excepting thought, had its own particular organ; so that in this respect there was no difference between sensitivity and intelligence; and every kind of soul, not the intellectual soul only, was immortal. All of which Aristotle concedes, presupposing that all such activities, even thinking, are organic, and that all souls are immortal. He only denies that such activities as sensation and joy are movements in the soul, asserting that they belong rather to the compound of body and soul. This alone he makes the point at issue.

§ 149. And here he does two things. First, he shows that the activities in question are not movements of the soul; secondly, he proves this with a special argument beginning at 'But intellect'.[3] His opponents, he says, maintain two points: (1) that joy and sorrow and so forth are movements; (2) that these movements are to be attributed to the soul; which therefore moves. But the conclusion does not necessarily follow; and in any case both propositions are false—the activities in question are not movements, nor are such things as anger, joy, sensation, to be attributed to the soul. But even granted, for the sake of argument, that they are movements, they should not be attributed to the soul; nor the soul, in consequence, be held to move in and with them.

[1] *Phys.*, III, cc.4–8.
[2] *De Coelo*, I, c.3; 269^b 15–270^a 10.   [3] § 163; 408^b 18.

§ 150. For it is obvious that, even if these activities are movements and are of the soul, they are not of the soul except with respect to certain definite parts of the body: thus sensation only takes place in certain parts of the body, such as the eye, the organ o sight; and anger in the heart; and so with the rest. It is clear that they are movements not of the soul alone, but of soul and body together. Yet they are *from* the soul; for example, when the soul thinks that anything is worthy of anger, the animal organ called the heart is disturbed and the blood gets heated around it. So also with fear; it makes a definite part of the body contract and change. And likewise with the rest. In these cases, then, the soul in itself does not move, but only moves in the movement of another thing, e.g. the heart. But in view of a point which Aristotle is going to prove later on,[1] namely that understanding[2] is an act of the soul alone, in which the body has no share, he observes here that perhaps understanding should be distinguished from all those activities which occur in the compound of soul and body. He says 'perhaps' because he is speaking tentatively. But in asserting that the other activities are of soul and body together he implies that they do arise *from* the soul.

§ 151. So, when he says 'Of these, etc.',[3] he means to show that these movements arise from the soul to the accompaniment of certain local changes; as in the case of anger, which occurs in the soul when parts of the body in and around the heart are moved: the blood heated by the heart is dispelled towards the extremities of the body. There may also be an 'alteration' or qualitative movement, as in fear, when the heart contracts and grows cold and one turns pale. What these passions are, and how they come about, is another question; but it is clear that as movements they are not in the soul alone, but in soul and body together.

§ 152. Hence just as any animal's bodily activities spring not from its soul alone but from its body, or from the compound of soul and body, so too sense-perception and joy and so forth should not be attributed to the soul alone, but to body and soul together. To say that the *soul* gets angry and is thereby moved is like saying that the *soul* weaves or builds or plays the harp. The soul indeed is the cause of these activities; for the acquired ability[4] to build or

[1] §§ 377; 684–5.   [2] *intelligere.* A *per se* incorporeal act.
[3] 408ᵇ 9.   [4] *habitus.*

weave or play the harp is in the soul, and the exercise of the ability in each case springs from the soul. But, as it is better to say that the builder, not the art of building, builds, though the builder builds by his art, so perhaps it is better to say that it is not the soul that feels pity or learns or thinks, but the man who does these things with his soul. He says 'perhaps etc.' for the reason given above.[1]

§ 153. But since the statement that the soul does not move, but man with his soul, might be taken to mean that movement exists in the soul as its subject, to forestall this Aristotle explains that when he says that man moves with his soul he means that movement is derived, as it were, *from* the soul, not that it is found in the soul itself.

§ 154. For when I say 'this moves with that', my statement can be taken in two senses: either that the source of a given movement is itself moving, as when I say that a man moves with his feet, the feet themselves moving; or that something motionless in itself moves another thing; and it is in this latter sense that a man is said to move with his soul.

§ 155. Now this movement is two-fold.[2] Sometimes the soul represents the term, to which the movement tends, as in sensation; for in the act of the soul's apprehending exterior sense-objects, the sensitive faculty in the bodily organ is aroused and, moving, transmits 'to it', i.e. to the soul, images and notions of sensible things. But sometimes the soul behaves as the starting point of movement, as in remembering, when the latent, buried images and notions of things are brought to light, in order that sensible things may be understood through them. Whether the inward storing away of images should itself be called a movement or a resting is not immediately relevant.

§ 156. Movements of this sort, then, are not to be attributed to the soul, but to the soul and body together; if they spring *from* the soul, this does not imply movement *in* the soul.

§ 157. But observe that this solution of the problem is only provisional; it does not leave us with the truth perfectly defined. For movement is attributed to the soul's activities in different ways by different people. In fact, three kinds of movement are discernible therein. In some of these activities movement in the strict sense is

---

[1] § 150.   [2] 408[b] 15.

found. In others it is found in a less exact sense of the term. And in others in a still looser sense.

§ 158. For movement proper occurs in the activities of the vegetative soul and in sensuous desire. In vegetative activity the material substance itself moves, in consequence of assimilating food. This movement is growth; wherein the vegetative soul plays the active part, the body a passive one. In sensuous desire also movement proper occurs, both through qualitative alterations and also through changes of place. No sooner does a man desire anything than he is affected by certain changes—becoming angry, as in the desire for revenge, or glad as in the pursuit of pleasure. And, accompanying this, the blood moves outwards from the heart to the extremities of the body; besides the fact that the whole man moves from one place to another in pursuit of what he desires.

§ 159. In a less strict sense, however, movement occurs in the acts of the sensitive soul. Here there is no movement of the material substance itself, but only a 'spiritual' movement of cognition: for example, the act of seeing is not a material modification; it is 'spiritual' reception into the eye of sensible forms. Yet it does involve some material change, because the faculty of sight is lodged in the body: and to this extent it involves movement, though it is not movement in the strict sense. Movement in the strict sense is not ascribed to the soul's activities except when a modification of the material substance is the direct term of the activity.

§ 160. Least strictly of all, and indeed only by a metaphor, is movement to be ascribed to the act of the intellect, in which there is no movement of the material substance, as in the case of vegetative activities, nor even any alteration of the subject of 'spiritual' operations, as in the case of sense-awareness. There is only an activity which is *called* movement simply because the mind goes from potency into act. This differs from movement proper; for whereas the latter connotes an imperfection in the moving subject, this activity proceeds from the subject as already perfect and complete.[1]

§ 161. Clearly then the acts of the vegetative and sensitive souls are not exclusively of the soul, but of soul and body together; while those of the intellect are only called movements metaphorically, and are exclusively of the soul, without the use of any particular bodily organ.

[1] cf. § 82.

§ 162. Note too that, as desire and cognition are both found in the sensitive part, the same division appears in the intellectual part also. Hence love, hatred, delight and so forth can be understood either as sensitive, and in this sense they are accompanied by a bodily movement; or as exclusively intellectual and volitional, without any accompanying sensuous desire; and understood in this sense they are not movements, for they involve no accompanying bodily change. In this latter sense they pertain even to immaterial substances, as will be shown more clearly later.

§ 163. Then, at 'But intellect',[1] Aristotle sets out to prove what has been shown, namely that even if activities of this kind are movements (as the philosophers he is discussing maintained) still they are not movements of the soul alone, but involve the body also. So he takes one of their opinions (famous in his time), namely that not the intellect only, but every kind of soul without exception, is immortal. According to this view the intellect was a substance in the making, still incomplete,[2] and was immortal. For it is a fact of experience that all the weakening and decay that affect the intellect or the senses come from the side of the bodily organ, not from the soul itself. Whence it would seem to follow that the intellect and every other sort of soul was incorruptible; if its activities grow feeble that does not imply its own decay, but the decay of the organs of the body.

§ 164. If the soul itself decayed it would decay especially in old age; that is when the organs of sense grow feeble. Yet in fact the soul itself is unaffected by old age; if an old man could be given a young man's eye he would see just as well as a young man. The decline of old age, then, is not due to a decline in the soul or in the faculties of sense, but to the body; just as in sickness or drunkenness it is the body, not the soul, that is enfeebled. Hence 'understanding',[3] i.e. simple apprehension, and 'thinking',[4] i.e. the intellectual activity of combining and distinguishing ideas, grow weak, not through a weakness in the intellect, but through 'the decay of something else within', i.e. the intellect's organ or instrument. Understanding 'in itself cannot be affected'.[5]

---

[1] 408[b] 18.

[2] *quaedam substantia quae est in fieri et nondum completa.* This curious phrase certainly adds to the plain meaning of the text. But *see* Introd., p. 33.

[3] *intelligere.*   [4] *considerare.*   [5] 408[b] 25.

§ 165. Now in saying this Aristotle is not giving it as his opinion that the intellect has a special bodily organ, but, in the manner already explained,[1] he is arguing on the supposition that the views of the philosophers whom he is criticising are sound; and it was their view, as we have seen, that each of the soul's activities, and even intellect itself, had its special bodily organ. Assuming this, therefore, he gives as the reason for the decay of the understanding that it is one of those activities (like hating and loving) which are not of the soul alone, but of 'that which has it',[2] i.e. of the compound of body and soul, or the bodily organ—precisely, he adds, in so far as this compound has 'it', i.e. understanding, and so forth. Consequently when 'this' (i.e. the bodily organ) 'decays' its activities, such as loving or understanding, decay likewise, and the soul itself neither remembers nor loves any more. The reason is that such processes did not only involve the soul, but 'that which was common', i.e. the whole compound being; which has now decayed and passed away. Clearly, then, if all such movements and activities decay through the body's decay, not the soul's, they are not themselves exclusively of the soul, but of the soul and body together; and not the soul, but soul and body together, is what moves.

§ 166. But to remove any impression that he himself believes the intellect to be what the argument he is using supposes it to be, he adds these words, 'Perhaps intellect is something more godlike and unalterable',[3] i.e. some sort of nobler power than any we are considering now, whose activity is exclusively of the soul. He says 'perhaps' because the question has not been decided yet; it will be cleared up in Book III.[4] So much to show that he is arguing on a supposition.

§ 167. Finally, he concludes from all this that it is now clear that the soul itself cannot be the subject of movement. And if so, then the soul is obviously not a self-mover with movements of the kinds here discussed, as the philosophers he is criticising had maintained.

[1] cf. § 147.   [2] 408[b] 27.   [3] 408[b] 29.   [4] § 671ss.

BOOK I, CHAPTER IV, CONTINUED

SOUL AS A SELF-MOVING NUMBER

MUCH THE MOST UNREASONABLE THING SAID about the soul is that it is a number moving itself. In this there are several impossibilities. First, what follows upon 'being moved', as they say; and then the special difficulties that follow their assertion that it is a number. How is one to conceive a unity, indivisible and undifferentiated in itself, as moving? Or by what? Or in what way? For if it is both moved and mover, there must be some difference in itself. §§ 168–9

Further, since they say that a line, being moved, makes a plane, and a point, being moved, a line, the movements of the units will be lines. Now a point is unit having position; so that the number of a soul must be in some place and have position. § 170

Further, if one subtracts from a number a number or a unit, another number is left. Plants, however, and many animals, live on after being divided, and seem to retain specifically the same soul. § 171

It would seem to be a matter of indifference whether one says 'units' or 'small bodies'. For if the spheres of Democritus were to become points, and only quantity remained, there would remain in them a moving and a moved, as in extended matter. For the distinction spoken of is not due to largeness

or smallness, but to quantity as such. Hence there must necessarily be something moving the units. But if it is the soul
which moves the animal, so also in the case of number: then
the soul is not a moving thing which is also moved, but a
mover only.   § 172

Now this would have somehow to be a unit.[1] If so, it must
have some principle of differentiation from other units. But
how can one isolated point differ from others, but in position?
But if there are many different units and points in a body,
they will be units in the same subject, and will occupy space
as points. But, if there are two in the same place, what is
there to prevent an infinity of them together? That of which
the place is indivisible is itself such. But if the points in the
body are the 'numbers' of the soul, or if the 'number' of
body-points is that of the soul, why are there not souls in all
bodies? For in all things there seem to be points, even to
infinity.   § 173

Furthermore, how is it possible for these points to be
separated and released from the body? Since lines cannot be
divided up into points?   § 174

CHAPTER V

This amounts to saying (as we said before), either, under
one aspect, the same as those who posit the soul as a body of
very refined elements, or, under another aspect, what Democritus said of the movement of the soul,—a thing intrinsically absurd. For if the soul is in all the body as sentient, there
must be two bodies in the same place, if the soul is some sort
of body. And for those who say it is a number, there are
many points in one point, or else every body has a soul;

---

[1] 'But how can such a thing be a unit?' is a possible rendering of the Greek,
409ᵃ 19.

unless the soul's 'number' be other than that of the points in the body. The animal would then come to be moved by a number, precisely as Democritus said. What difference does it make whether one says small spheres or large units, or, in general, that units are in motion? In any case it must needs be that the animal moves when these are moving. §§ 175–6

These and many other consequences result for those who would combine number and movement in a single principle. It is impossible for such to be not only a definition of the soul, but even one of its accidents—as is clear if one attempts by this procedure to account for the soul's activities and modifications, such as pleasure, pain and so forth. As we said before, on these principles it is not easy even to hazard a conjecture.   § 177

§ 168. After refuting those who asserted that the soul was a thing that moved, the Philosopher goes on now[1] to criticise the view of Xenocrates who said, in addition, that soul was a self-moving number; a far less rational opinion than the others already mentioned. For it involves many absurdities. First of course there are those arising from 'being moved', the irrationalities, namely into which all who say that the soul itself moves are led; and then, in addition, there are the special difficulties involved in the notion that soul is a number. Therefore in Xenocrates' definition of soul the Philosopher criticises, not merely the terms employed, but the meaning itself. This critique has two parts. First he shows that the definition does not fit the soul itself or its substance; and then that it does not fit its accidental qualities,—this at 'These and many other consequences'.[2] The former part subdivides into reasons for (a) rejecting the said definition,[3] and (b) for thinking that it involves all the difficulties implicit in the views of the other philosophers already criticised; this part beginning at 'This amounts to saying'.[4]

§ 169. He shows the unsuitability of the definition by six arguments; the first being as follows. You call the soul a self-moving number; but number is composed of units; the soul then, in your view, consists of units which move themselves. Now in any self-moving thing there are two parts (as is shown in Book VIII of the *Physics*)[5] one moving, the other moved. Therefore you must mean that each unit or point is composed of two parts, one moving, the other moved. But this is impossible. Therefore the soul is not a

---

[1] 408ᵇ 32.   [2] § 177; 409ᵇ 11.   [3] 409ᵃ 1–30.
[4] 409ᵃ 30.   [5] *Phys.*, VIII, c.5; 257ᵃ 30ss.

self-moving number. To show the impossibility of a unit having a moving part and a moved part: what is wholly indivisible and undifferentiated cannot be thought of as moving itself in such a way that one part moves and another is moved. For the motive or moving factor and the mobile or moved factor cannot exist without differing. Since, then, the unit is indivisible and undifferentiated, it cannot have such parts as these. Therefore the soul is not a self-moving number.

§ 170. The second argument, at 'Further, since',[1] runs thus. You say the soul is a number; and therefore composed of units, as has been said. Now the only difference between a unit and a point is that a point has position—it is a unit in position. But if the soul is a number, this number must exist somewhere in position. Therefore the soul is a unit in position, that is to say a point. But according to the Platonists a point in movement makes a line, a line in movement makes a surface, and a surface a body. If then the soul is a self-moving number each of its units is self-moving, and each of these is a self-moving point. But such a point can only make a line; therefore the same is true of the movement of the soul. Hence not life, but a line is the effect of the soul; which is not true. Therefore the soul is not a self-moving number.

§ 171. The third argument, at 'Further, if',[2] is the following. If, as you say, the soul is a number, it must have the nature and attributes of number. Now it is evident that whenever a unit is taken from or added to a number, the number is essentially changed. If you add 1 to 3 you alter the number *in kind*: 4 differs in kind from 3. Similarly if you take 1 from 3, leaving 2. Now it is agreed that living things are specified by their soul; since it is through the *form* that things are specified. If, then, the soul is a number, any addition to, or subtraction from, it must alter it in kind. But this is not true: for if plants and segmented animals[3] are cut up the divisions go on living, the same in kind as before. Therefore the soul is not a self-moving number.

§ 172. The fourth argument, at 'It would seem to be',[4] is as follows. You say the soul is a number; whence it follows, as we know, that it consists of units in position, i.e. points. But on this supposition it is obvious that there is no difference between saying, with Democritus, that the soul consists of small indivisible bodies

[1] 409ᵃ 2.   [2] 409ᵃ 7.   [3] e.g. worms.   [4] 409ᵃ 10.

and saying that it is composed of units in position. For each unit in position is a quantity and indivisible.

Very well then; the soul, in your view, is a self-moving number and, consequently, consists of units and points moving themselves. Let us suppose then that the indivisible bodies of Democritus are points (there is no difference, as we have seen) and are quantities (as they must be, since only quantities, properly speaking, move). Now these points will move themselves if the soul is 'a self-moving number'. But every self-mover, as has been said,[1] is two-fold; hence each point itself is two-fold, having a moving part and a moved part; and this, no matter whether they be large parts or small, provided they have some quantity; for every self-moving continuum contains the two factors, a moving one and a moved one. So there must be a mover of the units. But in living things the mover is the soul; therefore the mover of the number would be the soul; whence it follows that the soul is not a *moved* but a *mover*, and thus the definition of it as a self-moving number is incorrect. It should rather be defined as a number moving another number.

§ 173. The fifth argument begins at 'Now this would have somehow to be a unit'.[2] In Xenocrates' opinion the soul is a unity. But if so, then it is a point; for it must, as a unity, differ from other unities and it cannot differ except through position. For what is it that differentiates 'isolated points', i.e. unities as here understood, excepting[3] their position? Moreover, only through position are unities points. The soil, then, is not a mere unity, but a point. Yet it exists in the body and every body as such has its own points. Well then, are the soul-points identical with the body-points or not? If they are not, then every part of the body will contain also soul-points, and in every such part there will be two points[4] at the same time in the same place. And if two, why not more than two *ad infinitum*? Things whose place is indivisible are themselves indivisible; and require no increase of space if they increase in number; so that if two can be in an indivisible place, there is no reason why an infinite number should not be there. On the other hand if body-points are identical with soul-points, then every body has a soul,

[1] § 169.   [2] 409ᵃ 18.   [3] *id est, unitatis intellectae.*

[4] Pirotta has *et sic erunt duo puncta animae in eodem loco*, but the context requires that we omit *animae*.

since every body has points. But this is false; therefore the soul is not a self-moving number.

§ 174. The sixth argument, at 'Furthermore, how',[1] continues the preceding one. It follows from Xenocrates' theory that the soul is composed of points. Points are obviously inseparable and undetachable from bodies; for lines are not separable from surfaces, nor points from lines. But this is not true of the soul; hence it is not a point or a number. Clearly then, Xenocrates' definition is intrinsically inappropriate.

§ 175. Then, at 'This amounts to saying',[2] he finds this definition objectionable in its consequences. These consequences involve all the objectionable consequences flowing from the theories of all who have philosophised about the soul.[3] For some of these fell into the mistake of saying that the soul was a body made up of extremely fine parts,[4] whence it would follow that two bodies would be together in the same place; for the soul is wherever sensation occurs, and this is everywhere in the body. And the same would follow, as has been said,[5] if the soul were composed of points: two points, or even an infinite number of points, would exist together in the same place at the same time. This would follow if the soul-points differed from body-points. And if 'the number be other', i.e. if there is no difference between soul-points and body-points, then every body contains a soul, since it must contain points.

§ 176. Others, like Democritus,[6] erred in saying that the soul itself moved, and the body because of the soul. And from Democritus' statement that the soul was made up of indivisible spheres whose movement caused the body to move it followed that indivisible bodies were the cause of bodily movements. The same difficulty follows from the definition which states that an animal is moved by a number and so by points. It makes no difference what size we give to the moving spheres or units; for 'in any case', i.e. with spheres or with units, the origin of the soul's movement is the movement of bodily spheres and points.

§ 177. Next, at 'These and etc.',[7] he shows the weakness of the above definition with respect to accidental qualities. A complete

---

[1] 409ª 29.   [2] 409ª 30.

[3] He seems to mean the theories of all the philosophers criticised in the preceding chapters.

[4] cf. § 68.   [5] § 173.   [6] cf. § 34ss.   [7] 409ᵇ 11.

definition, he says, must give knowledge of the accidents as well as of the substance of the thing defined. But if we combine number and movement in our definition of the soul, we shall find ourselves involved in many difficulties besides those that concern the soul's substance. For these two things, number and movement, not only cannot belong to the substance of the soul, but are not even accidental qualities of it, nor are they means to a knowledge of these qualities. Hence the definition itself is unsuitable; it does not help us to know the accidental qualities of the thing defined. This will be evident to anyone who, relying on this definition, tries to attribute to the soul affections and activities such as reasoning, pleasure, pain and the like. If we started from number and movement, we should not only find it hard to reach any knowledge of the soul's accidental qualities and passions and activities, but we could not even begin to hazard any conjecture about them.

BOOK I, CHAPTER V, CONTINUED

EMPEDOCLES'S THEORY OF COGNITION
SOUL NOT COMPOSED OF THE
ELEMENTS

THERE ARE, THEN, THREE WAYS IN WHICH MEN HAVE defined the soul: some declaring that it is the principal mover, being self-moving; some, that it is the most subtle of bodies, or the least corporeal of things (what contradictions and problems these views entail we have briefly reviewed); so what is left for us to consider is how it is said to be constituted from the elements. They say this is so because the soul perceives things that are and knows each one. But many irrational consequences follow upon this. For they suppose that like is known by like, as if they meant to identify things themselves with the soul. But those [elements] are not the only things; there are many others, perhaps infinite in number, derived from them.

Granted, then, that the soul knows and perceives the elements of which each of these is formed, yet it will not know or perceive wholes, such as what a divinity is, or a man, or flesh, or bone, or anything else compounded. For the elements of these are not interrelated at random, but by some ratio or principle of composition, as Empedocles said of bone,

'*The earth all gracious in its ample caverns*
Took two parts out of eight of water and light,
But four from the god of fire,[1] *and then*
White bone was made.'

So it is no use supposing elements to be in the soul unless
there are in it also principles and co-ordination. Let each
know its like, it will not know bone or man unless these be
in it. It is hardly necessary to say, however, that this is impossible; who would ever think of enquiring if there is a stone
in the soul, or a man? Likewise, the good or the not-good;
and similarly with other things.   §§ 178–80

Further, 'that which is' can be predicated in several ways:
in one way, substance, in another, quality, in another, quantity; and in any other way according to the categories that
have been distinguished. Will the soul be made up of all these
or no? But it does not seem that there are elements common
to all these. Is it from those of substance only? How then will
it know anything of the other kinds? Or is one to say that
there are elements and principles proper to each category of
which the soul is composed? then there will be quality and
quantity and substance in the soul. But it is impossible that
of the elements of quantity be derived substance, and not
quantity. For those who hold that the soul is composed of all
things, these (and other such) difficulties arise.   §§ 181–2

It is unreasonable to say that one thing cannot be acted on
by its like, and yet that sensation and knowledge is 'like by
like'. For they posit sensation as being moved and affected,
and knowing and understanding likewise.   § 183

What has now been said witnesses to the many difficulties
and doubts to be faced by one who, with Empedocles, says
that each thing is known through its corporeal elements and

[1] *Vulcanus,* Ἥφαιστος.

[their relation] to its likeness. For whatever things in the body are obviously earthy (bones, sinews, hair) seem to perceive nothing; nor therefore even their likenesses; and yet they ought [on this hypothesis]. 　　　　§ 184

Again, each one of the principles will have more ignorance than understanding. For it will know a single principle and be ignorant of many others, indeed of all others. 　　§ 185

Further, for Empedocles, the Divinity must be the least knowing of all things, for he alone will not know one of the elements, namely Strife; but mortals, all; for every individual is composed of all. 　　　　§ 186

In general then, why is it that everything has not a soul? For all things are either elements or are made of one, or of several, or of all. They ought accordingly to know one, or several, or all. 　　　　§ 187

One might wonder what gives unity to them. For the elements are comparable to matter, and that which holds them together, whatever it is, is the most essential principle. That it should have a higher function or be more excellent than the soul is impossible; still more impossible that it be higher than intellect. For that this is the primordial and most exalted and godlike thing by nature is in full accord with reason. Yet these men say that the elements have priority among beings. 　　　　§ 188

Not one of those who maintain that the soul is constituted from elements because it perceives and knows realities, and that it is primary among moving forces, considers every kind of soul. For not all sentient beings move; for certain species of animals are observed to remain in one place, although it would seem that the soul moved the animal with this one motion only [i.e. locally]. Likewise with those who would make of elements the sensitive and intellectual powers; for plants seem to live, but are not endowed with local motion or perception; and many animals lack intelligence. Even setting this fact on one side, and admitting that intellect is a part of the soul, and the sensitive power likewise, they would not be speaking of every soul, nor of the whole of any soul, nor of one [entire soul].[1] The same objection tells against a notion expressed in the Orphic hymns, where it is said, 'The soul enters from the universe, breathed in by the winds.' This cannot occur in the case of plants and certain animals: unless, indeed, all use respiration; a fact overlooked by those who put forward this view.   §§ 189–90

But if one must constitute the soul from the elements, there is no need to use them all; for one term of contraries suffices for the discernment of itself and its opposite; thus by the straight line we know both itself and the oblique;[2] the criterion of both is the rule, but the curved is a criterion neither of itself nor of the straight.   § 191

[1] 'of every kind of soul or of the whole of any one soul', 410^b 26.
[2] *obliquum* for τὸ καμπύλον.

ST. THOMAS'S COMMENTARY
LECTIO TWELVE

§ 178. Having in the preceding sections explained that the early philosophers pursued their enquiry into the soul by three ways, that of movement, of knowledge and of incorporeal being, and having pressed certain objections against those who took the way of movement, and against those who identified soul with something bodiless and entirely simple, the Philosopher now turns to criticise the upholders of the principle that the soul knows everything because everything is included in itself.

§ 179. With their theory that all knowledge takes place by means of assimilation these philosophers had caught, as it were, a far-off glimpse of the truth; but they expressed this by saying that the reason why the soul knew all things was that all things entered into its composition, and that the soul possessed the likeness of all things according to the mode of existence, i.e. a corporeal one, which things have in themselves outside it. Hence, if things consist of elements, the same is true, they said, of the soul; and that is the cause of sensation and knowledge. The chief upholder of this view was Empedocles, who posited more elements in the soul than anyone else; and therefore the Philosopher is more concerned here to refute him than anyone else. So he first attacks the opinion of Empedocles,[1] and only then, at 'And some say',[2] that of certain others.

§ 180. Against Empedocles he brings ten arguments. The first is as follows. Empedocles argues that the soul must be composed of all the objects of its knowledge because knowledge takes place by means of similitude. But this involves many difficulties and absurdities. For clearly the elements are not all that any given thing contains; it includes much else besides, such as the proportion in which

---

[1] 409^b 23–411^a 7.   [2] Lectio 13, § 192; 411^a 7.

its elements are combined and the formulable essence of each one in particular,[1] and there may even be an infinity of accidents belonging to things made up of elements. Take, for example, bones. To understand bones we need to know, not only the elements of which they are composed, but also how these elements combine in them, and the functional pattern of bones; for the order of elements in compound things is not a random one, it involves a certain definite proportional arrangement. If bone, as Empedocles says, is composed of eight parts, each bone has eight parts into which the various elements enter in unequal measure: for earth, he says, contributes two parts, air and water one each, and fire four—to which predominance of fire is due the whiteness of bone, while from earth comes its dryness. Thus in compound things there are, besides the elements, certain proportions and patterns. Well then, either these proportions are in the soul together with the elements, or not. If they are in the soul, then bones and flesh and so forth, and therefore men and stones and bodies and things quite contrary to one another, are all in the soul; and this nobody dreams of conceding. But if only the elements are in the soul, then it does not in fact know the proportion in things nor compound things as such; and how can it know God (i.e. the Heavens as a whole) or man or stone or bone? It cannot possibly know these things; it knows only the elements which compose them, according to this view.

§ 181. The second argument,[2] starting at 'Further, that which is', runs thus. You say the soul is made up of elementary principles. But these differ according to the different categories of things, such as substance, quality, quantity and the rest. Is then the soul made up of the elementary principles of substance alone, or does it include those of the other categories? If the first alternative is right, then the soul only knows substance; yet the supposition is that it knows everything. But if it includes the elements of all the categories, then, since whatever has the elementary principles of substance is a substance, and whatever has those of quantity is a quantity, and so on likewise with the rest, it follows that the soul is at once both a substance, and a quality, and a relation, and so on and so forth.

§ 182. It might be answered that the elementary principles of

[1] But perhaps *ratio*, 'formulable essence', means only the proportion already mentioned.   [2] 410^a 13.

substance are also those of quantity, quality, etc., since everything is grounded in substance; hence the soul need only possess the principles of substance to know everything. But I say that things have both remote and proximate principles, and should be known by means of the latter. The principles of substance may be the remote, but they are not the proximate, principles of the other categories; hence they cannot give knowledge of anything except substance.

§ 183. The third argument,[1] starting at 'It is unreasonable', is this. The reason why the soul is said to be composed of all the elements is that it knows all things and knowledge is by similarity. Against this is the admitted fact that sensation and knowledge are a sort of being acted upon; and it seems unreasonable to say that like is acted upon by like, and not rather by its contrary; and consequently, to say that sensation or knowledge are by similarity.

§ 184. The fourth argument,[2] at 'What has now', is this. What has been said already is enough to show that Empedocles's theory is highly questionable and his manner of expressing it slipshod. But there is a yet stronger objection. If the soul, as he says, knows by similarity, then the element air will know air, and so on for the other elements. But we know that animals' bodies have many earthy parts which lack sensation, such as hair, bones and nerves; yet they ought to have sensation according to this theory. Therefore knowledge is not by similarity nor the soul composed of the elements.

§ 185. The fifth argument,[3] at 'Again etc.', runs thus. Another objection to this view is that it implies that principles as such are more ignorant than percipient. For if knowledge is only by similarity, and if every principle is quite simple, having no likeness to anything but itself, it follows that each principle only knows itself and is ignorant of everything else.

§ 186. The sixth argument[4] comes at 'Further'. This theory also implies the doubtful consequence that God is the most ignorant of all living beings. For, as we have seen,[5] Empedocles thought that everything on this earth could be reduced to the four elements together with Strife and Friendship, these last being the causes of coming-to-be and passing-away. But the sky he called God and said it was composed of the four elements and Friendship, but not

[1] 410^a 23.   [2] 410^a 27.   [3] 410^b 2.   [4] 410^b 4.   [5] §§ 45; 133.

of Strife; and was therefore incorruptible. If then knowledge is by similarity, God cannot know Strife, since it does not form part of him, and God is therefore less percipient, strictly speaking, than other living beings which know Strife because they include it.

§ 187. The seventh argument[1] comes at 'In general, why'. If the soul is made of all the elements, then all things have souls; for all things are made of either all or some elements. Now whatever is made up of elements or of compounds of elements[2] is a body. Hence all bodies, indeed all beings, have souls; which is false.

§ 188. The eighth argument[3] begins at 'One might wonder'. The elements are many and contrary; but whenever contrary things come together in a composition there must be some *other* thing which includes and unifies them. Hence if the soul is made up of the elements there must be something in it which unifies them. But it is extremely doubtful what this can be; for it must be something in the soul nobler than the soul, which is an impossibility, at least as regards that which it is reasonable to consider the supremely noble and divine thing, namely the mind. Besides, this other thing would have to be prior to the elements, whereas Empedocles and the rest have asserted that the elements were the first of all beings. Therefore the soul is not made up of elements.

§ 189. He begins the ninth argument[4] at 'Not one of those', showing the weakness of Empedocles's view and that of all the others who have enquired about the soul, whether by way of movement or by way of sense-perception. For (1) there is a gap in the arguments of all who defined the soul in terms of local movement. Many living beings, such as plants and things resembling plants, do not move locally at all but are fixed in one place. And (2) there is a like inadequacy in the definition of the soul in terms of intellect or sensation; for plenty of living things neither sense nor think. And if local motion, intellect and sensation are taken separately and regarded as distinct parts of the one soul, this will not apply to soul in general, since not all souls are intellectual; nor to the *whole* of any one soul, since only parts of it will be intellectual and sensitive; nor to any one *single* soul, since this description does not enumerate all the characteristics of any given soul;

[1] 410^b 7.

[2] Adopting Pirotta's proposal to read *ex elementis aut ex elementatis*.

[3] 410^b 10.   [4] 410^b 16.

for in any soul there are other things besides understanding and sensation.

§ 190. And a certain philosopher named Orpheus having fallen into a rather similar error in what he said about the soul, he too is mentioned here. Orpheus was one of those three early thinkers who were, so to say, poet-theologians; for they wrote in verse on philosophy and about God. The other two were Museus and a certain Linus. Orpheus, a wonderful orator whose words had power to civilise wild and brutish folk, was the first man to induce his fellows to live together in society. For this reason it is said of him that he could make rocks dance to the sweet sounds of his harp, which really means that his eloquence could melt the hardest hearts. And after these three poet-philosophers came the seven sages, of whom Thales was one. Now this Orpheus thought that the whole air was alive, was indeed a sort of living soul, and that the so-called souls of living bodies were really nothing but the air these bodies breathed; and this idea he expressed in verse. But the Philosopher objects to the Orphic theory, saying that it is just as inadequate as the others he has criticised; for there are many animals that do not breathe at all, 'a fact', he says, 'which was overlooked' by those who held this opinion. The criticism touches the inadequacy of the theory.

§ 191. At 'But if one'[1] comes the tenth argument; which convicts the Empedoclean theory of unnecessary complication. The soul's capacity for knowledge is explained by its composition from elements. Now it is a matter of experience that knowledge of anything rests on few, rather than many, principles; hence even if we grant that the soul is composed of elements we ought not to suppose that these are all the elements, but at the most two. And that knowledge rests on few rather than many principles is clear if we consider that in composite things, consisting of two principles, one of perfection, the other of imperfection, it is in the light of the former that we know the latter; and that in contraries, which can be reduced to a quality and its privation, it suffices to understand the term denoting quality and perfection in order to understand also the other term denoting privation and imperfection. Thus by the idea of straight line we know and form judgements about both straight and crooked lines; for 'the rule', i.e. the measure, is the

[1] 411ᵃ 2.

means of knowing both; but the crooked line is the means of knowing neither itself nor the straight. Hence there was no need to regard the soul as made up of all the elements; enough to adduce two only, fire and earth, as its means of knowing both itself and contrary things. Through fire it could know both cold and hot objects, and through earth the dry and the moist.

BOOK I, CHAPTER V, CONTINUED

THE ELEMENTS HAVE NO SOUL

ND SOME SAY THAT THE SOUL IS INTERMINGLED generally with the Universe. That is perhaps why Thales thought that the whole world was full of divinities. § 192

This, however, involves several difficulties. For why does the soul in fire and air not result in an animated being, whereas it does so in composite beings?—and that, even though it is thought to be more excellent in the former. (And one might well query why the soul in the air should be nobler and more enduring than that in animals.) On either count the theory is absurd and unreasonable. To say that air or fire is an animal is among the most wanton of absurdities; and if there is a soul in them, it is inconsistent not to call them animals. §§ 193–5

They seem to have held that there was a soul in these on the ground that the Universe is made up of homogeneous parts; so that if animals become animate by partaking of the containing element, they must say that the soul [of the Whole] is homogeneous with its parts. § 196

If then the air, divided off thus, be homogeneous, but the soul be composed of heterogeneous parts, something of it [the soul] will exist and something not.[1] It is necessary then, either that it be of homogeneous parts, or that it be not in any and every part of the whole. § 197

It is evident then, from what has been said, that the cause of knowledge being in the soul is not that soul is made up of the elements; and that it is neither true nor apposite to say that it is in motion. § 198

---

[1] That the distinction here referred to between parts of 'soul' refers to mortal and immortal existence is St. Thomas's interpretation of this passage (§ 197). The above translation has been made with this in mind. *See* Introd., p. 33.

§ 192. Having stated and rejected the theories and arguments of those who maintained that the soul was composed of elements, the Philosopher is now led, by the same train of thought, to discuss the notion, upheld by some, according to which a soul is intermingled with the elements. First, then, he states this opinion, and then, at 'They seemed to have held', the argument used to support it. And the opinion itself is first stated and then, at 'This, however,'[1] attacked.

There are, he says, some who see a soul intermingled with everything, whether simple elements or things composed of these. This perhaps is what Thales meant when he said that everything was full of gods; perhaps he thought that the entire Universe was alive and its life was divine; that just as soul exists everywhere in each living thing so a god was everywhere in the Universe and everything therefore was 'full of divinities'. And perhaps this was the notion that underlay idolatry.

§ 193. At 'This, however,' he points out, against this opinion, that it presents certain difficulties. For instance, if a soul exists in air and in fire (and of these two especially this was asserted) it is hard to see why it does not make 'animated beings' of them, i.e. why air and fire are not animals. Things composed of several elements are animals precisely because they contain a soul; and one would expect the soul to be all the more powerful where the element is pure and simple.

§ 194. Again,[2] one might ask, he says, why the soul which they place in the elements should be considered higher and more immortal than the soul of things composed of elements. For the latter constitute knowing, sentient animals; not so the former.

[1] 411ª 9. [2] 411ª 11.

§ 195. But, however the objections are put, the result is damaging to this theory. To say that fire or air is a living body is most improbable in itself; is contradicted by experience; and is unsupported by any good reason. And to deny that things which have souls need be living bodies is most unreasonable; for it would follow that there was no difference between souls that exist in bodies and those that do not.

§ 196. Then, at 'They seem to have held',[1] he states the reason used in support of this theory and refutes it; after which, at 'It is . . . evident'[2] he draws a general conclusion from all the foregoing discussions. The reason, he says, why some philosophers seem to have thought that a soul existed in 'these', i.e. in all the elements, was that they thought that the whole and the parts in elements were of the same nature, since the elements are simple. Observing that that part of 'the containing element', i.e. the air, which came into contact with the bodies of animals through their breathing, was the cause and principle of animal life, they thought it necessary to conclude that the soul of the whole was 'of the same specific nature as the parts', that is to say, that all the containing air was alive.

§ 197. At 'If then'[3] he refutes this argument. The assumption is that, because the portion of the air removed and inhaled by an animal is of a like nature to the air as a whole, the soul of the animal itself is, as it were, a portion of the soul of the whole air. But on their own principle this is clearly false; for, according to them, the soul of air 'exists', i.e. is immortal, as that which has never ceased from vivifying all animate beings, whereas the soul of this or that particular animal 'does not exist', i.e. is not immortal.[4] Therefore either of two awkward consequences flow from this theory. If all the parts of air, those outside and those breathed in, are homogeneous, then the same is true of the soul; but this has been disproved. But if the soul's parts are heterogeneous while the air's are homogeneous, then the soul is not in every part 'of the whole', i.e. of the whole air; which is against those who said that all the air had a soul.

§ 198. Then at 'It is evident'[5] Aristotle concludes this part of the

[1] 411ᵃ 16. [2] 411ᵃ 24. [3] 411ᵃ 20.
[4] 'existet', i.e. immortalis est: cf. transl. of text, note, and Introd., p. 33.
[5] 411ᵃ 24.

discussion of earlier opinions. Neither of these two predications made by the ancients was, he says, either true or well-expressed; namely that knowledge in the soul is a consequence of its being composed of elements, and that movement is in it for the same reason. So much should be clear to anyone who has followed the discussion up to the present.

BOOK I, CHAPTER V, CONTINUED

THE UNITY OF THE SOUL

SINCE KNOWLEDGE PERTAINS TO THE SOUL, AND SEN-
sation, and thinking, as well as desiring and deliberating
—in a word, all appetition; and as in animate beings
there also occur local motion, and growth, and preservation,
and decay, all from the soul, is each of these in the whole
soul, and do we understand and perceive and do and undergo
every particular experience, with the whole soul? Or does
each require a different part? And is life itself in any one of
these? Or in several? Or in all? Or is it from some quite
distinct cause?   §§ 199–203

Some say the soul is divisible, understanding by one part
and desiring by another.   §§ 204–5

If then the soul is of its very nature divisible, what holds it
together? Not the body, certainly: much rather the contrary
seems to be true, that the soul holds the body together; for
when it departs, the body expires and decomposes. If there is
some other thing which makes it one, this other is rather the
soul. One would then have to ask, concerning this other,
whether it be one or of many parts. If it is one, why not call
it the soul straightway? But if it is divisible, reason again
demands, what it is that holds this together? And so on *ad
infinitum*.   § 206

A further query arises about the soul's parts: what power has each in the body? If the whole soul holds together the whole body, it would be fitting if each of the parts controlled some part of the body. But this looks like an impossibility. It is difficult even to imagine what part the intellect would hold together, or how.   § 207

It is also held[1] that plants live after being divided, and certain divided animals also;[2] as if they had a soul specifically one, but not numerically. For each of these parts is endowed with sensation and moves locally for a certain time. If they are not long-lived, that is no objection: they have not the organs requisite for the preservation of their natures. Nevertheless, in each of the parts are to be found all the parts of the soul; and those separated parts are specifically the same as each other and as the whole; as each other, as if they were not separable; as the whole, as having an indivisible unity.[3]

§ 208

It would seem that the principle in plants is some sort of soul. Plants have only this in common with animals, and while this is independent of the sensitive principle, nothing has sensation without having this.   §§ 209–10

[1] 'It is observed that plants . . .', 411^b 19.
[2] 'and certain insects', *ibid*. St. Thomas follows M., § 208.
[3] 'the whole soul being divisible', 411^b 27.

ST. THOMAS'S COMMENTARY
LECTIO FOURTEEN

§ 199. Having reviewed and criticised earlier opinions on the soul the Philosopher proceeds now to put certain questions of his own;[1] which at 'Some say' he begins to answer.[2] But first we have to realise that the activities of the soul, such as sensation, understanding, desire, movement in space, and growth, can be considered in two distinct ways.

We can consider the *mode* of these activities; and from this point of view we can distinguish, underlying these activities, three powers of the soul: the vegetative, the sensitive and the intellectual.

§ 200. And these powers differ. For whilst the vegetative or nutritive power acts through active and passive qualities of matter,[3] such as heat and cold and the like, the sensitive power requires no such sensible qualities for its sentient activity, though it does depend on corporeal organs; while the intellectual power acts through neither sensible qualities nor a corporeal organ, for it functions in an entirely incorporeal way.

§ 201. But if we consider the *kinds* of activities within the soul's range, then we distinguish five powers with five corresponding activities: the nutritive, sensitive, locomotive, appetitive and intellectual powers.

§ 202. Having then discussed and criticised earlier opinions on the soul in general, Aristotle begins now an enquiry into the parts and particular activities of the soul. And he proposes two problems. The first is whether activities like sensing, rational judgement, desiring, deliberating, and also appetition (which he related to special parts of the soul in a more general way than these, placing the irascible urge in both the sensitive and the rational parts),

[1] 411ª 26.   [2] 411ᵇ 5.
[3] 'Of matter' is inserted for clarity.—(Transl.)

157

together with local motion and rest, growth and decline, whether all these pertain to the whole soul in such a way that each one occurs in every part of the soul, so that with each part we both understand and sense and move and desire and assimilate food; or whether the truth is not rather that each activity has its own special part, that is to say, that with one part we understand, with another we sense, and so on

§ 203. The second problem is this. Granted that each activity has its special part of the soul, is this true of the activity of simply being alive? Is *this* activity proper to any one of these parts? Or to many? Or to all at once? Or does it perhaps belong to some other part?

§ 204. Then at 'Some say'[1] he answers these questions in order. As to the first one, he states and then rejects a view of certain philosophers that the activities in question spring severally from the soul's parts, not from the soul in general; that the soul is so divided into parts that it understands with one and desires with another, just as some people hold that the sensitive power is in the brain and the vital power in the heart, and so on.

§ 205. Now this is partly true and partly false. If you take it to mean that the soul has different parts potentially, it is quite true that its parts and powers are distinct and that one of them understands and another senses. The soul is a whole in the sense that it has a total capacity with partial capacities subordinate to the whole. But if you take it quantitatively, as though the soul were of a certain size with parts of certain sizes, then this opinion is false. And this was how the philosophers in question thought of the soul— even to the extent that they made out the soul's different powers to be different souls.

§ 206. Next, at 'If then the soul'[2] Aristotle attacks this last hypothesis, with three arguments. The first is this.[3] Different things cannot be unified except by something else that unites them. If the one body contained several souls, these would have to be joined together and contained by something else. But there is nothing else that can do this; therefore the hypothesis is groundless. That there is no other unifying principle is shown thus. Whatever contains and unifies the soul will be either the body or some other thing. Now it is not the body. Rather, the body is contained and unified by its soul and falls to pieces when the soul leaves it. Then

[1] 411^b 5.   [2] 411^b 6.   [3] 411^b 6-13.

it is something else; but this must be a soul if it pertains especially to soul to unify and control. Is then this unifying soul itself intrinsically one, or made of several parts? If of several parts, then what unites them? And so on *ad infinitum*. But if this unifying soul is intrinsically one, then 'why not call it the soul straightway', i.e. why not concede at the beginning that the soul is intrinsically one? The soul, then, is not, as they thought, quantitatively divisible.

§ 207. The second argument comes at 'A further query'.[1] If the different parts of the soul are in different parts of the body, then each soul-activity has its own corporeal part or organ. But the intellect has no special corporeal organ. Hence their conception of the soul's parts is false.

§ 208. The third argument starts at 'It is also held'.[2] If each of the various activities of soul is proper to a special part of the body, then no one part is the organ of several distinct activities, nor are there several parts in an animal's body the same in kind. But experience proves that certain living things have parts with several activities each, and a soul that is identical in kind in the whole and in all the parts; e.g. in plants and in certain (segmented) animals which go on living after being cut up, the cut off parts retaining their feelings and movement for some time. It does not matter if these parts live for only a short time through lack of the organs of self-preservation. The point is that several soul-activities exist in several distinct corporeal parts at once, and the latter are specifically similar to each other and to the whole. Therefore the soul is not divided according to the different parts of the body.

The reason why such animals go on living after being divided is that the number and diversity of activities complete in themselves varies in direct proportion to the perfection of the soul in living things. The higher the soul the wider is the range of its activities; and the wider its active range the more, and the more distinctly diversified, organs or bodily instruments are required by it. So the relatively greater nobility of the rational soul calls for a greater diversity of its bodily organs, whilst the far lower soul of a segmented animal or a plant has only a narrow field of activity and therefore needs a body that is more uniform and less articulated, and in any part of which, taken separately, it can maintain its being.

[1] 411^b 14.   [2] 411^b 19.

§ 209. Then, at 'It would seem',[1] he answers the second question; concerning which we must realise that life belongs, properly speaking, to things that move and act of themselves and are not caused to do so by others. So 'to live' has two meanings. It can mean the *being* of a living thing, and in this sense Aristotle says that living is the being of living things. And also it can mean *activity*.

§ 210. Now the soul of plants, the vegetative soul, seems to be a sort of primary manifestation of life among things here on earth; for nothing lives without it and all living things share in it, though in other ways their modes of life differ. Animals and plants have only this in common. It can exist without sense or intelligence, but not sense or intelligence without it; no animal has sense or reason except it first have vegetative life. Thus it bears the same relation to life as touch to sensation.[2] Not that living things only live by this principle, but it is the point where life first appears.

[1] 411^b 27.   [2] cf. Bk. III, cc. 12, 13; lectios 17 and 18.

BOOK TWO

BOOK II, CHAPTER I

THE DEFINITION OF THE SOUL

HITHERTO WE HAVE SPOKEN OF WHAT OUR PRE-
decessors handed down to us about the soul. But let
us now re-open the enquiry from the beginning and
endeavour to determine what the soul is and what is its most
comprehensive definition.   § 211

Now, we say that one of the kinds of things that are is substance. Of this, there is one element, matter, which of itself
is no particular thing; another, the form or species according
to which it is called 'this particular thing'; and a third, that
which is from both of these. Matter is, indeed, potency, and
the form, act; and this latter has two modes of being, one,
like knowledge possessed, the other, like the act of knowing.
                                                          §§ 212–16
Bodies especially seem to be substances; and, among these,
natural bodies, for these are the principles of the others. Of
natural bodies, some possess vitality, others do not. We mean
by 'possessing vitality', that a thing can nourish itself and
grow and decay.   §§ 217–19

Therefore every natural body sharing in life will be a substance, and this substance will be in some way composite.
Since, however, it is a body of such and such a nature, i.e.
having vitality, the soul will not itself be the body. For the
body is not one of the factors existing in the subject; rather,
it *is* as the subject and the matter. It is necessary, then, that the

163

soul be a substance in the sense of the specifying principle of a physical body potentially alive. Now, substance [in this sense] is act; it will therefore be the act of a body of this sort.

§§ 220–6

Now this can mean one of two things: one, as is the possession of knowledge; another, as is the act of knowing. It is plain that it is like knowledge possessed. For the soul remains in the body whether one is asleep or awake. Being awake is comparable to the act of knowing, sleep to possession without use. Now knowledge possessed is prior in the order of generation, in one and the same thing. The soul, therefore, is the primary act of a physical body capable of life. §§ 227–9

Such a body will be organic. Parts of plants, indeed, are organs, though very elementary—the leaf is the covering of the pericarp and the pericarp of the fruit: roots, too, are like mouths, for both draw in nourishment. §§ 230–2

If, then, there is any one generalisation to be made for any and every soul, the soul will be the primary act of a physical bodily organism. § 233

Hence it is unnecessary to enquire whether the soul and body be *one*, any more than whether the wax and an impression made in it are one; or in general, the matter of anything whatever, and that of which it is the matter. For while *one* and *being* are predicated in many ways, that which is properly so is actuality. § 234

ST. THOMAS'S COMMENTARY
LECTIO ONE

§ 211. Having reviewed, in Book One, other men's opinions on the soul, Aristotle now begins Book Two of his Treatise, in which he sets out what he himself holds on the matter. First, then, linking up with what has gone before, he states his general aim;[1] and secondly, at 'Now we say that one', he starts to carry it out.[2] He begins by saying that despite all the previous accounts of the soul it is necessary to go into the whole matter again from the beginning. The subject is so difficult that it is wiser to assume that the truth about it has not yet been discovered. And in answer to the question raised in the Introduction to Book One, whether one should first define the soul, and afterwards its parts, he decides now to define the essence of the soul before coming to conclusions about its parts.[3] As though explaining this decision, he adds that we shall thus have acquired the most comprehensive idea of soul. For the definition of the soul itself comprises what is most common or general, whereas that of each of its parts or potencies comprises only some special aspect of it. And as he explains at the beginning of the *Physics*, the right way to teach is to begin with what is most general and end with precisions in detail.

§ 212. Beginning then at 'Now we say', his treatment divides into two parts, in the first of which he shows what soul in general is,[4] and in the second, starting at 'Of the soul's powers',[5] what are its parts or powers. The first part subdivides into (*a*) a definition that concludes,[6] and (*b*) one that introduces, a demonstrative

[1] 412ᵃ 1–5.   [2] 412ᵃ 6.
[3] The 'parts' begin to be examined at 414ᵃ 29: Lectio 5, § 279ss.
[4] Lectio 1, § 212–Lectio 4, § 278; 412ᵃ 5–414ᵃ 25.
[5] Lectio 5, § 279; 414ᵃ 29.
[6] Lectio 1–Lectio 2, § 244; 412ᵃ 5–413ᵃ 10.

argument;—this latter part comes at 'Since it is from the less clear'.[1]
Note in passing that any definition, as he says in Book I of the
Posterior Analytics,[2] is either the conclusion of a demonstration, e.g.
'Thunder is a continuous noise in the clouds', or it is the demonstration's starting point, e.g. 'Thunder is the extinction of fire in
the clouds', or it is the demonstration itself, but thrown into a different order, e.g. 'Thunder is a continuous noise etc., caused by the
extinction of fire etc.' in which the conclusion and the starting
point both appear, though not in syllogistic order.

As to (*a*), it includes first a definition of the soul,[3] and then, at
'It has been stated then',[4] an explanation of the definition. And to
clear the ground before the defining proper begins (at 'Therefore
every natural body')[5] he makes some preliminary distinctions.

§ 213. It should be noted here that, according to the teaching of
Book VII of the *Metaphysics*,[6] there is this difference between defining substance and defining accidents that in the former case
nothing *extrinsic* is included: every substance is defined in terms
merely of its material and formal principles; but in the latter case
something extrinsic to the thing defined is referred to, i.e. the subject of the accidents in question—as when one defines snubness as
'curvature of the nose'. The reason is that a definition must express what a thing is, and while substance is something complete
in its being and kind, accidents have being only in relation to a
substance. In the same way no *form* as such is complete in kind;
completeness in this sense belongs only to the substance composed
of form and matter; so that the latter's definition is complete without reference to anything else, whilst that of the form has to include a reference to its proper subject which is matter. Hence, if
the soul is a form its definition will not be complete without reference to its subject or matter.

§ 214. So, in the first part of this section, he makes certain distinctions, first in view of the work of defining the soul's *essence*,[7]
and then, at 'Bodies especially seem to be substances . . .'[8] in view
of defining its *subject*. As regards the former point he alludes to
three distinctions, of which the first is that of being into the ten

---

[1] Lectio 3, § 245; 413ᵃ 10.   [2] I, c.8; 75ᵇ 30. *See* Introd., p. 30.
[3] 412ᵃ 15–412ᵇ 9.   [4] Lectio 2, § 235; 412ᵇ 10.
[5] 412ᵃ 15.   [6] VII, c.1; cf. VI, c.1; 1025ᵇ 30ss.
[7] 412ᵃ 5–11.   [8] 412ᵃ 11.

categories; this he hints at when he says that substance is reckoned to be 'one of the kinds of things that are'.[1]

§ 215. The second distinction[2] alluded to is that of substance into matter, form and the compound of both. Matter is that which is not as such a 'particular thing',[3] but is in mere potency to become a 'particular thing'. Form is that by which a 'particular thing' actually exists. And the compound is 'the particular thing' itself; for that is said to be a 'particular thing' (i.e. something you can point to) which is complete in being and in kind; and among material things only the compound is such. For although immaterial substances are not compounds of matter and form, still they are particular things, having actual existence in themselves, and being complete in their own nature. Not so the rational soul; for though it has the existence in itself which belongs to a 'particular thing', it is not a complete nature by itself; it is rather a *part* of a specific nature. Hence it is not in all respects a 'particular thing'.

Matter, then, differs from form in this, that it is potential being; form is the 'entelechy' or actuality that renders matter actual; and the compound is the resulting actual being.

§ 216. Thirdly,[4] he distinguishes two senses of the term 'act'. In one sense knowledge is an act, in the other thinking is an act; and the difference can be understood by relating these acts to their potencies. Before one acquires the grammatical habit and becomes a grammarian, whether self-taught or led by another, one is only potentially so; and this potency is actualised by the *habit*. But once the habit is acquired one is still in potency to the *use* of it, so long as one is not actually thinking about grammar; and this thinking is a further actualisation. In this sense, then, knowledge is one act and thinking another.

§ 217. Then at 'Bodies especially' he alludes to three distinctions which are presupposed by his enquiry into the meaning of the definition of the soul, so far as the *subject* endowed with soul is concerned. The first is the distinction between corporeal and incorporeal substances.[5] Now the former are the most evident to us: for, whatever the latter may be in themselves, they do not impinge on our senses, but are only discoverable by an exercise of the reason. Hence he says that 'bodies especially seem to be substances'.

[1] 412ᵃ 5.   [2] 412ᵃ 7.   [3] *hoc aliquid.*
[4] 412ᵃ 10.   [5] 412ᵃ 11.

§ 218. The next distinction[1] is between physical or natural bodies and artificial bodies. Man and wood and stone are natural bodies, but a house or a saw is artificial. And of these the natural bodies seem to be the more properly called substances, since artificial bodies are made out of them. Art works upon materials furnished by nature, giving these, moreover, a merely accidental form, such as a new shape and so forth; so that it is only in virtue of their matter, not their form, that artificial bodies are substances at all; they are substances because natural bodies are such. Natural bodies therefore are the more properly called substances, being such through their form as well as through their matter.

§ 219. Thirdly,[2] he distinguishes between living and non-living natural bodies; and the living are those which of themselves take nutriment and grow and decay. Note here that this is said by way of example rather than definition. For, besides growth and decay, living things may exhibit sensation and intellectual knowledge and other vital activities. Immaterial substances, as is proved in the *Metaphysics*, Book XI,[3] have the life of intellect and volition, though they cannot grow and do not take food. But because, in the sphere of things that are born and die, the plant-soul (the principle of nutrition and growth) marks the point where life begins, this soul is here taken as the type of all living things. However, life is essentially that by which anything has power to move itself, taking movement in its wide sense so as to include the 'movement' or activity of the intellect. For we call those things inanimate which are moved only from outside.

§ 220. After this, at 'Therefore every natural body',[4] he begins to define the soul, presupposing the distinctions already made. And his enquiry here has three parts: (*a*) he enquires into the elements of the definition taken separately;[5] (*b*) at, 'If, then, there is any one generalisation',[6] he states his definition; and (*c*) at 'Hence it is unnecessary',[7] he uses it to refute an objection. As to (*a*) he first deals with the elements that refer to the soul's *essence*, and then to those that refer to its *subject*, at 'Such a body will be organic',[8] and in the part that concerns the essence he considers first the statement

---

[1] 412ᵃ 13.   [2] 412ᵃ 13.   [3] Perhaps XII, c.7; 1072ᵇ 1ss.
[4] 412ᵃ 15.   [5] 412ᵃ 15–412ᵇ 4.   [6] 412ᵇ 4.
[7] 412ᵇ 6.   [8] 412ᵃ 29.

that the soul is an 'act',[1] and then, at 'Now this can mean one of two things', that it is a 'primary act'.[2]

Aristotle's first conclusion, then, in line with what has been said already, is that if physical bodies are substances in the fullest sense, all living bodies are substances too, for they are physical bodies. And as each living body is an actual being, it must be a compound substance.[3] But just because to say 'living body' is to imply two things, the body itself and that modification of body by which it is alive, it cannot be said that the element in the composition referred to by the term body is itself the principle of life or the 'soul'. By 'soul' we understand that by which a living thing is alive; it is understood, therefore, as existing *in* a subject, taking 'subject' in a broad sense to include not only those *actual* beings which are subjects of their accidental modifications, but also bare matter or potential being. On the other hand the body that receives life is more like a subject and a matter than a modification existing in a subject.

§ 221. Since, then, there are three sorts of substance: the compound; matter; and form; and since the soul is neither the compound—the living body itself; nor its matter—the body as the subject that receives life; we have no choice but to say that the soul is a substance in the manner of a form that determines or characterises a particular sort of body, i.e. a physical body potentially alive.[4]

§ 222. Note that he does not say simply 'alive', but 'potentially alive'. For by a body actually alive is understood a living compound; and no compound as such can enter into the definition of a form. On the other hand the matter of a living body stands to the body's life as a potency to its act; and the soul is precisely the actuality whereby the body has life. It is as though we were to say that shape is an actuality; it is not exactly the actuality of an actually shaped body—i.e. the compound of body and shape—but rather of the body as able to receive a shape, of the body as in potency to an actual shape.

§ 223. But lest it be thought that soul is an actuality in the manner of any merely accidental form, he adds that it is a

---

[1] 412ᵃ 15.   [2] 412ᵃ 22.

[3] i.e. composed of Matter and Form, cf. § 215.

[4] 412ᵃ 20. *See* Introd., pp. 28–31.

substantial actuality or form.[1] And since every form has the matter proper to it, the soul must actualise just this special sort of body.

§ 224. The difference between accidental form and substantial form is that whereas the former does not make a thing simply be, but only makes it be in this or that mode—e.g. as quantified, or white—the substantial form gives it simple being.[2] Hence the accidental form presupposes an already existing subject; but the substantial form presupposes only potentiality to existence, i.e. bare matter. That is why there cannot be more than one substantial form in any one thing; the first makes the thing an actual being; and if others are added, they confer only accidental modifications, since they presuppose the subject already in act of being.

§ 225. We can therefore reject the view of Avicebron (in the Book called *Fons Vitae*) that according to the way in which any given thing can be divided into genera and species so it can be divided into substantial forms. Thus an individual man would have one form that made him a substance, another that gave him a body, another that gave him life, and so on. But what our premisses compel us to say is that it is one and the same substantial form that makes a man a particular thing or substance, and a bodily thing, and a living thing, and so on. For the higher form can give to its matter all that a lower form gives, and more; the soul gives not only substance and body (as a stone's form does) but life also. We must not think, therefore, of the soul and body as though the body had its own form making it a body, to which a soul is superadded, making it a living body; but rather that the body gets both its being and its life from the soul. This is not to deny, however, that bodily being as such is, in its imperfection, material with respect to life.

§ 226. Therefore, when life departs the body is not left specifically the same; the eyes and flesh of a dead man, as is shown in the *Metaphysics*, Book VII,[3] are only improperly called eyes and flesh. When the soul leaves the body another substantial form takes its place; for a passing-away always involves a concomitant coming-to-be.

§ 227. Then, at 'Now this can mean',[4] he examines the second term in the definition. He observes that there are two kinds of

---

[1] 412^a 21.   [2] *facit esse actu simpliciter.*

[3] VII, c.10; 1035^b 15ss.   [4] 412^a 22.

actuality, as we explained above,[1] the kind that is like knowledge
and the kind like thinking. And clearly the soul is of the former
kind; for it is due to the soul that an animal is able to be both
awake and asleep; and while waking is similar to thinking (for it is
a use of the exterior senses just as thinking is a use of knowledge
already possessed), sleep is more like the knowledge which lies
dormant in the mind so long as it is not actually being used; for in
sleep an animal's faculties are quiescent.

§ 228. Now, of these two actualities, knowledge comes first in
the order of coming-to-be in the same person; for it stands to
thinking as potency to act. But in the order of nature or essence
act is prior to potency (see the *Metaphysics*, Book IX)[2] as the end
and complete perfection of potency. And even in the temporal
order of coming-to-be, act, in a quite general sense, is prior; for
the potential is actualised only by something already in act. But in
this or that particular thing considered in itself potentiality may
come first; the thing may be actualised by degrees. Hence his remark that 'knowledge . . . is prior (i.e. to thinking) in the order of
generation in one and the same thing'.[3]

§ 229. So he concludes that soul is the primary act of a physical
body potentially alive, where act means the same sort of actuality
as knowledge.[4] He says *primary* act, not only to distinguish soul
from its subsequent activities, but also to distinguish it from the
forms of the elements;[5] for these retain their own proper activities,
unless impeded.

§ 230. Next, at 'Such a body',[6] he examines that part of the definition which has to do with the soul's *subject*, observing that the
'physical body' referred to is any organic body, i.e. any body
equipped with the various organs required by a living body in
consequence of the life-principle's various vital activities. For from
this principle (the soul) which is the richest of embodied forms,
spring many different activities, so that it requires, in the matter
informed by it, a full equipment of different organs. Not so the
less perfect forms of inanimate things.

§ 231. Now plants, the least perfect of animate things, exhibit
less organic diversity than animals. That is why Aristotle chooses

[1] § 216.   [2] IX, c.8; 1049^b 5ss.
[3] '. . . in the history of the individual' (Oxford transl., 412^a 26).
[4] 412^a 29.   [5] i.e. in the body.   [6] 412^a 29.

plants to illustrate his assertion that every animate body is organic, saying that even plants have organically diversified parts. But these parts are very simple, i.e. like to one another; they lack the differentiation that we find in animals. Thus the foot of an animal is made up of different parts, flesh, nerves, bones and so forth, but the organs of plants are composed of less diverse sets of parts.

§ 232. The organic character of the parts of plants is displayed in their diverse functions. Thus a leaf functions as a covering for the pericarp[1] or fruit-bearing part, i.e. for the part in which the fruit is born. The pericarp, again, protects the fruit itself. So too the roots have a function in a plant similar to that of the mouth in an animal; they draw in nourishment.

§ 233. Next, at 'If, then,'[2] he gathers all these observations into one definition, saying that if any definition covers all types of 'soul' it will be this: *the soul is the primary actuality of a physical bodily organism*. He does not need to add 'having life potentially'; for this is implied in 'organism'.

§ 234. Then at 'Hence it is'[3] he applies this definition to solve a difficulty. There had been much uncertainty about the way the soul and body are conjoined. Some had supposed a sort of medium connecting the two together by a sort of bond. But the difficulty can be set aside now that it has been shown that the soul is the *form* of the body. As he says, there is no more reason to ask whether soul and body together make one thing than to ask the same about wax and the impression sealed on it, or about any other matter and its form. For, as is shown in the *Metaphysics*, Book VIII,[4] form is directly related to matter as the actuality of matter; once matter actually *is* it is *informed*. Moreover, although, as he goes on to say, being and unity are variously predicated (in one way of potential, and in another way of actual, being), that is primarily and properly a being and a unity which has actuality. Just as potential being is only a being under a certain aspect, so it is only a unity under a certain aspect; for unity follows being. Therefore, just as the body gets its being from the soul, as from its form, so too it makes a unity with this soul to which it is immediately related. If, on the other hand, we regard the soul in its function as the *mover* of the body, then there is no reason why it should not move by means of a medium, moving one part of the body by means of another.

[1] *corticis vel fructiferi.*   [2] 412^{b} 4.   [3] 412^{b} 6.   [4] VIII, c.6; 1045^{b} 15.

BOOK II, CHAPTER I, CONTINUED

THE DEFINITION EXPLAINED
SOUL AND BODY

IT HAS BEEN STATED, THEN, WHAT THE SOUL IN general is. It is 'substance' as definable form; and this means what is the essence of such a kind of body. If some utensil, for example an axe, were a natural body, then 'being-an-axe' [axeishness] would be its substance, and this would be its soul. Apart from this, it would no longer be an axe, save equivocally. As it is, it is really an axe. And the soul is not the essence or 'what-it-is' of such a body as this, but of a *natural* body, such as has in itself the principle of motion and rest. §§ 235–8

Now what has been said should be considered with respect to parts. For if the eye were an animal, sight would be its soul. For this is the substance, in the sense of the definable form, of the eye. The eye is the matter of sight, and apart from this it is an eye no longer save equivocally, as with a painted or stone eye. What, therefore, holds of a part, we ought to apply to the whole living body: for the relation of a part [of the soul] to part [of the body] corresponds to that of sensitivity as a whole to the whole sensitive body, considered as such. § 239

Not that which has cast off its soul is 'capable of life', but that which possesses it. But seed and fruit are only in potency such a body. As cutting or seeing is act, so is consciousness. The soul is like sight and the capacity of a tool; the body, like the thing in potency. But as an eye is a pupil together with the power of sight, so is there a living thing where there are both body and soul. §§ 240-1

Therefore it is evident enough that the soul is inseparable from the body—or certain parts of it, if it naturally has parts; for it is of certain bodily parts themselves that it is the act. But with respect to certain of its parts there is nothing to prevent its being separated, because these are acts of nothing bodily. Furthermore, it is not clear that the soul is not the 'act' of the body in the way that a sailor is of his ship. Let these remarks serve to describe and define the soul, in outline. §§ 242-4

ST. THOMAS'S COMMENTARY

LECTIO TWO

§ 235. The Philosopher now begins to explain the definition of the soul given in Lectio 1; after which, at 'Therefore it is evident',[1] he draws a conclusion from it. The explanation has two parts, in the first of which he is concerned directly with the soul itself, while in the second, where he says 'Not that which has cast off',[2] he explains that part of the definition which refers to the subject which has a soul. With regard to the soul itself, he begins by illustrating the definition by a comparison with artificial things; and then goes on, at 'Now what has . . .',[3] to explain it by considering the parts of the soul separately.

In artificial things, made by human skill, the forms imposed on the material are accidental forms; and since these are easier for us to perceive than is substantial form, as being more accessible to the senses, it is obviously reasonable to approach the soul, which is a substantial form, through a comparison with accidental forms. And again, the soul's parts or potencies are more readily perceptible to us than its essence; for all our enquiry into the soul has to start from the objective terms of its activities and then proceed from these activities to their potencies, and thence to an understanding of the soul in its essence; that is why a study of the soul's parts can throw light on the definition of it.

§ 236. First, then, he observes that the definition given above is 'general', i.e. it applies to any soul.[4] It posits the soul as a substance which is a form; and this means that it presents to us the idea of the essence of something. For there is this difference between a form that is substance and one that is not, that the latter sort are not strictly of the essence or 'whatness' of a thing: whiteness is not of the essence of a white body; whereas substantial form is essential

[1] 413ᵃ 2.　　　[2] 412ᵇ 25.　　　[3] 412ᵇ 17.　　　[4] 412ᵇ 10.

175

and quidditative. To call the soul a substantial form, therefore, is to imply that it is of the essence and 'whatness' of the body it animates. Hence he says 'this', i.e. this quidditative substance, 'is the essence of this body',[1] i.e. of the body that is what it is precisely through having this particular form. For this form is essential to the thing, and is denoted by the definition of what the thing is.

§ 237. And because substantial forms, including the forms of natural[2] bodies, are not evident to us, Aristotle makes his meaning clear with an example taken from the forms (accidental) of artificial things. 'If', he says, 'some utensil (i.e. an artificial instrument) for example an axe, were a physical (i.e. a natural) body,' it would possess a form in the manner already explained.[3] So he continues: 'Then being-an-axe would be its substance,' i.e. would be the substantial form of the axe, which is that to which we refer our idea of axe as such.[4] This idea of axe as such he identifies with the essence of the axe, with what causes it to *be* an axe; and this essential form he identifies with the substance of the axe. He says 'substance' because the forms of natural bodies are substantial forms. Furthermore, if the axe were not merely a natural, but also an animate, body, its form would be a *soul*; and if it lost this soul it would no longer be an axe, except in name; just as when the soul leaves the body there is no longer an eye or flesh, except in name. Of course the axe, not being in fact a natural body, has no axe-form which is of the essence of the body that it is; so that if it lost the form of axe, the axe would still exist *substantially*, because the substance of artificial things is their matter which remains when the artificial form and, with this artificial form, the actuality of the artificial body as such, is removed.

§ 238. Then he explains[5] why he has distinguished between the axe as it actually is and as it would be were it a physical (that is, a natural)[6] living body: for the soul is not the essence and idea, i.e. the form, of an artificial body like an axe, but 'of such a physical body', i.e. of a body that is alive. To make this clearer he adds 'as has in itself the principle of movement and rest'—which is charac-

---

[1] 412b 11. St. Thomas reads simply *huic corpori*, but Moerbeke *hujusmodi corporis*.

[2] i.e. not artificial ones.

[3] § 218.

[4] 412b 13.

[5] 412b 15.

[6] Parenthesis added.—(Transl.)

teristic of *natural* things. For Nature is this sort of principle, as he says in the *Physics*, Book II.[1]

§ 239. Then at ' Now what has been said',[2] he applies what has been concluded about the soul as a whole, and the animate body as a whole, to the parts of each. If, he says, the eye were a whole animal, its soul would be sight; for sight is the essential form of the eye; which in itself is the material condition of sight; in the same way as an organic body is the material condition of a soul. Once sight is lost, the eye is no longer an eye, except in the sense that a stone or painted eye may be *called* an eye equivocally (this term is used when the same name is given to essentially different things). Remove, then, what makes an eye really an eye, and there is left only the name. And the same argument applies to the animate body as a whole: what makes it an animate body is its form, the soul. This removed, you have a living body only equivocally. For as one part of the sensitive soul is to one part of the sensitive body, so the faculty of sense as a whole is to the whole sensitive body as such.

§ 240. Next, at 'Not that which has cast off',[3] he explains what was meant by defining the soul as the 'act of a potentially animate body'. Now 'potentially' may be said about a thing in either of two senses: (*a*) as lacking the power to act; (*b*) as possessed of this power but not acting by it. And the body, whose act is the soul, is potentially animate in the second sense only. So, when he calls the body a thing potentially alive he does not mean that it has *lost* the soul it had and now lacks a life-principle altogether; he is speaking of what still has such a principle. On the other hand, seeds and the fruits that contain them are only potentially living bodies with souls; for a seed as yet lacks a soul. It is 'potential' therefore like that which has lost its soul.

§ 241. And to show just how the body is potential to the actuality that comes from its soul he adds that being awake is the actuality of the sensitive soul in the same way as cutting is the actuality of a knife and seeing is that of an eye; for each of these acts is the activity and use of a principle already there. But the soul is the first and underlying actuality; like the faculty of sight itself or the capacity of any tool; for each of these is the operative principle itself. So the body, complete with its soul, is potentially animate in

---

[1] *Phys.*, II, c.1, 192[b] 10ss.   [2] 412[b] 17.   [3] 412[b] 25.

the sense that, though it has its first actuality, it may lack the second. And as the eye is a thing composed of a pupil as its matter and the faculty of sight as its form, so an animal is a thing composed of soul as its form and body as its matter.

§ 242. Then, at 'Therefore it is evident',[1] he deduces a truth from the foregoing. Having shown that the soul is the whole body's actuality, its 'parts' being the actualities of the body's parts, and granted that an actuality or form cannot be separated from that which is actual and has form, we can certainly conclude that no soul can be separated from its body,—at least certain parts of the soul cannot be separated, if the soul can be said to have parts. For obviously some 'parts' of the soul are nothing but actualities of parts of the body; as we have seen in the case of sight, that it is the eye's actuality.[2] On the other hand, certain parts of the soul may well be separable from the body, since they are not the actuality of any corporeal part, as will be proved when we come to treat of the intellect.

§ 243. As to Plato's opinion that the soul is the act of the body not as its *form* but as its *mover*, he adds that it is not yet clear whether the soul is the act of the body as a sailor of a ship, i.e. as its mover only.

§ 244. Finally, recapitulating,[3] he says that the foregoing is an 'outline' description of the soul, meaning that it is extrinsic, as it were, and superficial and incomplete. It will be completed when he comes to define the innermost nature of the soul and the nature of each of its parts.

[1] 413^a 2. [2] § 239. [3] 413^a 9.

BOOK II, CHAPTER II

THE DEFINITION JUSTIFIED
MODES OF LIFE

SINCE IT IS FROM THE LESS CLEAR, THOUGH MORE obvious, facts that what is certain and more evident to thought emerges, let us attempt to approach the matter afresh.   § 245

For it is not enough that a defining principle should merely show a fact, as do most formulae, but also there should be contained and made plain the causes involved. Usually the constituent terms are like conclusions: for instance, what is a square[1] that is equal to an oblong? An equilateral orthogon. Such a term is of the nature of a conclusion. But to say that a square is the discovery of a mean line states the reason why.

§§ 246–52

Going back, then, to the beginning of our enquiry, let us say that the animate is distinguished from the inanimate by being alive.

To live, however, is predicated in several ways; and even if one only of these is present, we say there is life; as, for example, intellection, sensation, or movement and rest in

---

[1] *Tetragonismus*, which St. Thomas takes to mean 'square', not 'squaring'; and comments accordingly, §§ 248–51. *See* Introd., pp. 33–4. Pirotta places the question-mark after 'square', but the Commentary supposes that it comes after 'oblong'.

place; as well as the movement and rest involved in nourishment,[1] and growth and decay.   §§ 253–5

Hence all plants seem to live. They appear to have in themselves a power and principle of this kind, by which they increase or decay in various directions—that is to say, they do
not grow up but not down, but alike either way; and in all
their parts they are continually nourished, and they live so
long as they can take nourishment.   §§ 256–7

It is possible for this power to exist apart from the others;
but for the others to exist apart from it is impossible, at least
in mortal beings. This is evident in plants; for there is in them
no other soul-power. To live by this principle, then, is common to all living things.   § 258

But an animal is such primarily by sensation. For we also
call animals things that do not move or change their place,
provided they have sensation, and do not merely live.
There seem to be many of this sort: by nature they stay in
one place, but they have one of the senses.[2]   § 259

Touch is in all, primarily. As the vegetative powers can
be separated from touch and all sensation as a whole, so can
touch from the other senses. (We give the name 'vegetative'
to that part of the soul in which plants participate). All
animals are seen to possess the sense of touch.   § 260

For what cause each of these facts is so we shall say later on.
At present only this need be said: that soul is the principle of
the qualities we have discussed, and is characterised by the
vegetative, sensitive, intellective and motive powers.   § 261

[1] The second 'and rest' is not in the Greek, nor presupposed by the Commentary, § 255.
[2] This sentence is not in the Greek, 413[b] 4.

§ 245. Having defined the soul the Philosopher now sets out to prove his definition. First he says what he intends to do, and then, at 'Going back, then,'[1] proceeds to do it. As to the former point, he first determines the method of demonstration that he intends to use; after which, at 'For it is not enough',[2] he explains how certain types of definition can be proved. With regard to the method to be used we should note that, since we can only come to know the unknown if we start from what we know, and since the purpose of demonstration is precisely to cause knowledge, it follows that every demonstration must begin from something more knowable to us than the thing to be made known by it. Now in certain subjects, such as mathematics, which abstract from matter, what is the more knowable is such both in itself and relatively to us; hence in these subjects, demonstration can start from what is absolutely and of its nature more knowable, and therefore can deduce effects from their causes; whence the name given it of *a priori* demonstration.[3] But in the quite different sphere of the natural sciences, what is more knowable is not the same thing in itself and relatively to us; for sensible effects are generally more evident than their causes. Hence in these sciences we generally have to begin from what is, indeed, absolutely speaking less knowable, but is more evident relatively to us (*see* the *Physics*, Book I).[4]

§ 246. And this is the kind of demonstration which will be used here. So he says that what is of its nature more certain, and is more evident to thought, becomes certain to us by means of things less certain in nature but more certain to us; and that this shows us the

[1] 413ᵃ 20.
[3] *demonstratio propter quid.*
[2] 413ᵃ 13. cf. Introd., pp. 24-31.
[4] *Phys.*, I, 1; 184ᵃ 15.

method to use in enquiring once more into the soul and showing the grounds of the definition given above.[1]

§ 247. Then, at 'For it is not enough', he tells us why the question must be taken up again. Certain definitions can, he says, be demonstrated, and in these cases it is not enough for the defining formula to express, as most 'formulae', i.e. definitions, do, the mere fact;[2] it should also give the cause of the fact; and this being given, one can then proceed to deduce the definition which states the mere fact. At present many definitions are given in the form of conclusions; and he gives an example from geometry.

§ 248. To understand which we must note that there are two kinds of four-sided figure: those whose angles are all right angles, and these are called rectangles;[3] and the kind with no right angles, and these are called rhomboids.[4] Of the rectangles, again, there is one with four equal sides—the square or tetragon; and another which, without having all four sides equal, has two pairs of equal and opposite sides—the oblong. Thus:

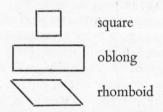

square

oblong

rhomboid

§ 249. Note further, that in any rectangular surface the two straight lines enclosing the right angle are said to contain the whole figure; because, the other two sides being equal to these two, each equal to its opposite, it follows that one of the enclosing lines measures the length of the whole figure, and the other its breadth: so that the whole figure is given in the contact of the two lines. If we imagine one of these lines moving along the other we see the whole figure form itself.

§ 250. Note also that if, between the two unequal sides that contain the oblong, one takes the proportional mean and squares it, one gets a quadrilateral equal to the oblong. This would take too long to prove geometrically, so let a numerical argument do for

[1] § 233.

[2] *hoc est quod quia.*

[3] *orthogonia.*

[4] *rhomboydes.*

the present. Let our oblong then have its longer side 9 feet and its
shorter side 4 feet. Then the proportional mean line will be 6 feet;
for as 6 is to 9, so 4 is to 6. Now the square of this line must equal
the oblong; which is obvious numerically: $4 \times 9 = 36, 6 \times 6 = 36$.

§ 251. Now it is thus, he says,[1] that the question, What is a
square[2] (i.e. the quadrilateral equal to an oblong)? is answered; it is
said 'to be an orthogon', i.e. a right-angled plane figure, which is
'equilateral', i.e. having all its sides equal, and so on. 'Such a term',
i.e. a definition of this sort, is really 'of the nature of a conclusion',
namely of a presupposed demonstration; whereas if one were to
say that a square is 'the discovery of a mean line', i.e. of the proportional mean between the two unequal sides of the oblong,
meaning that a square is what is constructed from this line, then at
last the definition would disclose the 'reason why' of the thing
defined.

§ 252. Note, however, that this example is only relevant to the
definition of the soul in so far as this definition is simply to be
demonstrated; it must not be taken to imply that our demonstration can proceed *a priori* from causes to effects.

§ 253. Next, at 'Going back then',[3] he begins to prove the definition of the soul given above; and this in the way indicated, i.e.
from effects to causes. This is how he sets about it: the first principle of life in things is the actuality and form of living bodies; but
soul is the first principle of life in living things; therefore it is actuality and form of living bodies. Now this argument is clearly *a
posteriori*; for *in reality* the soul is the source of vital activities because it is the form of a living body, not *e converso*. So he has to do
two things here; first, to show that soul is the source or principle of
vitality, and secondly, to show that the first principle of vitality is
the form of living bodies (this comes at 'Since that whereby etc.').[4]
With regard to the first point he does three things: (*a*) he distinguishes modes of life,[5] (*b*) he shows that the soul is the principle
of living activities—at 'Hence all plants';[6] and (*c*) he explains
how these parts of the soul are interrelated, by means of which it

[1] 413ᵃ 16.
[2] *Tetragonismus.* St. Thomas understands 'square', not 'squaring' or 'quadra-
ture' as the Greek requires. *See* Introd., pp. 33–4.
[3] 413ᵃ 20.   [4] Lectio 4, § 271; 414ᵃ 4.   [5] 413ᵃ 20–5.
[6] 413ᵃ 25.

originates vital activities. This is at 'We now ask whether each of these'.[1]

§ 254. He starts then by saying that to carry out our intention of proving the definition of the soul, we must assume as a kind of principle that things with souls differ from those without souls in being alive. Life is the test; and as life shows itself in several ways, if a thing has life in only one of these ways it is still said to be alive and to possess a soul.

§ 255. Life, he says, shows itself in four modes: (1) as intellectual; (2) as sensitive; (3) as the cause of motion or rest in space; (4) as cause of the motions of taking nourishment, decay and growth. He distinguishes only these four modes, although he has already distinguished five main types of vital activity,[2] and this because he is thinking here and now of the degrees of animate being. There are four such degrees, distinguished in the same way as the four modes in which life is manifested: for some living things, i.e. plants, only take nourishment and grow and decay; some have also sensation, but are always fixed to one place—such are the inferior animals like shell-fish; some again, i.e. the complete animals like oxen and horses, have, along with sensation, the power to move from place to place; and finally some, i.e. men, have, in addition, mind. The appetitive power, which makes a fifth type of vitality, does not, however, imply a distinct degree of living being; for it always accompanies sensation.

§ 256. Next, at 'Hence all plants',[3] he shows that a soul is involved in all these modes of life. He does this with regard (1) to plants, and (2) to animals, at 'But an animal is such, primarily'.[4] Then (3), he summarises, at 'For what cause', what has been said and remains to be said.[5] As to (1) he does two things. First he shows that the life-principle in plants is a soul. We have remarked, he says, that whatever evinces one of the four modes of life mentioned above can be said to live. Therefore plants are alive; for they all possess some intrinsic power or principle of growth and decay.[6]

§ 257. Now this principle is not mere nature.[7] Nature does not move in opposite directions, but growth and decay are in opposite directions; for all plants grow not only upwards or downwards,

---

[1] Lectio 4, § 262; 413^b 13.   [2] § 201.   [3] 413^a 25.   [4] 413^b 2.
[5] 413^b 9.   [6] 413^a 25.   [7] natura.

but in both directions. Hence a soul, not nature, is clearly at work in them. Nor do plants live only when actually growing or decaying, but, as things that take nourishment, they live so long as they can assimilate the food that induces growth.

§ 258. Next, at 'It is possible',[1] he shows that this principle of feeding and growing can exist apart from other life-principles, but these cannot exist apart from it, at least in things subject to death. He adds this last clause because of immortal beings like immaterial substances or heavenly bodies; because, if these have a soul, it is intellectual; it is not a capacity to take nourishment. And the separability of this life principle from others is clearly evident in plants which have, in fact, no other one but this. It follows that what first of all causes life in mortal things is this principle of growth and nourishment, the so-called vegetative soul.

§ 259. Then, at 'But an animal is such primarily',[2] he shows that a soul is the source of living in animals. And here he does two things. First he observes that what primarily distinguishes animals is sensation, though there are animals which have local movement as well; for we call those things *animals* (not just living beings) which have sensation, even if they are fixed to one place. For there are many such animals whose nature restricts them to one place, but which have the power of sense, e.g. shell-fish, which cannot move from place to place.

§ 260. Then at 'Touch is',[3] he shows that touch is the primary sense in animals. For just as the vegetative soul, he says, is separable from all the senses including touch, so touch is separable from all the other senses. For many inferior animals have only the sense of touch; but there are no animals without this sense. Now that degree of soul in which even plants participate we call the vegetative. Hence we can distinguish three degrees of living beings: first, plants; secondly, the inferior animals fixed to one place and with no sense but touch; and, thirdly, the higher, complete animals which have the other senses and also the power to move from place to place. And a fourth degree consists, evidently, of beings which have all this and mind as well.

§ 261. Finally, at 'For what cause',[4] summarising what has been said and remains to be said, he remarks that the cause of both these phenomena, namely the separability of the vegetative principle

[1] 413ᵃ 31.   [2] 413ᵇ 2.   [3] 413ᵇ 4.   [4] 413ᵇ 9.

from sensation and of touch from the other senses, will be given later on. He does this at the end of the whole Treatise.[1] For the present it suffices to say that 'soul' is the one principle underlying the four distinct modes in which life is manifested, namely the vegetative mode which belongs to plants and to all living things; the sensitive mode in all animals; the intellectual mode in all men; and fourthly, the mode that is a power to move from place to place, which exists in all the higher animals, both those with senses only and those with intellect as well.

[1] §§ 847–74.

BOOK II, CHAPTER II, CONTINUED

DIFFERENT KINDS OF SOUL

WE NOW ASK WHETHER EACH OF THESE [POWERS] is a soul, or a part of a soul: and if a part, whether it is separable only in thought or has also a distinct place.   § 262

Concerning some of these powers it is not difficult to see [the answers to our questions]; others, however, give rise to doubts. For, as in the case of plants some, on being divided, seem to go on living in separation from one another, as if there were in each plant one soul in act, but several in potency; so we find it happens in the case of other differentiations of soul, for instance in divided animals[1] each division has sensation and local motion; and if sensation, phantasm and appetition; for where there is sensation there is pleasure, and pain, and where these are there must necessarily be appetition.
§§ 263–7

But as regards intellect and the speculative faculty, nothing has so far been demonstrated; but it would seem to be another kind of soul, and alone capable of being separated, as the eternal from the perishable. It is evident, however, from the foregoing, that the other parts of the soul are not separable, as some have said.   § 268

By definition, however, they are obviously distinct. For if feeling is other than opining, the sense-faculty will differ

---

[1] 'in insects cut in two', 413^b 20: cf. *supra*, Bk. I, l. 14, § 208.

from the capacity to form opinions. Likewise with each of
the other powers mentioned. § 269

Further, all these powers are in some animals; in others,
some only; in yet others, only one. This makes the varieties
of animal. Why this should be so will be considered later.
The same obtains with regard to the senses: certain species of
animal have all; certain others, some; yet others have only
the one most necessary, touch. § 270

Since 'that whereby we live and perceive' can mean two
things,—like 'that by which we know', for we name one
thing knowledge, and another, the soul, though we are said
to know by both of these; and likewise as 'that by which we
are healthy'; for health is one thing, while a part of the body
(or the whole of it) is another; and in these cases knowledge,
or health, is the form and specific essence or ratio, and, as it
were, the act of such as can receive knowledge in the one case
and health in the other (for the action of an agent seems to
exist in the recipient or disposed material)—and *soul* being
that by which we primarily live and perceive and move and
understand, it follows that the soul will be a sort of species
or ratio; not, as it were, a matter or substratum. Substance is
predicated in three ways, as we have said: in one way as the
form; in another as the matter; and in another as what is from
both. Of these, matter is the potency, form the act; hence if
what is from both is the animate being, the body is not the
act of the soul, but the soul of the body. §§ 271–5.

And on this account they were right who thought that the
soul is neither apart from the body nor the same as the body;
for it is not, indeed, the body; yet is something of the body.
And therefore it is in a body, and a body of a definite kind;
and not as some earlier thinkers made out, who related it to a
body without defining at all the nature and quality of that
body; despite the fact that it is apparent that not any subject

whatever can receive any form at random. And that such is the case is confirmed by reason: the act of any one thing is of that which is in potency to it, and it occurs naturally and fittingly in matter appropriate to it.[1]

That the soul, then, is an actuality and formal principle of a thing in potency to exist accordingly, is evident from these considerations.   §§ 276–8

[1] 'fittingly' is not in the Greek, 414ª 26.

ST. THOMAS'S COMMENTARY
LECTIO FOUR

§ 262. After showing that 'soul' is the one principle common to the several types of vitality, the Philosopher now enquires into the various principles of the latter, asking how they are related both to the soul and to each other. And he does two things here. First, he puts two questions[1] (a) If the soul, the life-principle, is realised actually as a vegetative, sensitive, locomotive or intellectual principle, is each of these principles to be identified with the soul proper, or is each no more than a *part* of the soul? Now obviously, where the thing's vitality consists entirely in growing and taking nourishment (as in plants) the vegetative principle is simply the soul or life-principle itself. But where the thing also has sensation, this vegetative principle is only a part of the soul. And the same reasoning applies to other cases. (b) If each of these principles is a part of the life-principle, as in the human soul which contains all of them, are they parts in the sense that they are merely diverse powers of the one soul, existing in one thing though they can be *thought* of apart from one another, or are they distinct *beings* having each its distinct locality, so that the sense-power is in one part of the body, appetition in another, locomotion in another, and so on; as some indeed have thought.

§ 263. Secondly, when he says 'Concerning some of these',[2] he answers the above questions: first the second one; then, at 'Further, all these powers',[3] the first. The second question is answered in two parts: (a) with respect to the local separability of the parts of the soul, and (b) at 'By definition',[4] concerning their separability in the mind. As to (a) he says that some parts of the soul raise no difficulties, but that others do.[5]

§ 264. And he illustrates this by a comparison with plant-life.

[1] 413ᵇ 13.   [2] 413ᵇ 15.   [3] 413ᵇ 32.   [4] 413ᵇ 29.   [5] 413ᵇ 15.

Certain parts, he says, of plants can be cut off and yet seem to go on living; for the cuttings, grafted or replanted, unite with a new stem or with the soil. In these cases the life-principle appears to be actually single but potentially many. The same sort of thing is observable in the forms of inanimate physical bodies; as each such body is actually one and potentially many, so in the lower animate bodies whose parts are still undifferentiated, the soul exists as one whole actually, but as many potentially. For inanimate bodies can be divided into parts which each retain the same specific nature (e.g. air, water, minerals) and this nature was also the nature of the whole body; and it is somewhat the same with plants, the lowest order of animate beings; they require very little differentiation in their parts, and the life-principle of the whole survives, as such, in some of the separated parts.

§ 265. So also with those animals which remain alive after being cut up. Each division still has a sensitive soul: it will shrink back if you prick it. And obviously it can move about. So the same part retains, evidently, the principle of sensation and local movement. And if sensation, then it must also have imagination which is simply a certain motion derived from actual sensation, as we shall see later.[1] Again, it must also have appetition, since sensation necessarily involves satisfaction or dissatisfaction, i.e. pleasure or pain, because it involves a contact with the congenial or the uncongenial. And pleasure and pain involve desire and appetition. So the divided parts of such animals are able to desire.

§ 266. Now if each such divided part contains the vegetative, sensitive, appetitive and locomotive principles all together, it is clear that these principles are not to be located in any special parts of the animal's body. Yet certain powers are obviously so located: seeing is only in the eye, hearing in the ear, smelling in the nostrils, taste on the tongue and palate. But the fundamental and most necessary sense of touch is found over the whole body.

§ 267. A doubt may occur about imagination; for some assign to it a special organ of the body. But note that imagination (as will be shown later)[2] in the lower animals is *indefinite*; it is *definite* only in the higher animals. Hence if we assign a special organ to imagination, this is because the special completeness and definiteness of its activities[3] call for a special organ of the body, just as seeing

[1] §§ 632; 659; 666; 792.   [2] §§ 644; 839.   [3] i.e., in the higher animals.

requires an eye. But as to some powers of the soul it is not difficult to decide whether they are located in distinct parts of the body.

§ 268. Then, at 'But as regards intellect',[1] he points to one part of the soul over which doubts may arise. About the intellect, or whatever we call the percipient or speculative faculty, we are still, he says, uncertain. No proof has yet been given of its location in any special or particular organ of the body. Yet even at first sight it would seem to be of a different nature from the other parts of the soul, and to exist in a different way; and that it alone is separable from the rest of the soul (and may even exist apart from any organ of the body) as what is immortal from what is mortal. That the other parts of the soul are not *locally* separated is now clear.

§ 269. Then at 'By definition',[2] he shows that they are *mentally* separable from one another. For we distinguish potencies by their relation to acts; if the acts are specifically distinct, then so are the potencies. Hence he says here that the sensitive and opining, i.e. intellectual, principles are diverse; meaning that, as sensing is other than forming opinions, the faculties implied have distinct definitions. And the same is true of the other principles already mentioned.

§ 270. Then, at 'Further, all these powers',[3] he answers the first of the two questions proposed above,[4] observing that animals differ in this, that in some are found all the four vital principles mentioned above, in others only some of them, and in some only one. And where one only of these principles is found it is the soul itself; but where several are found together each is a part of the soul and the soul itself is named after the principal part, whether sensitive or intellectual as the case may be (the reason why animals differ in this way will be shown later).[5] And as with the powers of the soul, so with the particular senses; for some animals (the higher) have all the senses; some (e.g. moles) have some, but not all; while some (the lowest animals) have only the most necessary one, touch.

This passage might also be understood as referring to the statement, made a few lines earlier, that the parts of the soul which coexist in any one animal are not distinct *beings* nor in different places. For from this one might argue that they are not separable

[1] 413^b 24.   [2] 413^b 29.   [3] 413^b 32.
[4] § 262.   [5] §§ 288–94.

as between one animal and another; which error this passage removes.

§ 271. Next, at 'Since etc.',[1] he concludes, from the fact, that the soul is the first principle of life, to the definition of it already given; first proving this definition, and then, at 'And on this account',[2] drawing some further conclusions. The proof runs thus. Granted that there are two principles of our being and activity, one (the form) will be prior to the other (the matter). Now both body and soul are principles of life in us, but the soul comes first in this respect. The soul then is the form of the living body; which agrees with the definition already given: the soul is the primary actuality of a physical body capable of life.[3] Clearly, the middle term of this argument is the definition of the soul as the primary principle of life.

§ 272. The argument itself he sets out in four parts. (1) Explaining the major, he observes that we can speak of the principle of life and sensation from two points of view, formally or materially.[4] Just as we speak of the act of knowing as proceeding either from knowledge itself or from the soul; or as we speak of becoming healthy either with respect to health itself, or with respect to some part of the body, or to the whole of it. In both these cases, one of the principles is formal and the other material. For knowledge and health are forms or actualities of certain subjects: knowledge is a form of the part of the soul that knows, health of the body capable of health. Thus he says 'capable of knowing' and 'capable of health' in order to indicate the particular subject's aptitude to its particular form. For the actuality of an active principle, such as the form transmitted to matter by an agent, always appears to exist in what receives it and is adapted to it, i.e. in the subject, whose nature it is to receive from some one particular active principle, and which is adapted to attain the final term of the receiving-process, namely the form in question.

§ 273. (2) At 'and soul being that by which',[5] he states the minor, saying that the soul is the primary principle of our life and feeling and movement and understanding—these being the four chief manifestations of vitality already mentioned[6] (for by 'life' here is meant the vegetative principle which, as has been said,[7] is common

[1] 414ᵃ 4.   [2] 414ᵃ 19.   [3] § 233.   [4] 414ᵃ 4.
[5] 414ᵃ 12.   [6] § 255.   [7] §§ 258; 261.

to all living things). Now though it is in the body that we enjoy health, health itself is that by which we are called healthy primarily. Only in so far as the body has health are we said to be healthy. So too our souls are not said to know except in so far as they have knowledge; thus knowledge itself is that by which, primarily, the soul is said to be in the state of knowing. And the same is true of our body and its life; we are not said to live by the body except in so far as the body has a soul. Therefore he calls the 'soul' here the first principle of life and feeling, etc.

§ 274. (3) He concludes at 'it follows that the soul',[1] linking this phrase with the previous one, that the soul is a sort of nature or specific form; not the material for, or mere subject of, anything.

§ 275. (4) Then at 'Substance is predicated',[2] he shows how this conclusion follows from the premises. For it might have seemed to follow that the body no less than the soul was a form, since we call the body also a principle of life. So, to clinch the argument, he adds that if, as we have said,[3] the term 'substance' can refer to three things, to matter, to form, and to the complex of both (the matter being the potential element; the form the actuality; and the complex the thing that is alive in this way) the body is clearly not the soul's actuality, but rather the soul is the body's; for the body is potential with respect to the soul. And if the foregoing argument has led us to the alternative that the specifying principle is either the soul or the body, we can now conclude that it is the soul; for it is now clear that the body is not the form of the soul.

§ 276. Then at 'And on this account',[4] he deduces from the foregoing: (a) that they were right who thought that the soul required the body and yet was essentially distinct from it. It is not the body, for it is not matter; but it is essentially involved with the body, because it is its actuality; whence too it follows, as he says here, that it exists in that body whose actuality it is.

§ 277. (b) Being then in the body, and in a special kind of body, namely physical and organic, it is not, however, in it as the old natural philosophers fancied when they spoke of it. For they did not specify the *kind* of body that it has. Yet it does in fact have only one kind of body. And this we should expect *a priori*, it being

[1] 414ᵃ 13.　　[2] 414ᵃ 14.　　[3] § 221.　　[4] 414ᵃ 19.

natural to any act to be realised in some definite and appropriate material. So also, then, with the soul.

§ 278. Summarising, he concludes that the soul is a certain actuality and formal principle of that which exists accordingly, namely as potentially animate.

BOOK II, CHAPTER III

THE SOUL'S POWERS IN GENERAL

OF THE SOUL'S POWERS ALREADY SPOKEN OF ALL are present in some, certain only are present in others, and one only in yet others. By the powers of the soul we mean the vegetative, the sensitive, the appetitive, the locomotive and the intellectual.   §§ 279–87

In plants there is only the vegetative; in other living things, this and the sensitive; but if the sensitive is present, so must the appetitive be. For appetition means desire, and anger and will. Now all animals have the sense of touch; and where sensation is found there is pleasure and pain, the pleasant and the repugnant. What has these has appetite, this being desire for a pleasurable object.   §§ 288–9

Further; all have a sense of nutriment, inasmuch as touch is this sense. For all living beings are nourished by things dry and wet or hot and cold; and the sense of touch is of these. But they are nourished by the other sense-objects only indirectly.[1] Sound, colour and smell contribute nothing to nutrition; and as for savour, it is found in objects of touch. Hunger and thirst being appetites, hunger for the hot and dry and thirst for the cold and liquid, savour is as it were the delectable in these. We must settle these questions later; for the present let us only say that animals endowed with touch

[1] 'They are nourished' is not in the Greek, which may be rendered, 'touch is of these, and of other sense objects only indirectly', 414^b 9.

have appetition also. The case of imagination is not clear and must be examined later. Some animals, again, have local motion; some intellect and mind—such as men and whatever other beings there are of a like nature, or of one even more excellent.   §§ 290–4

It is therefore clear that the idea of soul must be one in the same way as that of figure: for as there is no figure other than the triangle and those that derive from it, so there is no soul apart from the aforesaid. There will be, however, in the case of figures a general idea applicable to all figures, yet proper to none. Likewise with these souls just mentioned. Hence it is absurd to seek a common definition in this matter (or in any other) which will be that of no existing thing, and on the other hand, to seek to define in terms of the individual species without taking into account such a common definition. There is indeed an analogy between what holds of figures and what holds of the soul. For in that which is consequent there is always potential that which is primary, both in figures and in animate beings. As the triangle is contained in the square, so is the vegetative in the sensitive.   §§ 295–8

§ 279. After defining the soul in general Aristotle comes to treat of its 'parts'. Now the soul has no parts except in the sense that its potentialities are parts of it; in that one subject, being in potency to many activities, its power with respect to each in particular can be called a part of it. To treat of its parts then is to treat of its various potencies. This he does here in two main sections: the first treats of the soul's powers in general and their distinction from one another; the second, at 'Hence we must speak first',[1] takes them one by one. The former subdivides into (a) a division of the powers of the soul; and (b) at 'So we must enquire . . .',[2] a discussion of what has to be proved about them, and how and in what order. The division itself of the powers (at 'It is therefore clear')[3] necessitates showing how the soul as a whole is related to its parts; but before we come to this, the powers enumerated have to be related to each other, which he does at 'In plants there is etc.'[4] First of all, then, he observes that, of the powers already enumerated, all are in some beings (men); some are in some beings (the other animals); and one only is in some others (plants). And having previously called them, not 'powers', but 'parts' of the soul, he clearly implies that the two terms mean the same. Now of these parts or powers there are five main types: the vegetative, sensitive, appetitive, locomotive and intellectual.[5]

§ 280. Regarding this five-fold division two things must be made clear: (1) why the usual threefold division of potencies into vegetative, sensitive and intellectual is set aside; and (2) why he has already made a fourfold division.[6]

§ 281. As to (1) we should note that all potencies are defined by

---

[1] Lectio 7, § 309; 415ᵃ 22.   [2] Lectio 6, § 299; 414ᵇ 32.   [3] § 295; 414ᵇ 20.
[4] § 288; 414ᵃ 32.   [5] 414ᵃ 29.   [6] §§ 255; 260.

their proper acts, and operative potencies by activities. The soul, being a form, has *operative* potencies; hence by differences between its activities we have to differentiate between its potencies. Now, as the activity of anything is consequent upon and corresponds to its being, we have to study vital activities precisely in the living beings which display them.

§ 282. The being of things whose actuality is 'soul', i.e. of the animate beings that exist on this earth and are the subject of the present discussion, this being includes two factors: one, material, in which it resembles the being of all other material things; and the other, immaterial, by which it has something in common with the world of the higher substances.

§ 283. Now there is this difference between these two divisions of being, that in so far as a thing is *material*, it is restricted by its matter to being this particular thing and nothing else, e.g. a stone; whilst in so far as it is *unmaterial*, a thing is free from the restriction of matter and has a certain width and infinity, so that it is not merely this particular subject but, in a certain sense, it is other things as well. That is why everything pre-exists, somehow, in the higher immaterial substances, as in universal causes.

§ 284. But in the lower terrestrial natures there are two degrees of immateriality. There is the perfect immateriality of intelligible being; for in the intellect things exist not only without matter, but even without their individuating material conditions, and also apart from any material organ. Then there is the half-way state of sensible being. For as things exist in sensation they are free indeed from matter, but are not without their individuating material conditions, nor apart from a bodily organ. For sensation is of objects in the particular, but intellection of objects universally. It is with reference to these two modes of existence that the Philosopher will say, in Book III, that the soul is somehow all things.[1]

§ 285. The activities, therefore, appropriate to living things in their *material* being are those we attribute to the vegetative soul. They fulfil the same purpose as the actions of inanimate beings, i.e. to attain and maintain existence; but they do this in a higher or nobler way. Inanimate bodies are brought into being and maintained by an *exterior* moving principle, whereas animate beings are generated by an *intrinsic* principle, i.e. seed, and are kept in

[1] Bk. III, lectio 13, §§ 787; 788.

existence by an intrinsic nutritive principle. It seems characteristic of living things that their activities should thus proceed from within themselves. But the purely immaterial activities of living things we identify with the intellectual part of the soul; while those in between belong to its sensitive part. Hence it is usual to distinguish three kinds of soul: vegetative, sensitive, intellectual.

§ 286. But since everything exists as *formed* in a certain way, the being of the sensible must have a sensible form, and the being of the intelligible an intelligible form. Now every form has by nature a certain trend or tendency whence proceed its activities or operations. Thus the form of fire tends naturally upwards (giving to fire its lightness) whence follows fire's *activity* which is the movement upwards. Now the trend that proceeds from a sensible or intellectual form is called sensitive or intellectual *desire*; as that of any form in nature is called a natural desire. And from this desire follows the activity of local movement. Here then is the explanation we required of the five-fold division of the powers of soul.

§ 287. And as to the second point, note that when Aristotle wished[1] to show that soul was the life-principle in things that live, he divided these into *grades*; which are not the same as those different kinds of vital activity whence we get our division of the powers of the soul. For, since all things that sense also desire, desire or appetition does not constitute a distinct *grade* of animate being; so we are left with only four such grades.

§ 288. Then, at 'In plants there is only', he shows the interconnection of the powers of the soul, thus explaining what he said previously,[2] that all these powers are in some things, some of them in some, and only one in some others. Here we have to consider that the completeness of the Universe requires that there should be no gaps in its order, that in Nature there should everywhere be a gradual development from the less to the more perfect. Hence, in the *Metaphysics*, Book VIII,[3] Aristotle likens the nature of things to numbers; which increase by tiny degrees, one by one. Thus among living things there are some, i.e. plants, which have only the vegetative capacity,—which, indeed, they must have because no living being could maintain an existence in matter without the vegetative activities. Next are the animals, with sensitivity as well as vegetative life; and sensitivity implies a third power, appetition,

[1] §§ 253–60.   [2] §§ 270; 279.   [3] VIII, c.3; 1043^b 30–1044^a 10.

which itself divides into three: into *desire*, in the stricter sense, which springs from the concupiscible appetite; *anger*, corresponding to the irascible appetite—both of these being in the sensitive part and following sense-knowledge; and finally *will*, which is the intellectual appetite and follows intellectual apprehension.

§ 289. That appetition exists in all animals he demonstrates in two ways.[1] (1) All animals have at least one sense, touch; but where there is any sensation there is pleasure and pain, joy and sorrow. Now while joy and sorrow seem to spring from inward apprehension, pain and pleasure come from external sensations, especially from touch. But joy and sorrow necessarily imply some sweet or disagreeable object, i.e. something pleasant or painful. For everything touched is either congenial to the one touching, and then it gives pleasure; or uncongenial, and then it gives pain. But whatever can feel pleasure and pain can desire the pleasant. Since then all animals, without exception, have a sense of touch, all can desire.

§ 290. (2) This second argument begins at 'Further, all have',[2] and runs thus. All animals have the sense that is aware of food; and this is touch; which is as necessary therefore to every animal as eating the food that agrees with it. The fact that it is touch that perceives food is clear if we consider that, as living bodies are made up of warm, moist, cold and dry elements it is of these that their food must consist; and these elements are just what touch is aware of. But 'other sense-objects', he says, do not, save indirectly, nourish living bodies; they do so only so far as they are involved in the objects of touch. Sound, colour, smell have nothing to do with food as such; they occur in food only in so far as things that sound or are coloured or odorous, are also hot, or cold, moist or dry. Savour, however, is reckoned a tangible quality—so that tasting is a sort of touch. Clearly, then, all animals have a sense-awareness of food.

§ 291. But whatever has this awareness can feel the two desires of nourishment, hunger and thirst. Hunger is desire for the hot and the dry elements, i.e. food; thirst for the cold and the moist, i.e. drink. Savour is a certain delectability in food and drink indicating a proper balance of the hot and cold, the moist and dry elements. It

[1] 414^b 1–6.   [2] 414^b 6.

is more of a pleasure added to eating than a necessity. Desire, then, always accompanies touch.

§ 292. What imagination has to do with desire and sensitivity will be shown later.[1]

§ 293. Now besides these three powers, the vegetative, the sensitive and the appetitive, some animals also have the capacity to move from one place to another. Some, too, i.e. human beings and any other kind of beings, if such exist, resembling or even perhaps excelling mankind, have, in addition to these four capacities, the power of understanding or intellect. The beings 'more excellent' are the immaterial substances and the heavenly bodies, the latter, however, only if they are alive. Among living corruptible beings the human race alone is endowed with intellect.

§ 294. For as intellect has no bodily organ, intelligent beings cannot be differentiated according to a physical diversity in the constitution of their bodily organs, as are the different species of animals (whose different constitutions cause them to sense in different ways).

§ 295. Then at 'It is therefore clear'[2] he shows how his definition of soul is related to the 'parts' that we have enumerated. To understand him here we must remember what Plato said about universal ideas, that they had a separate existence of their own. He did not say, however, that objects which follow successively from each other, such as numbers and geometrical figures, had a universal idea, i.e. he did not posit a universal idea of Number apart from particular numbers—as, for him, there was a universal idea of Man in addition to all existing men; and this because the classes of number are, of their nature, derived successively from each other, so that the first of these, duality, is the cause of all the rest. There is no need to posit a general idea of Number as the cause of the numerical species. The same argument applies to geometrical figures. They follow each other in the same way as numbers: from the triangle comes the tetragon, and from the latter the pentagon.

§ 296. Aristotle, then, says that the idea of Soul is one in the same way as that of geometrical figure is one. Just as there is no figure existing apart from the triangle and the rest, as their common idea, so it is with the soul. There exists no soul apart from the parts which have been enumerated.

[1] §§ 637–54.　　　　　　　　　　[2] 414^b 20.

§ 297. But while there is (even for the Platonists), no figure existing apart from all figures, nevertheless one common definition can be found which answers to all figures, without being proper to any particular one. And the same is true of living beings. It would be ludicrous therefore to seek a common definition, whether of animals or anything else, which did not fit any particular living thing actually existing. On the other hand it will not do to look for a definition that will fit only one sort of soul, ignoring what all have in common. We need a common definition which must, however, be applicable to souls in particular.

§ 298. He goes on now[1] to show the resemblance between the two definitions, namely of soul and of geometrical figure. In both cases what comes first is potentially in what follows. In figures the three-sided figure exists potentially in the square; for the square is divisible into two triangles. Likewise the sensitive life-principle contains the vegetative, both as potential, as it were, with respect to sensitivity, and also as a certain life-principle in itself. The same holds good with the other figures and the other divisions of soul.

[1] 414^b 28.

BOOK II, CHAPTER III, CONTINUED

THE SOUL'S POWERS CONTINUED
THEIR INTERRELATION
HOW TO DEFINE EACH

S O WE MUST ENQUIRE IN EACH PARTICULAR CASE
what the soul is of each: of plant, of man, of beast.

§ 299

It must be considered why they stand in this order: for there is no sensitive soul without the vegetative, yet in plants the vegetative exists apart from the sensitive. Again, there can be no sense apart from that of touch, but touch exists without the others; for many animals have no sight or hearing or sense of smell. Again, among sentient beings, some have local motion, others not. Last and least extensive of all [the species] that reasons and understands (as man and any other such).[1] For mortal beings which possess reason have also all the other [powers], but reason is not found in all that have any one of the latter; some indeed have not even imagination, others live by this alone. The speculative intellect is another issue.

Clearly then, whatever is the most precise definition with respect to each of the above will be that also of the soul.

§§ 300–2

[1] This parenthesis is doubtful, 415^a 8.

CHAPTER IV

It is necessary for the student of these [parts of the soul] to discover what is the nature of each, and only then to investigate habits and other matters.   § 303

But if one is to say what each of them is (namely the intellectual power or the sensitive or the vegetative) one must first say what it is to understand or perceive by sense; for actions and operations are prior to faculties in the order of thought. And if this is so, one ought first to consider the appropriate objects; which are prior even to the operations, and correspond to them; and thus to determine, in the first place, what these objects are—for instance, food and the sense-object and the intelligible.   §§ 304-8

§ 299. After enumerating the powers of the soul and showing how the general definition given above is related to the particular divisions of soul, the Philosopher now explains what remains to be cleared up and in what order. There are, he says, still two points to be made clear, one of which links up with the argument just given. For we have seen that, just as we must not be satisfied with a completely general definition of soul, such as will not express any of its particular realisations, so too we cannot rest content even with a definition which does answer in some way to these latter; we must pursue our enquiry until we shall have defined precisely what is *proper* to each of these divisions of soul in particular. Whence it follows that we have to ask about each particular type of living being—plant or man or animal—what is its own particular life-principle; thus applying and particularising our common notion of soul.

§ 300. Then at 'It must be considered',[1] he states the next point to be decided. He has already said that the parts of the soul follow each other in a series like the kinds of geometrical figure; and it remains to consider the reason for this. This reason will be given at the end of the Treatise;[2] here he only shows how the parts of soul follow one from the other successively. The sensitive part, he says, cannot exist without the vegetative, but the latter can, in plants, exist without the sensitive. And this is not surprising; for, as we have seen,[3] the purpose of the vegetative activities is to attain and retain existence itself, which is the ground of all the rest, as it were. And the senses display a like sequence; there are no senses at all unless there is touch; but touch itself can exist without the others. Many animals neither see, nor hear, nor smell, but only touch.

[1] 414[b] 34.   [2] Bk. III, lectionis 17 and 18; §§ 847-74.   [3] § 285.

And this will appear quite reasonable if we consider that by touch an animal is aware of the elements of which its substance consists (what it consists of and is nourished by), with which elements the other senses are only indirectly concerned. Hence the latter are not necessary for all animals, and in fact are found only in the higher animals.

§ 301. Again, there is the connection between sensitive and motive powers. Motive power cannot exist without sensitive, but the converse is not true. Some sentient beings move from place to place, but not all. We are speaking of the *progressive* movement of animals from one place to another; which is not found in all animals; though such as lack it show certain local movements of expansion and contraction—for instance, shellfish.

The ultimate division of soul—and the least extensive since it is not subdivided into different species—is that which has the power of reason and understanding; because where reason exists in mortal beings, there also are found all the other aforesaid powers. He says 'mortal' to exclude immaterial substances and the heavenly bodies (if these are alive) which, as neither being born nor dying, do not need the vegetative power; and as being able to understand by a direct intuition of the intelligible object, do not require sense-knowledge as a preliminary condition of understanding; whereas in corruptible natures all the sub-intellectual powers are presupposed as instruments preparing the way for intellect, which is the final perfection of Nature. But these sub-intellectual powers do not necessarily imply reason in the subjects that possess them. And in view of the affinity between intellect and imagination (as he said above, intellect either is, or is accompanied by, imagination)[1] he adds that some animals lack not only intellect but also imagination.

§ 302. Now this might seem to contradict a previous remark of his, that if a part cut from an animal retains sensation and desire, it retains also images[2]—if the latter imply imagination, as seems likely. We must therefore say that (as will be shown in Book III)[3] the lower animals have indeed a sort of imagination but *indeterminately*: i.e. the activity of imagining does not, in them, outlast actual sense-apprehension, as it does in the higher animals, which retain images of things sensed after these have been removed. Thus, as he says here, imagination varies in different animals. Some animals,

[1] § 18. [2] § 265. [3] §§ 644; 839.

lacking reason, live only by imagination, being led by it as we are led by reason. And though certain other animals lack both imagination and speculative intelligence, these two powers are not the same, as we shall see.

Clearly, then, the definition of the soul which has been given applies very precisely to each part of the soul.[1]

§ 303. Then, at 'It is necessary'[2] he shows the order to be followed in examining the parts of soul. From one point of view, he explains, the first thing to do is to define the nature of each of these parts; and then consider 'habits', i.e. whatever other parts of soul derive from them, and anything else pertaining to them and to whatever they animate, such as the organs of the body and things of that kind. This procedure is necessary to avoid confusion.

§ 304. Then, at 'But if etc.',[3] he observes that, from another point of view, our definition of any part of the soul—intellect or sensitivity or vegetativity—must begin from the *act* of the part in question, e.g. understanding or actual sensation; because in *idea* acts and operations precede potentialities. Potentiality is nothing but a capacity to act or be acted upon; it essentially involves a relation to actuality and can only be defined in such terms. And if this is the case with acts and potencies, acts in their turn connote something prior to themselves, i.e. their *objects*.

§ 305. For the *type* of every act or operation is determined by an object. Every operation of the soul is the act of a potentiality—either active or passive. Now the objects of *passive* potentialities stand to these as the causal agents which bring each potentiality into its proper activity; and it is thus that visible objects, and indeed all sensible things, are related to sight and to the other senses. But the objects of the *active* capacities are related to these as the final terms attained by their activities; for in this case the object is what each of these activities effectively realises. It is obvious that whenever an activity effectively realises anything besides the activity itself, the thing thus realised is the final term of the activity (cf. the *Ethics*, Book I);[4] for example a house is the final term of building. Hence all the *objects* of the soul's activities are either causal agents or final terms; and in both respects they specify those activities.

[1] Such seems to be St. Thomas's meaning; it differs from the Greek (415^a 12) and also, apparently, from M.

[2] 415^a 14.   [3] 415^a 16.   [4] E.N., I, c.7; 1097^a 15ss.

For, obviously, specifically diverse causal agents do specifically diverse things—as heat heats and cold chills. And so also with the final term of activity: becoming well or becoming ill differ as 'doings', because health differs from illness. Thus in the work of seeking definitions we have to consider the objects of the soul's operations before these operations themselves.

§ 306. We ought, therefore, to reach conclusions about objects before activities for the same reason as leads us to define activities before potencies. The 'objects' in question are such things as food and sensible being and intelligible being, with respect to the vegetative, sensitive and intellectual faculties respectively.

§ 307. But note that the activities and powers of soul are not distinguished with respect to distinct objects except precisely in so far as these are *objects*. For instance, visible being differs from audible being precisely as object. But if there is no difference *as object*, then it does not matter what other differences there may be; they will not essentially affect the *kind* of activity or potentiality. Thus by the same faculty we see a coloured man and a coloured stone; the difference is merely incidental to the object of the faculty.

§ 308. Note too that our intellectual potency is, as such, only potentially intelligible; in order to be understood it must be actualised through an idea drawn from sensible images. A thing is knowable only in the degree that it is actual; hence our intellectual potency attains to self-knowledge only through possessing an intelligible object in a concept (as will be explained in Book III),[1] and not by directly intuiting its own essence. This is why the process of self-knowledge has to start from the exterior things whence the mind draws the intelligible concepts in which it perceives itself; so we proceed from objects to acts, from acts to faculties, and from faculties to essence. But if the soul could know its essence in itself and directly it would be better to follow the reverse procedure; for in that case the closer anything was to the soul's essence, the more directly could it be known by the soul.

[1] §§ 724–6.

BOOK II, CHAPTER IV, CONTINUED

THE VEGETATIVE PRINCIPLE
HOW SOUL CAUSES BODY

HENCE WE MUST FIRST SPEAK OF NUTRITION AND generation. For the vegetative soul is present in others, and is primary, and is that most general power of the soul by which life is present in anything: its operations being reproduction and the use of nutriment.

§§ 309–10

For the most natural of the operations of such living beings as are mature, and not defective nor spontaneously generated, is to produce others like themselves: an animal an animal, and a plant a plant. To this extent do they participate as far as they are able, in the imperishable and the divine. For this all things seek after, doing all that they do by nature for the sake of this. Now 'that for the sake of which' anything takes place, is twofold, one, the end 'for which', the other the end 'in which'. Since then they cannot share by a continuous being, in the divine and everlasting (since nothing corruptible remains for ever numerically one and the same) each shares in this as far as it is able, one, however, more, and another less. And thus it endures, not the same, but *as if* the same; one indeed, but in species, not numerically.   §§ 311–17

The soul is the cause and principle of the living body. Now these words can be used in many ways. The soul, however, is a cause in three established senses: for it is that whence comes movement; that 'for the sake of which'; and as the essence of living bodies. § 318

That it is as the essence is evident. For in all things, the essence is the cause of existence. In things that live, to live is to be; and the cause and principle of this is the soul. § 319

Further: of that which is in potency, the act is the [immanent] idea. § 320

It is manifest that the soul is also a cause 'for the sake of which'. For Nature operates for a purpose, in the same way as mind; and this is its end. Such is the soul in living things, according to Nature. For all natural bodies are instruments of the soul: whether of animals or of plants, they exist as for the sake of the soul. 'For the sake of' is a phrase used in two ways, as 'that for which', and 'that in which'. §§ 321–2

But also the soul is the principle whence comes local motion. Yet this power is not present in all living things. Change and growth are, however, due to a soul, while sensation seems to be a kind of alteration, and nothing senses unless it has a soul. The same holds good of growth and decay; for nothing undergoes growth or decay physically, unless it is nourished; and nothing is nourished which does not share in life. § 323

§ 309. Having distinguished the capacities of 'soul' from one another, and explained how and in what order he means to discuss them, the Philosopher now treats of them in the order indicated. This he does in two stages. First, he examines one by one the divisions into which he has analysed soul, coming to certain conclusions about all of them. After that, in the penultimate chapter of this book, where he says, 'All living things have the vegetative soul',[1] he explains the interrelation of these 'parts' of soul.

The former section divides into four treatises:

(1) On the *vegetative* principle.
(2) Starting at 'These questions being settled',[2] on the *sensitive* principle.
(3) At 'As to the part of the soul by which it knows',[3] on the *intellect*.
(4) At 'We must now consider',[4] on the principle of *local movement*.

To the *appetitive* principle is assigned no special treatise, because it does not of itself constitute any special grade of animate being. It is treated, along with motion, in Book III.[5]

Treatise (1) divides into two parts: the first part contains certain preliminaries to the study of the vegetative principle; the second, beginning at 'Since the vegetative and generative',[6] contains Aris-

---

[1] Bk. III, lectio 17, §§ 847–64. [2] Bk. II, lectio 10, § 350ss.
[3] Bk. III, lectio 7, § 671.
[4] Bk. III, lectio 14, § 795. 'Since the soul is defined . . .'
[5] § 795ss. [6] Bk. II, lectio 9, § 333ss.

totle's conclusions on this matter. The former section again divides into (*a*) a statement of his aim,[1] and (*b*) at 'For the most natural',[2] an exposition of certain things which an understanding of the vegetative principle presupposes.

§ 310. (*a*) First of all, then, he remarks that if, as we saw in the last chapter, objects and acts have to be defined before potencies, and the fundamental potency before those which follow from it, we ought in consequence to begin by discussing nourishment, the object with which the vegetative principle deals, and generation, which is this principle's activity. Now this principle should be discussed first; because, whenever it coexists in one subject with the other parts of 'soul', it is as it were their foundation; for through its activities the physical reality, underlying both sensitivity and intelligence, is maintained. Besides, this part of 'soul' is common to all living things, and while it can exist apart from the others, they cannot exist without it; and it is always best to start with the more general *datum*. Its activities, then, being reproduction and taking nourishment, it is with these that we begin.

§ 311. (*b*) Next, when he says 'For the most natural'[3] he settles a few preliminary questions; and this in two stages. First, he shows that to generate one's kind is an act of the vegetative principle. This he had not yet shown, having spoken so far only of growth and decay in this connection. Next, at 'The soul is cause',[4] he proves that a soul is the principle of all vegetative activities (for indeed these activities might have seemed to come from mere nature, and not from a life-principle, since it is of their essence that they make use of the active and passive physical and corporeal qualities; and still more, because life in plants is hard to discern and latent).

§ 312. The first point is proved thus. All activities found to be natural to *all* living things spring, as we have seen, from the vegetative principle as the fundamental condition of there being any life at all;[5] and reproduction being one such activity, it must spring from the vegetative principle. Indeed, he relates reproduction to this principle because it is, as he says, the activity most natural to all living things; and this because in a certain way the process of generation is common to all beings, even to inanimate things. Of course the latter are generated differently; still, they *are* generated.

---

[1] §§ 309–10; 415ª 22.   [2] § 311; 415ª 26.
[3] 415ª 26.   [4] 415ᵇ 8.   [5] § 288.

But with them the generating principle is something quite exterior to the thing that comes into being, whereas animate things proceed from an interior principle inasmuch as they spring from the seed with its potentiality for new life.

§ 313. There are, however, three exceptions to the general rule that living things reproduce their kind. First, the immature; for children do not beget. Secondly, those defective in some essential requirement, such as the impotent and eunuchs. Thirdly, the case of spontaneous generation from putrefying matter. In this last case the life resulting is of a type so inferior that the *general* environment suffices to cause it, i.e. the influence of the heavenly bodies and the right material conditions. But these causes alone are not sufficient to generate the higher animals: this requires also the activity of *particular* causes of the same species as the animals generated.

§ 314. Hence he says that any living thing can reproduce its kind provided that it is 'mature' (excluding children) and not 'defective' (excluding eunuchs and such like) and that the effect generated is not 'spontaneously generated' (excluding things produced by putrefaction, which are said to come to be 'spontaneously' because they spring up without seed, which is something like the way things are done, as we say, spontaneously, i.e. not under exterior compulsion). And what he means by living things producing their like is that animals produce animals and plants plants; and more precisely that each species produces its like, men producing men and olive-trees olive-trees. And the reason why living things produce their like is that they may continuously participate, so far as they can, in what is divine and immortal, i.e. that they may become as like to the divine as possible.

§ 315. For just as there are degrees of perfection in one and the same being, inasmuch as it develops from potentiality into act, so there are more and less perfect beings; and therefore the more perfect a given thing is in itself, the more does it resemble the more perfect beings. Hence just as, while a thing is moving from potency to actuality, and as long as it is still in potency, it has a natural relation and inclination towards actuality, and when it attains incomplete actuality it still desires a more complete actuality, so, in the same way, everything in a lower form of existence is inclined to the maximum possible assimilation to the higher form. Hence

Aristotle adds that 'all things seek this',[1] i.e. an assimilation to what is divine and imperishable, and this is that 'for the sake of which they do all that they do by nature'.

§ 316. Now 'that for the sake of which' something is done can mean two things: (*a*) the end aimed at *directly* by an activity, as health is the direct aim of doctoring; and (*b*) as the end aimed at *indirectly*; and this again may be taken in two ways. For we might take the 'end' to include also that subject in which the activity's direct aim is realised, and in this sense the end of doctoring would be not health merely, but a healthy body. Alternately, we could mean by 'end' not only what is principally intended, but also the means to be employed; we might say, e.g. that the end of doctoring was to keep the body warm, because warmth preserves that harmony of elements in the body which *is* health. So then, when it is said here that perpetuity of being is the reason for the activity in question, we are referring either to some imperishable nature which material things strive, by reproducing their kind, to resemble, or to the reproductive process itself, which is the means to this end.

§ 317. Because, then, the lower forms of life are unable to share in the perpetual, divine being by way of continuity of their individual identity—since it is absolutely and intrinsically necessary (not merely a necessity imposed from without) that all corruptible things should individually pass away since they are intrinsically material—it follows that they can only share in it so far as their nature allows; the more lasting natures more, the less lasting less; but all sharing in it continuously by way of reproduction; each remaining one and the same, not indeed literally, but 'as if the same',[2] in the sense that one and the same species remains. Hence he adds that it does not remain one thing *numerically*, i.e. in the strict sense of the terms, but only *specifically*; and this because each individual reproduces its like according to species.

§ 318. Then, at 'The soul is the cause',[3] he shows the connection between the activities attributed to the vegetative principle and the soul. And he does two things here: first, he establishes a truth; secondly, at 'Empedocles',[4] he points out an error. The proof of the truth, again, has two stages. First, he states his aim, asserting that the soul is principle and cause of the living body; and since

[1] 415b 1.   [2] 415b 5.   [3] 415b 8.   [4] 415b 28. Lectio 8, § 324ss.

these terms are ambiguous, going on to distinguish three senses in which this proposition is to be taken. Soul, he says, is cause of the living body, (*a*) as the source of its movements, (*b*) as 'that for the sake of which', or end, and (*c*) as its 'essence' or form.[1]

§ 319. In the second place, at 'That it is',[2] he proves his proposition; and first with regard to soul being the cause of the living body as its form. Here he uses two arguments: first, the cause of anything as its 'essence', i.e. form, is the same as the cause of its being, for everything has actual existence through its form. Now it is the soul that gives being to living things; for their being is precisely their life, which they have from the soul. Hence the soul causes the body as its form.

§ 320. Then the second argument, at 'Further':[3] the actuality of anything is the immanent idea[4] and form of the thing as in potency. Now the soul, as we have seen, is the living body's actuality. Therefore it is the form and immanent idea of the living body.

§ 321. Next, at 'It is manifest',[5] he shows that the soul is a *final* cause of living bodies. For Nature, like mind, acts for a purpose, as was shown in Book II of the *Physics*.[6] But the mind, in its constructions, always orders and arranges materials in view of some form. So also, then, does Nature. If then the soul is the living body's form, it must also be its final cause.

§ 322. Moreover the soul is the end not only of living bodies, but also of all sublunary natural bodies. For it is evident that all such bodies are, as it were, instruments of 'soul'—not only of animals' souls but of the plant soul as well. Thus men turn to their own purposes both animals and inanimate things; animals make use of plants and inanimate things; and plants of the inanimate things which support and feed them. If then the action of things is an index to their nature it seems that all inanimate bodies are naturally instruments of animate things and exist for their sake. And, incidentally, the lower animate things exist for the higher. After this he distinguishes 'for the sake of' into the two aspects which have already been explained.[7]

§ 323. Thirdly, at 'But also the soul',[8] he shows that the soul is

---

[1] 415[b] 10.   [2] 415[b] 12.   [3] 415[b] 14.   [4] *ratio* (λόγος).

[5] 415[b] 15.   [6] *Phys.*, II, c.8; 198[b] 15ss.   [7] § 316.   [8] 415[b] 20.

the source of movement in the body. The form of every natural body, he explains, is the principle of the characteristic movement of that particular kind of body—e.g. the form of fire is cause of fire's movement. Now certain movements are characteristic of living bodies; such, for instance, as that by which animals move themselves about from place to place, though this, to be sure, is not found in all living things. Similarly sensation involves a certain alteration of the body not found except in beings that have soul. So too with growth and decay; these movements imply the use of food and therefore also a soul. The soul, then, is the principle of all these movements.

BOOK II, CHAPTER IV, CONTINUED

THE VEGETATIVE PRINCIPLE CONTINUED
TWO ERRORS REFUTED

EMPEDOCLES IS MISTAKEN HERE, ADDING THAT growth occurs in plants by their sending a root downwards, because earth is by nature below, and also upwards because of fire. § 324

Nor did he understand aright 'up' and 'down'; for these are not for all things the same as for the Universe; but roots of plants correspond to the head[1] in animals, if it is permissible to identify organs by their functions. For we reckon those organs to be the same which perform the same operations.

§§ 325–7

Besides, what holds fire and earth together if they tend in contrary directions? They must come apart if there is nothing to prevent this. But if there is such a thing, it must be the soul; and be also the cause of growth and nourishment.

§ 328

Now it seems to some that the nature of fire is the sole cause of growth and nutrition; for it certainly seems to be the only one of the bodies and elements that is self-nourishing and self-increasing. Whence the notion that it is this that is operative in plants and animals. §§ 329–30

It is indeed a concomitant cause, but the cause absolutely is not fire, but rather the soul. For the increase of fire is in-

---

[1] M. omits 'head', which is in the Greek and is presupposed by St. Thomas.

218

finite so long as there is anything combustible. But there are limitations to all things that subsist naturally, and some definite principle governs their dimensions and growth. And this belongs to the soul, not to fire, and to a specific principle rather than to matter. §§ 331-2

§ 324. The Philosopher has just shown that the activities we call vegetative have their origin in the soul. He now proceeds to refute two errors on this subject, which he deals with respectively in two sections; the second of which begins at 'Now it seems to some that the nature of fire'.[1] In the first section he begins by stating the error[2] and then, at 'Nor did he understand' attacks it.[3] Regarding the error itself, we should note that just as Empedocles refused to explain other cases of purposeful arrangement in Nature by any natural finality—for example he said that animals had the sort of feet they have, not in order to help them to walk, but simply because the matter of that part of their bodies happened to be arranged in that sort of way; so also the growth of living things he ascribed merely to the motion of light and heavy bodies. Observing that living things increase their size in different directions, e.g. up and down—as is evident in plants, which thrust their roots down and their branches up—he said that the downward growth of plants was due to the earth in their composition, which is heavy and therefore necessarily tends downwards; whilst their upward growth was due to fire which, being light, must tend upwards.

§ 325. Aristotle, then, at 'Nor did he', brings two arguments against this opinion of Empedocles. First, he says that Empedocles misunderstood 'up and down'. To see what he means here we should note that 'up and down', and the other differences of position(before and behind, right and left) are differentiated in some objects naturally, whilst in others they are merely relative to ourselves. In things which have definite parts as the natural principle of their various movements, these positions are based on Nature itself. Thus the Cosmos as a whole has a mid-point to which heavy

[1] § 329. [2] 415[b] 28. [3] 416[a] 1.

things naturally tend, and a circumference to which light things naturally rise; which makes a natural cosmic difference between up and down, according to the natural resting places of the light and the heavy. Again, in living things and mortal beings up and down follow growth and decay: the upper is that part which takes in food, and the lower the opposite part which ejects superfluities.

§ 326. Again, in some animals before and behind are determined in relation to their senses, and the right and the left by their movements in space. But things, no part of which is a special source or term of movement, have no natural differences of position in themselves; these are fixed simply by the thing's position relative to us. So is it with inanimate objects: the same pillar is said to be on the right or the left according as it is to the right or left of a man. Now in certain living things the *natural* upper and lower parts are fixed in the same way as in the Cosmos as a whole. It is so in man whose head is turned towards the top of the Cosmos and his feet to its bottom. But the reverse is found in plants, whose roots correspond to the head in man, since they function (as the part which takes in food) in the same way as the head in man. For we reckon that instruments are similar or dissimilar if their functions are so; hence the likeness between a plant's roots and the head of an animal, although *they* point downwards. Up and down, then, mean opposite things in plants and in the Cosmos as a whole. But brute animals are different; their heads are turned neither up nor down in relation to the Cosmos as a whole. This is what he means when he says that up and down are not for all things (i.e. living things) what they are for the Cosmos.

§ 327. But Empedocles took up and down to be the same for all living things and for the Cosmos. And indeed, if the movement of growth, by which we fix the upper and lower in living beings, followed the movements of the heavy and the light, by which the same relations are fixed for the Cosmos as a whole, then up and down would mean the same in all living beings and in the Cosmos. This is what led Empedocles to say that the roots of plants grew downwards.

§ 328. The second argument against Empedocles begins at 'Besides, what holds'.[1] To understand it, we should note that each element in a mixture is present not actually but virtually, and

[1] 416ᵃ 6.

therefore lacking the movement proper to itself. The whole mixture moves with the movement of the element that predominates. If each, as Empedocles seems to have thought, retained its own movement, then, since the elements have natural movements in contrary directions, it follows that they would become quite separate from one another, unless some containing force held them together. Now it is just this container of the element which seems to be the chief cause of growth. For though, to be sure, the increase of the body in its various parts is due to diverse motions of the elements, yet,[1] given the contrariety of elemental motion, growth is inconceivable unless the elements remain conjoined; otherwise there would be division, not growth. But in living things the soul is what holds the elements together; it is also, therefore, the source of their growth.

§ 329. Next, at 'Now it seems to some',[2] he states another theory; which, at 'It is indeed',[3] he then disproves. Unlike the theory of Empedocles, which put the causes of growth and nutrition in both earth and fire, this theory ascribes them only to fire.

§ 330. The reason given is that the cause of anything's modifications or motion would appear to be whatever had such modifications or motions essentially—e.g. fire, being essentially hot, is the cause of heat in things that contain other elements as well; and in the same way earth is the cause of heaviness. Now of the elements fire alone seems to 'feed' itself and to 'grow'; if we take these terms in a superficial sense. Therefore fire alone would seem to cause growth and nutrition in plants and animals. But whether fire really feeds itself and grows will be made clear later.[4]

§ 331. Then he attacks the above opinion. But note its grain of truth. All food has to be cooked, and this is done by fire, so that fire does play a part in nutrition, and consequently in growth also; not indeed as the principal agent (which is the soul) but as a secondary, instrumental agent. To say then that fire is a sort of concurrent or instrumental cause of growth and nutrition is true. But it cannot be the principal cause or agent, as he goes on to show.

§ 332. The principal agent in any action is that which imposes the term or natural limit upon what is done; thus in artificial things

---

[1] Pirotta prints *non enim*, which does not connect with the previous sentence. The sense seems to require *non autem*.

[2] 416[a] 9.   [3] 416[a] 14.   [4] §§ 341-2.

like boxes or houses the limit or term is fixed, not by the instruments used in the work, but by the art itself. The instruments, as such, are quite indifferent as to whether they are used to produce a thing of this shape and quantity or of that. A saw, as such, can be used to cut wood for a door or a bench or a house, and in any quantity you please; and if it cuts wood in this or that particular shape and quantity, this is due to the man who uses it. Now in Nature each thing obviously has certain limits to its size and its increase; each thing grows to a certain fixed pattern. For as each species of thing requires its own accidental modifications, so it needs its own measure of quantity, though some margin must be left to material differences and other individual factors. Men are not all equal in size. But there is a limit both to their largeness and their littleness; and whatever determines this limit is the true *principal* cause of growth. But this cannot be fire, because the growth of fire has no naturally fixed limits; it would spread to infinity if an infinite amount of fuel were supplied to it. Clearly, then, fire is not the chief cause of growth and nutrition, but rather the soul. And this is reasonable enough, for the quantitative limits of material things are fixed by form—the specific principle—rather than matter. Now the soul of a living being is to the elements it contains as form is to matter; the soul, then, rather than fire, sets the term and natural limit to size and growth.

BOOK II, CHAPTER IV, CONTINUED

THE VEGETATIVE PRINCIPLE CONTINUED

NUTRITION

SINCE THE VEGETATIVE AND GENERATIVE FACULTIES of soul are a single power, it is first necessary to fix the nature of nutrition. For it is by this operation that [this power] is distinguished from the others.   § 333

It would appear that food is a contrary to that which is fed: yet not every contrariety [involves feeding]; but only such contraries as find their increase as well as their origin in each other. For there are many things which originate from opposites: but not all derive their increase thus; (for instance, health coming from sickness). Nor, it seems, do all that do so nourish one another in the same way. For water is a food to fire, but fire does not feed water. And with uncompounded bodies this seems especially to be the case; that which feeds is one thing and that which is fed another.   §§ 334–5

But a difficulty arises here. For some say that anything is nourished by what is similar to it; just as it is increased thus. But to others, as we have said, it seems, on the contrary, that a thing is nourished by its opposite,—as though it were impossible that like [should be altered] by like; whilst food is altered and digested. Change in all things is either [to] an opposite or to a mean state. Moreover nutriment is acted upon by that which is nourished: not the latter by the nour-

ishment; any more than a craftsman by his material; but this
is acted on by him—the craftsman changing only from repose
to activity.   §§ 336–8

It makes all the difference indeed whether food is considered as what it is at first or as what it becomes finally. But
if as both, in the one sense as undigested, in the other as
digested, then certainly both the [above] theories of food can
be upheld: for as it is undigested, one of two contraries is
nourished by the other: but in so far as it is digested, one of
two similars is nourished by the other. Whence it is clear
that both parties speak in one way rightly, and in another
way wrongly.   § 339

Since only what is alive is nourished, what is nourished is
the animate body as such. Wherefore nutriment means something related to what is animate, and this not incidentally
only.   §§ 340–2

To be nutritive and to be active[1] are two distinct things.
In so far as the living being is quantitative, food is active; but
in so far as it is substantial, food is nutritive. It preserves the
substance, and this just so long as it is fed.   § 343

And it is productive of generation, not of the one nourished, but of such a one as the one nourished—for this latter
is already a substance; and nothing generates itself; it only
maintains itself in being.   § 344

Wherefore, this soul-principle is a power able to preserve
what possesses it as a thing of such a kind; and food is preparatory to the operation; hence the being cannot continue,
deprived of food.   § 345

[1] *Activo esse*, 'to be active', is in Pirotta's text, but St. Thomas, § 343, reads, as
in Aristotle, 'To be *augmentative*', 416^b 11.

Since there are three factors: what is nourished; that by which it is nourished; and that which nourishes; what nourishes is the primary soul, that which is nourished is the body containing it, and that by which it is nourished is food.

§ 346

Since all things are rightly named from their end and the end [of this soul] is to have generated another being like itself, then the primary soul is generative of what is like itself.[1]

§ 347

'That by which' in nourishment is twofold, as 'that by which' in steering is the hand or the rudder: the one moving and moved, the other moving only.[2] Now of necessity all food must be such that it can be digested, and what effects digestion is heat. Hence every animate being has heat.

In outline, then, we have stated what nutriment is: the subject must be further examined later in a special discussion.

§§ 348–9

[1] 'The primary soul would be generative etc.', 416^{b} 24. Aristotle is giving a definition, which is obscured in the Latin by the omission of 'would be'.

[2] St. Thomas reads (§ 348) 'moving', as here. The better reading of the Greek is 'moved', 416^{b} 27.

§ 333. After showing that the activities called vegetative originate in the soul, the Philosopher proceeds to examine these activities. And first he examines their subject-matter, which is food.
Next he shows how the activities and their subject-matter correspond—this at 'Since only what is alive'.[1] Thirdly, at 'Wherefore
this soul-principle',[2] he defines the faculties brought into play in
these activities. As regards the first point he does three things: (a)
he states the plan of the present argument;[3] (b) at 'It would appear
that food',[4] he says what at first sight appears true about nutrition;
to which (c) at 'But a difficulty',[5] he brings an objection.

In the first place, then, (a) he observes that, as the vegetative and
reproductive powers are included in the same general vegetative
power ('vegetative' as a *special* power being really the nutritive
power), we should discuss food first of all in relation to this power
as a whole. For it is taking food that characterises this part of the
soul as distinct from the intellectual or sensitive parts. For the other
vegetative activities all presuppose taking food.

§ 334. Then (b) he states in three points what appears at first
sight with regard to nourishment. First, food would always seem
to be the contrary of the subject fed; and this because it has to become the latter, and becoming is from one thing to its contrary.
Secondly, however, it seems to be clear that not *any* contraries will
do; they must be such as can change into one another. Food is
changed into the being of the one fed; hence all contraries which
alternate in a subject without the one ever actually changing into
the other have nothing to do with food. Thus sickness is not the

---

[1] § 340; 416[b] 9.   [2] § 345; 416[b] 17.   [3] 416[a] 19.
[4] 416[a] 21.   [5] 416[a] 29.

food of health, nor white of black. But how substances come to contain contraries is another question.

§ 335. (c) Again, since increase of bulk seems to follow nutrition, the contraries involved must be such as affect each other in this way. Water may be *generated* by fire and *e converso*, but we do not say that water is fed by fire. Yet we can say that fire is fed by water, inasmuch as watery vapour nourishes fire. When water comes from fire there is no new coming-to-be of water; but fire can make use of and grow by means of watery vapours. Among the elements, therefore, only fire seems to be fed and only water seems to be food, taking water to include all vapours and liquids.

§ 336. Then at 'But a difficulty'[1] Aristotle brings an objection against what he has just said. The difficulty concerns the statement that food is a 'contrary'. For some maintain that food should resemble the subject fed. Food causes growth, and a thing grows by what it resembles; otherwise the growth would be a mere addition of something extrinsic. Therefore like, it seems, is fed by like.

§ 337. To others, however, it seems that food must, as we have said, be contrary to what is fed. And they are moved by two reasons. (a) Food, being cooked, is transformed into the subject fed. But all transformation is either into a contrary or into an intermediate, as white into either black or grey. And the intermediate is a sort of contrary: grey compared with white, is black; and compared with black, is white; for it combines both. Therefore food is contrary to the subject into which it is transformed.

§ 338. (b) Again, every agent is contrary to that on which it acts; like is not *passive* to like. But food is passive to what is fed: it is transformed and digested. What is fed is not passive to its food, any more than an artist to his material (for it is the material that is altered, not the artist, except indirectly, in so far as he moves from potency to act). It would seem, then, that food is contrary to what is fed. Now the first of these two reasons is drawn from the contrariety between the two terns of a change; and the second from the contrariety between agent and patient. That which is fed, and itself acts upon the food, is the term into which the food is transformed.

§ 339. Then at 'It makes all the difference'[2] he solves the problem, saying that the answer depends on whether by 'food' we

[1] 416[a] 29.   [2] 416[b] 2.

mean what remains at the end of the process of heating and digesting, or what is received at first before this process begins. If food can be taken in both these senses—namely as the finished and as the raw product—then the two answers are both admissible. If it is taken in the latter sense, then subjects are fed by their contrary, which itself is acted upon and transformed; but if in the former sense, then like is fed by like; for the active agent assimilates what it acts upon, which is ultimately made like the agent and, as such, can increase the agent's bulk. Thus both the above opinions were in one way true and another way false.

§ 340. Next, at 'Since only',[1] he shows how food is related to the activities of the vegetative principle: to taking nourishment; to growth (at 'To be nutritive');[2] and to reproduction (at 'And it is productive').[3]

First, then, he observes that nothing is fed except what has life and soul; hence the besouled body is what is fed. Now food is potential with respect to the subject fed; for it is changed into this subject. It follows that, inasmuch as food is the material of feeding, it is essentially, not accidentally, related to the besouled body as in potency to this body.

§ 341. Nothing then is, properly speaking, fed excepting what has a soul. Fire might seem to resemble in some way things that are fed, but it is not fed, strictly speaking. For that is properly said to be fed which absorbs something else in order to maintain its own being; and though this appears to happen with fire, it does not really happen. Once a fire has started, if you add fresh fuel, a new fire starts in the new fuel; but not in such a way that the new fuel maintains the fire already started before it was added. By starting a fire in fresh wood you do not maintain the flame in the other wood already burning. For the one flame made up of many flames is not one in the simple sense of the term; it is only one by the aggregation of many units, like a heap of stones. And it is this sort of unity that gives to burning a certain likeness to taking food.

§ 342. Living bodies, on the other hand, are really fed; food maintains life precisely where it already existed. This also is why only living bodies, properly speaking, grow; for each and every part in them is fed and increases; whereas inanimate things increase only by addition of part to part; what existed already does not

[1] 416^b 9.   [2] 416^b 11.   [3] 416^b 15.

increase, it is merely made into a new whole together with some other thing added to it.

But if fire has a special likeness to living and growing things, this is because the formal principle in fire is stronger than in the other elements, and its active power greater. It seems, therefore, to feed and grow because it so obviously seizes and subdues to itself other things.

§ 343. Then, at 'To be nutritive',[1] he relates taking food to growth, observing that whilst the objective terms of feeding as feeding and of growing as growing are one and the same *thing*, they differ in idea. Food, we have seen,[2] is in potency to the living body; which itself is both a quantum and a definite particular thing or substance. As a quantum it receives its food (which itself is a quantum) as a cause of growth; but as a particular sort of substance it receives food precisely as food. For it is of the nature of food to maintain the substance of what is fed; which is required by the continuous using up of natural warmth and moisture. Hence the substance of the thing fed lasts just so long as it is fed.

§ 344. Then at 'And it is productive'[3] he relates nutrition to generation, as the latter's cause. For seed, the generative principle, is the residue of food. And food is an agent in generating, not the subject fed, but other subjects of the same kind; for the subject fed already exists and cannot be generated afresh. Nothing generates itself; only what does not yet exist is generated. This is not to say, however, that things cannot maintain themselves.

§ 345. Next, at 'Wherefore, this soul-principle',[4] he concludes with a definition of the powers of the vegetative soul: first, of the nutritive power, and then, at 'Since all things',[5] of the whole vegetative principle. As to the nutritive power, he observes that it is simply that faculty by which a living being is able to maintain itself as such; while food is the condition of this faculty's activity, that by means of which it maintains its subject. Hence loss of being follows lack of food.

§ 346. And, having remarked[6] that the source of nutritive activity is a capacity in the soul relating essentially to food, he goes on, at 'Since there are three'[7] to show how that power and the food itself differ as sources of nutrition. Nutrition, he says, involves three fac-

[1] 416b 11.   [2] § 340.   [3] 416b 15.   [4] 416b 17.
[5] 416b 23.   [6] § 323.   [7] 416b 20.

tors: what is fed; that wherewith it is fed; and the primary agent in feeding: this primary agent is the primary, i.e. vegetative, soul. What is fed is its body; and that wherewith it is fed is food. Thus a capacity in the soul is the cause of taking food as the principal agent; but food as the instrumental agent.

§ 347. Next, at 'Since all things',[1] he defines that primary or vegetative soul (the entire soul of plants, but only part of any animal's soul). To understand his definition, we must realise that the three vegetative activities fall into a certain order. First is taking food, by which things are maintained in being; the second and more perfect activity is growth, by which a thing increases in both quantity and capacity; while the third and most perfect and ultimate vegetative activity is reproduction, by which a being, already pretty complete in itself, gives existence and perfection to another being. For each thing is at its best, as is said in the *Meteorologica*, Book IV,[2] when it can reproduce its likeness in another. If then all things are rightly defined and named in terms of their end, and the end of all the activities of the vegetative soul is to generate its likeness in another, it follows that we can suitably define this 'primary soul' as that which is reproductive of another, like to itself in kind.

§ 348. And in view of his previous remark that this primary soul's instrument was food, to prevent anyone thinking that it had no other instrument, he shows, at 'That by which',[3] that the subject fed has another instrument wherewith it is fed; just as in steering a ship there are two instruments. For the pilot steers with both hand and rudder. Now the hand is a conjoined instrument which has the soul for its form. Whilst, then, the rudder is an instrument which moves the boat and itself is moved by the hand, the hand itself is not moved by an exterior motive force, but by an interior one; for it is a part of the man and the man moves himself. Similarly, the instrument of nutrition is twofold. There is the separated instrument not yet informed by the soul; and this is food. But there must also be a conjoined instrument; for the food must be digested; and this requires heat. As then a pilot moves the rudder with his hand, and the boat with the rudder, so the soul moves the food with heat and, by means of the food, nourishes itself. The heat is the soul's conjoined instrument; a natural warmth inseparably rooted in the soul and necessary to all living things as the

[1] 416^b 23.   [2] *Meteor.*, IV, c.3, 380^a 11ss.   [3] 416^b 25.

condition of their digesting their food. And it is because this primary soul is, unlike the intellect, the actuality of a part of the body that it has a conjoined instrument.

§ 349. Summarising, Aristotle says that he has defined 'in outline', that is in general, what food is; later he will treat of it with more precision and finality. For he wrote a special book on food,[1] as also on the generation and movement of animals.

[1] Not extant.

BOOK II, CHAPTER V

SENSITIVITY

POTENCY AND ACT IN SENSATION

THESE QUESTIONS BEING SETTLED, LET US SPEAK OF sensation in general. As has been said, sensation occurs in a being moved and acted upon; for it appears to be a kind of alteration. Some say, 'like is acted on by like'. How far this is possible or impossible has been stated in our general discussion of activity and passivity. §§ 350–1

It may be asked why there is no sensation of the senses themselves; and why they do not produce sensation without something extraneous, seeing that they contain within themselves fire and earth and the other elements that give rise to sensation, either of themselves or through their accidental qualities. It becomes evident that the sensitive power is not an actuality, but is only potential; which explains why it does not sense[1] [without an exterior object] as the combustible does not burn of itself without something to make it burn. Otherwise it would burn itself, and not need a fire already alight. § 352–4

But as we speak of sensing in two ways, (for we say that one who sees and hears in potency sees and hears, even when he happens to be asleep; and also that one does so actually)

---

[1] This clause is not in the Greek, 417^a 7.

so we may speak of 'sense' in two ways,—as in potency and as in act. Likewise, to perceive[1] is both potential and actual.

§ 355

To start with then, let us speak as if being acted upon and moved were the same as action and moving. For movement is a kind of activity, though imperfect, as has been stated elsewhere.

§ 356

All things are moved and affected by an agent, or something in act. Hence it is, that a thing is affected both by its similar and also by its dissimilar, as we have said. What *is* being affected is dissimilar: what *has* been affected is similar.

§ 357

---

[1] Or perhaps 'the sense-object', αἰσθητόν rather than αἰσθάνεσθαι, which M. renders as *sentire*.

ST. THOMAS'S COMMENTARY
LECTIO TEN

§ 350. After treating of the vegetative part of soul the Philosopher now begins to examine the sensitive part. This treatment divides into two sections, the first of which deals with what is most apparent in sensitivity, i.e. the exterior senses, while the second, beginning at 'That there is no other sense',[1] treats of what is latent therein. In the former section Aristotle first explains how sense-faculties are related to sensible objects, and then, at 'In treating of each sense' he defines[2] both faculty and object. Regarding the former point, he first repeats some earlier observations,[3] and then, at 'It may be asked', proceeds to the present problem.[4]

First of all, then, he remarks that this is the place to start discussing the sensitive soul, beginning with a general view of the subject and going on later to a more detailed treatment. And he repeats two things already said: that to sense is to be moved or acted upon in some way, for the act of sensation involves a certain alteration of the subject; and secondly, that it was the view of some enquirers that the passivity of sensation was an instance of like being acted upon by like.

§ 351. For some early thinkers held that like is known and sensed by like: as Empedocles said, earth knows earth, fire knows fire, and so on. Now the general problem of the action of like upon like is discussed in the *De Generatione*,[5] where Aristotle's conclusion is that, although at the start of any action the agent and patient are contrary, when the action is finished they are similar. For the agent, in acting, assimilates the patient.

---

[1] Bk. III, lectio 1, §§ 565-7.   [2] Bk. II, lectio 13, § 383.
[3] 416^b 32.   [4] 417^a 1.
[5] *De Generatione et Corruptione*, I, c.7.

§ 352. Then, at 'It may be asked',[1] he proceeds to the present problem. He shows that in themselves the senses are in potency; then, at 'But since we speak of sensing in two ways',[2] that they are sometimes in act; and thirdly, at 'Distinctions however',[3] he shows how they move from potency into act.

To understand the first of these three points, note that all who, like Empedocles, said that like was known by like, thought that the senses were actually the sense-objects themselves,—that the sensitive soul was able to know all sense-objects because it consisted somehow of those objects; that is, of the elements of which the latter are composed.

§ 353. Two things follow from this hypothesis. (1) If the senses actually are, or are made up of, the sense-objects, then, if the latter can be sensed, the senses themselves can be sensed. (2) Since the presence of its object suffices to enable the sense-faculty to sense, then, if this object actually exists in the faculty as part of its composition, it follows that sensation can take place in the absence of external objects. But both these consequences are false. He introduces them here as specimens of the problems which the early philosophers could not solve. So he says, 'It may be asked why there is no sensation of the senses',[4] i.e. why the senses themselves are not sensed; for it seems they would be sensed if they, the faculties, were really like their objects.

§ 354. It is also hard to see 'why they do not produce sensation', i.e. why actual sensation does not occur, 'without something extraneous', i.e. without exterior sense-objects; since, in the opinion of the ancients, fire, earth and the other elements belong to the inner nature of the sense-faculty and are perceptible by sense, either in themselves, i.e. in their essence (as these philosophers thought, not distinguishing between the senses and the intellect which alone perceives essence), or in the accidental qualities proper to them, namely heat and cold and so forth, which are essentially sense-perceptible. Now since these difficulties are insurmountable if the sense-faculty consists of its objects in their actuality (as the early philosophers thought), Aristotle concludes that the sensitive soul is clearly not actually, but only potentially, the sense-object. That is why sensation will not occur without an exterior sense-object, just

[1] 417ª 1. [2] 417ª 9.
[3] Lectio 11, § 358; 417ª 21. [4] 417ª 1.

as combustible material does not burn of itself, but needs to be set on fire by an exterior agent; whereas if it were actually fire it would burn simply by itself.

§ 355. Then, at 'But as we speak of sensing',[1] he shows, by the two ways in which we speak of anyone sensing, that sensation is intermittently actual. For we sometimes say that a man sees or hears when he only does these things potentially, as when he is asleep; but sometimes we mean that what he is actually doing is seeing or hearing. Clearly, then, sensation and sensing may be referred to either in act or in potency.

§ 356. Next, at 'To start with then',[2] he explains the above. For to speak of sensation as 'in act' might seem contradictory to his previous statement that it was a certain passive being acted upon or moved; for to be in act seems to pertain to an active agent. So he explains that in calling sensation an 'act' he is referring precisely to the state of being acted upon or moved; inasmuch as this is a certain state of being actual. For movement has a certain actuality; which is the actuality (as he says in the *Physics*, Book III)[3] of the imperfect or potential, that is to say, of changeable being. In the same way, being moved and sensation itself are a sort of action, as implying an actuality of being. The phrase 'To start with', however, means that he will add something later to show how the senses become actual in fact.

§ 357. Thirdly, at 'All things are moved and affected',[4] he shows how it follows from the above that the old theory that like senses like cannot be true. Everything potential, he says, is acted upon and moved by some active agent already existing; which in its actualising function makes the potential thing like itself. In some sense, then, a thing is acted upon by both its like and its unlike (as we have already remarked).[5] At first, and while the transforming process is going on, there is dissimilarity; but at the end, when the thing *is* transformed and changed, there is similarity. And so it is as between the sense-faculty and its object. And the early philosophers went wrong because they missed this distinction.

[1] 417^a 9.   [2] 417^a 14.   [3] *Phys.*, III, c.1; 201^a 10ss.
[4] 417^a 17.   [5] § 351.

BOOK II, CHAPTER V, CONTINUED

SENSITIVITY
POTENCY AND ACT CONTINUED

DISTINCTIONS HOWEVER MUST BE MADE CONCERN-
ing potency and act; for at present we are speaking
of these in one sense only.   § 358

For there is such a thing as 'a knower', in one sense, as
when we say that man is 'a knower' because man is of the
class of beings able to have knowledge. But also as when we
speak of a man as 'knowing' because he possesses the science
of grammar. These two are not *capable* in the same way; but
the former's power is, as it were, generic and comparable to
matter; whereas the latter has the power to consider at will,
so long as no extraneous obstacle intervenes. Yet again, only
he who is actually attending to (say) the letter A, is in the
strictest sense *knowing*.   §§ 359–61

Therefore the first two are knowing in potency. But one
has undergone a change through being taught, and is often
altered from the contrary state,[1] whereas the other is moved
to action from simply having sense or grammar without
acting [accordingly]; but in a different way from formerly
when he had not yet acquired any habit [of knowing].[2]

§§ 362–4

[1] i.e., once his potency to know has been actualised. This is the first of the
three cases mentioned above.

[2] 'from formerly etc,' is not in the Greek, 417ᵇ 1; nor referred to by St.
Thomas, § 364.

Nor is 'being acted on' a simple term. It is one thing to be somehow destroyed by a contrary; quite another when what is in potency is maintained by what is in act, and is of a similar nature, being related to the latter as potency to act.

§§ 365–6

For when a man possessed of knowledge becomes actually thinking, there is certainly either no 'alteration'—there being a new perfection in him, and an increase of actuality;—or it is some novel kind of alteration. Hence it is as misleading a statement to say that a man is 'altered' when he thinks, as to say this of the builder when he builds. The process from being in potency to understand and think to actually doing so should not be called instruction, but has by rights some other name.   §§ 367–8

The change from being in potency, in one who learns and receives instruction from another (who actually has learning and teaches) either should not be called a 'being acted upon' (as we have said), or there are two modes of alteration, one a change to a condition of privation, the other to possession and maturity.   §§ 369–72

ST. THOMAS'S COMMENTARY

LECTIO ELEVEN

§ 358. Having explained how the sensitive faculties are both in act and in potency, the Philosopher now goes on to say how they are brought from potency into act. This he does in two parts: first distinguishing between act and potency, and between the diverse ways in which a thing may pass from one state to the other, taking his example from the intellect; and secondly, at 'The first change in the sensitive being',[1] he applies all this to the case of sensation.

As regards the first of these parts he does three things: (a) he states his intention; (b) he distinguishes, at 'For there is such a thing as',[2] between act and potency in the intellect; and (c) he explains, at 'Therefore the first two',[3] how what is potential, in both the two senses of the term which have been distinguished, becomes actual.

First of all,[4] then, he says he is about to discuss potency and act, in order to show the diverse ways in which things can be said to be actual or potential—because so far the two terms have been used 'in one sense only', i.e. without distinctions.

§ 359. Then at 'For there is such a thing as', he distinguishes act and potency in the intellect. We speak, he says, in one sense of potency when we say that man is a knower, referring to his natural capacity for knowledge. Man, we say, is one of that class of beings that know or have knowledge, meaning that his nature *can* know and form habits of knowing. In another sense, however, we say of someone that he knows, meaning that he knows certain definite things; thus we say of one who has the habit of some science—e.g. Grammar—that he is now one who knows.

§ 360. Now, obviously, in both cases the man's capacities are implied by calling him a knower; but not in the same way in both

[1] Lectio 12, §§ 373-4.   [2] 417ᵃ 22.   [3] 417ᵃ 30.   [4] 417ᵃ 21.

cases. In the first case man is said to be 'able' through belonging to a certain genus or 'matter', i.e. his nature has a certain capacity that puts him in this genus, and he is in potency to knowledge as matter to its form. But the second man, with his acquired habit of knowing, is called 'able' because when he wishes he can reflect on his knowledge—unless, of course, he is accidentally prevented, e.g. by exterior preoccupations or by some bodily indisposition.

§ 361. A third case would be that of a man who was actually thinking about something here and now. He it is who most properly and perfectly is a knower in any field; e.g. knowing the letter A, which belongs to the above-mentioned science of Grammar. Of the three, then, the third is simply in act; the first is simply in potency; while the second is in act as compared with the first and in potency as compared with the third. Clearly, then, potentiality is taken in two senses (the first and second man); and actuality also in two senses (the second and third man).

§ 362. Then where he says 'Therefore the first two',[1] he explains (1) how both these types of potency are actualised, and (2), at 'Nor is being acted on',[2] he discusses whether this actualisation is the result of a being acted upon.

First, then, he remarks that while in the two first cases there is potential knowledge, and while potency as such is able to be actualised, there is a difference, in respect of actualisation, between a primary and a secondary potency. One in primary potency to knowledge is brought into act through being, as it were, changed or altered by teaching received from another (the teacher) who already knows actually. And often, he says, this change is from a *contrary* habit; alluding to those who come to actual knowledge from a state of ignorance.

§ 363. Ignorance has two meanings. It can be purely negative: when the ignorant person neither knows the truth nor is involved in the opposite error; and in this case he is simply brought into actual knowledge, not changed by being rid of a contrary habit. On the other hand, ignorance may imply the bad condition of being involved in error contrary to the truth; and to acquire knowledge, then, one must be changed by being delivered from that contrary habit.

§ 364. But one in potency in the secondary sense—i.e. as already

[1] 417ª 30.   [2] 417ᵇ 1.

possessing the habit—passes from the state of having, indeed, sensations or knowledge but not exercising them, into the state of actually knowing something here and now. And this kind of actualisation differs from the other.

§ 365. Then at 'Nor is being acted on'[1] he discusses the question whether both kinds of actualisation can be called being acted upon. First, he explains the different meanings of 'being acted on'. Then at 'For when a man possessed of etc.',[2] he applies these distinctions to the present problem. First, then, he remarks that being acted upon has several meanings, like potency and act. In one sense it implies some kind of destruction caused by a contrary quality. For in the strict sense the state of being passive to action seems to connote, on the side of the patient, a loss of something proper to it through its being overcome by the agent; and this loss is a sort of destruction, either absolutely, as when the patient loses its substantial form, or relatively, as in the loss of an accidental form. And the loss implies a contrariety in the agent, the imposition upon the patient's matter, or being, of a contrary form from outside. In the first and strict sense, then, 'being acted on' means a destruction caused by a contrary agent.

§ 366. In another and looser sense the term connotes any reception of something from outside. And as a receiver is to what it receives as a potency to its actuality; and as actuality is the perfection of what is potential; so being acted upon in this sense implies rather that a certain preservation and perfection of a thing in potency is received from a thing in act. For only the actual can perfect the potential; and actuality is not, as such, contrary to potency; indeed the two are really similar, for potency is nothing but a certain relationship to act. And without this likeness there would be no necessary correspondence between *this* act and *this* potency. Hence potency in this sense is not actualised from contrary to contrary, but rather from like to like, in the sense that the potency resembles its act.

§ 367. Next at 'When a man possessed of',[3] Aristotle discusses whether the actualising of already acquired knowledge involves a being acted upon. And he takes first the transit from secondary potentiality into fullest actuality; and then at 'The change from being in potency',[4] that from primary potentiality into the

---

[1] 417[b] 1.   [2] 417[b] 5.   [3] 417[b] 5.   [4] 417[b] 12.

acquired habit of knowledge. Now, as to the former point, he asserts that this movement into actual thinking is not truly a *passive* being altered; for, as we have seen,[1] no movement into act, *as* movement into act, is such. The term applies, strictly, only to the alteration of a subject from one to the other of two mutually exclusive qualities. But this is not what happens when a man begins to exercise his mind on knowledge he already possesses; rather, he is developing a quality already possessed; as Aristotle says here, it is 'a new perfection in him and an increase of actuality'; for perfection increases with actuality. And if one insists on using the terms 'actuality' and 'being acted upon', they must be taken in a wider and less strict sense. And to illustrate the point he adds that it is just as inept to speak of a thinker being 'altered' when he actually thinks as to say of a builder that he is altered by building.

§ 368. A further conclusion:[2] if it be granted that to pass from habitual to actual knowing is not a reception of new knowledge, but rather a drawing out and perfection of knowledge possessed already, it remains true that to be taught is to acquire new knowledge. Therefore, when a man is brought simply to the *act* of knowing or understanding, this ought not, strictly speaking, to be called 'instruction'; it might be given some other name, though perhaps no other has in fact been found for it.

§ 369. Then at 'The change from being in potency', he discusses whether the transit from potency to act of one who acquires completely fresh knowledge is an 'alteration', in the sense of a 'being acted upon'. He says that when a learner, previously knowing only potentially, is instructed by a master already knowing actually, one should either call this simply *not* a case of alteration and being acted upon, or else distinguish two kinds of alteration. The one kind is 'a change to a condition of privation', i.e. into qualities opposed to those which the thing already has, and incompatible with these, and therefore until now excluded by them. The other kind is 'by a change to a possession and maturity', i.e. through receiving habits and forms which perfect the thing's nature and involve no loss of what it already has. And the learner is altered in this second sense, not in the first.

§ 370. Now this seems to contradict what was said above,[3] that learners often changed from a contrary habit, and thus, it would seem, acquired qualities opposed to their former ones. But really, when one is brought from error to the knowledge of truth there is indeed a certain likeness to the change from one quality to its opposite, but it is only a likeness. For where there is true alteration both the opposed qualities—the terms of the process—are necessarily and essentially involved, e.g. becoming white involves not only white, but also black, or some intermediary colour which in relation to white is a sort of blackness. But where knowledge is acquired it is quite accidental that the learner was previously in error. He could learn without first being in error. Hence it is not in the true sense an alteration.

§ 371. Another difficulty occurs where he says that the learner as such is taught by a master who already knows. For it does not always happen thus; a man may acquire knowledge by finding out for himself. To this we reply that whenever a potential knower becomes an actual knower, he must indeed be actualised by what is already in act. But this may be effected either by a purely extrinsic cause, as when air is lit up by an already actual light, or by an intrinsic cause as well, as when a man is healed both by nature and by a doctor. In this latter case both causes of healing are actual health; for obviously health exists both in the mind of a doctor and in some healthy part of the man's nature (i.e. the heart) in virtue of which the rest of the man recovers health. Doctors make use of such natural means to health as warmth or cold or other variable dispositions, so that we can say that the whole of their skill consists in helping nature to drive out sickness. If nature were strong enough she could do this by herself without a doctor's aid.

§ 372. And the case is the same when a man acquires knowledge. For here again there are two principles involved: an intrinsic one, which a man uses when he finds things out for himself; and an extrinsic one, as when he learns from others. But in both cases a potency is actualised by something already in act. The light of the agent intellect gives a man immediate actual knowledge of the first principles which we know by nature, and in virtue of this actual knowing he is led to actual knowledge of conclusions previously known by him only potentially. In like manner too a teacher can help him towards knowledge, leading him step by step from principles he already knows to conclusions hitherto unknown to him.

Nor would this external aid be necessary if the human mind were always strong enough to deduce conclusions from the principles it possesses by nature; and indeed the power so to deduce *is* present in men, but in varying degrees.

BOOK II, CHAPTER V, CONTINUED

SENSITIVITY
ACTUALISATIONS OF SENSE AND
INTELLECT COMPARED

THE FIRST CHANGE IN THE SENSITIVE BEING IS caused by the parent. When it is born it is already endowed as with knowledge. Actual sensation corresponds to the act of thinking.[1] §§ 373–4

They differ, however. For the actuation of sense-operations is from without; namely from the visible, the audible, and so on for the other senses. The cause [of the difference] is that sensation, even in act, is of particulars: whereas scientific knowledge is of universals. For the latter are, in a way, within the soul itself; hence the act of the intellect is interior and at will; whereas sensation is not from within the soul, and requires that a sense-object be presented. The same holds good of the sciences which concern sense-objects, and for the same reason, i.e. that sense objects are singulars and are external. But there will be time later to deal with these more conclusively. §§ 375–80

For the present it is sufficiently established that 'in potency' is not univocally predicated; but it means one thing when, for example, we say that a child is able to be a soldier, and

---

[1] Altering Pirotta's punctuation to agree with the Greek and the Commentary.

quite another thing when we say this of an adult. The same holds of the sensitive power. Since, however, this distinction has no name, and yet it is settled that the [two stages] differ, and in what way, it is necessary to use the expressions 'to be acted upon' and 'to be altered' as if they were precise terms. The sensitive power is potentially that which the sense-object is actually, as we have said. It is acted upon in so far as it is not like: it becomes like, in being acted upon; and is then such as is the other. §§ 381–2

§ 373. After distinguishing between potency and act, and eluci-
dating in terms of intellectual activity the transit from one state to
the other, the Philosopher now applies what he has said to the case
of sensation. First, he shows how there is a transit from potency to
act in sensing. Secondly, at 'They differ, however'[1] he explains the
difference between the two cases. Thirdly, at 'For the present it is
sufficiently established',[2] he recapitulates what has been said about
sensation.

Regarding the first point, we must take into account that, as in
intellectual cognition, so too in sensation, potency and act are each
two-fold. For what so far possesses no sense-faculty but is due by
nature to have one, is in potency to sensation; and what has the
sense-faculty, but does not yet sense, is in potency to actual sensation in the same way as we have seen in the case of acquired intellectual knowledge. Now, as a subject moves from primary potency
into primary actuality when it acquires knowledge through teaching, so too a subject's primary potency to the possession of a sense-
faculty is actualised by his birth. But whereas a sense-faculty is
natural to every animal,—so that in the act of being generated it
acquires a sense-faculty along with its own specific nature—the
case is not the same with intellectual knowledge; this is not naturally inborn in man; it has to be acquired through application and
discipline.

§ 374. This is what he means by saying that 'the first change in
the sensitive being' is caused by the parent. This 'first change', he
explains, is from sheer potency to the primary actuality; and it is
due to the parent; because there is a power in the semen to actualise
the sensitive soul with all its capacities. Once an animal has been

[1] 417[b] 19.   [2] 417[b] 29.

generated it has its senses in the same way as a man who has been taught possesses knowledge. And when it actually senses it corresponds to the man who actually exercises his knowledge by thinking.

§ 375. Then at 'They differ, however',[1] he sets himself to discriminate between actual sensation and thinking; and he finds the first reason for distinguishing these activities in the difference between their objects, i.e. the sense-objects and intelligible objects which are attained by actual sensation and actual thinking respectively. The sense-objects which actuate sensitive activities—the visible, the audible, etc.—exist outside the soul; the reason being that actual sensation attains to the individual things which exist externally; whereas rational knowledge is of universals which exist somehow within the soul. Whence it is clear that the man who already has scientific knowledge about certain things does not need to seek such things outside himself; he already possesses them inwardly, and is able, unless prevented by some incidental cause, to reflect on them whenever he pleases. But a man cannot sense whatever he pleases; not possessing sense-objects inwardly, he is forced to receive them from outside.

§ 376. And as with sense-activities, so with the sciences of sense-objects; for the latter are individual things existing outside the soul. Therefore a man cannot speculate scientifically on *any* sense-objects, but only on such as he perceives in sensation. But there will be time to treat conclusively of this matter later on, in Book III, where we discuss the intellect and its relation to the senses.[2]

§ 377. Concerning what is said here, we have to ask ourselves (*a*) why sensation is of individual things, whereas science is of universals; and (*b*) how exactly universals exist in the soul.

As to (*a*) we should note that while the sense-faculty is always the function of a bodily organ, intellect is an immaterial power— it is not the actuality of any bodily organ. Now everything received is received in the mode of the recipient. If then all knowledge implies that the thing known is somehow present in the knower (present by its similitude), the knower's actuality as such being the actuality of the thing known, it follows that the sense-faculty receives a similitude of the thing sensed in a bodily and material way, whilst the intellect receives a similitude of the thing

[1] 417^b 19.   [2] §§ 622-36; 671-99; 765-78.

understood in an incorporeal and immaterial way. Now in material and corporeal beings the common nature derives its individuation from matter existing within specified dimensions, whereas the universal comes into being by abstraction from such matter and all the individuating material conditions. Clearly, then, a thing's similitude as received in sensation represents the thing as an individual; as received, however, by the intellect it represents the thing in terms of a universal nature. That is why individuals are known by the senses, and universals (of which are the sciences) by the intellect.

§ 378. As to (*b*), note that the term 'universal' can be taken in two senses. It can refer to the nature itself, common to several things, in so far as this common nature is regarded in relation to those several things; or it can refer to the nature taken simply in itself. Similarly, in a 'white thing' we can consider either the thing that happens to be white or the thing precisely as white. Now a nature—say, human nature,—which can be thought of universally, has two modes of existence: one, material, in the matter supplied by nature; the other, immaterial, in the intellect. As in the material mode of existence it cannot be represented in a universal notion, for in that mode it is individuated by its matter; this notion only applies to it, therefore, as abstracted from individuating matter. But it cannot, as so abstracted, have a *real* existence, as the Platonists thought; man in reality only exists (as is proved in the *Metaphysics*, Book VII)[1] in this flesh and these bones. Therefore it is only in the intellect that human nature has any being apart from the principles which individuate it.

§ 379. Nevertheless, there is no deception when the mind apprehends a common nature apart from its individuating principles; for in this apprehension the mind does not judge *that* the nature exists apart; it merely apprehends this nature without apprehending the individuating principles; and in this there is no falsehood. The alternative would indeed be false—as though I were so to discriminate whiteness from a white man as to understand him *not* to be white. This would be false; but not if I discriminate the two in such wise as to think of the man without giving a thought to his whiteness. For the truth of our conceptions does not require that, merely apprehending anything, we apprehend everything in it.

[1] VII, c.11; 1036ª 25ss.

Hence the mind abstracts, without any falsehood, a genus from a species when it understands the generic nature without considering the differences; or it may abstract the species from individuals when it understands the specific nature, without considering the individuating principles.

§ 380. It is clear, then, that universality can be predicated of a common nature only in so far as it exists in the mind: for a unity to be predicable of many things it must first be conceived apart from the principles by which it is divided into many things. Universals as such exist only in the soul; but the natures themselves, which are conceivable universally, exist in things. That is why the common names that denote these natures are predicated of individuals; but not the names that denote abstract ideas. Socrates is a 'man', not a 'species'—although 'man' is a 'species'.

§ 381. Finally, at 'For the present etc.'[1] he recapitulates his remarks on sensation and observes that only now has it become clear that what we call potency has more than one meaning. It is in one sense that we say that a boy *can* be a soldier, i.e. by a remote potentiality. But in another sense we say that a grown man can be a soldier, i.e. by proximate potentiality. And the same distinction applies to sense-perception; as we have seen,[2] there are two ways of being in potency to sense anything. Though we have found no terms to express this difference, we have seen, nevertheless, that the two kinds of potency differ, and how they differ.

§ 382. And in spite of the fact that a thing which passes from the second stage of potency into act, through actualising its sense-faculty, ought not, strictly speaking, to be said to be 'altered' or 'acted upon', we cannot help using these terms; and this because the sense-faculty is potentially such as the sense-object is actually. It follows that, whilst at the start of the process of being acted upon the faculty is not like its object, at the term of the process it has this likeness. It was because they failed to make this distinction that the earlier philosophers thought that sense-faculties were composed of the same elements as their objects.

[1] 417^b 29.   [2] §§ 373-4.

BOOK II, CHAPTER VI

SENSE OBJECTS IN GENERAL

IN TREATING OF EACH SENSE WE MUST FIRST DISCUSS sense-objects. We speak of a sense-object in three ways: two [kinds of sense-objects] are perceptible *essentially*; one *incidentally*. Of the two former, one is proper to each sense, the other common to all. § 383

Now, I call that the *proper* object of each sense which does not fall within the ambit of another sense, and about which there can be no mistake,—as sight is of colour, and hearing of sound, and taste of savour; while touch has several different objects. Each particular sense can discern these proper objects without deception; thus sight errs not as to colour, nor hearing as to sound;[1] though it might err about *what* is coloured, or *where* it is, or about what is giving forth a sound. This, then, is what is meant by the proper objects of particular senses. §§ 384–5

Now the sense-objects *in common* are movement, rest, number, shape, dimension. Qualities of this kind are proper to no one sense, but are common to all; thus a movement is perceptible both by touch and by sight. These, then, are the essential objects of sensation. § 386

To be a sense-object 'incidentally' is said, for example, of

[1] 'sight' and 'hearing' are not in the Greek, the subject of 'errs not' being 'each sense'; 418ª 15.

a white object that is the son of Diares. This is perceived incidentally because whiteness happens to belong to what is perceived: but the sense[1] is unaffected by that object as such. Of objects *essentially* sense-perceptible, the proper are properly such; and to these the essence of each sense is naturally adapted. §§ 387–98

[1] 'sense' is not in the Greek, 418ᵃ 23.

§ 383. Having explained in general terms how sense-faculties are related to their objects, the Philosopher now begins his examination of objects and faculties separately. This enquiry divides into two parts, of which one is concerned with the sense-objects, and the other, starting at 'It must be taken as a general rule',[1] with the faculties. The first part again divides into (a) a discrimination of the proper or special sense-objects[2] from the rest, and (b) at 'That of which there is sight',[3] an examination of the special objects of each sense. As to (a) he first makes a division of the sense-objects, and then, at 'Now I call that the proper object,'[4] explains this division piecemeal.

Beginning, then, he observes that before we decide what the senses themselves are we must discuss the objects of each sense; for objects are prior to faculties. Now the term sense-object is used in three ways, in one way incidentally[5] and in two ways essentially or absolutely;[6] and of the latter we use one in referring to the special objects proper to each sense, and the other in referring to objects that are common to more than one sense in all sentient beings.[7]

§ 384. Then at 'Now I call that',[8] he explains the members of the division, and first what he means by a special sense-object. He says that he means by this term what is perceived by one sense and by no other, and in respect of which the perceiving sense cannot err; thus it is proper to sight to know colour, to hearing to know sound, to taste to know flavour or savour. Touch, however, has

---

[1] Lectio 24, §§ 551ss. [2] *sensibilia propria.*
[3] Lectio 14, § 399. [4] § 384; 418ᵃ 11.
[5] *per accidens.* [6] *per se.*
[7] *sensibilia illa quae communiter sentiuntur ab omnibus quae sentiunt,* i.e. the *sensibilia communia* (cf. § 385). [8] 418ᵃ 11.

several objects proper to itself: heat and moisture, cold and dryness, the heavy and the light, etc. Each sense judges the objects
proper to itself and is not mistaken about these, e.g. sight with
regard to such and such a colour or hearing with regard to sound.

§ 385. But the senses *can* be deceived both about objects only
incidentally sensible and about objects common to several senses.[1]
Thus sight would prove fallible were one to attempt to judge by
sight *what* a coloured thing was or *where* it was; and hearing likewise if one tried to determine by hearing alone *what* was causing
a sound. Such then are the special objects of each sense.

§ 386. Next, at 'Now the sense-objects',[2] he says, touching the
second member of the division, that the common sense-objects
are five: movement, rest, number, shape and size. These are not
proper to any one sense but are common to all; which we must
not take to mean that all these are common to all the senses, but
that some of them, i.e. number, movement and rest, are common
to all. But touch and sight perceive all five.

It is clear now what are the sense-objects that are such in themselves or absolutely.

§ 387. Then, at 'To be a sense-object incidentally',[3] he takes the
third member of the division. We might, he says, call Diarus or
Socrates *incidentally* a sense-object because each happens to be
white: that is sensed incidentally[4] which happens to belong to
what is sensed *absolutely*.[5] It is accidental to the white thing, which
is sensed absolutely, that it should be Diarus; hence Diarus is a
sense-object incidentally. He does not, as such, act upon the sense
at all.

While it is true, however, that both common and special sense-
objects are all absolutely or of themselves perceptible by sense,[6]
yet, strictly speaking, only the special sense-objects are *directly* perceived,[7] for the very essence and definition of each sense consists
in its being naturally fitted to be affected by some such special
object proper to itself. The nature of each faculty consists in its
relation to its proper object.

§ 388. A difficulty arises here about the distinction between
common and incidental sense-objects. For if the latter are only

[1] *sensibilia communia*; cf. § 383 (fin.).   [2] 418a 17.   [3] 418a 20.
[4] *sentitur per accidens*.   [5] *sentitur per se*.   [6] *per se sensibilia*.
[7] *proprie per se sensibilia*.

perceived in so far as the special objects are perceived, the same is true of the common sense-objects: the eye would never perceive size or shape if it did not perceive colour. It would seem then that the common objects themselves are incidental objects.

§ 389. Now there are some who base the distinction between common and incidental sense-objects upon two reasons. They say that (*a*) the common objects are proper to the 'common sense',[1] as the special objects are to the particular senses; and (*b*) that the proper objects are inseparable from the common objects, but not from the incidental objects.

§ 390. But both answers are inept. The first is based on the fallacy that these common sense-objects are the special object of the 'common sense'. As we shall see later,[2] the common sense is the faculty whereat the modifications affecting all the particular senses terminate; hence it cannot have as its special object anything that is not an object of a particular sense. In fact, it is concerned with those modifications of the particular senses by their objects which these senses themselves cannot perceive; it is aware of these modifications themselves, and of the differences between the objects of each particular sense. It is by the common sense that we are aware of our own life, and that we can distinguish between the objects of different senses, e.g. the white and the sweet.

§ 391. Moreover, even granted that the common sense-objects were proper to the common sense, this would not prevent their being the incidental objects of the particular senses. For we are still studying the sense-objects in relation to the particular senses; the common sense has not yet been elucidated. As we shall see later,[3] the special object of an interior faculty may happen to be only *incidentally* sensible. Nor is this strange; for even as regards the exterior senses, what is in itself and essentially perceptible by one of these exterior senses is *incidentally* perceptible by another; as sweetness is incidentally visible.

§ 392. The second reason is also inept. Whether or no the subject of a sensible quality pertains essentially to that quality makes no difference to the question whether the quality itself is an incidental sense-object. No one, for instance, would maintain that fire, which is the essential and proper *subject* of heat, was directly and in itself an object of touch.[4]

[1] *sensus communis.*   [2] §§ 575–8; 601–14.   [3] §§ 395–6.   [4] As heat is.

§ 393. So we must look for another answer. We have seen[1] that sensation is a being acted upon and altered in some way. Whatever, then, affects the faculty in, and so makes a difference to, its own proper reaction and modification has an intrinsic relation to that faculty and can be called a sense-object in itself or absolutely. But whatever makes no difference to the immediate modification of the faculty we call an incidental sense-object. Hence, the Philosopher says explicitly that the senses are not affected at all by the incidental object as such.

§ 394. Now an object may affect the faculty's immediate reaction in two ways. One way is with respect to the *kind* of agent causing this reaction; and in this way the immediate objects of sensation differentiate sense-experience, inasmuch as one such object is colour, another is sound, another white, another black, and so on. For the various kinds of stimulants of sensation are, in their actuality as such, precisely the special sense-objects themselves; and to them the sense-faculty (as a whole) is by nature adapted;[2] so that precisely by *their* differences is sensation itself differentiated.

On the other hand there are objects which differentiate sensation with respect, not to the *kind* of agent, but to the *mode* of its activity. For as sense-qualities affect the senses corporeally and locally, they do so in different ways, if they are qualities of large or small bodies or are diversely situated, i.e. near, or far, or together, or apart. And it is thus that the *common* sensibles differentiate sensation. Obviously, size and position vary for all the five senses. And not being related to sensation as variations in the *immediate* factors which bring the sense into act, they do not properly differentiate the sense-*faculties*; they remain common to several faculties at once.

§ 395. Having seen how we should speak of the absolute or essential sense-objects, both common and special, it remains to be seen how anything is a sense-object 'incidentally'. Now for an object to be a sense-object incidentally it must first be connected accidentally with an *essential* sense-object; as a man, for instance, may happen to be white, or a white thing happen to be sweet. Secondly, it must be perceived by the one who is sensing; if it were connected with the sense-object without itself being perceived, it could not be said to be sensed incidentally. But this implies that with respect to *some* cognitive faculty of the one sensing

[1] §§ 183; 350–1.   [2] Parenthesis inserted.—(Transl.)

it, it is known, not incidentally, but absolutely. Now this latter faculty must be either another sense-faculty, or the intellect, or the cogitative faculty,[1] or natural instinct.[2] I say 'another sense-faculty', meaning that sweetness is *incidentally visible* inasmuch as a white thing seen is in fact sweet, the sweetness being directly perceptible by another sense, i.e. taste.

§ 396. But, speaking precisely, this is not in the fullest sense an incidental sense-object; it is incidental to the sense of *sight*, but it is essentially *sensible*. Now what is not perceived by any special sense is known by the intellect, if it be a universal; yet not *anything* knowable by intellect in sensible matter should be called a sense-object incidentally, but only what is at once intellectually apprehended *as soon as a sense-experience occurs*. Thus, as soon as I see anyone talking or moving himself my intellect tells me that he is alive; and I can say that I see him live. But if this apprehension is of something *individual*, as when, seeing this particular coloured thing, I perceive this particular man or beast, then the cogitative faculty (in the case of man at least) is at work, the power which is also called the 'particular reason' because it correlates individualised notions, just as the 'universal reason' correlates universal ideas.

§ 397. Nevertheless, this faculty belongs to sensitivity; for the sensitive power at its highest—in man, in whom sensitivity is joined to intelligence—has some share in the life of intellect. But the lower animals' awareness of individualised notions is called natural instinct, which comes into play when a sheep, e.g., recognises its offspring by sight, or sound, or something of that sort.

§ 398. Note, however, that the cogitative faculty differs from natural instinct. The former apprehends the individual thing as existing in a common nature, and this because it is united to intellect in one and the same subject. Hence it is aware of a man as this *man*, and this tree as this *tree*; whereas instinct is not aware of an individual thing as in a common nature, but only in so far as this individual thing is the term or principle of some action or passion. Thus a sheep knows this particular lamb, not as this lamb, but simply as something to be suckled; and it knows this grass just in so far as this grass is its food. Hence, other individual things which have no relation to its own actions or passions it does not

---

[1] *vis cogitativa.*   [2] *vis aestimativa.*

apprehend at all by natural instinct. For the purpose of natural instinct in animals is to direct them in their actions and passions, so as to seek and avoid things according to the requirements of their nature.

BOOK II, CHAPTER VII

SIGHT. ITS OBJECT

THAT OF WHICH THERE IS SIGHT IS THE VISIBLE; and the visible is colour, and also something which, though it has no name, we can state descriptively. It will be evident what we mean when we have gone further into the matter. § 399

For the visible is colour, and it is this of which visibility is predicated essentially; not, however, by definition, but because it has in itself the cause of being visible. For every colour is a motivating force upon the actually transparent: this is its very nature. Hence nothing[1] is visible without light; but by light each and every colour can be seen. Wherefore, we must first decide what light is. §§ 400–3

There is, accordingly, something transparent. By transparent I mean that which is, indeed, visible, yet not of itself, or absolutely, but by virtue of concomitant colour. Air and water and many solids are such. But transparency does not depend on either air or water as such, but on the same quality being found in both, and in the eternal sphere above as well. § 404

Light is the act of this transparency, as such: but in potency this [transparency] is also darkness.[2] Now, light is a kind of colour of the transparent, in so far as this is actualised by fire

---

[1] 'Hence it (colour) is not visible without light', 418ᵇ 1.

[2] Or perhaps rather: 'where this transp. is potential, there is darkness', 418ᵇ 10.

or something similar to the celestial body; which contains indeed something of one and the same nature as fire.   § 405

We have then indicated what the transparent is, and what light is; that light is not fire or any bodily thing, nor any emanation from a body—[if it were this last,] it would be a sort of body, and so be fire or the presence of something similar in the transparent.[1]   § 406

For it is impossible for two bodies to exist in the same place at the same time.   § 407

Light seems to be the contrary of darkness; and the latter is the privation of this quality in the transparent. So it is plain that the presence of this is light.   § 408

Empedocles (or anyone else who may have said the same) was wrong when he said that light was borne along and extended between the earth and its envelope, unperceived by us. This is in contradiction alike to sound reasoning and to appearance. Such a thing might happen unobserved over a small space: but that it should remain unnoticed from the east to the west is a very extravagant postulate.   §§ 409–26

---

[1] '... nor any emanation from a body (for then it would still be a sort of body) but the presence of fire or something of that kind in the transparent', 418^b 15–17. St. Thomas agrees with M., § 406.

ST. THOMAS'S COMMENTARY
LECTIO FOURTEEN

§ 399. Having distinguished the proper sense-objects from the common, and from those that are sensible incidentally, the Philosopher now treats of the proper object of each sense: first of the proper object of sight; then, at 'Now let us start',[1] of that of hearing; then, at 'It is not so easy', of that of smell;[2] then, at 'The tasteable',[3] of that of taste; and lastly, at 'The same reasoning holds', of that of touch.[4]

As to sight, he discusses, first, its object, and then, at 'At present what is clear',[5] how this object comes to be seen. Touching the object of sight, he does two things. First, he determines what is the visible, dividing it into two. Secondly, he deals with either visible, at 'For the visible is colour'. He says then, first,[6] that, the proper sense-object being that which each sense perceives *of itself exclusively*, the sense-object of which the special recipient is sight is the visible. Now in the visible two things are included; for both colour is a visible, and also something else, which can be described in speech, but has no proper name; which visible belongs to things which can be seen by night, such as glow-worms and certain fungi on oak-trees and the like, concerning which the course of this treatise will inform us more clearly as we gain a deeper understanding of the visible; but we have to start from colour which is the more obvious visible.

§ 400. Then, at 'For the visible',[7] he begins to define both objects of sight: first colour and then, at 'Not all visible things',[8] that of which he says that it has no proper name. As to colour he does two

---

[1] Lectio 16, § 439ss.   [2] Lectio 19, § 479ss.
[3] Lectio 21, § 501ss.   [4] Lectio 22, § 517ss.
[5] Lectio 15, § 431ss.   [6] 418^a 26.
[7] 418^a 29.   [8] Lectio 15, § 429; 419^a 1.

things: first, he shows what colour has to do with visibility; secondly, at 'There is, accordingly, something transparent'[1] he settles what is required for colour to be seen.

First of all, then, he says that, colour being visible, it is visible of itself, for colour as such is essentially visible.[2]

§ 401. 'Essentially'[3] is said in two ways. In one way, when the predicate of a proposition falls within the definition of the subject, e.g. 'man is an animal'; for animal enters into the definition of man. And since that which falls within the definition of anything is in some way the cause of it, in cases such as these the predicate is said to be the cause of the subject. In another way, on the contrary, when the subject of the proposition falls within the definition of the predicate, as when it is said that a nose is snub, or a number is even; for snubness is nothing but a quality of a nose, and evenness of a number which can be halved; and in these cases the subject is a cause of the predicate.

§ 402. Now colour is essentially visible in this second manner, not in the first; for visibility is a quality,[4] as being snub is a quality of a nose. And this is why he says that colour is visible 'essentially', but 'not by definition'; that is to say, not because visibility is placed in its definition, but because it possesses of itself the reason why it should be visible, as a subject possesses in itself the reason for its own peculiar qualities.

§ 403. Which he proves by this, that every colour as such is able to affect what is actually diaphanous. The diaphanous is the same as the transparent (e.g. air or water), and colour has it in its nature to actualise further an actual transparency. And from this, that it affects the actually transparent, it is visible; whence it follows that colour is of its nature visible. And since the transparent is brought to its act only by light, it follows that colour is not visible without light. And therefore before explaining how colour is seen, we must discuss light.

§ 404. Then, at 'There is, accordingly',[5] he discusses those things without which colour cannot be seen, namely the transparent and light; and this in three sections. First, he explains the transparent. Secondly, at 'Light is',[6] he treats of the transparent's actuality, i.e.

---

[1] § 404; 418^b 4.   [2] 418^a 29–418^b 2.   [3] *Per se*; or *secundum se* (§ 400).

[4] *est quaedam passio.*   [5] 418^b 4.   [6] 418^b 9.

light. Thirdly, he shows how the transparent is receptive of colour, at 'Now that only can receive colour'.[1]

To begin with, therefore, he says that if colour is that which of its nature affects the transparent, the latter must be, and in fact is, that which has no intrinsic colour to make it visible of itself, but is receptive of colour from without in a way which renders it somehow visible. Examples of the transparent are air and water and many solid bodies, such as certain jewels and glass. Now, whereas other accidents pertaining to the elements or to bodies constituted from them, are in these bodies on account of the nature of those elements (such as heat and cold, weight and lightness, etc.), transparency does not belong to the nature of air or water as such, but is consequent upon some quality common, not only to air and water, which are corruptible bodies, but also to the celestial bodies, which are perpetual and incorruptible. For at least some of the celestial bodies are manifestly transparent. We should not be able to see the fixed stars of the eighth sphere unless the lower spheres of the planets were transparent or diaphanous. Hence it is evident that to be transparent is not a property consequent on the nature of air or water, but of some more generic nature, in which the cause of transparency is to be found, as we shall see later.[2]

§ 405. Next, at 'Light etc.',[3] he explains light, first stating the truth, then dismissing an error. He says, to begin with, that light is the act of the transparent as such. For it is evident that neither air nor water nor anything of that sort is actually transparent unless it is luminous. Of itself the transparent is in potency to both light and darkness (the latter being a privation of light) as primary matter is in potency both to form and the privation of form. Now light is to the transparent as colour is to a body of definite dimensions: each is the act and form of that which receives it. And on this account he says that light is the colour, as it were, of the transparent, in virtue of which the transparent is made actually so by some light-giving body, such as fire, or anything else of that kind, or by a celestial body. For to be full of light and to communicate it is common to fire and to celestial bodies, just as to be diaphanous is common to air and water and the celestial bodies.

§ 406. Then, at 'We have then indicated',[4] he rejects a false opinion on light; and this in two stages. First, he shows that light is

---

[1] 418ᵇ 27, § 427.　　　[2] § 422.　　　[3] 418ᵇ 9.　　　[4] 418ᵇ 13.

not a body; then he refutes an objection brought against the arguments which prove that light is not a body, at 'Empedocles . . .
was wrong'.[1] As to the first point he does three things.

(*a*) He states his own view, saying that, once it is clear what the
transparent is, and what light is, it is evident that light is neither
fire (as some have said, positing three kinds of fire, the combustible, and flame, and light); nor a body at all, or anything flowing
from a body, as Democritus supposed, asserting that light consisted of atomic particles emanating from luminous bodies. If there
were these emanations from bodies, they would themselves be
bodies, or something corporeal, and light would thus be nothing
other than fire, or something material of that sort, present in the
diaphanous; which is the same as to say that light is a body or an
emanation from a body.[2]

§ 407. (*b*) At 'For it is impossible',[3] he proves his own hypothesis
thus. It is impossible for two bodies to be in one place at one time.
If therefore light were a body, it could not co-exist with a diaphanous body; but this is false; therefore light is not a body.

§ 408. (*c*) At 'Light seems',[4] he shows that light does co-exist
with the diaphanous body. For contraries exist in one and the same
subject. But light and darkness are contraries in the manner in
which a quality and its privation are contraries, as is stated in the
Metaphysics, Book X.[5] Obviously, darkness is a privation of this
quality, i.e. of light in the diaphanous body—which is therefore
the subject of darkness. Hence too, the presence of this quality is
light. Therefore light co-exists with the diaphanum.

§ 409. Then at 'Empedocles . . . was wrong',[6] he refutes an answer to one argument which might be urged against those who
hold that light is a body. For it is possible to argue thus against
them: if light were a body, illumination ought to be a local motion
of light passing through the transparent; but no local movement of
any body can be sudden or instantaneous; therefore, illumination
would be, not instantaneous but successive, according to this view.

§ 410. Of which the contrary is a fact of experience; for in the
very instant in which a luminous body becomes present, the transparent is illuminated all at once, not part after part. So Empedocles,
and all others of the same opinion, erred in saying that light

[1] 418[b] 20.   [2] 418[b] 13-17.   [3] 418[b] 17.
[4] 418[b] 18.   [5] X, c.4; 1055[a] 30ss.   [6] 418[b] 20.

was borne along by local motion, as a body is; and that it spread out successively through space, which is the medium between the earth and its envelope, i.e. the sky;[1] and that this successive motion escapes our observation, so that the whole of space *seems* to us to be illuminated simultaneously.

§ 411. For this assertion is irrational. The illumination of the transparent simply and solely presupposes the placing of a luminous body over against the one illumined, with no intervening obstacle.

§ 412. Again, it contradicts appearances. One might indeed allow that successive local motion over a small space could escape our notice; but that a successive movement of light from the eastern to the western horizon should escape our notice is so great an improbability as to appear quite impossible.

§ 413. But as the subject matter under discussion is threefold, i.e. the nature of light, and of transparency, and the necessity of light for seeing, we must take these three questions one by one.

On the nature of light various opinions have been held. Some, as we have seen, held that light was a body; being led to this by certain expressions used in speaking of light. For instance, we are accustomed to say that a ray 'passes through' the air, that it is 'thrown back', that rays 'intersect', and so forth; which all seem to imply something corporeal.

§ 414. But this theory is groundless, as the arguments here adduced of Aristotle show, to which others might easily be added. Thus it is hard to see how a body could be suddenly multiplied over the whole hemisphere, or come into existence or vanish, as light does; nor how the mere intervention of an opaque body should extinguish light in any part of a transparent body if light itself were a body. To speak of the motion or rebounding of light is to use metaphors, as when we speak of heat 'proceeding into' things that are being heated or being 'thrown back' when it meets an obstacle.

§ 415. Then there are those who maintain, on the contrary, that light is spiritual in nature. Otherwise, they say, why should we use the term 'light' in speaking of intellectual things? For we say that intellectual things possess a certain intelligible 'light'. But this also is inadmissible.

[1] *caelum.*

§ 416. For it is impossible that any spiritual or intelligible nature should fall within the apprehension of the senses; whose power, being essentially embodied, cannot acquire knowledge of any but bodily things. But if anyone should say that there is a spiritual 'light' other than the light that is sense-perceived, we need not quarrel with him; so long as he admits that the light which is sense-perceived is not spiritual in nature. For there is no reason why quite different things should not have the same name.[1]

§ 417. The reason, in fact, why we employ 'light' and other words referring to vision in matters concerning the intellect is that the sense of sight has a special dignity; it is more spiritual and more subtle than any other sense. This is evident in two ways. First, from the *object* of sight. For objects fall under sight in virtue of properties which earthly bodies have in common with the heavenly bodies. On the other hand, touch is receptive of properties which are proper to the elements (such as heat and cold and the like); and taste and smell perceive properties that pertain to compound bodies, according as these are variously compounded of heat and cold, moisture and dryness; sound, again, is due to local movement which, indeed, is also common to earthly and heavenly bodies, but which, in the case of the cause of sound, is a different kind of movement from that of the heavenly bodies, according to the opinion of Aristotle. Hence, from the very nature of the object it would appear that sight is the highest of the senses; with hearing nearest to it, and the others still more remote from its dignity.

§ 418. The same point will appear if we consider the *way* in which the sense of sight is exercised. In the other senses what is spiritual in their exercise is always accompanied by a material change.[1] I mean by 'material change' what happens when a quality is received by a subject according to the *material* mode of the subject's own existence, as e.g. when anything is cooled, or heated, or moved about in space; whereas by a 'spiritual change' I mean, here, what happens when the likeness of an object is received in the sense-organ, or in the medium between object and organ, *as a form causing knowledge,* and not merely as a form in matter. For there is a difference between the mode of being which a sensible form has in the senses and that which it has in the thing sensed. Now in the case of touching and tasting (which is a kind of touching) it is clear

[1] *immutatio naturalis.*

that a material change occurs: the organ itself grows hot or cold by contact with a hot or cold object; there is not merely a spiritual change. So too the exercise of smell involves a sort of vaporous exhalation; and that of sound involves movement in space. But seeing involves only a spiritual change—hence its maximum spirituality; with hearing as the next in this order. These two senses are therefore the most spiritual, and are the only ones under our control.[1] Hence the use we make of what refers to them—and especially of what refers to sight—in speaking of intellectual objects and operations.

§ 419. Then again some have simply identified light with the manifestation of colour. But this is patently untrue in the case of things that shine by night, their colour, nevertheless, remaining obscure.

§ 420. Others, on the other hand, have said that light was the substantial form of the sun, and that the brightness proceeding therefrom (in the form of colours in the air) had the sort of being that belongs to objects causing knowledge as such. But both these propositions are false. The former, because no substantial form is in and of itself an object of sense perception; it can only be intellectually apprehended. And if it is said that what the sense sees in the sun is not light itself but the splendour of light, we need not dispute about names, provided only it be granted that what we call light, i.e. the sight-perceived thing, is not a substantial form. And the latter proposition too is false; because whatever simply has the being of a thing causing knowledge does not, as such, cause material change; but the rays from the heavenly bodies do in fact materially affect all things on earth. Hence our own conclusion is that, just as the corporeal elements have certain active qualities through which they affect things materially, so light is the active quality of the heavenly bodies; by their light these bodies are active; and this light is in the third species of quality, like heat.

§ 421. But it differs from heat in this: that light is a quality of the primary change-effecting body,[2] which has no contrary: therefore light has no contrary: whereas there is a contrary to heat. And because there is no positive contrary to light, there is no place for a contrary disposition in its recipient: therefore, too, its matter, i.e.

[1] *et soli disciplinabiles.*

[2] *qualitas primi corporis alterantis, quod non habet contrarium.*

the transparent body, is always as such immediately disposed to its form. That is why illumination occurs instantaneously, whereas what can become hot only becomes so by degrees. Now this participation or effect of light in a diaphanum is called 'luminosity'.[1] And if it comes about in a direct line to the lightened body, it is called a 'ray';[2] but if it is caused by the reflection of a ray upon a light-receiving body, it is called 'splendour'.[3] But luminosity is the common name for every effect of light in the diaphanum.

§ 422. So much being admitted as to the nature of light, we can easily understand why certain bodies are always actually lucent, whilst others are diaphanous, and others opaque. Because light is a quality of the primary change-effecting body, which is the most perfect and least material of bodies, those among other bodies which are the most formal and the most mobile to actualisation are always actually lucent; and the next in this order are diaphanous; whilst those that are extremely material, being neither luminous of themselves nor receptive of light, are opaque. One may see this in the elements: fire is lucent by nature, though its light does not appear except in other things. Air and water, being more material, are diaphanous; whilst earth, the most material of all, is opaque.

§ 423. With regard to the third point (the necessity of light for seeing), note that it has been the opinion of some that not merely seeing, but the object of seeing, i.e. colour as such, presupposed the presence of light; that colour as such had no power to affect a transparent medium; that it does this only through light. An indication of this was, they said, that one who stands in the shadow can see what is in the light, but one who stands in the light cannot see what is in shadow. The cause of this fact, they said, lay in a correspondence between sight and its object: as seeing is a single act, so it must bear on an object formally single; which would not be the case if colour were visible of itself—not in virtue of light—and light *also* were visible of itself.[4]

§ 424. Now this view is clearly contrary to what Aristotle says here, 'and . . . has in itself the cause of being visible';[5] hence,

[1] *lumen.*   [2] *radius.*   [3] *splendor.*

[4] Pirotta's correction of *et item lumen* to *et tantum lumen* is not acceptable in view of the context.

[5] §§ 400–3; 418ª 30.

following his opinion, I say that light is necessary for seeing, not because of colour, in that it actualises colours (which some say are in only potency so long as they are in darkness), but because of the transparent medium which light renders actual, as the text states.

§ 425. And in proof of this, note that every form is, as such, a principle of effects resembling itself. Colour, being a form, has therefore of itself the power to impress its likeness on the medium. But note also that there is this difference between the form with a complete, and the form with an incomplete, power to act, that the former is able not merely to impress its likeness on matter, but even to dispose matter to fit it for this likeness; which is beyond the power of the latter. Now the active power of colour is of the latter sort; for it is, in fact, only a kind of light somehow dimmed by admixture of opaque matter. Hence it lacks the power to render the medium fully disposed to receive colour; but this pure light can do.

§ 426. Whence it is also clear that, as light is, in a certain way, the very substance of colour, all visible objects as such share in the same nature; nor does colour require to be made visible by some other, extrinsic, light. That colours in light are visible to one standing in the shade is due to the medium's having been sufficiently illumined.

BOOK II, CHAPTER VII, CONTINUED

SIGHT. HOW COLOUR IS SEEN

OW THAT ONLY CAN RECEIVE COLOUR WHICH has none, as only that which is soundless, can receive sound. What is without colour is the transparent and the invisible, or what is barely seen, being dark.[1] The transparent is precisely of this nature when it is not in act, but in potency. For the same substance is sometimes dark, sometimes light. §§ 427–8

Not all visible things, however, are visible in light, but only the colour proper to each. There are certain things which are, indeed, not seen in light, but which produce a sensation in darkness, such as those which burn or are luminous. These are not called by any one term. Such are the fungi of certain trees, horn, fish-heads, scales, and eyes. But the *colour* proper to each of these is not perceived. Why these things are thus seen is matter for another enquiry. §§ 429–30

At present what is clear is that what is seen in light is colour; [and that] therefore it is not seen without light. For to be colour is to be able to move the transparent into act; and this act of the transparent is light. A plain proof whereof is that if one places on the sight itself a coloured object, it is not seen. But colour moves the transparent medium (say, air); and the sensitive organ is moved by this extended continuum. §§ 431–2

[1] 'such as what is "dark" ', 418^b 29.

Democritus put forward the erroneous opinion that if the medium were a vacuum, perception would be everywhere exact, even of an ant in the sky. This is, however, impossible; for only when the sensitive faculty is affected does vision occur. This cannot, however, be effected by the colour seen, in itself. It must therefore be due to the medium. If there were a vacuum, a thing, so far from being perceived clearly, would not be seen at all. We have stated, then, why it is necessary that colour be seen in light.   §§ 433–5

But fire is seen in both darkness and light: necessarily, for the transparent is made light by it.   § 436

The same account holds for both sound and smell. No sensation is produced when either of these touches the organ: but a *medium* is affected by sound and smell, and the sense organ of one or the other sense by the medium. But if one places an object that sounds or smells upon the sense-organ itself, no sensation occurs. The same holds good of touch and taste, although this is not obvious. The reason for this will be made clear later.   § 437

The medium of sound is air; that of smell has no special name. For as there is a common quality for colour, to wit, the transparent, in air and water, so there is a common quality in them for smell. For it seems that aquatic animals possess a sense of smell. But man, and whatever living things breathe, are unable to smell except when breathing. The cause of this will be dealt with later.   § 438

§ 427. After treating of colour and the transparent medium and luminosity, the Philosopher now proceeds to explain how the medium is related to colour. It is clear, from the foregoing, that the transparent medium is receptive of colour; for colour, we have seen, acts upon it. Now what is receptive of colour must itself be colourless, as what receives sound must be soundless; for nothing receives what it already has. The transparent medium is therefore colourless.

§ 428. But, as bodies are visible by their colours, the transparent medium must itself be invisible. Yet since one and the same power apprehends contrary qualities, it follows that sight, which apprehends light, also apprehends darkness. Hence, although the transparent medium of itself possesses neither light nor colour, being receptive of both, and is thus not of itself visible in the way that things bright or coloured are visible, it can, all the same, be *called* visible in the same sort of way as dark things and scarcely visible things are so called. The diaphanum is therefore a kind of darkness, so long as it is not actually but only potentially transparent: the same thing is the subject, sometimes of darkness, sometimes of light. Thus the diaphanum, while it lacks luminosity and is only potentially transparent, is in a state of darkness.

§ 429. Then at 'Not all',[1] having decided about colour, which is made visible by light, he reaches a conclusion about that other visible object of which he said above[2] that it had no proper name. He observes that not all things depend on light for being seen, but only the colour that is proper to each particular thing. Some things, e.g. certain animals that appear fiery and lucent in the dark, are not visible in the light, but only in darkness. There are many such

---

[1] 419ª 1.   [2] § 399.

things, including the fungi of oaks, the horn of certain beasts and heads of certain fish, and some animals' scales and eyes. But while all these things are visible in the dark, the *colour* proper to each is not seen in the dark. The *things* are seen both in light and in darkness; but in darkness only as bright objects, in light as coloured objects.

§ 430. The reason why they are seen shining in the darkness is another matter. Aristotle only mentions the fact incidentally, in order to show the relation of the visible to luminosity. This, however, seems to be the reason for their being visible in the dark, that such things have in their constitution something of light, inasmuch as the brightness of fire and the transparency of air and water is not entirely smothered in them by the opacity of earth. But having only a small amount of light, their brightness is obscured in the presence of a greater light. Hence in the light they appear not as bright, but only as coloured. The light in their constitution is so weak that it is unable perfectly to actualise the potentially transparent medium to receive the full effect of the colours which by nature it is fitted to receive. Hence, by this light neither their own colour, nor that of other things, is seen: but only their brightness. For brightness, being a more effective agent upon the medium than colour, and in itself more visible, can be seen with less alteration of the medium than colour requires.

§ 431. Next, at 'At present what is clear',[1] he explains how colour actually affects sight, first pointing out what this necessarily presupposes, and then, at 'The same account holds',[2] indicating a like necessary condition in the case of the other senses. As to the former point, he first decides what is the truth of the matter, and then at 'Democritus etc.',[3] sets aside an error. First, then, he says that we are now clear that what is seen in light is colour, and that colour is invisible without light; and this because, as has been explained, colour of its nature acts upon a transparent medium, and it does this in virtue of light, which is the latter's actuality. Hence light is necessary if colour is to be seen.[4]

§ 432. An indication of this[5] is the fact that if a coloured body is placed upon the organ of sight it cannot be seen; for then there remains no transparent medium to be affected by the colour. The pupil of the eye is indeed some such medium, but, so long as the

[1] 419ᵃ 7.   [2] 419ᵃ 25.   [3] 419ᵃ 15.   [4] 419ᵃ 7ss.   [5] 419ᵃ 11.

coloured body remains placed upon it, it lacks actual transparency. There has to be a medium, say air or something of the kind, which, being actualised by colour, itself acts upon the organ of sight as upon a body continuous with itself. For bodies only affect one another through actual contact.

§ 433. Then at 'Democritus etc.',[1] he sets aside an erroneous view. Democritus, he says, was wrong in thinking that if the medium between the eye and the thing seen were a vacuum, any object, however small, would be visible at any distance, e.g. an ant in the sky. This cannot be. For if anything is to be seen it must actually affect the organ of sight. Now it has been shown that this organ as such is not affected by an *immediate* object—such as an object placed upon the eye. So there must be a medium between organ and object. But a vacuum is not a medium; it cannot receive or transmit effects from the object. Hence through a vacuum nothing would be seen at all.

§ 434. Democritus went wrong because he thought that the reason why distance diminishes visibility was that the medium is of itself an impediment to the action of the visible object upon sight. But it is not so. The transparent medium as such is not in the least incompatible with luminosity or colour; on the contrary, it is proximately disposed to their reception; a sign of which is that it is illumined or coloured instantaneously. The real reason why distance diminishes visibility, is that everything seen is seen within the angle of a triangle, or rather pyramid, whose base is the object seen and apex in the eye that sees.

§ 435. It makes no difference whether seeing takes place by a movement from the eye outwards, so that the lines enclosing the triangle or pyramid run from the eye to the object, or *e converso*, so long as seeing does involve this triangular or pyramidal figure; which is necessary because, since the object is larger than the pupil of the eye, its effect upon the medium has to be scaled down gradually until it reaches the eye. And, obviously, the longer are the sides of a triangle or pyramid the smaller is the angle at the apex, provided that the base remains the same. The further away, then, is the object, the less does it appear—until at a certain distance it cannot be seen at all.

§ 436. Next, at 'But fire',[2] he explains how fire and bright bodies

[1] 419ª 15.   [2] 419ª 23.

are seen—which are visible not only, like coloured objects, in the light, but even in the dark. There is a necessary reason for this, namely that fire contains enough light to actualise perfectly the transparent medium, so that both itself and other things become visible. Nor does its light fade out in the presence of a greater light, as does that of the objects mentioned above.[1]

§ 437. Then, at 'The same account . . .',[2] he shows how the case of the other senses is similar to sight. No sound or odour, e.g., is perceived if there is *immediate* contact with the organ in question. There must be a medium affected by sound or odour, which itself then affects our sense of hearing or of smell. A sounding or odorous body placed upon the organ is not perceived as such. The same is true even of touch and taste, though, for a reason to be given later,[3] this is less evident.

§ 438. Finally, at 'The medium of sound',[4] he states what is the medium in hearing and smelling. That of hearing is air, and that of smelling is something common to air and water—just as both of these provide a medium for colour in so far as each is a transparency. There is indeed no name for the quality in air and water which provides the medium for odour; but it certainly is not transparency. And that both air and water are conductors of smell he shows from the fact that marine animals have a sense of smell. Man, however, and other animals that walk and breathe, only smell by breathing; which proves that air is the medium of smell. This fact will be explained later.[5]

[1] §§ 429–30.   [2] 419ᵃ 25.   [3] §§ 526–8; 542.
[4] 419ᵃ 32.   [5] §§ 491–500.

BOOK II, CHAPTER VIII

SOUND. ITS CAUSES. ECHO

NOW LET US START BY TREATING OF SOUND AND hearing. Sound is twofold: the sort that is actual, and the sort that is potential. For certain things, we say, have no sound, such as sponges, wool and fur; while others, such as bronze and all other smooth and hard things, have sound, because they are able to produce it, i.e. to cause actual sound in the medium and in the hearing. §§ 439–41

Sound in act is always of something, on something, in something: for it is caused by percussion. Hence it is impossible for anything by itself, as a single thing, to produce sound. For there must be one thing that strikes and another that is struck; hence whatever emits sound does so 'on something', i.e. by contact with something—which, when touched with a blow, sounds. And the blow necessarily implies movement.

§ 442

As we said before, it is not a blow upon anything whatever that gives sound: wool makes no sound, although it be struck; but bronze, or anything smooth and hollow, is such. Bronze because it is smooth; whilst hollow things by repercussion produce many 'blows' after the first, since what is set in motion cannot find an outlet. §§ 443–4

Further: sound is heard in air and water, but less in water. It is, however, neither air nor water that, properly, sounds; there must be a percussion of solid objects on each other, and on air. This happens if air is confined when struck, and cannot disperse. Hence if the striking is rapid and violent sound results. For the movement of what strikes must be sudden, if it is to out-run the breaking-up of the air; just as if one were to strike a rapidly-moving heap of sand or pile of stones.

§§ 445-6

Echo arises when air rebounds like a ball against air rendered a compact unity by a restraining vessel that prevents its dispersion.

§§ 447-9

It seems there is always some echo, but not always a clear one. For the same occurs with sound as with light; which also is always reflected: otherwise it would not spread to every part, but beyond the area illuminated by the sun there would be darkness. Still, it is not [always] reflected as it is reflected by water or bronze or other smooth things; hence it makes the shadow by which we discern the boundaries of light.[1]

§ 450

[1] This rendering is governed by the Commentary (§ 450). But in the Greek what 'makes the shadow etc.' is the reflection from water, etc.

ST. THOMAS'S COMMENTARY

LECTIO SIXTEEN

§ 439. Having disposed of the visible, the Philosopher now deals with the audible, that is, with sound. This section divides into two parts. In the first he deals with sound in general. In the second he deals with one kind of sound, namely voice, at 'Voice' etc.[1] The first part is again divided into two parts. First, he deals with sound itself; then with difference of sound, at 'Differences in sonorous things'.[2] The former part again subdivides. First, he reaches a conclusion on sound; then he raises a doubt about this conclusion, at 'Is it that which strikes'.[3] The former of these sections again divides into two conclusions, the first on the origin of sound, and the second on the way that sound affects the hearing, at 'Empty space'.[4]

Should it be asked why he now raises the question of the origin of sound, whereas he did not deal with the production of colour, but only with colour's effects on sense-organ and medium, the answer is that colour and odour and taste and the tangible qualities have a fixed and permanent existence in their subjects. The consideration therefore of these qualities in themselves is one thing, and that of the way they affect the senses is another. The two questions are quite distinct. So the Philosopher deals with the origin of colour, taste and smell in his work *De Sensu et Sensato*;[5] and with that of tangible qualities in the *De Generatione*,[6] and in part also in the *Meteorologica*;[7] whilst in the present book he is only considering the objects of sensation in so far as they affect the sense-organs. But as sound is caused by change and has no fixed and stable existence

---

[1] Lectio 18, §§ 466ss.   [2] Lectio 17, §§ 461ss.
[3] *ibid.*, § 459.   [4] *ibid.*, § 451.
[5] *De Sensu et Sens*, cc.3–5.   [6] *De Gen. et Corr.*, II, c.2; 329^{b} 5ss.
[7] *Meteor.*, I, c.3; 340^{b} 5ss.: and II, cc.8–12; 385^{a} 1ss.

in a subject, but actually *consists in* a movement or change, therefore it can be considered at one and the same time in its objective origin and in its effect on the senses. Its origin, then, is regarded under two aspects: first he deals with the primary origin of sound; and then, at 'Echo arises',[1] with its secondary origin, produced by reverberation. As to the primary origin, he first explains that sound is sometimes in act and sometimes in potency; after which he shows how sound comes to be in act, at 'Sound in act'.[2]

§ 440. He says, then, first that, before dealing with touch and taste, we must consider sound and smell; but first sound, because it is more spiritual, as has been shown.[3] We speak of sound in two ways: as in act and as in potency. We say a thing has a sound when it is actually sounding, and also when it is only able to make sounds; as when we say, 'this bell sounds well', though it may not be actually ringing. In the same way we say of some things that they have no sound, meaning that they have no power to produce sound, e.g. sponges and similar soft objects; whereas other things, on the contrary, are said to sound because they are especially apt to produce sound, such as bronze, and other smooth and even materials. So it is clear that sound is sometimes spoken of as potential, and sometimes as actual.

§ 441. But the actuality of sound involves the medium and the faculty of hearing. For we can speak of a sense-object as actual in two ways: (1) So far as the object is actually being sensed, i.e. when its likeness is affecting the sense-organ. In this way a sound is actual when it is heard. (2) So far as the object actually is such that it can be sensed, but is such simply in its own objective being, outside the senses. And in this way the other sense-objects, colour, odour, savour, etc., exist actually in coloured or odorous or savourable bodies. But not so sound; for in a sound-productive body there is sound only potentially: actual sound exists only when the medium is affected by a disturbance from that body. Therefore the act of sound exists, he says, in the medium and in the hearing, but not in the audible body.

§ 442. Then at 'Sound in act',[4] Aristotle shows how sound actually comes about: first with regard to the number of factors required for sound to come into act; and then, at 'As we said before',[5]

[1] § 447; 419^b 25.   [2] § 442; 419^b 9.   [3] §§ 417–18.
[4] 419^b 9.   [5] 419^b 13.

with regard to what these factors are. First then, there are three concurrent factors in sound: Sound is *of* something, *on* something, *in* something. Therefore no single thing by itself can produce sound—the reason (or sign) of this being that the cause of sound is percussion, which implies a thing struck and a striker. Hence his saying '*of* something, *on* something', i.e. *of* the thing striking and *on* the thing struck. What produces sound must touch something as with a sudden blow. Now a blow implies local movement, which implies a medium. Hence the need for a medium, if sound is to be produced actually. Hence his saying, '*in* something'.

§ 443. When he says 'As we said before',[1] he shows what sort of factors produce sound. And first he shows of what sort must the striking and the struck objects be; and then, at 'Further etc.',[2] what sort of thing the medium must be. First, then, as we have already noted, sound is not produced by striking any material body whatever. Wool and sponges and suchlike soft things cannot give out sound even when struck; the reason being that soft things yield to the impact, so that no air is expelled by it—no air in which a sound might be formed by the blow of a striker and the resistance of something struck. Yet when such soft things are compressed firmly enough to resist an impact, then a sound results, though only a dull one. But bronze objects, and bodies that are smooth and concave, give out sound when struck. Hardness is needed; else air will not be driven out by the blow, and consequently no sound be caused. And the body struck should also be smooth, so that the air expelled may hold compactly together in one, as will be explained below.[3]

§ 444. Hollow bodies give out sound very well, when struck, because they hold the air in, and, as this air first set in motion cannot at once come out, it disturbs the rest of the air, and thus by repercussion the impact and the sounding are multiplied. For this reason also materials with a suitable disposition of air in their composition are especially sonorous, such as bronze and silver; but materials in which air is less well disposed are less sonorous, like lead and such things as are more earthy and sedimentary.

§ 445. Then, at 'Further: sound is heard',[4] he explains the

[1] *ibid.*   [2] 419[b] 18.   [3] § 451.   [4] 419[b] 18.

medium in which sound is produced: observing that the medium of sound is air or water, but water less than air. The most suitable medium for both the production and the reception of sound is air. And since the medium of any sense must lack all the sensible qualities perceived by that sense, if it is to serve as the receiver of them, it is evident that neither air nor water has a sound of its own; but if sound is to be produced in air or water some firm and solid and hard objects must strike upon one another, and so cause an impact on the air.

§ 446. Now if the impact of solid bodies upon one another is to be simultaneous with the production of sound in the air, it is necessary that the air remain a whole and continuous, that it be not broke up before receiving the effect of the impact. Hence it is, as experience shows, that when two bodies are brought slowly together no sound occurs: for the air recedes and melts away before the contact is made. But if the impact is swift and violent, then a sound results; for if sound is to occur, the movement of what strikes must *precede* the division of the air, so that the air can be struck while still *en bloc*, or collected, and so a sound be produced in it. It is as when one strikes swiftly with a whip, hitting a whole heap of stones all at once, before they fall apart.[1] For the same reason, when anything passes rapidly through the air, it makes a noise as it goes, because the air itself, being compact, serves as the object struck, not merely as the medium.

§ 447. Next, at 'Echo arises',[2] he deals with the secondary production of sound, which is by reverberation. This sound is called echo. He settles, first, how echo itself is produced; and then, at 'It seems', how its varieties occur.[3] With regard to the former point, we may note that the production of sound in air follows the movement of air, as has been said.[4] What takes place in the air when sound is produced is like what happens in water when something is thrown into it. Obviously, circular undulations form in the water where it is hit; and these are small around the point of striking, but with a strong movement; whilst further away the undulations are large and the movement is weak. Ultimately, the movement disappears altogether and the undulations cease. But if

---

[1] . . . *percutere acervum lapidum antequam dissolvatur* . . . 'a heap or whirl of sand' (Oxford trans.).

[2] 419[b] 25.   [3] *ibid.*   [4] §§ 445–6.

the undulations meet an obstacle before they cease moving a contrary wave-movement is set up, so much the more violent as it is closer to the original impact.

§ 448. Now, in a similar way, when sounding bodies strike together the air is moved in a circular motion and the sound diffused in all directions. Near to the impact the air-circles are small, but are moving swiftly. Hence, there the sound will be very distinctly heard. Further away the circles are larger and the sound is less distinct; and at length it ceases altogether. But if, before the circles vanish, the air so moving and so carrying sound, is repulsed from some body, the undulations return on their tracks and a new sound comes in the reverse direction. And this is called 'echo'.

§ 449. This effect is realised most perfectly when the obstacle in question is concave, for then it acts like a vessel that holds the air together in its own unity, preventing its dispersal. For then the moving air, thus held together and unable to move further because of the obstacle, is thrown back on the air behind and a reverse movement begins—just as when a ball thrown against an obstacle rebounds.

§ 450. Then, where he says 'It seems',[1] he explains how echo occurs in various ways, saying that there would seem to be always *some* echo produced, but it is not always definite, i.e. clearly perceptible. This he shows by a simile drawn from light. Light, he says, is always reflected; but sometimes the reflection is perceptible, sometimes not. The reflection of light is visible when it comes from a shining body; for then the reflection is accompanied by some brightness, as was the original emission of light. The reflection is not visible when it comes from an opaque body, for then it takes place with no brightness or radiance. Yet unless the sun's rays were reflected by opaque bodies there would be no light at all in the air of any part of the upper hemisphere, but instead only darkness everywhere away from the sun, i.e. outside the places reached by the solar rays directly. But light is not reflected by opaque bodies in the same way as by water or air or any of the smooth and polished bodies which throw back light brightly and radiantly. The reflection from opaque bodies is 'dark', that is to say, it forms the shadow extending outside the limit of the clear

[1] 419^b 27.

light of the solar rays. So also, then, when the repercussion of sound takes place in a concave body, wherein sound cannot but be multiplied, a clear and distinctly perceptible echo results. But when the repercussion of sound is from other bodies which do not naturally redouble it, there is no perceptible echo.

BOOK II, CHAPTER VIII, CONTINUED

HEARING. ITS MEDIUM
HIGH AND LOW SOUNDS

EMPTY SPACE IS RIGHTLY SAID TO BE NECESSARY FOR hearing,—for by that is meant air which, when moved as a simple continuum, causes hearing. On account of its instability, however, it gives no sound unless what is struck be smooth; *then* it has the required unity, holding together on account of the even surface, for the surface of a smooth thing is uniform. The sonorous, therefore, is that which moves a compact mass of air continuous as far as the organ of hearing. §§ 451–452

Hearing is naturally conjoined with air; and because it is in air, therefore by a movement in the air outside is caused an interior movement also. Hence an animal does not hear all over its body, nor does air pass through every member. For the animate body and the part to be set in motion have not air throughout (as [also liquid is only in the eyeball]).[1] § 453

Of itself air is soundless; for, being mobile, it easily yields. But when its motion cannot be diffused a sound arises. There is air, built into the ears, so as to be immobile; and it accordingly registers every variety of motion with exactitude. § 454

---

[1] The parenthesis may be omitted, 420^a 7.

On this account therefore we hear also in water, for this does not penetrate to that inner air, nor, by reason of its many convolutions, into the ear. Should it do so, one would not hear; nor if the eardrum were ailing—just as we do not see if the cornea of the pupil is diseased.　　　　§§ 455–7

A test of good hearing on the contrary is whether there is a continual ringing in the ear, like a horn. For then the air in the ear is perpetually moving by a motion of its own; whereas sound is from without, and is not the ear's own. And for this reason they say that we hear by a "resounding vacuum", because we hear by what holds air in constraint.　　　§ 458

Is it that which strikes, or that which is struck, which sounds? Or both, but in different ways? For sound is a movement of something that can move in the way that a bouncing body flies off a smooth surface one flings it at. As has been said, not everything that strikes or is struck gives a sound, for instance one needle struck against another. But what is struck must have a plane surface smooth and regular so that the air rebound and be set in motion instantaneously.[1]　　§§ 459–60

Differences in sonorous things are apparent in the actual sounding. For just as colours are not seen without light, so there is no high or low note apart from sounding.　　§ 461

These terms are used by metaphor from things perceived by touch.　　　　§ 462

A high note moves the sense-organ much in a brief space of time; the low note, little, in a longer time.　　§ 463

But this does not mean that the fast is the high and the slow the low; rather, the former arises because of swiftness of motion, the latter because of slowness.　　　　§ 464

[1] 'But what is struck must be smooth, so that the air rebound and vibrate in a single mass', 420^a 25.

So there seems to be an analogy with the tangible, as sharp and blunt. For the 'sharp' pierces, while the 'blunt' thuds; and the reason is that the one moves in a brief period, the other in a greater. Hence it comes about that the former is swift, the latter slow.

Let this serve to define sound.   § 465

ST. THOMAS'S COMMENTARY

LECTIO SEVENTEEN

§ 451. After deciding about the origin of sound the Philosopher now comes to certain conclusions about sound's impression on sense: and first, at 'Hearing[1] is etc.', about its effect on the sense-organ.

First, then, he observes that, the medium of sound being air, it has been rightly said that the vacuum was an essential factor in hearing (for those who said this thought that 'the vacuum' *was* air). Now when air is disturbed it makes sound audible, provided that it is a single continuum such that a sound can be formed in it. For if sound is to be produced it requires a singleness and continuity in the air; therefore no sound occurs unless the sounding thing that is struck be smooth. A thing is smooth if no part of it juts out from the rest. A smooth surface, then, is a simple unity, upon which the air too exists in a single and uniform way. It is otherwise if the body in question has a rough surface; and since air is 'unstable',[2] that is, easily broken up, it follows that neither will the air be a continuous unity, and therefore that no sound will be formed in it.

§ 452. It is clear then that nothing sounds, i.e. produces sound, unless it sets in motion a single continuum of air between itself and the hearing. It follows that those who said that the 'vacuum' was adapted to the sense of hearing said something to the point; for to be adapted to hearing is a property of air, which they called a 'vacuum'. But they were not right in using the term 'vacuum' for that which is really full of air.

§ 453. Then, when he says 'Hearing is naturally conjoined',[3] he concludes about the impression made on hearing by sound, so far as the organ is concerned. And he does three things here. First,

[1] § 453; 420ᵃ 4.　　　[2] *frangibilis*. Moerbeke has *fragilis*.　　　[3] 420ᵃ 4.

he shows that air is adapted to the organ of hearing: secondly, he shows what sort of air this is (at 'Of itself air'),[1] and thirdly, he shows how hearing may or may not be obstructed by an impediment in the organ (at 'On this account therefore').[2]

First, then, he says that hearing has a natural congruity with air; air is adapted to the organ of hearing as watery fluid to the organ of sight. And this because, air pertaining to the organ of hearing, the same effect of sound can exist in the moving air both inside and outside the organ—the air inside acting as the instrument of hearing. This is why hearing does not occur in every part of the body, nor the sounding air produce a sound in, or penetrate into, every part of the animate body. The latter has not air in each of its parts so that *any* part might be set in motion by sound; in the same way as the living body has a certain watery fluid only in one special part (the pupil of the eye), not everywhere.

§ 454. Then, at 'Of itself air',[3] he shows what sort of air is instrumental in hearing. And he says that everything that sounds is by nature resistant to percussion. Obviously air is not of itself a sounding material, for it does not by nature resist what strikes it, but rather yields easily. However, its yielding or diffusion can be prevented by a solid body, and then the movement of the air gives out a sound. For we have seen[4] that, for the production of sound, two solids must strike against each other and against air. But the air proper to hearing is 'built into', or firmly set in, the ears with a certain stillness, in order that the animal may perceive distinctly every one of its movements. For, as the watery matter in the pupil lacks colour in order to take in all differences of colour, so must the air in the tympanum of the ear lack motion that it may discern every difference of sound.

§ 455. Next, at 'On this account',[5] he shows how hearing may be hindered by an impediment in the organ. He states two impediments, according to the two conditions which, he says, are necessary to the organ of hearing. Of these, the first is air, and the second that this air be still. The first impediment, then, will be any elimination of the air. It follows therefore that hearing can take place in water, provided that the water does not penetrate to that special air which, as he says, is 'built into' the ear. But in fact water

[1] 420ᵃ 7. [2] 420ᵃ 11. [3] 420ᵃ 7.
[4] § 442. [5] 420ᵃ 11.

does not enter into the ear at all; because of the spirals which prevent its entry.

§ 456. But if water should happen to penetrate to this inner air, the animal would cease to hear, because the air needed for hearing would then have been eliminated; just as sight is prevented if the aqueous matter of the pupil is destroyed by the entry of some alien body. And not only is hearing impeded by the loss of this air, but also 'if the ear-drum', that is, the skin enclosing this air, or some adjoining portion, 'is ailing';[1] just as in the case of sight, when the cornea of the pupil which holds the aqueous matter of the eye is injured.[2]

§ 457. Now, certain books maintain that we do not hear in water. This is contrary to what has been said here[3] (that we hear both in air and in water) and also to what the Philosopher says in the *Historia Animalium*,[4] that animals hear in water. For though the water does not penetrate to the interior air, it can set it in motion, and thus impress upon it some sort of sound.

§ 458. He states the second impediment to hearing at 'A test of good hearing'.[5] This impediment would come from a lack of stability in the air of the inner ear: so he says that a sign of one's good or bad hearing is whether one continually hears a ringing in the ear, like the sound heard when a horn is held up to the ear; which sound is due to the movement of air in the horn. One in this condition has poor hearing, for the air in his ears is continually moving by a motion of its own. Each sound ought to be adventitious to the organ of hearing, not intrinsic; just as the organ of sight should receive each colour from without, having none of its own. If it has any of its own, sight is impeded. And in the same way, if the air in the ear has a motion and sound of its own, hearing is impeded. And it is because hearing thus comes about through air that some (thinking that air is a vacuum) say that we hear through a 'resounding vacuum'; and indeed the organ by which we hear has its own special, motionless air, quite distinct from the air outside.

§ 459. Then, at 'Is it that which strikes',[6] he raises a question about the origin of sound: whether the active cause of sound is the

---

[1] *laborat.*

[2] The text is evidently corrupt here, but the meaning is clear.

[3] § 455.   [4] *Hist. Animal.*, IV, c.8; 533ᵇ 1ss.   [5] 420ᵃ 15.   [6] 420ᵃ 19.

thing that strikes or that which is struck. He concludes that both are causes, though in different ways; because as sound follows upon motion, whatever is an efficient cause of motion is so also of sound. Sound originates in the movement with which a thing striking rebounds from the resistance of the thing struck; just as 'bouncing' or resilient bodies rebound from hard smooth objects, when one impels them violently against the latter. Clearly then the thing striking is a cause of movement; and also the object struck, inasmuch as it makes the latter rebound: and thus both are efficient causes of the motion.

§ 460. And, because to produce sound it is necessary that there be a rebound from a struck thing's resistance, consequently not everything that strikes or is struck gives out sound (as was said to begin with):[1] e.g. if one needle is struck against another. To produce sound what is struck must be 'smooth', that is, so disposed that the air spreads and moves at once when the thing struck resists. Such a movement will cause sound.

§ 461. Then, at 'Differences', he examines the differences of sounds. First, he shows how these differences are perceived; and secondly,[2] how they are named (at 'These terms are used'). He says first,[3] then, that different things produce different sounds. But these varieties in sounding bodies' capacity to produce sound are only manifested in act, not in potency. For as colours are not perceived without light, so high or low tones are not perceived until a sound is actual.

§ 462. Then, where he says 'These terms are used',[4] he shows how differences of sound are named. And he does four things here. First, he states whence the names of sounds are taken, saying that they are taken by metaphor from tangible qualities; for obviously high and low are reckoned as tangible qualities.[5]

§ 463. Next, at 'A high note moves',[6] he explains these names, saying that a sound is 'high' which moves the sense of hearing much in a short time: while a 'low' sound is one which moves it little in a longer time.

§ 464. Thirdly, at 'But this does not mean',[7] since the above descriptions would seem to apply to the fast and the slow (the fast

[1] §§ 443-4. [2] 420ᵃ 29. [3] 420ᵃ 26.
[4] 420ᵃ 29. [5] The Latin terms are *acutum* and *grave*.
[6] 420ᵃ 30. [7] 420ᵃ 32.

being that which in a short time moves much, the slow that which in much time moves little), he shows how the high and low in sounds are related to the fast and slow in motions. The fast, he says, is not the same as the high-toned, nor the low-toned the same as the slow, any more than sound, differentiated by the high and the low, is the same as movement, differentiated by the fast and the slow. But, as movement causes sound, so speed of movement is the cause of high tones, and slowness of low; in the case of sounds caused by a single movement. But when sound is produced by many movements, it is frequency of movements that causes the high tones, whilst their slowness[1] causes the low, as Boethius says in the *De Musica*.[2] Hence the tauter is a string, the higher is its note; because at a single stroke it vibrates more frequently.

§ 465. Fourthly, at 'So there seems to be',[3] he likens differences of sounds to the tangible qualities from which they are named: observing that these qualities do resemble the sharp or flat in sounds; for the high note 'pierces' the hearing, in that it disturbs it quickly; whilst the low tone 'thuds' on it, so to speak, because it takes a longer time to disturb it. So the one takes place rapidly, the other slowly. Concluding, he says that he has sufficiently examined sound.

[1] The term is still *tarditas*, 'slowness'; as used in the case of sounds caused by one movement.

[2] *De Musica*, I, c.3 (P.L., vol. LXIII, col. 1173; cf. *ibid.*, cols. 1175–6).

[3] 420ᵇ 1.

BOOK II, CHAPTER VIII, CONTINUED

VOICE

VOICE IS THE SOUND OF A LIVING THING. NO IN-animate being utters voice, though, by analogy, the flute and the harp are said to 'speak'; and so, too, other inanimate objects which sound with duration, harmony and significance. The resemblance arises from voice also having these qualities.   §§ 466–9

Many animals have no voice, such as the bloodless, and, among those with blood, fish. And this is reasonable if, in fact, sound is a movement.[1] But the fish that are said to have voice, such as those in the Achelous, make a sound through their gills, or in some other such way.   §§ 470–1

Voice is a sound made by an animal, but not from *any* part of its frame. Since all things sound by something striking another in a medium (which is air), it is reasonable that those only will have voice which inhale air.   § 472

For Nature employs air inhaled for two operations; as it does the tongue for both taste and speech; of which one, taste, is a necessity; whence it exists in more species; while the other, self-expression, is for well-being. So with breath: it [regulates] interior heat—and this is necessary to existence,

---

[1] 'movement of air', 420^b 11.

(the reason for this will be stated elsewhere); and it also serves voice, which is for well-being.   § 473

Now the organ of respiration is the windpipe, and the purpose of this organ is to serve the lungs. Quadrupeds have more heat in this part than in others,[1] so respiration is needed, and first of all around the heart. Hence it is necessary that air enter when [an animal] draws breath.   §§ 474–5

Hence a striking by the soul (in these parts) upon air inhaled through the windpipe is voice.   § 476

For not every animal sound is voice, as we have said; there is clicking the tongue, and the noise made by coughing. There is needed a living being to utter the sound, and some accompanying phantasm. For voice is a significant sound; not that (merely) of air respired, as coughing is; rather, with it the air in the windpipe is struck against the windpipe.   § 477

A sign of this is that we cannot produce voice while inhaling air nor while exhaling it, but only while retaining it. For what holds the air also sets it in motion. It is thus clear why fish have no voice; for they have no windpipe. They lack this member because they do not inhale air or breathe. Those who say otherwise are wrong.[2] The cause of this, however, is another question.   § 478

[1] 'than other animals', 421^b 25. But St. Thomas follows M. (§ 474).
[2] Not in the Greek, 421^a 5.

ST. THOMAS'S COMMENTARY
LECTIO EIGHTEEN

§ 466. After discussing sound the Philosopher deals with voice which is a kind of sound. His treatment divides into two parts: first, he gives certain facts preliminary to a definition of voice; which he then defines, at 'Hence a striking'.[1] In the former part he does two things. First, he points out what things have voice: and secondly, what is the particular organ of voice, at 'Voice is a sound'.[2] The former division subdivides: first, he shows that only animate beings have voice, and then states which of these have it, at 'Many animals'.[3]

First, then,[4] he observes that voice is a kind of sound,—the sound of the living being; and not of any, but of certain species, as will be explained later.[5]

§ 467. No inanimate thing has a voice. And if sometimes such are said to have voice, this is by way of similitude, as when we speak of the voice of flutes and lyres and suchlike instruments. There are three respects in which the sounds made by these are comparable to voice. The first is *prolongation*; for while the sound of inanimate bodies is produced by a simple percussion, which is no sooner ended than the sound quickly passes away without continuing, voice, on the contrary, is produced by a percussion of air in the windpipe (as will be explained later),[6] which can be maintained by the soul according to its desire, and so be prolonged and continued. The instruments mentioned above have, then, some likeness to voice in the relatively prolonged character of their sounds.

§ 468. The second respect in which they resemble voice is *me lody*. The sound of an inanimate body, since it arises from simple

[1] § 476; 420^b 27. [2] 420^b 12–13. [3] 420^b 9.
[4] 420^b 5. [5] §§ 470–1. [6] § 476.

percussion, is uniform, with no variations of high and low pitch; and therefore without harmony. But in voice the percussions occur differently according to the varying feelings of the animal that is producing it; hence it is diversified by high and low pitch. And something like this occurs in the melodies produced by the said instruments.

§ 469. The third resemblance their sounds bear to voice consists in a certain likeness to *speech* in the way these sounds are co-ordinated. Human speech is not a continuous sound (hence in the *Predicaments*[1] it is counted as a species of 'discrete quantity'). Speech is divided into words, and words into syllables—and this by the separate percussions made upon air by the soul. In a similar way the said instruments, by means of separate strokes or breathings, etc., produce sounds successively.

§ 470. Next, at 'Many animals',[2] he points out which animated beings have voice. Even many animals, he says, have none. These are the bloodless animals, of which there are the four genera enumerated in the *De Animalibus*,[3] namely: the 'soft-bodied', having soft flesh externally, such as cuttlefish and molluscs; those with a soft shell, like crabs; those with a hard shell, like oysters; and those with anular bodies, like bees, ants, and so forth. None of these have voice.

§ 471. And even some sanguineous animals lack voice—namely fish. This is natural enough if sound is a movement of the air (as we have seen);[4] for animals of this sort do not breathe air, and therefore produce no sound which could be their voice. And if it is asserted that certain fish, like those in the Achelous (the name of a river), have a voice, this is not true properly speaking; they merely make a sound with the gills by which they expel water and draw in air, or perhaps with some other moving instrument.

§ 472. Then, at 'Voice is a sound made by an animal',[5] he points out the organ of voice. First, he shows that the organ of voice is the same as that of respiration. Secondly, he explains the use of respiration, at 'For Nature employs'.[6] Thirdly, he shows what is the organ of respiration, at 'Now the organ'.[7]

He observes first, then, that, while voice is an animal sound, not any sound of any part of the animal is voice. And since the produc-

[1] *Categ.*, c.6; 4^b 31ss.   [2] 420^b 9.   [3] *Hist. Animal.*, I, c.6; 490^b 5–15.
[4] § 443.   [5] 420^b 12–13.   [6] 420^b 16.   [7] 420^b 23.

tion of sound requires the striking of something *against* something *in* something (i.e. in the air) it is understandable why those animals only have a voice which take in air by respiration, and that they have voice in the part through which they breathe.

§ 473. Then, at 'For Nature employs air',[1] he says that Nature uses air inhaled for two operations, as it uses the tongue for both tasting and speech. Of these two last activities, tasting is a necessity, since by it the animal discerns the nutriment that maintains it in mere existence (which is why taste is found in most animals). But the expression of meaning by means of speech is for the sake of a more complete existence. In a similar way, Nature uses inhaled air both for the mitigation of natural heat, which is simply necessary (the cause of this is given in the *De Respiratione et Expiratione*)[2] and also for the production of voice, which is for a more complete existence.

§ 474. Next, at 'Now the organ of respiration',[3] he says that this organ is the windpipe, the function of which is to serve the lungs by enabling them to draw in air. It is necessary that air be taken into the lungs because animals that can move about have more heat in this part than in others. The lungs are connected with the heart, wherein lies the source of the natural warmth of the body; consequently the parts around the heart need to be cooled; and this is done by respiration.

§ 475. These parts he says need to be cooled 'first', either because the lungs come first after the heart as being next to it, or because the heart comes first among the animal's parts, both in origin[4] and in the process of causing movement: which is why it is necessary that air enter the lungs to cool the heart's natural heat. Or indeed the comparison may be between 'this part'[5] in animals that move upon feet, and the same parts in other animals. For it is clear that animals with blood have more natural heat than those without; and among those with blood, fishes have the least; which is why neither bloodless animals nor fishes breathe, as has been said.[6]

§ 476. Then, at 'Hence a striking',[7] he draws from the foregoing observations a definition of voice; first stating the definition and then, at 'For not every animal',[8] explaining it. First, then, he says

---

[1] 420^b 16.   [2] *De Respir.*, c.21–2; 478^a 10ss.   [3] 420^b 23.
[4] *quantum ad generationem, et quantum ad causalitatem motus.*
[5] i.e. the lungs.   [6] §§ 470–1.   [7] 420^b 27.   [8] 420^b 29.

that, since voice is the sound of the animate being, proceeding from the part through which it breathes air (for every sound implies some striking on air), it follows that voice is a striking upon air breathed in through the windpipe; which striking is caused by the soul as animating these parts, but especially the heart. For while the soul exists everywhere in the body of an animal (as its form), yet its *motive* power is principally in the heart. Note that he is defining in terms of the *cause* of the thing defined; for voice is not in fact the striking itself, but a sound made by striking.

§ 477. Next, at 'For not every animal sound',[1] he explains the definition with regard to his assertions (1) that the vocal impact came from the soul; and (2) that its material is breath, at 'A sign of this'.[2] Three factors have entered into his definition of voice: that which impels, i.e. the soul; that which is impelled, i.e. the air respired; and that in which the vocal impact occurs, i.e. the windpipe. The third of these he has explained above;[3] so there remain the first two. He observes, then, first, that, as he has said,[4] not every animal sound is a voice. Sometimes the tongue makes sounds which are not voice. Again, coughing is not voice. For voice to be produced it is required that what strikes the air should be something alive, or with a soul, and also, accompanying this, that an image be present which is meant to signify something. For voice must be a *significant* sound,—significant either by nature or conventionally. Hence the statement that vocal impact proceeds from the *soul*; for operations proceeding from imagination can be said to be from the soul. It is clear, then, that voice is not the mere impact of breath such as occurs in coughing; and that the principal cause of the production of voice is the soul, using this air, i.e. air inhaled, to force against the windpipe the air within it. Not air, then, is the principal factor in the formation of voice, but the soul, which uses air as its instrument.

§ 478. Then, at 'A sign of this',[5] he explains the other element in his definition, namely that voice is the impact of breath, saying that there are two signs of this. One sign is that no animal can produce voice either while inhaling air, or while expelling it, but only while it retains air; because while it retains air, this air, being withheld and striking against the air in the windpipe, causes a move-

[1] 420ᵇ 29.   [2] 421ᵃ 1.   [3] §§ 474-5.   [4] §§ 466-9.   [5] 421ᵃ 1.

298

ment that results in voice. Another sign is that fishes have no voice; for they have no windpipe or vocal passage, and this because they neither inhale nor exhale air. Those who say that fishes breathe are mistaken; but why they do not breathe is another matter, belonging to the science which deals with the particular attributes of animals.

BOOK II, CHAPTER IX

SMELL. ITS OBJECT

I T IS NOT SO EASY TO COME TO CONCLUSIONS ABOUT
odour and the odorous as about the sense-objects already
discussed. What odour is is less obvious than what sound
is, or the visible or light; the reason being that our sense of
smell lacks precision; it is inferior to that of many animals.
For man smells but feebly, discerning nothing odorous save
with some special pleasure or disgust, as though our organ
for the perception of smells were defective. It is arguable indeed that, as hard-eyed animals see colour, yet so that delicate
differences are not sharply defined to them, except as these
cause fear or not, so are smells to the human species.

§§ 479–80

For it seems that while smell has an analogy with taste,
and the species of savour with odours, yet we have a sharper
perception of taste, because this is a sort of touch,—the sense
which man possesses to the highest degree of precision.
Whereas in the other senses he is inferior to many animals,
by touch he can discriminate with exactness far beyond the
rest of the animal world. Hence man is the most sagacious of
animals. A sign of this is that within the human race, men
are gifted or not intellectually in virtue of this sense, and of
no other. For coarse-bodied people are mentally inert, whilst
the tenderly-fleshed are quick of understanding.   §§ 481–6

As some flavours are sweet, some bitter, so with odours.
But some things are analogously endowed with savour and

300

odour: I mean, have a pleasant taste and pleasant smell. In
others, however, these qualities are contrary. Likewise odours
are pungent, harsh, sharp or oily: but since, as we have said,
odours are not very distinct, whereas flavours are, they take
their names from the latter, according to resemblance. For a
sweet smell comes from saffron and honey: a pungent smell
from thyme; and so in other cases.   §§ 487-9

Furthermore, as hearing (and the same obtains in each of
the senses) bears on the audible and the inaudible (and sight
on the visible and the invisible), so smell is of the odorous and
the odourless. The odourless is either that which simply cannot have a smell at all, or that which has smell but a poor one
and feeble in quality. The same can be said of the tasteless.

§ 490

§ 479. Having dealt with the visible and the audible, the Philosopher now considers smell and its object. His treatment has two parts: he first examines this object as such, and then at 'Smelling also'[1] the manner in which it impinges upon the sense. And as to the object as such, having considered it in itself, he turns, at 'Furthermore, as hearing',[2] to consider a certain odourless object which falls within the range of smell. The former consideration again subdivides: first, he shows the difficulty of reaching definite conclusions about smell; secondly, he explains how we can come to know about the odorous, at 'For it seems that smell has an analogy'.[3]

First then he observes that it is harder to reach conclusions about smell and its object than about the sense-objects discussed hitherto, the audible and the visible. For what odour is is not as clear to us as what sound is, or the visible, or light, or other things of that sort.

§ 480. The reason, he says, is that our sense of smell is not so strong that we can distinctly and unerringly discern its object; for this sense is weaker in us than in many other animals; the reason being that, as the sense-organ corresponds to the sense-object, and as smell is produced by the warm and dry, therefore a good organ of smell will be predominantly a warm, dry organ. Now the brain of man, close to which lies the organ of smell, is, as the Philosopher says in the De Animalibus,[4] larger in proportion to his body than that of any other animal; and since the brain itself is cold and moist, the human sense of smell is proportionately the less. Man smells weakly—indeed only what is strongly odorous and causes pleasure or disgust; and this because his sense of smell is lacking in

[1] Lectio 20, § 491; 421^b 9.   [2] § 490; 421^b 2.   [3] 421^a 16.
[4] Hist. Animal., I, c.16; 494^b 25.

a keen and exact discernment of its object. Hence one may reasonably opine that human beings stand with respect to odours in the same case as hard-eyed animals, such as locusts and certain types of fish stand with respect to colours; for these animals, on account of their weak vision and ill-disposed organs, see only what is very obviously visible and as such is apt to frighten them, or the contrary.

§ 481. Then at 'For it seems that . . .',[1] he shows how differences of odour are made known to us. First, he shows how differences of odour are brought home to us by comparison with differences of taste. Secondly, he shows how differences of odour correspond to differences of taste, at 'As some flavours'.[2]

First, then, he remarks that the sense of smell in man seems to have some relation and correspondence to taste; and, likewise, the varieties of flavour (i.e. savour) to those of odour. Now things hidden become known through what is more evident. Since, then, the varieties of flavour are clearly evident to us, those of smell, which are not so, but which have a certain affinity to those of flavour, are brought home to us through this resemblance.

§ 482. Now the varieties of flavour are especially evident to us because man has a more acute sense of taste than other animals, taste being a modality of touch and touch being possessed by man at a far higher degree of precision than by any other animal; although in respect of the other senses man falls short of some animals. For certain animals see and hear and smell better than man: but the touch of man is far superior to that of other animals in exactitude of apprehension.

§ 483. This pre-eminence of touch in man is the reason why man is the wisest of animals; moreover, among men it is in virtue of fineness of touch, and not of any other sense, that we discriminate the mentally gifted from the rest. Those whose bodily constitution is tough, and whose sense of touch is therefore poor, are slow of intellect; whilst those of a delicately balanced constitution with, in consequence, a fine sense of touch are mentally acute. This too is why the other animals have flesh of a coarser texture than man.

§ 484. Yet it might seem that mental capacity corresponded rather to excellence of sight than of touch, for sight is the more spiritual sense, and reveals better the differences between things.

[1] 421ᵃ 16.   [2] 421ᵃ 26.

Still, there are two reasons for maintaining that excellence of mind is proportionate to fineness of touch. In the first place touch is the basis of sensitivity as a whole; for obviously the organ of touch pervades the whole body, so that the organ of each of the other senses is also an organ of touch, and the sense of touch by itself constitutes a being as sensitive. Therefore the finer one's sense of touch, the better, strictly speaking, is one's sensitive nature as a whole, and consequently the higher one's intellectual capacity. For a fine sensitivity is a disposition to a fine intelligence. But an exceptionally good hearing or sight does not imply that the sensitivity as a whole is finer, but only that it is so in one respect.

§ 485. The other reason is that a fine touch is an effect of a good bodily constitution or temperament. For as the organ of touch is itself necessarily endowed with tangible qualities (being composed of the elements) it needs to be in a condition of potency to extremes of the tangible at least by itself constituting a mean between them. Now nobility of soul follows upon a well-balanced physical constitution; because forms are proportionate to their matter. It follows that those whose touch is delicate are so much the nobler in nature and the more intelligent.

§ 486. Another question that arises is why the differentiations of odour are named after those of taste, if it is touch that is the most exact of the senses. I answer that both the odorous and the tasty are caused to be so by some special *combination* of elemental qualities; consequently the former corresponds to the latter more than to the *simple* qualities which are the object of touch.

§ 487. Next, when he says 'As some flavours are sweet etc.',[1] he explains how the kinds of odour correspond to the kinds of flavour or taste, observing that as we distinguish these as sweet or bitter, so do we also with odours. But notice that, while some things reveal a harmony of flavour and odour, that is to say, they are sweet in both, others on the contrary have an agreeable flavour but a disagreeable smell, or the converse.

§ 488. The reason for this is that flavour pertains to an aqueous liquid partially digested; and odour to a dry gaseous matter partially modified by the surrounding atmosphere. Now it sometimes happens that both substances, the subtle gas and the grosser liquid, are each combined in a nice proportion; and then both odour and

[1] 421[a] 26.

flavour are pleasing. But if in one this balance is found, and not in the other, then the one will be pleasing but the other not so.

And what has been said of sweet and bitter, the extremities in flavour, can be applied also to the sour, the pungent, i.e. astringent or harsh, the acid and the oily: these flavour-qualities can be transferred to the odorous.

§ 489. And although odours and flavours do not always and in all respects correspond, nevertheless because odours are, as I have said,[1] only imperfectly distinct and evident, they are named after their resemblance to flavours; for on the whole there is a correspondence. Thus saffron and honey have both a sweet taste and a sweet smell, and thyme and suchlike have a pungent taste and smell; and so with other flavours and odours.

§ 490. Then, at 'Furthermore, as hearing',[2] he shows how odourless things are perceptible to smell. As hearing, he says, is of the audible and inaudible, and sight of the visible and invisible (because opposites are known by one and the same faculty, and a lack only by means of what is lacking), so smell is of the odorous and the odourless. There are two senses of the term odourless: it can mean what has no smell at all, such as all simple (i.e. uncompounded) bodies, or what has a little or a faint smell. And the same is true of the tasty and the tasteless.

[1] §§ 480–2.   [2] 421^b 3.

BOOK II, CHAPTER IX, CONTINUED

SMELL. HOW IT OCCURS

SMELLING ALSO TAKES PLACE THROUGH A MEDIUM, which is either air or water. For aquatic animals seem also to perceive odours, both those with blood and those without, like animals that live in the air; for some of them traverse long distances for their food, being drawn to it by smell. §§ 491–5

So there seems to be a difficulty. If operations of smell are of the same type, yet man smells by inhaling: when exhaling or holding his breath he smells nothing, neither from a distance, nor close at hand, not even if the object is placed inside the nose. (That a thing should be imperceptible when placed on the very organ of sensation, is indeed common to all,[1] but to be unable to perceive without breathing is peculiar to man. This is evident to those who make the experiment). Since, then, bloodless animals do not breathe, they would seem to have some other sense besides those which have been spoken of. § 496

But this is impossible, if it is odour they perceive. For the sense for odours, good odours or bad, *is* smell. Furthermore, they seem to be overcome by the same strong odours as man, such as asphalt, brimstone and the like. Therefore, even if they do not breathe, they must smell. §§ 497–8

[1] St. Thomas (§ 496) is not sure whether 'all' refers to other senses or other animals. The whole of this parenthesis is difficult, and alternative readings have been proposed. 421^b 17.

Now this sense seems to differ as between man and other animals, as human eyes differ from the hard eyes of some animals. The former have a covering or protection, the eyelids, and unless these are moved or withdrawn, one does not see. Hard-eyed animals have nothing like this; they see at once whatever happens to be present in the transparent medium. In the same way, then, the organ of smell is in some animals like an eye with no covering; in others, which inhale air, it has a covering that is withdrawn when they respire and so distend the veins and pores. And for this reason animals that breathe do not smell in water. For they must respire if they are to be affected by odour, and they cannot do this in a liquid.   § 499

Odour is of dry things as savour of liquid; and the sense-organ of smell is such in potency.   § 500

ST. THOMAS'S COMMENTARY

LECTIO TWENTY

§ 491. After concluding about the odorous as such, the Philosopher now deals with its impact on the sense; and first, as to the medium; secondly, at 'Odour is of dry things',[1] as to the organ of the sense of smell. As to the former point he does two things. First, he indicates the medium of the organ of smell; next, at 'So there seems to be a difficulty',[2] he raises a question about the conclusion reached.

First then he observes that the organ of smell is affected by the odorous through a medium, i.e. air or water. That air is a medium of smell is obvious, for we smell through the air. So we need only prove that water is such a medium. This he shows by the fact that aquatic animals, and not only the sanguineous but the non-sanguineous also, perceive odours, like animals that live in the air. A sign of this is that some of them[3] travel a long distance for their food, which could not happen unless they were attracted by smell —like vultures which are said to come long journeys to carrion: But just how smell is diffused to such a distance in space is not certain.

§ 492. An opinion which some have maintained should be noted here, that all sensation is consummated in a kind of touch: a contact, they said, must occur of sense and sense-object; but not in the same way in sight as in the other senses. For they said that from sight to the object seen certain 'visual lines' proceed; and that when these touch the object it is seen; whereas in the case of the other senses a reverse process takes place, and the sense-object comes to the faculty. This (they said) is particularly obvious in tasting and

---

[1] 422ª 6. [2] 421ᵇ 13.

[3] i.e., for St. Thomas animals that live in air, or perhaps animals generally. Aristotle is referring to aquatic animals.

touching, which perceive by a sort of contact; and would seem to occur also in hearing, which implies a movement of air to the ear; and also in smelling;—for they maintained that odours are conveyed to the sense of smell by a kind of fume that bodies give off by evaporation.

§ 493. The cause of their drawing this distinction between two modes of sensation seems to have been that these early thinkers had no theory or perception of a spiritual modification of a medium, but only of a material one. Now a material modification of the medium is evident in all mediated sensations other than sight: for, obviously, odours and sounds are carried or impeded by the wind; which is certainly not the case with colour. Also, in one and the same section of air contrary colours can appear, as when one man sees white and another black at the same time and through the medium of the same air; which is not the case with odour, for contrary odours impede one another, even in the medium. Therefore, knowing nothing about the way the visible object affects the medium, these philosophers maintained that sight was conveyed to the thing seen; whereas, observing in other sensations the changes that took place in the medium, they believed that in these cases the sense-objects came to the sense.

§ 494. But it is clear that this cannot occur in smelling. When vultures smell carrion at a distance of fifty miles or more, this cannot be due to any bodily evaporation from the carrion being diffused over so great a space. This is the more evident if we consider that a sense-object affects its medium for the same distance in all directions, if not impeded. There would not be enough of the object to occupy so much space, even if the whole corpse were to evaporate; for there is a fixed limit of rarification for all natural bodies,—the rarity of fire; and in any case, and especially, the corpse can smell and be smelt in this way without being sensibly altered.[1]

§ 495. We are therefore compelled to say that whatever gaseous vapour may come from an odorous substance, it does not reach as far as the point where the odour is perceived; but that beyond the point reached by this vapour the substance affects the medium 'spiritually'. That such 'spiritual' modification of the medium is effected by the object of sight more than by that of the other senses

[1] i.e. by evaporation.

is due to the fact that by their visible qualities corruptible bodies participate in the mode of being of incorruptible bodies; hence these qualities exist in a more formal and noble manner than do the other sense-objects which are proper to bodies precisely as corruptible.

§ 496. Then at 'So there seems to be a difficulty',[1] he states a problem suggested by what he has been saying; bringing forward objections, first from one side and then, at 'But this is impossible',[2] from the other; until, at 'Now this sense seems',[3] he provides a solution.

First, then, he observes that it is doubtful whether all animals smell in the same way, as having identically the same sense of smell (aquatic animals, for instance, smell through water). It would seem not indeed. Man smells when he breathes in air, but when he is exhaling air or holding his breath he cannot smell at all either at a distance or close to the object, even if the latter is put into his nose. Now, that the object is imperceptible if it is placed right against the sense-organ is of course common to all the senses in all animals; but that odours are imperceptible without respiration is peculiar to man, as experience shows. And as non-sanguineous animals do not breathe, it would seem to follow that they had some sense other than smell and the other senses attributed to man.

§ 497. Then, at 'But this is impossible, if it is odour that they perceive',[4] he adduces two arguments on the other side. (1) The senses are distinguished according to their objects; and since smell is the sense of odours, whether good or bad, and these are perceived both by the breathing and by the non-breathing animals, it follows that the sense of smell in man and these animals is the same.

§ 498. (2) The same things are destructive of the same senses: sight does not suffer from sounds nor hearing from colours. But the non-breathing animals seem to suffer in their senses from the same strong and oppressive odours as are grievous to man, e.g. from bitumen (a compound of the juice of herbs), sulphur and the like. Hence other animals, even if they do not breathe, have a sense of smell like man.

§ 499. Next, at 'Now this sense seems to differ',[5] he proposes his solution: this diversity in the mode of breathing is due, he says, not

[1] 421ᵇ 13.   [2] 421ᵇ 21.   [3] 421ᵇ 26.   [4] 421ᵇ 21.   [5] 421ᵇ 26.

to a difference in the senses, but to different constitutions of the organ; the organ of smell in man being different from that in other animals, as a man's eyes differ from the hard eyes of certain beasts. The human eye has a protective covering or envelope called the eyelid, which must be withdrawn before a man can see. This is not the case with hard-eyed animals; they see at once whatever appears in the transparent medium. And so it is with non-breathing animals; their olfactory organ is uncovered; whereas that of breathing animals is covered over until the pores are dilated in the act of respiration. The latter therefore cannot smell through water; for they cannot breathe in it.

§ 500. Then at 'Odour is etc.',[1] he indicates the organ of smell, saying that as the basis of odour is dryness (as that of taste is moisture) the organ of smell must be in potency to odour and dryness (as that of sight is to colours and light).

[1] 422ª 6.

BOOK II, CHAPTER X

TASTE. ITS MEDIUM, OBJECT, ORGAN
KINDS OF FLAVOUR

THE TASTEABLE IS A SORT OF TANGIBLE; HENCE, IT is not perceptible through an extraneous body as medium, any more than the object of touch. And the body in which is savour, i.e. the tasteable, is in liquid as its material, which is tangible.   §§ 501–4

Hence, if we were in water, we should taste a sweet thing put into it; not that the sensation would then operate through a medium, but because the savour would be mixed with the water, as in a drink. (Colour, however, is not thus seen because of any mixture or efflux.) There is then nothing corresponding to a medium [in tasting]. As colour is the visible, so savour is the tasteable.   §§ 505–7

It causes no sensation of taste except in liquid; but it must be moist, actually or potentially; as [with] saliva[1] which is very liquid and moistens the tongue.   § 508

As sight is of the visible and the invisible (for darkness is invisible, and sight discerns this also, as it does, in addition, the extremely bright, which is also invisible, but in quite

---

[1] 'for instance, what is salty', 422ª 18. Aristotle gives τό ἁλμυϱόν as an example of a 'tasteable' easily dissolved. M. renders it as *saliva*, which alters the sense. St. Thomas follows M.

another way); [and as] the same holds of hearing, which is of sound and silence, one being audible, the other inaudible, and [the latter includes] excess of sound, which is to hearing as brilliance is to sight; for as a feeble sound is in a way inaudible, so, in another way, is an extremely violent one. ('Invisible' indeed can mean either what is absolutely such, or [the term may also be used] as in other cases of 'the impossible' where [this concept] is applied both to what lacks what it ought to have by nature, and to what has this defectively,—as we say of a footless [animal] that it is motionless.[1]) So, in the same way, taste is of the savourable and the non-savourable, the latter being what has either only a faint savour, or one altogether destructive of the taste. It would seem that the principle of this is the drinkable or the non-drinkable; and taste is of both, but the latter has either a faint taste or one that destroys the sense: whilst the former is according to nature. The drinkable is common to taste and touch.   §§ 509-11

Since what is tasteable is liquid, it is necessary that the sense-organ be neither liquid actually, nor incapable of becoming so. For taste is affected by the savourable thing as such. It is therefore necessary that the sensorium be moistened, yet in such a way that it keeps its potentiality thereto; the tasting sense being non-humid.   § 512

There is a sign of this in that the tongue cannot perceive taste either when it is dry or when it is too moist. In the latter case contact takes place with the original moisture; as when one who has first tasted a very strong flavour then tastes another, or those burdened [with fever] taste all things as bitter because the tongue is saturated in a liquid of that sort.   § 513

The species of savour are, like colours, the simple contraries; sweet and bitter. Adjoining these, however, are, with the former, the succulent, with the latter, the saline. Then there

[1] 'answering to the footless (animal) and stoneless (fruit)', 422ᵃ 29.

are the intermediary flavours: pungent, harsh, stringent and piquant. These seem to be about all the varieties of savour that exist; to which taste, as such, therefore, is in potency; the savourable being what reduces it to act. §§ 514–16

§ 501. Having dealt with the visible, the audible and the odorous, the Philosopher now treats of the tasteable; and this in two parts, first considering the tasteable in general, and then, at 'The species of savour',[1] its division into flavours. As to the former point he does three things. First, he asks whether the tasteable is perceived through a medium; then he explains what is perceived by taste, i.e. the tasteable and the non-tasteable, at 'As sight etc.';[2] and thirdly, what is the organ of taste, at 'Since what is tasteable is liquid'.[3] For he has explained these three points with regard to the other senses, namely the medium, the object sensed and the sense-organ. As regards the medium, he first shows that the tasteable is not perceived through any extraneous medium; then, at 'Hence, if we were in water',[4] he answers an objection; and thirdly, at 'It causes no sensation',[5] he shows us the necessary condition of actual tasting.

§ 502. First, then, he says that the tasteable is something tangible, i.e. discerned by touch. That is why it is not sensed through a medium extraneous to the body, i.e. which is not part of the living body—differing in this from the sense-objects hitherto treated of, which are perceived through air or water outside the animal's body. Touch does not perceive through an extraneous medium, but through one that is conjoined with the subject, i.e. through flesh, as we shall see.[6] Therefore, as taste is a kind of touch, the tasteable is not perceived through any extraneous medium.

§ 503. That the tasteable is a sort of tangible he shows thus: flavour or savour exists in moisture as in the matter proper to it; and moisture is tangible.

[1] § 514; 422ᵇ 10.   [2] § 509; 422ᵃ 20.   [3] § 512; 422ᵃ 34.
[4] 422ᵃ 12.   [5] 422ᵃ 18.   [6] §§ 525–8.

§ 504. But if taste is a kind of touch, it would seem that it ought not to be placed in contrast to touch (for no species is opposed to its genus); and if so, then there are not five senses but only four. But, in truth, touch and taste can be considered in two ways: with regard to the mode of perception, and thus taste is a kind of touch, for it apprehends by contact; and with regard to the object, and then we have to maintain that as the object of taste is to the object of touch, so the sense of taste is to the sense of touch. For flavour (the object of taste) is evidently not one of the qualities of those elemental bodies of which the animal is composed, which constitute the specific object of the sense of touch; yet it is caused by them, and exists in one of them as in its matter, i.e. in moisture. Clearly then, taste is not the same as touch, but is somehow founded on touch. So a distinction is commonly drawn between taste, as discriminative of flavours, and taste as a kind of touch discerning certain tangible qualities, namely those of nourishment, of which touch is the sense, as has been pointed out.[1] Hence Aristotle's remark in the *Ethics* (Bk. III)[2] that there is no such thing as temperance in the pleasures of taste understood in the former of these senses, but only as understood in the latter.

§ 505. Next, at 'Hence, if we were in water'[3] he answers an objection. For it is obvious that if something tasty and soluble were placed in water (say, honey, or something of that kind) and we were in the water also, we would be aware of the thing's flavour, even though at a distance from it.[4] Taste, then, apparently perceives its object through an extraneous medium, water.

§ 506. To dispose, then, of this objection, Aristotle, arguing from the principle already stated, that taste does not use an extraneous medium, says that if we were in the water in the way described we should certainly perceive the sweet thing in the water at a distance from us, but that the sensation would not in fact reach us through a medium; for the flavour would be mixed with the liquid as in a drink (as when honey or the like is mixed with water or wine) and the water itself would be affected by the sweet object. Taste then would not perceive the thing's flavour at a distance except in so far as the water was affected by the thing.

---

[1] § 290.　　　　[2] E.N., III, c.10; 1118ᵃ 15ss.　　　　[3] 422ᵃ 12.

[4] This phrase Pirotta puts in quotation marks, but it does not appear in his text of Moerbeke.

§ 507. A sign of which is that the taste is not so strongly affected by such water as it naturally would be by the flavour of the thing that is at a distance, because the flavour is weakened by mixing with water. Colour, on the other hand, is not seen through its medium in such a way that the coloured body is mixed with the medium, or that anything from it flows to the eye, as Democritus supposed; it is seen rather through a spiritual modification of the medium. Hence, sight does not perceive colour as colour of the air or of water, but as colour of a distant coloured body, and to the same degree of intensity. Comparing, then, taste with sight, we cannot say that the *medium* of taste is like that of sight, but we can say that just as colour is the visible, i.e. the object of vision, so flavour is the tasteable, i.e. the object of taste.

§ 508. Then at 'It causes no sensation of taste',[1] he shows what is required for taste in the place of a medium, observing that nothing tasty is tasted without moisture. As colour becomes actually visible in light, so flavour becomes actually tasteable in moisture; for which reason all that is tasteable is either actually liquid already, like wine, or is potentially liquid, like things taken as food. Hence the necessity of saliva in the mouth; being very liquid it moistens the palate, so that what is eaten may be liquefied and its flavour perceived.

§ 509. Next, at 'As sight is of the visible',[2] he treats of the object perceived by taste, comparing taste with sight and hearing. For sight perceives both the visible and the invisible, as has been said;[3] the invisible being darkness, which is apprehended by sight. Also what is extremely bright, like the sun, is described as invisible, though in quite another way. For darkness is called invisible because of a lack of light, but brilliant objects on account of an excess of light which overcomes the sense. Similarly hearing is of the audible, i.e. sound, and of the inaudible, i.e. silence (the privation of sound) and also of the inaudible in the sense of what is heard with difficulty, either because of its excessive loudness or because it is too faint to affect the hearing sufficiently. And so it is with all things involving capacity and incapacity.

§ 510. For one can say of a thing that it is incapable, meaning either that it has not what it ought to have by nature, or that it has it only defectively. Thus an animal is described as unable to walk

[1] 422ᵃ 18.   [2] 422ᵃ 20.   [3] § 490.

either because it lacks legs or because it is weak on its legs. And so it is with taste and the tasteable and non-tasteable. The latter means either what has little or poor flavour, or what is so violently flavoured as to overcome the sense.

As the tasteable pertains to moisture, i.e. the drinkable, and moisture is the basis of savour, it would appear that the drinkable and the non-drinkable are fundamental in the process of tasting. For taste perceives both, the one, i.e. the non-drinkable, as bad and destructive of taste, but the other, i.e. the drinkable, as appropriate and congenial to taste. Yet while the tasteable is perceived by taste, precisely as a sense distinct from touch, the drinkable and non-drinkable are perceived by it inasmuch as it is a species of touch. For the drinkable is common to touch and taste, to touch in so far as it is liquid, to taste so far as it has savour.

§ 511. Obviously then, the pleasures afforded by food and drink, in so far as these are things perceptible and drinkable, accompany taste inasmuch as it is a kind of touch (*see* Book III of the *Ethics*).[1]

§ 512. Then at 'Since what is tasteable is liquid'[2] he examines the organ of taste, first stating the fact and then, at 'There is a sign of this',[3] pointing out a sign of its truth.

First, then, he says that because the tasteable is liquid and has savour, the organ of taste must itself be neither actually moist nor actually flavoured. Yet it must be able to become moist—like the organ of sight, which must be colourless, but able to receive colour. This is because the taste is affected by the tasteable precisely as such, as any other sense by its proper object. Since then the tasteable as such is liquid, the organ of taste, in the act of receiving the savour, must become moist; and yet preserve its quality of being able to taste, when it is not actually, but only potentially, moist.

§ 513. Next, at 'There is a sign',[4] he observes that an indication of the truth of the foregoing is that the tongue is able to taste nothing when it is either quite dry, or extremely liquid; for when it is excessively liquid through the presence and predominance of some liquid already tasted, then for the time being no new moisture can be tasted; as when after tasting a strong flavour one can taste nothing else, because the sensation of the former flavour remains on the tongue. Similarly to the 'burdened' or sick, all things

---

[1] Probably E.N., III, c.10; 1118ª 25ss.   [2] 422ª 34.
[3] 422ᵇ 5.   [4] 422ᵇ 5.

taste bitter because their tongues are covered with a feverish or bitter moisture.[1]

§ 514. Then at 'The species of savour'[2] he concludes about the species of taste, observing that, as in the case of colour simple colours are contrary, such as white and black, so in flavours the simple are contrary, as the sweet and the bitter. Those 'adjoining', that is, those immediately following upon the simple species, are the succulent following on the sweet, and the salty following on the bitter. Intermediary are the sour, the pungent, the astringent and the acid, which two last are reducible to the same. To these seven species of flavour most of the others seem to be reducible.

§ 515. Note, with regard to these species, that whilst flavours are caused by the hot and the cold, the moist and the dry, and although contraries connote terms furthest apart, yet the contraries in the species of flavour do not follow the maximum differences of hot and cold or of moist and dry, but are related precisely to the natural capacity of the sense of taste to be affected by savour either to disgust or to delight. There is no need then for the sweet or the bitter to be particularly hot or cold or moist or dry, but much that it be in a state that corresponds somehow to the sense of taste. As for the origin of flavours, that is explained in the *De Sensu et Sensato*.[3]

§ 516. He concludes, finally, that taste, i.e. the sense of taste, or its organ, is in potency to savour and the species of savour; and that the tasteable is what can bring it into act.

[1] *plenam humiditate . . . scilicet cholera, quae est amara.*
[2] 422^b 10.   [3] *De Sensu et Sens*, c.4.

BOOK II, CHAPTER XI

TOUCH. ONE SENSE OR MANY?
ITS MEDIUM

THE SAME REASONING HOLDS FOR THE TANGIBLE and touch. If touch is not one sense, but several, then the tangible sense-objects must necessarily be several. But it is a problem whether it is one sense or several: and what the organ is—whether it is the flesh, or what corresponds to flesh in other [animals],[1] or not; and if not, then this [flesh] would be the medium, while the primary sense organ would be something else within.   §§ 517–18

For every sense seems to be of a single contrariety, as sight of white and black, hearing of high and low, taste of sweet and bitter. But in the tangible order there are several contrarieties, hot and cold, dry and wet, hard and soft, and the like.   § 519

Here is a partial solution of this problem: that in other senses also there are several contraries; as in voice there is not only high and low but also loud and soft, smooth and rough, and other such qualities. There is also a like variety of differences in colour.   § 520

But it is not clear what is the underlying unity of touch, as sound is of hearing.   §§ 521–4

[1] i.e. in animals without flesh.

It is not evidence as to whether the sense-organ is interior or is the flesh, immediately, that the sensation arises simultaneously with contact. For if, as things are, one were to stretch a covering or membrane over the skin, a sensation would still arise immediately on making contact; yet it is obvious that the sense-organ was not *in* this membrane. And if it were ingrown the sensation would reach the sensorium even sooner.   §§ 525-6

Therefore it appears that the relation of this part of the body [to the whole] is comparable to that which air would have if it formed a natural covering that grew all round our bodies. For then it would appear that we perceived sound and odour and colour through some one common medium, and even that there were but one sense for hearing, seeing and smelling. Since in fact, however, there exists something definite through which the motions [of these senses] are produced, it is evident that each of these senses is diverse. But in the case of touch, this is still far from clear. It is impossible that an animated body be constituted from air or water, for it must be solid. It can, then, only be a mixture from earth and the other elements, as flesh (or its counterpart) requires. Wherefore it is necessary that the medium of touch be a body conjoined [to the organism] through which its sensations, which are several, may come about.   §§ 527-8

That they are several is proved by the fact that there is touch in the tongue; for that same member feels all kinds of tangible objects, as well as savours. If every part of the flesh perceived savours it would seem that touch and taste were one and the same. But we know that they are two, in that one organ cannot be substituted for the other.   § 529

§ 517. Having considered the objects of the other senses, the Philosopher finally treats of the object of touch, examining this sense last of all because it appears to be the least spiritual of the senses, though it is the foundation of all the others. This section divides into two parts: first he settles certain questions about touch; after which he states the truth about it, at 'It would seem then in general'.[1] The first part again divides into, first a statement, and, secondly, a solution, at 'For every sense',[2] of the problems in question.

He observes then, first, that in the matters to be examined, the same reasoning holds whether we treat of the tangible or of touch. What is said of one holds good of the other; and if touch is not one sense but several, then the tangible must be, not one kind of sense-object, but several. This he says because, while his intention in general is to define the sense-object first, and after that the sense itself, in the case of touch he is going first to enquire into the sense; and this because the questions he wants to answer are more conveniently dealt with in this way than by treating first of the tangible object. So he prefaces his remarks with a kind of explanation, asserting that it does not matter whether we speak of the tangible or of touch.

§ 518. Of the two questions about touch and the tangible, the first is whether there are several senses of touch or only one; and the second is, what is the place or organ of feeling in touch? i.e. whether flesh is the touch-organ in animals that have flesh (which are those that have blood), and, in those that lack blood, something analogous to flesh; or, on the contrary, is flesh, or what corresponds to flesh, merely the medium of the sense of touch, while

<hr/>

[1] Lectio 23, § 545; 423ᵇ 17.   [2] 422ᵇ 23.

its primary organ is something internal, close to the heart? The second opinion is the one maintained in the *De Sensu et Sensato*.[1]

§ 519. Next, at 'For every sense seems',[2] he begins to answer these questions. With regard to the first he does three things: (*a*) he gives an argument for the view that there are several senses of touch; (*b*) he presents a solution of the problem at 'Here is a partial solution';[3] and (*c*) he criticises this solution at 'But it is not'.[4] The preliminary argument runs as follows: each single sense appears to bear upon a single pair of contraries, as sight upon white and black, hearing upon high and low, taste upon sweet and bitter; but included in the object of touch are several such pairs, hot and cold, moist and dry, hard and soft, and others of the same kind, besides heavy and light, sharp and blunt and so on. Therefore touch is not one sense, but several.

§ 520. Then, at 'Here is etc.',[5] he gives what might seem to be a solution, saying that one might answer that even in the other senses there appear to be several contrarieties; e.g. in hearing; for in the voice one can observe not only the contrariety of high and low, but that also of loud and soft, rough and smooth, and the like. Similarly colour presents various differences besides the contrariety of black and white, as that one colour is intense, another dull, one beautiful, another ugly. Yet these facts do not mean that either vision or hearing is not a single sense; nor then need the tangible's many contrarieties imply that touch is not a single sense.

§ 521. Then, at 'But it is not clear',[6] he sets aside this solution, saying that all the contraries found in the audible have but one subject, sound; and so too with colour in the visible. But no common subject can be found of all the contraries connected with touch; hence there does not seem to be one genus of tangible, and one sense of touch.

§ 522. To understand this passage we must consider that there is a proportion involved in the distinction between potencies and objects: if a single sense is a single potency, the corresponding object must be a single genus. Now it is shown in the *Metaphysics*, Book X,[7] that each genus includes one primary contrariety. Hence

---

[1] *De Sensu et Sens.*, c.2; 438^b 30–439^a 3.   [2] 422^b 23.
[3] 422^b 27.   [4] 422^b 33.
[5] 422^b 27.   [6] 422^b 33.   [7] X, 4; 1055^a 5–20.

there must be one primary contrariety in the object of any one sense; and that is why the Philosopher says here that one sense is of one contrariety.

§ 523. However, it is possible for one genus to include several contrarieties beside the primary one, and this either by a process of *subdivision*—as in the genus body, the first contrariety is between animate and inanimate; and since animate bodies are divided into the sensitive and insensitive, and the sensitive yet again into rational and irrational, contrarieties multiply in the genus body;—or *incidentally*, as, to take the genus body again, we find the contrariety of white and black, not to mention all the other corporeal accidental qualities. It is thus therefore that we must understand, as regards sound and voice, that, besides the primary contrariety of high and low, which is essential, there are other accidental contrarieties.

§ 524. Now in the genus of tangible things, there are several essential primary contrarieties, which can all in one way be reduced to a single subject, but in another way not; for in one way the subject of the contrariety can be found in the genus, which is related to the various contrary differences as potency to act. In another way the subject of the contraries can be found in the substance, which is itself the subject of the genus in which the contraries are included,—as when we call coloured body the *subject* of black or white. Speaking then of the subject which is the *genus*, it is plain that there is no one same subject of all tangible qualities. But speaking of the subject which is *substance* there is one subject of all these, i.e. the body that pertains to the substance of a given animal. And therefore Aristotle will say[1] that tangible qualities belong to body precisely as body, i.e. they are the qualities by which the elements of body are distinguished from one another. For the sense of touch discriminates among the factors that combine to constitute the animal body. Hence, *formally* speaking and in the abstract, the sense of touch is not one sense, but several; but it is one *substantially*.

§ 525. Next, at 'It is not evidence',[2] he deals with the second question; and this in two stages. First, he states the true answer; secondly, he comes to a conclusion that throws some light on the former question, at 'Therefore it appears'.[3] Note then, in the first

---

[1] §§ 529; 546.   [2] 422^{b} 34.   [3] 423^{a} 6.

place, that it might appear that flesh was the organ of sensation in touch, because we feel tangible things on the instant of contact.

§ 526. But, setting this argument aside, he remarks that to decide whether the organ of touch be interior or not (in the latter case the flesh would be the immediate organ of touch) it does not seem sufficient proof that, as soon as the flesh is touched, there occurs a tactual sensation, i.e. one feels; because if one were to extend a skin or tenuous web over the flesh the tangible would be felt immediately on contact with it; yet obviously the organ of touch would not be *in* the covering membrane. And again, if this web could become a part of one's nature,[1] one would feel all the sooner through it. Hence though at the touch of natural flesh the tangible is felt at once, still it does not follow that the flesh is the organ of touch, but only that it is a natural medium for it.

§ 527. Next, at 'Therefore, it appears',[2] he comes to a conclusion that throws light on the first question, saying that, flesh being a medium adapted to the sense of touch, it would seem that this part of the body has the same sort of relation to sensation as the air around us would have if it were a natural part of us. For though this air is but the *medium* of sight, smell and hearing, it would appear in that case to be the *organ* of these senses; and thus it would seem to us that we saw and smelled and heard by a single organ and with a single sense. But in fact just because, as a medium for such sensations, it is 'definite', i.e. distinct from ourselves, we see clearly that it is not an organ. Moreover there are obviously diverse organs for the three senses aforesaid, and therefore a clear distinction of three senses. But it is not so clear in the case of touch; for here the medium is a natural part of us.

§ 528. And he gives a reason for this difference. Air and water, the media of the other senses, could not be a natural part of us, for a living body cannot be constituted of pure air or pure water. These substances, being watery and fluid, are not solid or definite by themselves; they need to be terminated by other things, whereas a living body must be solid and self-contained. Hence the latter needs to be composed of earth and air and water, as required, i.e. as flesh requires in animals that have flesh, and correspondingly for those that have it not. So the body which serves as the medium in touch, i.e. flesh, is able to be naturally conjoined or united with

[1] *connaturalis homini.*   [2] 423[a] 6.

touch in such a way as to transmit the manifold sensations of touch.

§ 529. Then at 'That they are several',[1] he states another fact in support of this. By the tongue also, he says, we obtain several tactile sensations; for by it we feel all the objects of touch that are felt in other parts of the body, and we feel, besides, the flavour or savour that is not perceived in other parts of the body. If the other parts of flesh perceived savours, we should not discriminate between taste and touch, just as we do not in fact discriminate between the touch that discerns hot and cold and that which discerns wet and dry. But it is quite clear that touch and taste are two senses, because they are not mutually transferable: taste does not occur in every part where touch can occur. And the reason why taste is not to be found wherever there is touch is that savours are not qualities of those elements which constitute the bodies of animals; hence they are not, like tangible qualities, of the very substance of an animal.

[1] 423ᵃ 17.

BOOK II, CHAPTER XI, CONTINUED

THE MEDIUM OF TOUCH CONTINUED
ITS ORGAN AND OBJECT

A PROBLEM ARISES, ON THE ASSUMPTION THAT EVERY body has depth, that is, the third dimension. Bodies having [between them] a medium which is a body cannot touch one another. Now every liquid involves body, and so does everything moistened; it must either be water or contain water. But things in contact with one another in water must necessarily have water as a medium covering their extremities, unless these last be dry.[1] If this is true, it is impossible for one body to touch another in water. The same holds good of air (for air is to the things that are in it as water to things in water) although this fact is less evident to us, just as animals that live in water are unaware that bodies that touch in water are all wet. §§ 530-40

The question then is, whether there is one way of sensing for all objects of sense, or different ways for diverse objects. The latter at first sight seems to be the case,—taste and touch being effected by contact, the others from a distance. But this is not so: we perceive the hard and the soft through something intervening, just as we do the audible and the visible and the odorous. But of these objects, some operate at a distance, others close at hand. That is why the fact escapes us: we do perceive everything through a medium, but the fact

---

· [1] The Greek has 'these not being dry', 423ᵃ 26. St. Thomas (§ 531) follows M,

is not evident in the latter cases. Indeed, as we said before, if we were to perceive all tangible objects through a membrane, not knowing what was interpolated, we should think we touched the objects themselves, as we now do in air and water: for in these cases we think we touch the objects and that there is no medium. §§ 541–2

But the tangible differs from the visible and the audible; for we perceive the latter in that the medium itself produces some effect in us; whereas the tangible does not affect us *through* the medium so much as *with* the medium, simultaneously, as when one is struck on a shield. For the shield does not strike its holder *after* it is itself struck; but the two are struck at once. §§ 543–4

It would seem in general that flesh and the tongue stand to the sense-organ precisely as water and air to sight and hearing and smell, each to its respective sense. When the sense organ is touched (as when one places a white object on the surface of the eye), no sensation is produced in either case. Hence the organ of the tangible is internal; for the same thing happens in this sense as in the others; what is placed on the organ they do not perceive.[1] What, however, is placed on the flesh they do perceive;[2] flesh, then, is the medium of touch. § 545

Tangible objects vary therefore with differences of body as such—I mean the differences by which the elements are distinguished as hot and cold, wet and dry, as is stated in our work on the elements. The sense organ for these, the tactile, in which the sense called touch is principally lodged, is the part in potency to these qualities. For to perceive is to receive an impression. Hence whatever makes the organ to be such as itself is actually, does so, the organ being in potency thereto. Hence we do not perceive what has heat, or cold or hardness or softness to an exact similitude of our own heat, and so

[1] 'is not perceived', 423^b 25. [2] 'is perceived', *ibid.*

forth, but rather the extremes of these: the sense being, as it were, in a mean state between the contrary extremes in the objects perceived; which is how it discriminates between them. For a mean is discriminative; in the presence of either extreme it becomes the contrary one. Hence, as whatever is to perceive black or white must have neither of these in itself actually, but both potentially (and so with the other sense-objects), so touch must be actually neither hot nor cold.

§§ 546-8

Further: as sight is, in a way, of the visible and the invisible (and similarly with the rest of such opposites), so touch is of both the tangible and the intangible. The intangible is that which has the distinguishing quality of tangibles to a very small extent, as air is affected;[1] and also the excessively tangible, such as things destructive.

We have now said in outline something about each of the senses.

§§ 549-50

[1] The Latin renders clumsily a Greek idiom which simply means 'as with air', 424[a] 14.

§ 530. Having shown how the sense of touch requires a medium that is of the nature of the one who touches, the Philosopher goes on to ask whether it needs an extraneous medium. And his answer contains two points: first, he shows that touch does not occur without an extraneous medium; next, at 'The question, then, is whether',[1] he shows how touch and taste differ from other senses which perceive through an extraneous medium.

First, then, he remarks that in the case of touch one might doubt whether it has an extraneous medium, since we have seen[2] that the medium of touch is a natural part of us. The doubt assumes that every body has depth, i.e. a third dimension. And indeed it is clear that every body *has* three dimensions, length, breadth and depth; whence it follows that whenever two bodies have another between them, the former bodies are not in direct contact; they must be divided by a dimension.

§ 531. It is also evident that wherever there is a liquid or wet medium, there must be a body of some sort. For wetness is a quality and must exist in a body as its subject. Either then it resides in a body essentially, and then there is a liquid, e.g. water; or it exists in virtue of some adventitious body, in which case there is something that is wet, i.e. having water either on its surface only, or on its surface and throughout as well; so he says that every humid or wet body must either be liquid or 'contain' liquid. Now it is clear that bodies which touch in water have water as a medium between them covering their outer surfaces—otherwise they would be dry in water, which is impossible; for whatever things are in water must be wet, in the sense that water covers their surfaces. Water, then, is the medium between two

<hr>

[1] § 541; 423[b] 1.   [2] § 527.

things touching in water; whence it follows that it is impossible that one body should touch another in water immediately. And the same holds good for air, which is a fluid like water.

§ 532. For the air flows round the things that are in the air as water around things which are in water; but it is much less noticeable to us that air is a medium of this kind than that water is, on account of our being continually in the air so that it envelops us imperceptibly. In the same way, animals that live in water are not aware that when two bodies touch one another their surfaces are wet; for, being habitually in water, they do not notice the water between them and the bodies they are touching. There is also this other reason why the fact is less evident to us in the case of air than water: that air is more subtle and less perceptible to sense. Whenever, then, we touch anything there is always a medium between ourselves and the thing touched, whether air or water.

§ 533. But a question suggests itself. The medium for any sense should be lacking in the sensible qualities perceived by it,—like the colourless diaphanum. But obviously air and water have tangible qualities; so it seems they cannot be the medium for touch.

§ 534. Averroes answers that we are not affected by pure air or pure water. Nothing is passively affected, he says, save by its opposite, in accordance with the principle of passivity; but air and water are not contrary to us, they are indeed akin to us, in the same way as place to what is located in it. Hence our touch is not affected by air and water, but by qualities extraneous to them. What tangible qualities are perceived in air and water are due to their combination with extraneous bodies. As fire never loses its heat, so water never loses the quality proper to water; and if we ever perceive heat, this is due to the admixture of some extraneous body.

§ 535. Now this reply contains several errors. First, it is false to assert that air and water do not affect our bodies, as being akin to these in the manner of a locality to what is placed in it. For, clearly, our bodies get their place in nature, as also their natural movement, from the element that predominates in them; and, consequently, are related to locality and material environment as elements located to elements locating. But contiguous elements mutually affect one another at the points of contact, as is shown in the *Meteorologica*, Book I.[1] Our bodies therefore are naturally subject to the influence of the elements.

§ 536. Again, everything in potency is, as such, disposed to receive the influence of what is in act; and our bodies, being in a mean state between the extremes of the tangible qualities in the elements, are related to these qualities as potency to act. For, as we shall see,[2] a mean is in potency to extremes. It is evident, then, that our bodies are disposed to be influenced by the elemental qualities, and to perceive them.

§ 537. This error of Averroes comes from his failing to distinguish between the elements as contrary to, and as akin to and containing (as the locality contains the located), one another.

§ 538. Note then that the elements can be considered in two ways: in one way, in terms of active and passive qualities, and in this sense they are contrary to one another and act upon one another at their points of contact; but in another way, in terms of their substantial forms derived from the influence of the heavenly bodies. Now the elements are formal in the degree that they are akin to the heavenly bodies; and since it is of the essence of form to have the character of an inclusive whole, it follows that a superior body as such contains its inferior, and stands to the latter as a whole to a part which, though a part, is yet a distinct being; which is precisely the relation of locality to the located. And therefore the function of locating and containing is derived to the elements from the primary locating principle, the heavenly body. Whence it follows too that locality and local motion pertain to the elements in virtue of their substantial forms, not of their active and passive qualities.

§ 539. Another error is this, that he says that air and water undergo no changes save by mixing with something extraneous. For it is evident that air and water are in some degree destructible; but destruction and generation can take place in the elements without any mixing and yet involve change, as is proved in the *De Generatione*.[3] Therefore, so long as water remains water, its natural quality can be changed without the admixture of anything extraneous. The case of fire is quite different; being the

---

[1] *Meteor.*, I, c.2.   [2] §§ 547-8.
[3] *De Gen. et Corr.*, I, c.4; cf. II, c.7.

most formal and active of the elements, the rest are material in relation to it, as Aristotle says in Book IV of the *Meteorologica*.[1]

§ 540. It may be said, then, that air and water are easily changeable by extraneous qualities, especially in small quantities such as the amount of air and water between two bodies that touch one another. This is why the sense of touch is not impeded by the medium of water or air. And, of the two, air is less an impediment than water, for its tangible qualities are scarcely perceptible at all. But an intensification of the tangible qualities of air or water, as when they become extremely hot or cold, does of course impede the sense of touch.

§ 541. Then, when he says 'The question, etc.',[2] he shows the difference between touch and taste on the one hand, and the rest of the senses on the other: first rejecting a supposed ground of differentiation; secondly, stating the true difference, at 'But the tangible differs.'[3] In the first place, then, he says that this question of the extraneous medium of touch leads one to ask whether the sensation of all sense objects occurs in the same way, or diversely for diverse objects—as, at first sight, it does seem that touch and taste perceive by immediate contact, whilst the other senses apprehend their objects at a distance.

§ 542. But this difference is illusory; we do in fact perceive the hard and the soft and other tangible qualities 'through something intervening',[4] an extraneous medium, like the objects of other senses, the audible, the visible and the odorous. But whilst the latter objects are sometimes a long way from the sense, the tasteable and tangible are so close that the medium is practically imperceptible and passes unnoticed. We perceive all sense-objects through an extraneous medium, but this is not noticeable in taste and touch; to repeat what we said before,[5] if the medium of touch were a membrane that covered us without our noticing it, we should feel through a medium in a manner similar to the way we do actually feel in air or water. For as it is, we fancy we touch the sense objects themselves,[6] and that there is no medium.

§ 543. Then at 'But the tangible differs',[7] having rejected the false difference he states the true one, observing that tangible

[1] *Meteor.*, IV, c.1; 379ᵃ 15.
[2] 423ᵇ 1.   [3] 423ᵇ 12.
[4] 423ᵇ 6.   [5] § 526.   [6] i.e., immediately.   [7] 423ᵇ 12.

objects differ from visible and audible in that, whereas we perceive the latter because they set in motion the medium, and the medium in turn moves us, we perceive tangible objects, not because the medium has first moved us, but as being moved *simultaneously* with the medium, by the sense-object. It is as when a man is struck on his shield; the shield, being struck, does not then strike the man; man and shield are struck simultaneously.

§ 544. Nor is this simultaneity to be understood in the order of time only; for in sight the medium is affected by the visible and the eye by the medium, and yet sight occurs without succession in time. Smelling and hearing, however, take place with some temporal succession, as it is said in the *De Sensu et Sensato*.[1] The succession is due to the way the cause of the action operates; for whereas in the other senses a change in the medium is itself the cause of the sense being affected, it is not so in touch; for in other sensations the medium is present of necessity, whilst it is only as it were an accidental accompaniment of touch, due to the fact, for example, that the bodies in contact are moist.

§ 545. Next, when he says 'It would seem in general',[2] he concludes to the truth about the sense of touch: with regard (*a*) to the medium; (*b*) to the organ, at 'Tangible objects vary',[3] and (*c*) to the object apprehended by this sense, at 'Further: as sight etc.'.[4] First, then, he observes that the flesh and the tongue seem to be related to the organ of touch as air and water to the organs of sight, hearing and smell. Now in none of these latter senses can sensation occur if the organ itself is touched; thus a white body placed on the surface of the eye is invisible. Whence it follows that the organ of touch is within; for this sense works in the same way as in others; and if animals *can* perceive sense-objects placed on their flesh, it is evident that if flesh is not precisely a sense-organ it is certainly a *medium* of sensation.

§ 546. Then, at 'Tangible objects . . .',[5] he explains the nature of the organ of touch. Tangible qualities, he says, are the differentiations of body precisely as body, i.e. those differences which diversify the elements, namely dry and wet, hot and cold, of which Aristotle treats in his work on the elements, the *De Generatione et Corruptione*.[6]

[1] *De Sensu et Sens.*, c.1; 436ᵇ 20–1.   [2] 423ᵇ 17.   [3] 423ᵇ 27.
[4] 424ᵃ 10.   [5] 423ᵇ 27.   [6] *De Gen. et Corr.*, II, cc.2 and 3.

§ 547. For it is clear that the organ of touch, wherein the sense called touch primarily resides, is a part of the body in potency to these differentiations. Every sense-organ is passive to its object, because sensation is a kind of receiving; if the sense-object, which is the agent in the operation, reduces the sense to a condition similar to itself, the sense was previously potentially such. This is why, in the degree that the organ of touch already actually has any quality, it does not perceive this quality. We do not feel a thing as hot or cold, hard or soft, in so far as these qualities are already present in the organ of touch; rather, we perceive such tangible qualities as exceed that mean state between contrasted tangibles in which this sense properly consists. For as a mean is potential to extremes, so the organ of touch can discern the extremes of tangible qualities. It can be affected by either extreme because, as compared with either, it has the nature of the other: e.g. as compared with heat the tepid is cool, but as compared with cold it is warm. Thus the mean is passive to both extremes, being in a way the opposite of each. As the organ that knows white and black has neither of these actually and both of them potentially (and the like is true of the other senses) so also is it, and necessarily, in the sense of touch: its organ is neither hot nor cold, but in potency to both.

§ 548. But this occurs in a special way in touch. In sight, for instance, the organ in potency to black and white is quite free from both black and white, for it is quite colourless. But in the case of touch the organ cannot be completely deprived of heat and cold, moisture and dryness, for it is composed of elements having these qualities essentially. Rather, the organ of touch is in potency to its objects as a mean between extremes, potential to either extreme. Whence it follows that the closer an animal's composition approaches the state of perfect balance, the finer will be its sense of touch; and that is why man, of all animals, has the finest touch, as we have seen.[1]

§ 549. Next, at 'Further: as sight',[2] he concludes about the *object* of touch. As sight, he says, is of the visible and invisible, and the other senses are also of opposites (as hearing of sound and silence), so touch is of both the tangible and the intangible. 'Intangible' is said in two ways: either of that which has a tangible

[1] §§ 482-3.   [2] 424[a] 10.

quality to an excess which destroys the sense, like fire; or of that which has very slight tangibility, like air. Both are called intangible because both are hard to perceive by touch.

§ 550. Summing up, he says that he has treated 'in outline', that is, in a summary manner, of each of the several senses. For he deals with them more in detail in the *De Sensu et Sensato*.[1]

[1] cc.1ss.

BOOK II, CHAPTER XII

GENERAL CONCLUSIONS
ON SENSATION

IT MUST BE TAKEN AS A GENERAL RULE THAT ALL SENSA-
tion is the receiving of forms without matter, as wax receives a seal without the iron or gold of the signet-ring.
It receives an imprint of the gold or bronze, but not *as* gold
or bronze. Similarly the sense of any sense-object is acted
upon by a thing having colour or flavour or sound; not,
however, in respect of what each is called as a particular
thing, but in so far as each has a certain quality and according
to its informing principle. §§ 551–4

The primary sensitive part is that in which a power of this
sort resides. They [part and power] are indeed the same thing,
but differ in mode of being. What receives sensation will be
an extended magnitude, but neither being sensitive nor sensation is a magnitude. Each is, rather, a certain ratio and
power *of* a magnitude. § 555

It is clear from these facts why the excess of sensible qualities destroys the sense-organs. For if the change is too violent
for the sense-organ, the ratio [of the latter] is lost,—which
[ratio] *is* the sense. It is as with tone and harmony when the
strings are violently struck. Also it is plain why plants have
no sensation, though they have some share in soul, and are
affected by tangible objects to become hot or cold. The

reason is that they lack a mean or principle of this kind, able to receive the forms of sense-objects; they are acted upon materially.   §§ 556–7

It might be asked, is anything affected by odour if it cannot have the sense of smell?—or by colour, if it is unable to see? And so in the other cases.   § 558

But if what can be smelt is odour, whatever causes smell *is* odour.[1] Hence things incapable of smelling cannot be affected by odour. The same argument holds for the other senses. And of subjects that can perceive, the ability belongs to them only in virtue of each being sensitive.   § 559

The same is evident thus: neither light or darkness or sound or odour affect bodies; but only what they occur in does so; e.g. it is the air which accompanies thunder that smashes trees.   § 560

But things tangible and savours do so affect things. If not, what is it that inanimate things are affected and changed by?[2]
                                                    § 561
Therefore, do not also the other sense-objects have a like effect? But not every body is affected by odour or sound,—such recipients being only things indefinite and unstable like air: which may smell as though affected somehow.   § 562

What then is to smell, save to be 'affected somehow'? But to smell is to sense. Air, however, being so affected, becomes rapidly sensible.   § 563

[1] Or 'whatever odour causes, it causes smelling'. St. Thomas notes both senses, § 559.

[2] If Aristotle is here putting an objection to his own view, St. Thomas misses this nuance (§ 561). He takes this objection to be simply Aristotle's statement of one aspect of the matter as he saw it.

ST. THOMAS'S COMMENTARY
LECTIO TWENTY-FOUR

§ 551. Having examined each of the senses separately the Philosopher proceeds now to conclusions about sensitivity in general; and this in three stages: first he explains the nature of sense; then, at 'It is clear',[1] he solves certain problems connected with that explanation; and thirdly, at 'It might be asked',[2] he raises certain questions touching the way a sense is affected by its object. As regards the first point he explains (a) the nature of sense, and (b) the nature of sense-organs, at 'The primary sensitive part'.[3]

First, then, he says that it must be maintained in general, as true of all the senses without exception, that the senses receive forms without matter, as wax receives the mark of a ring without the iron or gold. This, however, would seem to be common to all cases of passive reception; every passive thing receives from an agent in so far as the agent is active; and since the agent acts by its form, not its matter, every recipient as such receives form without matter. Which indeed is sensibly apparent; e.g. air does not receive matter from fire acting upon it, but a form. So it would seem not to be peculiar to sensation that it receives form without matter.

§ 552. I answer that, while it is true that every recipient receives a form from an agent, there are different ways of receiving form. Form received in a patient from an agent sometimes has the same mode of existence in the recipient as in the agent; which occurs when the patient is disposed to the form in the same way as the agent. For whatever is received is received into the being of the recipient; so that, if the recipient is disposed as the agent is, the form comes to be in the recipient in the manner in which it exists in the agent. And in this case the form is not imparted without

---

[1] 424ᵃ 28. [2] 424ᵇ 2. [3] 424ᵃ 24.

the matter. For although the numerically one and the same division of matter that is in the agent does not become the recipient's, the latter becomes, in a way, the same as the material agent,[1] inasmuch as it acquires a material disposition like that which was in the agent. And it is in this way that air receives the influence of fire, and any other passive thing in Nature the action that alters its natural quality.

§ 553. Sometimes, however, the recipient receives the form into a mode of existence other than that which the form has in the agent; when, that is, the recipient's material disposition to receive form does not resemble the material disposition in the agent. In these cases the form is taken into the recipient 'without matter', the recipient being assimilated to the agent in respect of form and not in respect of matter. And it is thus that a sense receives form without matter, the form having, in the sense, a different mode of being from that which it has in the object sensed. In the latter it has a material mode of being,[2] but in the sense, a cognitional and spiritual mode.

§ 554. Aristotle finds an apt example of this in the imprint of a seal on wax. The disposition of the wax to the image is not the same as that of the iron or gold to the image; hence wax, he says, takes a sign, i.e. a shape or image, of what is gold or bronze, but not precisely *as* gold or bronze. For the wax takes a likeness of the gold seal in respect of the image, but not in respect of the seal's intrinsic disposition to be a gold seal. Likewise the sense is affected by the sense-object with a colour or taste or flavour or sound, 'not in respect of what each is called as a particular thing',[3] i.e. it is not affected by a coloured stone precisely as stone, or sweet honey precisely as honey, because in the sense there is no such disposition to the form as there is in these substances; but it is affected by them precisely as coloured, or tasty, or as having this or that 'informing principle'[4] or form. For the sense is assimilated to the sensible object in point of form, not in point of the disposition of matter.

[1] i.e. the same as the agent in respect of its materiality as well as of its form.

[2] *esse naturale.*

[3] Oxford transl.: 'it (the sense) is indifferent what in each case the *substance* is', 424[a] 23-4.

[4] *vel secundum rationem*, i.e. *sec. formam.*

§ 555. Next, at 'The primary sensitive part',[1] he concludes about the organ of sense. Since from his teaching that sense receives forms into cognition immaterially, which is true of the intellect also, one might be led to suppose that sense was an incorporeal faculty like the intellect, to preclude this error Aristotle assigns to sense an organ, observing that the 'primary sensitive part', i.e. organ of sense, is that in which a power of this sort resides, namely a capacity to receive forms without matter. For a sense-organ, e.g. the eye, shares the same being with the faculty or power itself, though it differs in essence or definition, the faculty being as it were the form of the organ, as was said above.[2] So he goes on to say 'an extended magnitude', i.e. a bodily organ, is 'what receives sensation', i.e. is the *subject* of the sense-faculty, as matter is subject of form; and yet the magnitude and the sensitivity or sense differ by definition, the sense being a certain ratio, i.e. proportion and form and capacity, of the magnitude.

§ 556. Then, when he says 'It is clear etc.',[3] he infers from these premisses a reply to two questions which might arise. What has been said, he observes, explains why an excess in the object destroys the sense-organ; for, if sensation is to take place there must pre-exist in the organ of sense 'a certain ratio'[4] or, as we have termed it, proportion. But if the impact of the sense-object is stronger than what the organ is naturally able to bear, the proportion is destroyed and the sense itself, which precisely consists, as has been said, in the formal proportion of the organ, is neutralised. It is just as though one were to twang cords[5] too violently, destroying the tone and harmony of the instrument, which consists in a certain proportion.

§ 557. His analysis also gives us the answer to another question, namely why plants do not feel, though they have some share in soul and are affected by certain sense-objects, i.e. tangible things, as well as by heat and cold. The reason why they do not feel is that they lack the proportion needed for sensation, in particular that balance between extremes of the tangible qualities which is a prequisite of the organ of touch, apart from which there can be no sensation. Hence they have no intrinsic principle for

[1] 424a 24.   [2] §§ 234-41.
[3] 424a 28.   [4] *ratio*, cf. § 555.
[5] i.e. of some stringed instrument.

receiving forms 'apart from matter', that is to say, no sense. They are affected and undergo changes only materially.

§ 558. Next, when he says 'It might be asked'[1] he raises a question touching the sense-object's action on the senses. Having just remarked that plants are affected by certain sense-objects, he raises the question whether a subject can ever be affected by objects other than those of which it possesses the sense; say, by odour if it has no smell, or by colour, if it has no sight, or by sound, if it is without hearing.

§ 559. Then, at 'But if what can be smelt is odour',[2] he brings two reasons against this suggestion. In the first place, it is proper to what can be smelt to cause smell; but odour is such; therefore if anything causes smell, it causes it by odour (or, according to another reading, odour causes smell). The proper action of odour as such is to cause a smell or occasion a smelling. Whence it follows that whatever receives the activity of odour as such has a sense of smell; and whatever lacks a sense of smell cannot be affected by odour. And the same argument holds of other beings that it is impossible that anything whatever might be affected by sense-objects; this can only happen in things endowed with sense.

§ 560. At 'The same is evident thus'[3] he states the second reason, as follows. The above argument is confirmed by experience. Light and darkness, smell and sound, produce no effect on sensible bodies, except incidentally, inasmuch as the bodies *with* those qualities do something, like the air that cleaves wood when it thunders; for it is not this *sound* that affects the wood, but the moving air.

§ 561. Then at 'But things tangible and savours'[4] he shows that it is otherwise with tangible qualities; tangible things and 'savours', i.e. flavours, do indeed produce, he says, an effect on sensible objects. But this is to be understood of the flavours, not precisely as such, i.e. as tasteable, but just in so far as the tasteable is something tangible, and taste a kind of touch. For if (insensible)[5] bodies were not affected by tangible qualities, there would be no question of inanimate bodies being affected and altered at all, these tangibles being the elemental active and passive qualities in virtue of which all bodily alterations take place.

[1] 424[b] 2.   [2] 424[b] 6.   [3] 424[b] 9.
[4] 424[b] 12.   [5] *Si . . . corpora insensibilia non paterentur*, etc.

§ 562. Next, at 'Therefore, do not also',[1] he shows that other sense-objects act on inanimate things, though not on all. For in asking: 'Therefore, do not' other sense-objects affect inanimate things as odour does?, he implies that they do. Yet not every body is affected by odour and sound, though all are by heat and cold. By such sense-objects are affected only unstable, impermanent bodies, such as air and water, which, being fluid, are not very self-contained; and that air can be affected by odour is obvious enough when it stinks.[2] Another reading says 'bears',[3] meaning that the phenomenon[4] is carried or borne to the sense by sensible objects other than itself.[5] The reason for this difference is that, as tangible qualities are productive of the other sensible qualities, they have more active power than the others, and can operate on bodies in general, whereas the other sense-objects, having less active power, can act only on things that are especially impressionable. The same principle applies to the light of the heavenly bodies, with its effect on terrestrial ones.

§ 563. Lastly, at 'What then is to smell?',[6] he solves the problem raised by the argument stated above. If a thing, he asks, can be affected by odour and yet not smell it, what is there in smelling odour other than just being affected by it? And he answers that smelling happens when a thing is affected by odour in such a way as to perceive it. But air is not affected in this way, since it has no sensitive potency; it is affected only so as to become a sense-object, inasmuch as it affords a medium for sensation.

[1] 424^{b} 14.   [2] *foetet*.   [3] *feret*.
[4] *species*: presumably the odour.
[5] Presumably, in this case, the air.   [6] 424^{b} 16.

BOOK THREE

BOOK III, CHAPTER I

IS THERE A SIXTH SENSE?
THE 'COMMON' SENSE-OBJECTS

THAT THERE IS NO OTHER SENSE BESIDES THE FIVE enumerated—I mean, sight, hearing, smell, taste, touch—is tenable for the following reasons: § 564–7

For if we have sensation of all the objects of the sense of touch (all varieties of the tangible being in fact perceptible by us through touch) then, if we lack some [class of] sensation, we must be lacking also in some sense-organ. Now whatever we perceive by contact is perceptible to us through that sense of touch which we do in fact possess. But whatever we perceive through a medium and without contact is perceived through intervening simple elements (I mean such as air and water); and [in this case] things are so disposed that if several sense-objects, differing generically from one another, are perceptible through one medium, then, necessarily, what has a sense-organ of this kind can perceive either object—e.g. if the organ is constituted of air, then air is medium for both colour and sound. But if there are several media for the same sense-object, as air and water are for colour (both being transparent), what is possessed of either [medium] alone will perceive what comes through either or both.[1] §§ 568–70

---

[1] 'through both', 425^a 2. Our rendering of this difficult paragraph is of course governed by the Commentary.

The sense-organs are formed of these two simple bodies only, air and water. For the pupil is of water; the [organ of] hearing, of air; and smell of either. But fire is found in none, or is common to all; for nothing without heat is sensitive. Earth either belongs to none, or is especially involved in touch. Whence it remains that there is no sense-organ without air and water. Now these organs certain animals do in fact possess. All the senses therefore are found in animals neither incomplete or defective (for even the mole is observed to have eyes beneath its skin). Therefore, if there is no other kind of body, and no qualities other than those of the bodies here present[1] no sense will be lacking to any [such] animal.[2]

§§ 571–4

But there cannot be a sense proper to the common qualities which we perceive by any one sense, yet not incidentally merely: such as movement, rest, shape, size, number, unity.

§§ 575–6

For we know all these by motion: that is, we know size by movement and from size, shape; for shape is itself a kind of size.

§ 577

What is at rest we know as not moving, and number as the negation of continuity and identity.[3] For each sense perceives some one thing, so that it is impossible that there should be a sense specially adapted to any of these.[4]

§ 578

The situation would, in that case, be as when we perceive what is sweet by sight. This happens because we take account of the sensation of both these, so that when they coincide we

[1] i.e. of this world.

[2] 'no s. will be lacking', 425ᵃ 13. St. Thomas adds 'to us' (§ 574), as do Hicks and Tricot in their versions.

[3] *negatione continui et proprii*. If M. réally wrote *propriis* he would agree with the Greek καὶ τοῖς ἰδίοις; but the Commentary (§ 578) hardly supports this reading.

[4] The Greek adds 'for example, movement', 425ᵃ 21.

are aware of it. If it were not so, we should perceive this only incidentally, as when we see the son of Cleon not as the son of Cleon but as something white; with which object there happens to coincide the fact of being the son of Cleon. But we have a general sense for common qualities, and this not merely incidentally. Hence, there is not a proper sense [for them]. [If there were] we should never perceive them except in the way we have said that we see the son of Cleon. The senses perceive incidentally what is proper to one another; [perceiving] not in their specific capacity, but in so far as they form one sense,—as in the perception of bile as both reddish in colour and bitter.[1] It does not pertain to either sense to judge that these are qualities of one thing. Hence arises the mistaken view that, if a thing is reddish, it is bile.   §§ 579–81

One might ask why we have several senses and not one only. Is it in order that the common qualities, which are consequent on the proper, should be less obscure—movement, dimension, number? For if there were no sense but sight alone, and that only of white as an object, these qualities would certainly be very obscure to the apprehension, and all things would appear alike, because colour and dimension always accompany each other. But the fact that there are common qualities attained by various senses, makes it evident that each of them is a distinct object.   §§ 582–3

---

[1] Bile=*cholera*, which M. puts for χολή. He puts *rubicunda* for ξανθή.

ST. THOMAS'S COMMENTARY
LECTIO ONE

§ 564. Here begins Book III in the Greek text; for the good reason, apparently, that it is here that Aristotle begins to examine the intellect. Now there have been philosophers who denied all difference between intellect and senses. But clearly the intellect cannot be any one of the exterior senses already considered;[1] for its apprehension is not restricted to any one particular class of sense-objects. So the question is whether sensitivity includes any other cognitive faculty such as might lend support to the view that intellect is somehow one of the senses.

§ 565. This section divides into three. First, he asks whether there is any other sense besides the five exterior senses. Next, at 'Now, if the soul is defined',[2] he proves that the intellect is entirely distinct from the senses. Thirdly, at 'As to the part of the soul',[3] he examines the intellectual part of the soul, by now clearly distinguished from the senses. The first of these sections has two parts: (a) he shows that there are no other *particular* senses besides the five exterior ones; and (b) he shows that, besides these, there is a *common* sense,—this comes at 'Since we perceive that we see'.[4] With regard to (a), after proving that there are only five particular senses, he shows why there are several of them and not one only. The former proof itself divides into two: first he shows that only the five senses apprehend particular 'sensibles'; and then at 'But there cannot be',[5] that the same five are the only senses to apprehend common 'sensibles'.

§ 566. To prove the first of these two points he argues thus. If a subject has a sense-organ in virtue of which a certain definite

[1] §§ 399–563.
[2] Lectio 4, § 615; 427ª 16.
[3] Lectio 7, § 671; 429ª 10.
[4] Lectio 2, § 584; 425ᵇ 11.
[5] § 575; 425ª 14.

range of sensible objects is naturally perceptible, this organ is the medium by which it perceives those objects. But the higher animals are endowed with all the organs of sense; therefore they can perceive the entire range of sensible objects; and as these organs are only five in number, the whole range of particular sensible objects is covered by the five organic senses.

§ 567. In proposing this argument Aristotle begins by stating his purpose in using it, i.e. to convince anybody that there are no other senses besides the five aforesaid.

§ 568. Next at 'For if . . .', he explains the major premiss of the argument: that a subject possessed of any sense organ can know all that can be known by that organ. This he shows from the sense of touch. There are obviously certain tangible qualities, namely (as has been said)[1] the various modifications of elemental bodies as such; for what has been said about the four elements has made it clear that there are such modifications. And all these tangible qualities, as such, fall within the range of our sensation.

§ 569. He then applies the same principle—that we are aware of precisely such objects as correspond to a given sense-organ in us—to the other senses. So he says: if we sense anything tactually perceptible, so that all tangible qualities, as such, are sensed by us, we can go on to argue in general that, if we do not in fact perceive a sensible quality, the reason must be that we lack the sense-organ to which it corresponds; precisely because if we have a sense-organ we do perceive certain sensible qualities. And this generalisation he then supports with particular examples.

§ 570. And first with respect to things we apprehend without any extrinsic medium; for he says that whatever we sense 'by contact', i.e. without an extrinsic medium, is reached by the organ of touch (under which he includes taste). But where, as in the other senses, certain extrinsic media, simple substances like air and water, come between us and the object, it is relevant to observe that one and the same organ may convey apprehensions of several objects different in kind; and in that case, the subject having the organ apprehends things different in kind. For example, if a sense-organ contains air, and air naturally retains and conveys both colour and sound, then a subject with an air-containing organ will be able to sense both colour and sound. If, on the contrary,

---

[1] §§ 546–8.

several different organs can attain the same sensible object—as happens in the case of organs composed, the one of air, the other of water, which are both transparent and therefore both receptive of colour,—then a subject with any one of such organs is able to perceive whatever is perceptible through, or by means of, all of them. The reason for his saying this is that the sense-organs which function through an extrinsic medium always correspond to that medium; and the fact is that the same sensible object, for instance odour, can reach different animals through different media, e.g. through water as well as air.

§ 571. Thirdly, at 'The sense-organs are formed',[1] he makes and explains a further statement: that the higher animals possess all the organs of sense. These organs, he says, are by nature composed of only two of the simple bodies, namely air and water—these being the two most passive simple bodies, and a ready passivity to the sensible object being the condition required in a sense-organ. Thus the pupil of the eye contains water, enabling the eye to receive a likeness of the thing it sees; the organ of hearing contains air (as we have noted already);[2] whilst the sense of smell is related by some to air and by some to water. Fire, on the other hand, by reason of its extreme activity, plays no part in the organs of sense, though in a certain way its presence is felt in all the senses; for sensitivity always presupposes warmth because it always presupposes life.

§ 572. Whilst earth as such has nothing to do with the sense-organs as such, it is in a special way a *condition* of touch: for it is mixed in with the body in a certain definite proportion which itself determines that mean between tangible extremes which gives the body a sense of touch at all; whence it follows that the organ of touch contains all the elements mixed in a certain proportion. But precisely as sensitive the sense-organs are made of air and water and of these only; and the air or water-composed organs are found in those animals we call 'higher animals'.[3] So he concludes by saying that, apart from naturally inferior organisms, such as the immobile animals which have only the sense of touch, all animals are endowed with all the organs of sense.

§ 573. Apart, too, from the 'defective',[4] i.e. animals lacking a

---

[1] 425ᵃ 2–3.   [2] § 453.

[3] *quaedam animalia . . . scilicet perfecta*; cf. § 255.   [4] 425ᵃ 10.

sense which should be theirs by nature, like blind or deaf men. But moles, for example, are 'higher animals', having eyes under their skin. Living underground they do not need sight; and if their eyes were uncovered the soil would aggravate them.

§ 574. Clearly this argument assumes a definite number of elements. It infers that, because there are only so many elements, the sense-organs that reach their objects through an exterior medium must be composed exclusively of air and water. Again, it presumes a fixed number of elemental qualities which are also the tangible qualities; and infers that all the latter are known to us; and that therefore we are equipped with all the sense faculties that exist. These conclusions could only be disproved by showing, either that there was some other corporeal element besides the four known to us, or that there were other tangible qualities (in the things around us and known to us), other than those which we do in fact perceive by touch. But there is no need to entertain such hypotheses, and we can safely conclude that the five senses we possess are the only senses that exist.

§ 575. Then where he says, 'But there cannot be',[1] he rejects the suggestion that the 'common sensibles' are the object of another and distinct sense. For the proper and direct object of any one sense is only known *indirectly* by any other sense; but the common sensibles are not known *indirectly* by any sense at all; rather, they are each *directly* known by several senses. Therefore they cannot be the proper objects of any *one* sense.

§ 576. Note how this argument proceeds. Aristotle first states the conclusion, that there cannot be any one organ specially adapted to the perception of the 'common sensibles' perceived directly, not indirectly, by all the senses, namely movement, rest and so forth.

§ 577. Then, at 'For we know',[2] he shows that these common sensibles are directly, not indirectly, perceived.[3] What enters sensation precisely by disturbing the sense-organ is directly, not indirectly, sensed; for to sense directly is simply to receive an impression from a sensible object. Now all these common sensibles are sensed in this way, which is why he says that we apprehend

---

[1] 425ᵃ 14.   [2] 425ᵃ 17.

[3] But *see* § 387, where *per accidens*, rendered here by 'indirectly', is rendered as 'incidentally'.

them by 'motion', i.e. through some disturbance of the organ.
Size, for example, is obviously sensed in this way: it is the subject
of such sensible qualities as colour or savour, and no quality is able
to act in separation from its subject. From which it follows that
shape also is known in this way, for shape is an aspect of size;
it is size as terminated. As Euclid says, shape is what is contained
in a limit.

§ 578. Rest also is perceived by means of movement, as darkness by means of light, for rest is the lack of movement. Number
also, since it comes from dividing a continuum or continuous
magnitude, is apprehended as the latter's negation, and its properties are known through those of the continuum; for as the continuum is infinitely divisible, so numbers can go on to infinity, as
is shown in Book III of the *Physics*.[1] Now it is clear that all the
objects of any sense go to make up one single direct object of
that sense, in so far as they concur in affecting the organ of that
sense; whence it follows that these 'common sensibles' belong to
the direct, not the indirect, objects of sensation; and further, that
no one of them is the object of any distinct and special sense.

§ 579. Then, at 'The situation etc.',[2] he shows that if they were
the object of any special sense they would be also indirectly
sensed. This is what he means by saying that the hypothesis in
question would imply that we perceived the common sensibles
in the same way as we see sweetness. For sweetness and (e.g.)
whiteness each answer to a distinct and special sense; hence, when
both qualities are found in the same thing each is known directly
by its own special sense and indirectly by that of the other. By
sight we know whiteness directly, sweetness indirectly.

§ 580. But if an object is not directly perceived by any special
distinct sense it can never *become* the indirect object of any other
sense through the concurrence of two senses or sensibles in the
same thing; it must always, in every respect, be indirectly perceived.[3] Thus I perceive indirectly that so and so is Cleon's son,
not because he is Cleon's son, but because he is white; whiteness
as such only *happens* to be connected with Cleon's son. Being the
son of Cleon is not (like sweetness) indirectly visible in such a
way as to imply its being directly perceived by some other sense.
On the other hand the common sensibles are not indirectly sen-

[1] *Phys.*, III, c.6.   [2] 425ᵃ 22.   [3] cf. § 395.

sible at all; they are a common yet direct object of several distinct senses. It follows that they answer to no special and distinct sense; if they did, they would be indirectly sensed, like the fact that so and so was Cleon's son.

§ 581. For the senses perceive each other's special objects indirectly, as sight that of hearing, and *vice versa*. Sight does not perceive the audible as such, nor hearing the visible as such (for the eye takes no impression from the audible, nor the ear from the visible) but both objects are perceived by each sense only in so far as 'one sense', i.e. one actual sensation so to say, bears upon an object which contains both. I mean that both the senses in question are exercised at once upon one and the same sensible thing, as when bile is at once seen as red and tasted as bitter; so that as soon as we see that this thing is red we judge that it is bitter. But there is no special sense of the *conjunction* of redness and bitterness, for this conjunction is quite incidental,[1] and what is incidental cannot be the object of any special faculty. And the fact that sight only indirectly knows savour helps us to understand why we are so often deceived in such cases, and jump to the conclusion that because a certain thing is, for example, red, it is therefore bile.

§ 582. Then at 'One might ask',[2] he goes on to enquire why there are many senses. As this is a question about a species as a whole it must be answered in terms of final causality (as he explains towards the end of the *De Generatione Animalium*);[3] not, like questions about individual peculiarities, in terms of material or efficient causality. So here he introduces the idea of purpose. The question might arise, he says, why we have several senses instead of only one; and he answers that it is to enable us to discern such things as movement, size and number, which are at once accompaniments of each distinct and proper sensible object and also common to them all. For suppose there were only the sense of sight, whose proper object is simply colour; then, since the impression of colour on the sense-organ immediately involves an impression of size, so that the two objects are inseparable, we should never be able to distinguish between colour

---

[1] *non est nisi per accidens*: incidental from the point of view of the senses brought into play.

[2] 425[b] 4.   [3] *De Gen. Anim.*, V, c.1; 778[a] 30–778[b] 19.

and size; they would appear to us as exactly the same. But the fact that size is also perceived by a sense other than sight, whilst colour is not, is enough to show us that size and colour are not the same. And the same holds good for the other common sensibles.

§ 583. To this one might add also the following reason. Since every potency as such implies an object, there must be a diversity of sensitive potencies if, and in the manner that, there is a diversity of sensible objects. But objects become sensible by impressing a sense-organ; hence to the different kinds of such impressions will correspond a diversity of sensitive potencies. Now one way in which the sense-organ is impressed by objects is by physical contact, whence arise both the sense of touch, perceiving what composes the physical constitution of an animal, and the sense of taste, perceptive of those qualities which indicate the suitability of an animal's nourishment for keeping its body in being. And another way by which the sense-organ can receive its impression is through a medium; and this involves either an intrinsic change in the object itself, as in the case of smell, which implies a certain disintegration of the thing smelt; or a change of place, as in the case of sound; or no change at all in the sensible object, but simply a spiritual impression upon the medium and the sense-organ, such as is made by colour.

BOOK III, CHAPTER II

SUBJECT AND OBJECT IN SENSATION

SINCE WE PERCEIVE THAT WE SEE AND HEAR, WE MUST
see that we see either by sight or by another sense.

§ 584

And if by another sense, then either this is the sense by
which we see, or another sense altogether.[1] But [then] the
same sense will bear on the coloured object and the sense of
sight. Hence, either there will be two senses for one object,
or one sense must be its own object. § 585

Further, if the sense perceptive of sight is other, either there
is a process to infinity, or there must be some sense which
takes account of its own operation: hence it is better to admit
this in the first instance. § 586

Here is a problem: if to perceive by sight is to see, and
colour, or what possesses it, is what is seen, then that which
first sees must be coloured. § 587

It is clear, then, that 'to perceive by sight' has not only one
meaning. For even when we are not seeing, it is by sight
that we distinguish between light and dark, though not in
the same way. § 588

Moreover, that which sees is, in a way, coloured; for each
sensitive faculty is receptive of the sense-object without its

---
[1] This sentence is not in the Greek.

357

material concomitant. Hence, in the absence of the sense-objects there remain sensations and phantasms in the sense-powers. The act of the sense-object and the sensation are one and the same: but these—I mean, for instance, sound in act or sight in act—are not identical in their being. For it happens that what has hearing does not hear all the time, and what has sound is not always sounding. But when that which is able to hear operates, and that which is able to sound sounds, both hearing in act and sound in act arise simultaneously. (Of which two, one might call one 'hearing', the other 'sounding'.)

§§ 589–91

If then movement and action and passion are in that which is acted upon, it follows that sound and hearing in act reside in that which *is* these potentially. For the act of what moves or causes is realised in the recipient; hence it is not necessary that what moves be itself in motion. The act of the sound-producing is therefore sound or a sounding; and of the hearing faculty, is hearing or audition.[1] For 'hearing' and 'sounding' are both twofold. And the same reasoning applies to the other senses and their objects. For as the action and the reception are in the recipient, not in the agent, so the act of the sense-object and of the sense faculty are in the sensitive recipient. However, whereas both are named in some cases (as sounding and audition) in others one or the other is nameless. Vision is the act of seeing, but that of colour has no name; and tasting is the act of the tasting faculty, but the act of savour has no name.

§§ 592–3

Since the act of the sense-object and of the sense faculty is one and the same (though each has its own being) it is necessary that they pass away or remain simultaneously, as in the above-mentioned case of hearing and sounding; and, therefore, of taste and flavour and the rest. It is not, however, necessary to hold this of the potency.

§ 594

[1] *aut auditus, aut auditio est*: 'hearing as completed or in process' (Wallace's transl.). St. Thomas takes *auditio* to be hearing as in act.

But on this point the earlier natural philosophers spoke erroneously, holding that there was no black or white without sight, no flavour without taste. In one way what they said was right, in another wrong. Inasmuch as both the sense-object and the sense-faculty exist in two ways, one in potency the other in act, what they alleged applies to the latter, but not to the former. But they made bald assertions about matters which call for distinctions.   §§ 595–6

Now, if voice is a harmony of some sort, and voice and the hearing of it are somehow one, and also, somehow, not one and the same; and if harmony is a proportion; then the hearing must be a kind of proportion. For this reason anything excessively shrill or deep destroys the hearing; and the same in flavours destroys the taste; and in colours, the sight, whether the excessively brilliant or the dark; and in smell, a strong odour, whether sweet or bitter; as if the sense were a certain proportion. Hence, too, those [savours] become delectable which, from having been pure and unmixed (e.g. the bitter or sweet or saline) are brought into a proportion.[1] Then indeed they give pleasure. And in general what is compounded is more of a harmony than the sharp or low [sounds] alone; or in the case of touch, what can be both heated and chilled.[2] Sense is a 'proportion' which is hurt or destroyed by extremes.   § 597–8

[1] Correcting *dicuntur* (Pirotta) to *ducuntur*.
[2] 'heated or chilled', 426^b 6.

ST. THOMAS'S COMMENTARY
LECTIO TWO

§ 584. Having shown that there are no more than five particular senses, the Philosopher next proceeds to ask whether these five senses spring from any one common potency. He is led to ask this by observing two activities which do not seem to be peculiar to any one sense, but to spring from some more general potency: for (a) we have some perception of the activities of the particular senses, e.g. we sense our own seeing and hearing; and (b) we distinguish between the objects proper to each of the different senses, between, for instance, sweet and white. So he enquires into the source of these two activities, first of the former, and then, at 'Each of the senses, then',[1] of the latter. The former enquiry divides into three parts. First[2] he states the problem, saying that the fact that we do perceive our own seeing and hearing and so forth implies either that sight (for example) is able to see its seeing, or that some other faculty has this power; and so also with the other senses.

§ 585. Next, at 'And if, etc.',[3] he brings objections against both these alternatives. But first he proposes two arguments to show that it is sight that sees its own seeing. (1) If one perceives one's seeing by a sense other than sight, then either that sense is a sense of colour, or the sense of colour and the sense of seeing colour are quite distinct. But if one and the same sense knows colour and the sight of colour, then the act of one and the same sense bears at once upon the sight of colour and the coloured thing. Whence follows one of two consequences. For if this sense of seeing and of colour is not the sense of sight, then there are two senses with the same object, namely the coloured thing; but if it is the same as sight, then sight is, after all, what perceives seeing—which is con-

---

[1] Lectio 3, § 599s.; 426ᵇ 8.   [2] 425ᵇ 11.   [3] 425ᵇ 13.

trary to the hypothesis. Nor could it possibly be maintained that the perception of seeing is not a perception of colour; without perceiving colour one cannot possibly perceive seeing, for seeing is only sensing colour.

§ 586. (2) The second argument begins at 'Further, if . . .'.[1] If the sense of seeing is other than sight, then the further question arises whether that sense of seeing also senses its own activity; and if it does not, then there must be a third sense which does this. And either this series goes on to infinity—which is impossible, both because no action could ever be completed which depended on an infinity of actions, and because no single subject can possess an infinite number of faculties—or we have to posit a sense which really does take account of itself, i.e. perceive its own sensation. But, by the same reasoning, there is no need to go beyond the first sense of all; there is no reason why sight should not sense its seeing. Therefore the sense of colour is the same as the sense of seeing colour.

§ 587. Then at 'Here is a problem'[2] he puts an objection from the other side in the form of a difficulty, which he proceeds to answer at once, because he has already, with the arguments given above, gone a long way towards settling the whole question. The objection runs thus. If it is by sight that we sense our seeing, then we simply *see* our seeing. Now nothing is seen except colour or coloured things; if then one sees that one sees, the first seeing (that which is subsequently seen), must itself be coloured; which would seem to be false in view of the principle already laid down,[3] that sight receives colour precisely in so far as it is colourless.

§ 588. Next, at 'It is clear then',[4] he answers this difficulty in two ways. In the first place, it is clear from what has been said that to see can mean different things—a perception of our seeing and a perception of mere colour; and this gives two distinct senses of the word. To make this clearer, observe that when we say that we are seeing we sometimes mean that our sight is, at the present moment, actually being impressed by the visible object, namely colour; but we can also sometimes mean that we are aware of the difference between light and dark even when we are not, at the moment, receiving an impression from an exterior sensible

[1] 425^b 15.　　[2] 425^b 17.　　[3] § 427.　　[4] 425^b 20.

object. But 'seeing' does not mean the same in both cases. So what this solution comes to is this, that the act of seeing can be regarded either as the disturbance of a sense-organ by an exterior sensible object, and in this sense colour *only* is seen; or as the act by which, after the said disturbance, and even on the disappearance of the sensible object, we form a judgement on the reception of the object into the sense-organ; and in this sense not only colour is seen, but also the sight of colour.

§ 589. Then, with 'Moreover, that which sees',[1] he proposes his second answer to the difficulty. This answer is required by the fact that colour has two modes of being: a material[2] mode in the object, a spiritual mode in sensation. The former solution implied only the first of these modes; this one depends on the second. And here he does three things: (1) he sets out the solution; (2) at 'If then there is movement' he proves what the solution assumes; (3) at 'Since the act' he applies it to the solution of certain other problems.

§ 590. First, then, he says that while one solution of the difficulty was found by maintaining that the subject seeing colour was not coloured, another might be argued on the assumption that the subject seeing colour is in a certain sense coloured, inasmuch as, in seeing, it takes in a likeness of colour, becoming like the coloured object. This is why the power by which one sees one's own seeing can still be strictly a power of sight. That the one who sees is, in a sense, coloured, he then proves from what was said above, i.e. that the sense-organ as such receives a form from the sensible object, but without matter;[3] which is why, when the object passes away, we retain sensations and images, i.e. the appearances in and by which animals somehow sense things.[4] So the one who sees becomes coloured in so far as he retains a likeness of colour and of the coloured thing; and not only sight, but any act of sense is identical in being with the act of the sensible object as such; although the mind can consider them apart.

[1] 425^b 22.

[2] *duplex esse: unum naturale in re . . . aliud spirituale in sensu.*

[3] §§ 551–4.

[4] *aliquo modo sentiunt animalia*: or perhaps '. . . animals in their various ways are sentient'.

§ 591. I say, the act of *sense*, meaning, for instance, actual hearing; and the act of the sensible *object*, meaning actual sound. For the two are not always in act: the hearer is not always hearing, nor the thing heard always sounding; but when the former goes into the appropriate act and the latter begins to sound, then together take place an actual sound and an actual hearing. Since, then, sight perceives an object and its actuality, and the one who sees is assimilated to the object, so that his act of seeing is the same being as the actuality of the object (though the mind can distinguish them), it follows that one and the same power in us sees colour, and the impression of colour on the sense-organ, and the visible actuality of the thing seen, and our sight of it. The power, then, by which we see our seeing is not really other than sight itself, though it can be thought of as distinct.

§ 592. (2) Next, where he says 'If then movement . . .',[1] he proves his assumption that the sensible object and the sentient subject are actually identical though they can be thought of apart; making use here of Book III of the *Physics*, in which it is proved that movement and action and passion exist in that upon which the action in question bears, i.e. in the thing that is moved by and passive to the action.[2] Now hearing is obviously passive with respect to sound. Therefore, the actual sound, no less than the actual hearing, exists on the side of the potency, in the organ of hearing; and this because the act of an active mover comes to full existence in what is passive to it, not in the agent as such. This is why it is not necessary that every mover be itself moved; for that is moved which has the movement; so that if the movement or action (which is a sort of movement) came to full existence in the mover,[3] the mover would also be moved. And as in the *Physics* it was laid down that action and passion are one single actuality of the same subject, though they differ in thought, so here he says[4] that the sensible object and sentient subject are actually identified in one subject, though they differ to thought. Hence the act of sound or of the sounding thing is the sensation of sound, while that of the hearer is hearing.

§ 593. For both hearing and sound can be regarded either as in act or as in potency; and what has been said of them in this

---

[1] 426ᵃ 2.   [2] *Phys.*, III, c.3; 202ᵃ 10ss.

[3] Which is not the case when, as he says, the mover is 'active'.   [4] §§ 590–1.

connection is true also of the other senses and sensible objects, namely that, as the *subject* of both action and passion is not the agent but the thing that receives the action—the agent being only the *source* of the action—so the act of the sensible object, no less than the act of the sense-faculty, exists in the latter as in its subject. But sometimes a distinct word is used for each act, as when the act of the object is called 'sounding'[1] and that of the faculty 'hearing';[2] while sometimes only the act of the faculty has a special name. Thus the act of sight is called vision, but that of colour is nameless; and the act of taste is called tasting, but that of savour has no name in Greek.

§ 594. Then (3) at 'Since the act', he uses the foregoing solution to answer two more questions. (*a*) Do the sense-faculty and its object together cease and together remain in being? Answering which, he observes[3] that, since the actualities of faculty and object are one actuality in one subject, though distinct to thought (as has been said),[4] therefore actual hearing and actual sounding must together cease to be and together persist; and so also with savour and tasting and the rest. But the same is not necessarily true of the faculties and objects as in potency.

§ 595. Which leads him[5] to reject an opinion of some early natural philosophers. They were wrong, he says, in supposing that nothing was white or black except when it was seen; or had savour except when it was tasted; and so forth. And because they thought that nothing existed except what was sensible, and that the only knowing was sensation, they concluded that the whole being and truth of things was a mere appearance; and further, that contradictories could both be true at the same time, if and because they seemed true to different people.

§ 596. Now this is partly true and partly false. Sense-faculty and sense-object can be taken in two ways, as in potency and as in act. From the point of view of act, what they said was correct: there is no sense-object without sensation. But it is not true from the point of view of potency. They made 'assertions', i.e. without distinguishing, in a matter which calls for distinctions.

§ 597. Then, where he says 'Now if voice',[6] he applies these principles to solve another problem: (*b*) why are certain objects,

[1] *sonatio.*   [2] *auditio.*   [3] 426[a] 15.   [4] §§ 590-3.

[5] 426[a] 20.   [6] 426[a] 27.

364

destructive of the senses, whilst others give them pleasure? And he says that since every harmonious and well-balanced sound is, as a sound, identical somehow with the faculty of hearing, the fact that the sound is a kind of harmony implies that hearing is the same. Now harmony or proportion is destroyed by excess; an excessive sense-object is therefore destructive of the faculty. An excessively sharp or heavy sound can destroy hearing; an excessively tasty thing destroys taste; too much brightness or darkness destroys the sight; over-powerful smells destroy the sense of smell. As though the sense itself in each case were a kind of proportion.

§ 598. On the other hand, if several sensible objects are mixed in due proportion the effect is pleasant. Thus savours mingled to a due sourness or sweetness or saltiness are extremely enjoyable. There is always more pleasure to be gained from combinations than from simplicity. Harmony is more enjoyable than mere high notes or mere low notes. So too in touch, with the combinations of hot and cold. For the sense-faculty delights in proportion as in its like, being itself a kind of proportion. But excess destroys it, or at least is disagreeable to it.

BOOK III, CHAPTER II, CONTINUED

THE COMMON SENSE

EACH OF THE SENSES, THEN, IS OF A SENSIBLE OBJECT [1] and in a sense-organ, precisely as such, and it discerns the differences within its object—for example sight, black and white; taste, sweet and bitter; and likewise with the other senses. §§ 599–600

Since we distinguish, however, between black and sweet, and any other of the sense-objects, comparing them and perceiving that they differ, there must be some sense for this operation too; for these objects are all in the sense-order. Hence it is also clear that flesh is not the ultimate sense-organ; for, in that case, this discrimination would have to be effected by touching. §§ 601–2

Nor could it be by divided [powers] that the sweet is discerned as other than the white: but both must be presented to some one faculty. For [otherwise] it would be like my perceiving one thing and you another: it would then certainly be evident that the two were different; but some one single [power] must say that they differ—i.e. sweet from white. Therefore it is one single power that asserts this; and as it asserts, so it understands and senses. It is patent that it is not possible to distinguish separate objects by faculties themselves separate. §§ 603–4

---

[1] Pirotta has *subjecti sens*. The Greek and St. Thomas (§ 600) have 'object'.

And the same holds with regard to separate points of time, as the following considerations show. For the faculty that says that good and bad differ says that they differ *now*, and this *now* is not extrinsic to the statement (I mean, as in saying *now* that they are different, but not that there is *now* a difference; whereas this [faculty] both says now and that the difference is now). Therefore they are discerned simultaneously; an undifferentiated principle distinguishes the two in an indivisible time.   § 605

But it is impossible for one and the same thing, if indivisible, to be moved by contrary movements in an indivisible point of time. For if the object be sweet, it so affects the sense or the mind, but if bitter, contrariwise, and if white, in another way.   § 606

Therefore [perhaps] what discriminates is numerically indivisible and inseparable, yet in essence distinct. For it is in one way capable of multiplicity because it perceives things divided off from one another: but in another way, it is indivisible. Thus in its essence indeed it is divisible, but it is indivisible locally and numerically.   § 607

But this is not possible;[1] one and the same indivisible thing can be in contrary states potentially, but not in its very essence. It can divide in its activities indeed; but it cannot *be* black and white at the same time; and therefore neither can it receive the forms of both—if this is how sensation and understanding occur.   § 608

But it is just as some speak of a point as one or as two, and in this sense as divisible. As indivisible [this faculty] is a unity making an instantaneous act of discernment. But as divisible, it is not a unity; for it uses the same point twice.

---

[1] 'Is not this impossible?' 427[a] 6.

In so far as it takes a third[1] as two, it takes account of two objects which are distinct, as in a separate principle. Yet in so far as it is one, it acts instantaneously and by a single act.

So much then by way of defining the principle by which we call any animal sentient.   §§ 609–14

[1] 'takes the boundary-point (τό πέρας) as two', 427ª 13.

LECTIO THREE

§ 599. So far the Philosopher's approach to an examination of the 'common sense' has been by way of our perception of our own seeing and hearing. But his scrutiny of this perception has so far only led him to the conclusion that seeing is itself perceived by the faculty of sight, though not in the same way as exterior objects are perceived. He has not yet decided that there is any one common faculty that takes account of the activities of the particular senses. But now he takes his enquiry a step further by pointing to another activity of the soul as evidence of the existence of a faculty with a common relationship to all the five senses: the activity of discriminating between various sense-objects. And here he does two things: first, he shows how far the particular senses can so discriminate; next, he investigates that discrimination of sensible objects which exceeds the scope of any particular sense (this begins at 'Since we distinguish').[1]

§ 600. He observes then, first, that we have seen that each sense is perceptive of its own proper object precisely in so far as a likeness of the object is formed within its own particular organ as such; for the organ of each sense is directly, not indirectly, impressed by the proper object of that sense. And within this proper object each sense discerns its characteristic differences; sight, e.g. discerning white and black, taste sweet and bitter; and so with the others.

§ 601. Then, at 'Since we distinguish',[2] he points out the faculty that discriminates, as the particular senses cannot discriminate, between the objects of the different senses. And here he does two things: first, he demonstrates his conclusion; then he puts and solves an objection (at 'But it is impossible etc.').[3] The demon-

[1] 426[b] 12. [2] 426[b] 12. [3] 426[b] 29.

stration has three parts: (*a*) he shows that there is a sense that perceives the differences between black and white and sweet; (*b*) that this sense is one faculty, not two; and (*c*) that it simultaneously perceives both objects between which it discriminates. First, then, he observes that whereas we are able to distinguish not only between black and white, or sweet and bitter, but also between white and sweet, and indeed between any one sense-object and another, it must be in virtue of some sense that we do this, for to know sense-objects as such is a sensuous activity; the difference between white and sweet is for us not only a difference of ideas, which would pertain to the intellect, but precisely a difference between sense-impressions, which pertains only to some sense-faculty.

§ 602. If this be true, the most likely sense-faculty would seem to be touch, the first sense, the root and ground, as it were, of the other senses, the one which entitles a living thing to be called sensitive. But clearly, if this discrimination were a function of touch, then the fundamental organ of touch would not be flesh; if it were, then by the mere contact of flesh and a tangible object, this object would be discriminated from all other sense-objects. Now this discrimination cannot be attributed to touch precisely as a particular sense, but only as the common ground of the senses, as that which lies nearest to the root of them all, the 'common sense' itself.

§ 603. Then, at 'Nor could etc.',[1] he shows that it is by one and the same sense that we distinguish white from sweet. For one might have supposed that we did it by different senses, by tasting sweetness and by seeing whiteness. But if this were true, he says, we could never perceive that white was other than sweet. If this difference is to appear it must appear to some one sense-faculty; so long as white and sweet are sensed by distinct faculties it is as though they were sensed by two different men, one perceiving sweet and another white; I this and you that. In this case sweet and white are obviously distinct, because I am impressed in one way by sweetness, and you in another by whiteness.

§ 604. But this would not *show* us their sensible difference. There must be one single faculty which 'says' that sweet is not white, precisely because this distinction is one single object of

[1] 426[b] 17.

knowledge. The 'saying' is the expression of an inward knowing; and as the saying is a single act, it must spring from a single act of understanding and sensing that what is sweet is not white. He says 'understands and senses', either because he has not yet established the distinction between sense and intellect, or perhaps because both these powers know the difference in question. As then the man who judges white to be other than sweet must be one man aware of both objects, so he must do this by means of one faculty; for awareness is the act of a faculty. Hence Aristotle's conclusion, that it is clearly impossible to perceive 'separate objects', i.e. that two things are distinct, by 'separate', i.e. by distinct, means; there must be one single power aware of both things.

§ 605. Next, at 'And the same',[1] he proves that this awareness is of both things simultaneously, not at 'separate', i.e. distinct, moments. This will appear, he says, from what follows; for as a judgement on the difference between things is single with respect to what is discerned, for example that good is distinct from bad, so is it single with respect to the *time* in which it is discerned. One judges that such and such a difference exists *when* one is judging. Nor is the time only accidentally connected with the difference itself, as it would be if 'when' referred to the subject judging and the meaning was 'he *now* judges that a difference exists' (and not ' . . . that now a difference exists'); in which case the 'now' would be merely incidental to the *object*. But the judgement of difference is in the present in the sense that there is difference at present; which necessarily implies a simultaneous apprehension of the two different objects; they are both known in the same instant as they are known to be different. Obviously, then, they are known at once and together. Hence, as one undivided faculty perceives the object's difference, so in one undivided moment both are apprehended.

§ 606. However, he now[2] puts an objection to himself;—concerning which he does four things. First, he states the objection, as follows. One and the same indivisible thing cannot move in different directions in one and the same indivisible moment of time. Now intellect and sense are moved by their objects, the one by an intelligible thing to understand it, the other by a sensible

[1] 426ᵇ 23–4.　　　　[2] 426ᵇ 29.

thing, to sense it. But distinct and mutually exclusive sense-objects cause distinct and mutually exclusive movements; therefore one and the same sensitive or intellectual faculty cannot know several distinct and mutually exclusive objects at the same time.

§ 607. Then, at 'Therefore what',[1] he suggests the following solution. That which perceives the difference between mutually exclusive objects does so simultaneously and is numerically indivisible, i.e. it is one as a subject of actions; but in its essence, and therefore to thought, it is divided. So, then, it is in one way an indivisible subject which perceives 'divided', i.e. distinct objects; but in another way, the percipient subject is itself divisible, inasmuch as in essence, and to thought, it is divisible—even while it does not cease to be locally and numerically one indivisible subject of actions. He says 'locally' referring to the fact that different faculties are found in different parts of the body.

§ 608. Thirdly, at 'But this is not possible',[2] he rejects this solution: because if a thing *really* is a self-identical and indivisible subject, even if it is not so in thought, it can indeed be in potency to diverse movements, but once it is actually 'in activity' or moving, it cannot do so in mutually exclusive ways; for this implies a *real* divisibility. One and the same indivisible thing cannot be white and black at the same time in the same respect; nor, for the same reason, can it receive simultaneous impressions from white and black objects. And the same is true of understanding and sensing, if these are a kind of reception of impressions.

§ 609. Fourthly, at 'But it is just as',[3] he gives the true solution, using the simile of a point. Any point between the two ends of a line can be regarded either 'as one or two'. It is one as continuing the parts of the line that lie on either side of it, and so forming the term common to both. It is two inasmuch as we use it twice over, to terminate one part and begin the other. Now sensitivity flows to the organs of all the five senses from one common root, to which in turn are transmitted, and in which are terminated, all the sensations occurring in each particular organ. And this common root can be regarded from two points of view: either as the common root and term of all sensitivity, or as the root and term of this or that sense in particular. Hence, what he means is that, just as a point, under a certain aspect, is not one only but also two,

[1] 427[a] 2.   [2] 427[a] 5.   [3] 427[a] 10.

or divisible, so the principle of sensitivity, if regarded as the root and term of seeing and of hearing, appears twice over under the same name, and in this way it is divisible.

§ 610. In so far then as this single principle receives and 'takes account of two distinct' and separate 'objects', these are known 'as in a separate', i.e. as by a divisible 'principle' of knowledge; 'but in so far as' it is single in itself it is able to know these objects and their differences together and simultaneously. It is a common sensitive principle, aware of several objects at once because it terminates several organically distinct sensations; and as such its functions are separate. But just because it is one in itself it discerns the difference between these sensations.

§ 611. Now all sensuous activity being organic, this common sensitive principle must have its organ; and since the organ of touch is all over the body it would seem to follow that, wherever the ultimate root of the organ of touch may be, there also is the organ of the common sensitive principle. It was with this in mind that Aristotle has said[1] that if flesh were the fundamental organ of touch, we should discriminate between various sense-objects by merely touching things with our flesh.

§ 612. We may note also that though this common principle is set in motion by the particular senses, all the impressions of which are transmitted to it as to their common term, this does not imply that the particular senses are nobler than the common sense; though certainly a mover or agent is, as such, nobler than what it moves or acts upon. Nor is the exterior sensible object nobler, strictly speaking, than the particular sense moved by it, though it is in a way nobler as having actually the white or sweet quality which the senses have only potentially; but of the two the sense is strictly the nobler thing, and this in virtue of sensitivity itself— hence in receiving the object immaterially it ennobles it, for things received take, as such, the mode of being of the receiver. And the common sense receives its object in a still nobler way because it lies at the very root of sensitivity, where this power has its point of greatest unity. Yet we must not suppose that the common sense appropriates *actively* the impressions received in the sense-organs; all sensitive potencies are passive; and no potency can be both active and passive.

[1] § 602.

§ 613. Observe too that each particular sense is able to discriminate between contrary sense-objects in virtue of its share in the power of the 'common sense'; each is one of the terminal points for the various influences which reach us from mutually exclusive exterior sense-objects through a medium. But the final judgement and discrimination belong to the 'common sense'.

§ 614. Concluding,[1] he says that he has now discussed the principle according to which an animal is said to have, or be able to have, sensations.

[1] 427ª 14.

BOOK III, CHAPTER III

DISTINCTION OF SENSE FROM INTELLECT

ERROR

IMAGINATION AND OPINION

NOW, IF THE SOUL IS DEFINED PRINCIPALLY BY TWO differences, by motion in place and by what it is to understand, discern and sense, it would seem that both to understand and to judge are a kind of sense-perception,—for in either case the soul discerns and knows reality.

§§ 615–16

The early philosophers, indeed, said that rational judgement and sensation were the same thing, as when Empedocles says: 'The will is increased in man in the present moment',[1] and in another place:[2] 'Whence it always affords them new objects of knowledge.' To the same purport is that line of Homer:

'The mind of mortals is such as the father of gods and men brings into light'.[3]   §§ 617–21

All these suppose the intellect to be something corporeal, like sensation, and that both sensing and judging are of 'like by like', as we explained at the beginning of this treatise.

§§ 622–3

[1] M. translates μῆτις as *voluntas*, 'will', better rendered as 'craft', 'skill', or 'practical reason'.

[2] St. Thomas takes *et in aliis* to mean 'in other animals'. The above rendering agrees with the Greek, 427ª 24.

[3] *Od.*, XVIII, 136: quoted more fully here than in the Greek, as St. Thomas points out (§ 620).

But they ought at the same time to have treated of error,—which is a state more natural to animals [than truth], and in which the soul spends the greater part of its time. So it must follow, either that all that seems to be really is (as some maintain) or that error is a contact with what is unlike—this being the contrary of knowing like by like.   §§ 624–7

It would appear, however, that error and knowledge are the same with respect to contraries.   § 628

Now it should be evident that rational judgement and sensation are not the same. The latter is in all animals, the former in but few.   § 629

Nor again is understanding [the same as sensation]. It may be correct or incorrect,—correct as prudence, science and sound opinion; incorrect as the opposite of these. This is not the same as sensation. For sensation is always true of its own proper objects, and is found in all animals, whereas intelligence is sometimes accompanied by error, and is found in no species that lack reason.   §§ 630–1

For imagination is other than both sensation and intellect. Yet it cannot occur without sensation, and without it there is no opinion.   § 632

It is evident that opinion and imagination are not identical. The latter state arises in us at will, as a picture before our eyes, like the imagery employed by those who cultivate memory training. But opinion is not within our power in this way; it must express the true or the false, of necessity.

§ 633

Further, when we think that anything is arduous or fearful, we are at once emotionally affected; and likewise, if there be occasion for confidence. But in imagining, it is as though we were regarding in a picture things arduous or encouraging.

§§ 634–5

These are, besides, the various modes of making a judgement: speculative science, opinion and prudence; with their contraries. Let the question of their differences be discussed elsewhere. § 636

ST. THOMAS'S COMMENTARY
LECTIO FOUR

§ 615. After showing that to perceive the acts of the particular senses, and to discriminate between their various objects, are activities not beyond the range of sensitivity as a whole, the Philosopher now addresses himself to the question whether rational judgement and understanding are beyond its range. And he does two things here: first, he proves that rational judgement and understanding are not activities of sense, which is the same as to show that sense and intellect are distinct faculties; secondly, at 'For imagination is other etc.',[1] he shows that the image-forming faculty, which is a kind of sense, is other than the power to form opinions, which pertains to reason. The former argument subdivides into (1) a statement of the theory of the identity of sense and intellect, and (2) a refutation of this theory.[2] To the statement itself he adds an explanation of the origin of this theory,[3] and also some remarks of certain philosophers, which seemed relevant.[4]

§ 616. First,[5] then, he says that as the early philosophers defined the soul especially in terms of local motion and knowledge—which includes rational discernment and sensation—it would seem to have been their view that understanding and judging were the same sort of activity as sensing; for in both there is discernment and knowledge.

§ 617. Next, where he says 'The early philosophers',[6] he shows that this is more than a mere inference from their general teaching, and that they explicitly taught that sensation and rational understanding were identically the same. But in order to understand the words which he quotes here of these philosophers, and their

---

[1] 427[b] 14; § 632.   [2] 427[b] 1.   [3] 427[a] 26.
[4] 427[a] 21.   [5] 427[a] 16.   [6] 427[a] 21.

relevance to the present argument, we have to consider that no body can act directly upon what is purely incorporeal. Now the sense-faculties are in part corporeal, because of the bodily organs in which they exist. Therefore they are subject to the influence of the heavenly bodies,—though, even so, only indirectly, for neither the soul itself nor any of its powers is directly subject to the action of corporeal matter. Consequently, the imagination and sense-appetite are modified in various ways by the influence of the heavenly bodies. Brute animals are generally governed by this influence, since they are led entirely by their senses. Hence to suppose that heavenly bodies act directly upon the intellect and will is to admit that these faculties are corporeal. And this is what some of the early philosophers seem to have said.

§ 618. Empedocles, for instance, said that in man, no less than in other animals, the 'will is increased', i.e. prompted to act, 'in the present moment', i.e. according to its time-context; which itself depends on the disposition of the stars. It is the present moment that 'always affords them', i.e. to men and the other animals 'new objects of knowledge'; for all the animals, men included, envisage things differently at different times.

§ 619. To the same effect Homer speaks of the mind of mortal man being 'such as the father of gods and men' (i.e. the sun) 'brings into light'. He calls the sun the 'father of men' because of the part it plays in human procreation; for man is born from man and the sun. And the sun he calls the 'father of gods', either following the old view that made gods of the other stars which, the astronomers tell us, are governed somehow by the sun, or following the view that certain men are divine because generated by solar influence. And the sun is, of course, strongest in the daytime while it is visible and is moving across the upper hemisphere; hence the name of 'day-planet' given it by astronomers. So what Homer is saying is that the sun is the cause of understanding in men, and that their knowledge of things varies with the movement, situation and appearance of the sun.

§ 620. In point of fact Aristotle quotes only the beginning of Homer's line; neither the Greek text nor the Arabic gives us the rest of it. Aristotle relies on his readers remembering the whole of it from a part, as when one quotes the first words of a well-known verse of any author. But Boethius cites the whole of

Homer's line, for the sake of his Latin readers who were not familiar with that poet.

§ 621. What has been said, then, makes it quite clear that if the stars do have a direct influence on the intellect and will, then there is no difference between the intellect and the senses. There is no difficulty, however, about admitting an indirect stellar influence upon intellect and will, in so far as these faculties act in conjunction with the faculties of sense. Thus any injury to the bodily organ of the imagination will impede the intellect; and the will is incited towards choosing or not choosing by sensuous desire. But since the will is never drawn of necessity, but remains free to follow or not the promptings of desire, human actions are never completely determined by astral influences.

§ 622. Next, he states the reason why this opinion arose. If you take away that by which things differ, they are left the same; and if rationality is removed from man he is left simply an animal. Now the difference between intellectual and sensuous cognition is that the latter is corporeal. Sensation cannot occur apart from the act of a bodily organ, whereas understanding, as we shall prove later,[1] does not take place by means of such an organ. But to the early philosophers understanding seemed a corporeal action like sensation; hence they supposed that intellect and sense were the same.

§ 623. And how they thought of both activities as corporeal he next explains,[2] saying that they maintained that the acts of discernment in both intellect and sensation arose from the presence of a likeness of an object (as it was said in Book I) in the knowing subject; and they thought this likeness was essentially corporeal, so that earth was known by earth and water by water, and so on with other objects. And consequently, sensing and understanding were both conceived of as functions of corporeal nature, and therefore as fundamentally the same.

§ 624. He goes on now, at 'But they ought',[3] to criticise this opinion, first with regard to the premiss on which it depends, and then at 'therefore it is evident', directly in itself. So he remarks, first, that the philosophers who explained knowledge by the presence of a likeness should have also given some explanation of error; for error seems to be even more natural to animals,

---

[1] § 684.   [2] 427ᵃ 26.   [3] 427ᵃ 29ss.

as they actually are, than knowledge. For experience proves that people easily deceive and delude themselves, whilst to come to true knowledge they need to be taught by others. Again, the soul is involved in error for a longer time than it spends in knowing truth, for to acquire this knowledge even a long course of study hardly suffices. (Now this argument is indeed valid against those early philosophers who regarded knowledge as natural to the soul in the sense that the soul, being constituted of the first principles of things, knew all that could be known, and knew it actually, not merely in potency.)

§ 625. But Aristotle's objection might be answered in two ways. One might say that since the early thinkers did not admit the existence of error (their view being, as we have seen,[1] that all that seemed to be true was true) they did not need to explain error.

§ 626. Secondly, it might be answered that to explain knowledge as a contact of the soul with what is like itself is implicitly to explain error as the soul's contact with what is unlike itself. Hence, from the fact that the early thinkers did not explicitly render an account of error, he infers that either they identified truth with appearances, or that they held that the soul went astray into error by touching things unlike itself; since to touch the unlike seems the opposite of knowing the like.

§ 627. The first alternative is refuted in Book IV of the *Metaphysics*.[2]

§ 628. So he proceeds to examine the second alternative, at 'It would appear'.[3] The like and the unlike are obviously contraries. But in knowledge and in error the relation to either of two contraries is the same: if you know one, you know the other; if you err about one, you err about the other. Hence he says that knowledge and error are apparently the same with respect to contraries. It follows that touching a like thing cannot cause true knowledge if touching an unlike thing causes error; for in that case one would know one of a pair of opposites and be mistaken about the other.

§ 629. Then, at 'Now it should be evident',[4] he attacks the theory in question directly, and shows that neither rational judgement nor understanding is the same as sensing; they belong to

[1] § 39; cf. §§ 595–6.   [2] IV, c.5, 1010ᵇ 1ss.   [3] 427ᵇ 5.   [4] 427ᵇ 6.

intellectual knowledge. Now the intellect as judging is said to have wisdom, whilst as apprehending it is said to understand. Showing therefore that rational judgement and sensation differ, he argues thus: sensation belongs to all animals, but wisdom is found in only a few; therefore they differ. And he allows wise judgement to 'a few animals', and not exclusively to man, because even certain brute animals have a sort of prudence or wisdom, in that they instinctively form correct judgements on what they need to do.

§ 630. Secondly, at 'Nor again',[1] he shows the difference between understanding and sensation; and this in two ways; the first being as follows. Understanding may be 'correct' or 'incorrect'. 'Correct' understanding bears either upon speculative and necessary truths, and then it is called scientific; or upon a right ordering of practical action in the sphere of the contingent, and then it is part of prudence; or upon one of two alternatives, but without deciding finally in favour of *this* one, and while still admitting that the *other* might be the truth; in which case it forms a reasonable opinion. 'Incorrect' understanding is in each case the opposite of correct understanding; it results in spurious science or imprudent decisions or foolish opinions. Sensation, on the other hand, can only be 'correct', for the senses are infallible with respect to their proper objects. Therefore sensation and understanding are different.

§ 631. And since it might be objected that 'correct' understanding, at least, is the same as sensation, he adds that sensation is found in 'all animals' whilst understanding is found only in rational animals, that is, in men. For it is proper to man to come to an understanding of intelligible truth by way of rational enquiry; whereas the immaterial substances, which are in a higher degree intellectual, apprehend truth immediately without having to reason about it. Therefore 'correct' understanding is not the same as sensation.

§ 632. Next, when he says 'For imagination',[2] he shows the difference between opinion, which is of the intellect, and imagining, which is of the senses. And here he does two things: first, he shows that imagining is not opinion; then he studies the nature of imagining, at 'Concerning understanding'.[3] The former sub-

---

[1] 427ᵇ 8.   [2] 427ᵇ 14.   [3] Lectio 5, § 637.

divides into three parts. First he states his aim, saying that another way to grasp the difference between sense and intellect is to consider that imagining differs from both, yet presupposes sensation (as will be shown later),[1] and itself is presupposed by opinion. For it seems that, as imagining is to the senses, so is opinion to the intellect. When we sense any sensible object we affirm that it *is* such and such; but when we imagine anything we make no such affirmation, we merely state that such and such *seems* or appears to us. The word 'imagining' itself[2] is taken from seeing or appearing. Similarly, when we understand an intelligible object we affirm that it *is* such and such; but when we form opinions, we say that such and such *seems* or appears to us. For, as understanding depends upon sensing, so opinion depends on imagining.

§ 633. In the second place, at 'It is evident',[3] he proves by two arguments the difference between opinion and imagination. The first is this. Images can arise in us at will, for it is in our power to make things appear, as it were, before our eyes—golden mountains, for instance, or anything else we please, as people do when they recall past experiences and form them at will into imaginary pictures. But we are not free to form opinions as we please; one cannot form an opinion without resting it on some reason, true or false. Therefore opinion is not the same as imagination.

§ 634. The second argument at 'Further, when'[4] is this. Opinion has an immediate effect on our affective nature; so soon as we opine that anything is disagreeable or frightening we feel sad or frightened. So also if anything is thought of as encouraging or promising, we at once feel hopeful or glad. But it is not so with imagining; for so long as anything appears merely imaginatively to us, it is as if we were merely looking at pictures of frightening or encouraging objects. Therefore opinion differs from imagining.

§ 635. Now the cause of this difference is that our affective nature is not impressed or swayed by the mere vision of things brought about by imagining; but only by things regarded as good or evil, useful or harmful; and this, in man, presupposes opinion with its positive or negative judgements as to the evil and terrible or the desirable and encouraging. Mere imagining passes no judgement on things. In brute animals, however, the affective power

[1] §§ 655-9.   [2] *phantasia*; cf. § 668.
[3] 427[b] 16.   [4] 427[b] 21.

is swayed by natural instinct; which plays the same part in them as opinion in man.

§ 636. Thirdly, at 'There are, besides',[1] he remarks that of the many forms of intellectual judgement, such as science, prudence and opinion, with their contraries, he does not intend to treat here. They are dealt with elsewhere, in the *Ethics*, Book VI.[2]

[1] 427^b 24.　　　　　[2] E.N., VI, cc.3–11.

BOOK III, CHAPTER III, CONTINUED

IMAGINATION
WHAT IT IS NOT

CONCERNING UNDERSTANDING, SINCE IT IS ONE
thing and sensation another, while imagination
seems to differ from both of these and from opinion
also, let us settle first what imagination is, and then speak of
the other matter]opinion].   § 637

If, then, imagination is that by which we say that some
phantasm arises within us, it follows (if we are not speaking
metaphorically) that it is one of the faculties or dispositions
in virtue of which we perceive and pronounce either falsely
or truly. Such faculties are sensation, opinion, knowledge,
understanding.   §§ 638–40.

That it is not sensation is evident. For sensation is either in
potency or in act: the faculty of sight, or the actual seeing.
But appearances occur when neither of these is present; as
when we dream.   § 641

Further, sensation is always to be found, in potency in all
animals that are not defective. Not so imagination.[1]

                                                              § 642
But if they were the same in act, it would happen that

---

[1] 'Again, sense is always present, imagination not', 428ª 8. St. Thomas
follows M.

imagination was present in all animals. But this apparently is not so—e.g. in the ant, the bee, the worm.   §§ 643-4

Again, sensations are always true: but many phantasms are false.   § 645

Again, we do not say, when we are functioning accurately with regard to sense-objects: 'that *seems* to us a man'; we say this rather when our sensation is indistinct; in which case it may be true or false.   § 646

And, as we said before, such appearances come to men in their sleep.[1]   § 647

And it is certainly not one of the qualities which are always truthful, such as knowledge or understanding: for imagination can be true or false.[2]   § 648

It remains therefore to consider whether it is opinion. For opinion can be either true or false. But belief follows immediately on opinion, for one never finds a man not believing the opinion that seems to him to be true. But there is no such thing as belief amongst animals, although there is imagination in many.   § 649

Further: belief attaches to all opinion, and is due to conviction, which in turn is due to reasoning. Now imagination is found in some beasts; but reason in none.   § 650

It is therefore evident, on these grounds, that neither opinion accompanying sensation, nor through sensation, nor a combination of opinion and sensation, will constitute imagination.   § 651

[1] 'when their eyes are shut', 428^a 16.
[2] 'can be false', 428^a 18.

And it is clear that opinion would have simply the same objects as sensation.[1] I mean, that an imagining of 'white' would be a combination of the sensed 'white' and the opinion that it is 'white'. For it would not be produced by an opinion of 'white' and a sensation of 'good'.[2] To imagine, then, would be having an opinion of the same thing as what one senses— the same absolutely speaking.   § 652

False appearances, however, are possible about which at the same time one holds a true opinion: and indeed the Sun seems to be a foot across, yet is believed to be greater than the inhabited world. Therefore it comes about, either that one discards the true opinion which one had formed, the thing itself remaining, and one neither forgets nor ceases to hold [that opinion]: or, if one still retains it, the same must be both true and false. But a false [opinion] is produced if there is an unnoticed transformation in the facts. Imagination therefore is neither one of these, nor constituted from these.

§§ 653–4

[1] This is an argument added to those referred to in the preceding section by *propter haec*, 'on these grounds'.

[2] 'an opinion of good and a sensation of white', 428^{a} 30.

ST. THOMAS'S COMMENTARY
LECTIO FIVE

§ 637. After saying that imagination is not the same as opinion he begins to examine it in itself, first stating the question to be treated before proceeding with it at 'If then'. We have seen, he says, that understanding differs from sensation, and that opinion is akin to the former, but imagining to the latter; and now, having finished with the senses, it will be convenient to discuss imagination before tackling the quite distinct problems touching the intellect and opinion.

§ 638. Then, at 'If then',[1] he begins to treat of imagination, and this in two main sections, first proving that the imagination is not to be numbered among those cognitive powers or dispositions by which we discriminate truth from falsehood, or judge things to be true or false; and then, at 'But since it can happen',[2] explaining what in fact the imagination is. The former section subdivides into three. To begin with, he enumerates our various powers or modes of discernment; secondly, he shows that imagination is not one of these,[3] and thirdly, that it is not even a combination of any of them —this part beginning at 'It is therefore evident'.[4]

First, then, he observes that if it is through imagination that we become conscious of phantasms or appearances (unless the term 'phantasm' is taken metaphorically) imagination would seem to be one of those cognitive dispositions or powers by which things are perceived together with their differences, or are judged according to this or that aspect, truly or falsely, i.e. with a correct or erroneous judgement. (Not that the appearance itself is the same as this discerning or judging.) Now there seem to be four powers or dispositions from which such discernment or judgement proceeds:

[1] 428ᵃ 1.   [2] Lectio 6, § 655.

[3] § 641; 428ᵃ 5.   [4] 428ᵃ 24.

sense, understanding, opinion and scientific knowledge. Imagination, then, is apparently one of these four.

§ 639. Aristotle mentions these four as being already familiar. Other factors (as they seem to be) in cognition were still, at the time he was writing, not defined with certainty. But having already[1] distinguished sensation from the intellect, he can enumerate here three factors distinct from sense: understanding, opinion and scientific knowledge.[2] Nor is he, apparently, speaking of the understanding as a faculty (i.e. of the intellect); else it would not be set apart from science and opinion, which both belong to it as a faculty. But 'understanding' means here an infallible, immediate and intuitive grasp of such intelligible objects as the first principles of knowledge; while 'scientific knowledge' means certain knowledge obtained by rational investigation; and 'opinion' means a knowing that falls short of scientific certainty.

§ 640. And in calling imagination one of these 'dispositions or powers' he implies that the cognitive factors here mentioned are either habits or powers. As to these four factors being the only principles of cognition known to the early philosophers, our evidence is the theory of Plato[3] who reduced only these four to numbers—understanding to 1, science to 2, opinion to 3, sense to 4.

§ 641. Next, when he says 'That it is not',[4] he distinguishes imagination from all the above four: first of all from sensation, then from understanding and science, and finally from opinion. As to sensation, he begins by proving that imagination is not one of the senses,[5] either potentially or actually. For imagination is active during sleep. This cannot be due to any sense as in potency, in which state the senses are aware of nothing at all; nor to any sense as in act, for in sleep the senses are not in act. Therefore imagination is neither a sense in potency nor a sense in act.

§ 642. Then, at 'Further etc.',[6] he argues as follows to show that imagination is not a sense in potency. The latter is always found in animals, but imagination, which implies an awareness of appearances, is sometimes lacking. Therefore . . .

§ 643. Then, at 'But if etc.',[7] he gives four reasons for distinguishing imagination from the senses as in act. (1) Sense as in act is

---

[1] §§ 630–1.   [2] *intellectus, opinio, scientia.*   [3] Bk. I, lectio 4, § 51.
[4] 428[a] 5ss.   [5] i.e. exterior senses.   [6] 428[a] 7–8.   [7] 428[a] 9.

found in all animals, i.e. irrational animals; so that if it were the same as imagination, this would be found in all irrational animals, which in fact is not true; for neither ants, nor bees, nor worms have imagination. Therefore . . .

§ 644. But note that all animals have imagination in some sense of the term; but the lower animals have it indeterminately, as Aristotle will explain later.[1] And if ants and bees seem to differ in this respect from the rest of the lower animals, through their apparent exercise of a great deal of intelligence, the truth is, nevertheless, that ants and bees behave so cleverly, not because they are aware of definite images distinct from exterior sensations, but by a natural instinct; for they only imagine so long as they are actually receiving sensible impressions. Their purposeful and, as it were, provident activities do not arise from any image of what is *going* to happen in the future; their present activities alone are represented inwardly to them, and it is a natural instinct rather than any distinct apprehension which orders these activities to an end. On the other hand, says Aristotle, those animals have imagination in the precise sense of the term which retain a distinct image of things even while they are not actually sensing things.[2]

§ 645. (2) This argument begins at 'Again, sensations'.[3] The senses in the act of sensing are always truthful; they cannot err about their proper objects. But phantasms are very often deceptive, when there is nothing real that corresponds to them. Therefore the imagination is distinct from every sense as in act.

§ 646. (3) This argument comes at 'Again, we do not say'.[4] When we are moved by an actual sense-experience to act immediately and without hesitation, we never say e.g. 'That seems to us a man'. We are more likely to speak thus when we are uncertain, as when we see things at a distance or in the dark. And in these cases the actual sensation is either true or false. For the senses (whatever sense it is which makes us aware of a man) are indeed sometimes deceived as to their *indirect* object. He adds this in order to show the affinity between imagination, which can also be either truthful or deceptive, and obscure sensations. But as soon as we are sure that we are only imagining, we say 'it *appears* to be a man', and that we do not know for certain that it *is* a man. Therefore imagination is distinct from any sense as in act.

[1] §§ 838-9.   [2] i.e. exteriorly.   [3] 428ᵃ 11.   [4] 428ᵃ 12.

§ 647. (4) Again,[1] phantasms come during sleep when the senses are not in act. Therefore a phantasm is not an actual sensation.

§ 648. Next, when he says 'And it is certainly',[2] he shows the difference between imagination and both simple understanding and science. Simple understanding bears upon first principles, and science upon demonstrated conclusions; and these are always true. But images are often false; therefore imagination is neither simple understanding nor science.

§ 649. Then at 'It remains',[3] he shows that imagination is not opinion (which it might seem to be, for opinion too is sometimes false) by two arguments. (1) The result of opinion is belief, if it is natural to believe in one's opinions. If belief is not found in brute animals, this is because they have no opinions. But many brute animals, as he has said,[4] have imagination. Therefore imagination is not opinion.

§ 650. (2) (At, 'Further, belief etc.')[5] Belief always follows opinion (as we have said) because one naturally believes in one's opinions. And the state of being persuaded is the outcome of belief; we believe those things of which we are persuaded. Now persuasion is always accompanied by rational inference, for one must have some reason for being persuaded of anything; hence from first to last reasoning goes along with opinion. But while some brute animals have imaginations, none of them have reason. Imagination, then, is distinct from opinion. Obviously, this argument confirms what the previous one assumes, i.e. that brute animals lack belief.

§ 651. Then at 'It is therefore evident',[6] he shows that imagination is not a combination of any of the factors mentioned above; and more particularly that it is not, as it might rather plausibly seem to be, a combination of sensation and opinion. And here he does three things. First, he states his conclusion, as a further inference from what has been said: that since imagination is neither one of the senses nor opinion, we can already see that it is neither opinion plus sensation—i.e. an opinion *essentially*, but with a *concomitant* sensation; nor opinion *through* sensation—i.e. an opinion essentially, but *caused* by sensation; nor a mixture of the two, as though both were of its essence. He does not say that imagination

[1] 428ª 15.   [2] 428ª 17.   [3] 428ª 19.
[4] §§ 643–4.   [5] 428ª 22.   [6] 428ª 24.

is not sensation plus opinion, because it has apparently more to do with opinion, which can be false, than with sensation which is always true.

§ 652. Secondly, at 'And it is clear',[1] he shows what the term opinion would mean if it were true that imagination were a blend of sensation and opinion. For since an image is always of some definite thing, and of nothing else at the same time, then clearly the opinion which, conjoined to sensation, was an act of imagination, would bear simply and solely upon the one object presented to it by the sensation. It is as if one were to say, e.g. that imagination combined an opinion of whiteness and a sense of whiteness; it could not combine an opinion of whiteness and a sense of goodness; for, in that case, the object *imagined* would not be one and the same. Therefore, if to imagine is to combine opinion and sensation, to be aware of images is simply and solely to have as the object of one's opinion the direct object of a sensation; not in any way the indirect object of that sensation.[2]

§ 653. Thirdly, at 'False appearances',[3] he refutes the above hypothesis. For it can happen that images derived from sensation present us with falsehoods of which, none the less, we form a true opinion. Thus our senses tell us that the sun measures only one foot across; which is false. But by our true opinion we believe that it is larger than 'the inhabited world', i.e. than the whole of our earth. Yet on the hypothesis that the image-appearances are only an opinion conjoined to sensation, one of two consequences must follow. The first is that in the act of conjoining opinion and sensation we reject the true opinion which we held till then, while the thing itself, of which we form our opinion, 'remains', i.e. stays exactly the same; and we ourselves neither forget nor cease to be persuaded of that true opinion. But this is impossible; for there are only three ways in which a true opinion, once held, can be lost: (*a*) When the object itself changes,—as when we truly opine that Socrates is seated while he is seated; but if, when he ceases to sit, we retain that opinion, it changes from being a true opinion to being false; (*b*) When we cease to hold an opinion we once held

[1] 428ᵃ 27.

[2] Because, since this would connote the direct object also, there would be two 'objects' involved in the one 'image'—which is impossible.

[3] 428ᵇ 2.

because we forget it; and (*c*) When we cease to hold an opinion we once held because, for some new reason, we cease from thinking it to be true. It is impossible to lose an opinion if none of these conditions is realised; and yet this is what the first alternative involves.

§ 654. And there is only one other conceivable alternative; which is that the true opinion is retained along with the false one; which would mean that, since the image-appearance is identical with opinion (as it must be if imagining is opining), the same image-appearance is both true and false. And if from being true it becomes false then the 'transformation' of the object, i.e. its alteration from what it was before, must be hidden from him who holds the opinion; otherwise, as soon as the object altered the opinion would alter too, and thus would not be false. He adds this to explain his earlier remark, about the 'remaining' of the object. And his conclusion is that imagination is neither one of the aforesaid four factors in cognition, nor any combination of them.

BOOK III, CHAPTER III, CONTINUED

IMAGINATION
WHAT IT IS

B UT SINCE IT CAN HAPPEN THAT, ONE THING moving, another is moved by it; and imagination seems to be a movement, and to arise only with sensation, and in sentient beings, and to be of such objects as are sensed; and since a motion may be caused by actual sensation, and such necessarily resembles sensation,—then imagination will be just this movement, never originated apart from sensation, incapable of existing in non-sentient beings, and enabling its possessor to act and to be affected in many ways, and being itself both true and false.   §§ 655–9

This happens because sense-perception is true of its own proper objects, or has the least possible amount of falsehood; but secondarily it bears on that in which these qualities inhere, and here it can be deceived. Sensation is reliable as to whether a thing is white or not, but not as to whether it is this or that. Thirdly, there are the common qualities consequent on the accidents in which the proper qualities inhere. I mean, such as movement and dimension, which belong to sense-objects—and about these deception very easily arises in sensing. The movement derived from actual sensation differs from the sensations by which these three objects are perceived.[1]

---

[1] Perhaps, rather, 'differs according as it (the movement) arises from one or other of the sensations etc.' St. Thomas follows M. (§ 664), 428^b 25.

Although the first [movement] is true, the sensation itself
being present, the others can easily be false, whether sensation
be present or not, and especially when the sense-object is distant. If, therefore, nothing except imagination possesses what
has been described, then the statement is true, namely that
imagination is a movement produced by sensation actuated.

§§ 660-7

Since sight is the most prominent sense, [imagination] has
taken its name from light, as there is no seeing without light.

§ 668

And since these images dwell within, and resemble sense
experiences, animals do many things in accordance with
them; some animals, as lacking reason, namely beasts; but
some, i.e. men, when their intellect is veiled either by passion,
or by sickness, or by sleep.

Let so much suffice, therefore, on imagination, its nature
and its function.   §§ 669-70

§ 655. After showing that imagination is not one of those four activities into which the earlier philosophers divided knowledge, the Philosopher now asks: what is imagination in itself? And he does two things. First, he says what imagination is; secondly, he explains its properties, at 'This happens because'.[1] And with a view to defining imagination he lays it down that anything moved may itself move something else (recalling the argument in the *Physics*, Book VIII, where it is shown that there are two kinds of mover, one that is itself without movement, and one that moves another through being moved itself).

§ 656. Then[2] he suggests that imagination is a sort of movement: that just as the sensing subject is moved by sensible objects, so, in imagining, one is moved by certain appearances called phantasms.

§ 657. Next,[3] he suggests an affinity between the imagination and the senses, in that imagination presupposes sensation and is found only in sentient beings or animals; and further, that it bears only upon things sensed, and in no way on things purely intelligible.

§ 658. Then[4] he suggests that the act of sensation can give rise to a sort of movement, in accordance with the principle first laid down, that a thing moved may move another. Actual sensation is a being moved by a sensible object; and the movement of the actuated sense itself causes another movement which, as it proceeds from sensation, must resemble sensation; for every agent as such is a cause of its own likeness. And that which, being moved, moves another, must cause a motion similar to its own.

§ 659. And this leads him[5] to the conclusion that imagination is a certain movement caused by the senses in their act of sensing. It

[1] 428^b 18.   [2] 428^b 11.   [3] 428^b 12.   [4] 428^b 12–14.   [5] 428^b 14.

cannot exist without sensation, nor in insentient beings. If there is any movement caused by actual sensation, it must resemble sensation, and imagining is the only activity of this kind. Hence it must be the movement in question. And, being such, it can give occasion to the imagining subject for a variety of actions and passions. And it can be either true or false, as we shall see.

§ 660. Next, at 'This happens',[1] he gives reasons for the characteristic properties of imagination, using the above analysis: (a) he gives a reason for his assertion that imagination is sometimes true and sometimes false; (b) he explains why it is called by this name; and (c) he explains why he said that animals are largely governed by their imaginations.

(a) First, then, he notes that the reason why imagination is sometimes true and sometimes false is implicit in the statement that its source is the act of the exterior sense; for the latter is related to truth in different ways, according to its varying relation to objects.

§ 661. For, in the first place, sense-perception is always truthful with respect to its proper objects, or at least it incurs, with respect to these, the minimum of falsehood; for natural powers do not, as a general rule, fail in the activities proper to them; and if they do fail, this is due to some derangement or other. Thus only in a minority of cases do the senses judge inaccurately of their proper objects, and then only through some organic defect, e.g. when people sick with fever taste sweet things as bitter because their tongues are ill-disposed.

§ 662. But the senses have also their indirect objects, and with regard to these they can be deceived. What seems to be white is indeed white as the sense reports; but whether the white thing is this or that thing, is snow, e.g., or flour, is a question often answered badly by the senses, especially at a distance.

§ 663. Thirdly, there are the 'common sensibles', found in things some of whose accidental qualities are 'proper sensibles'. Thus size and movement accompany, as 'common sensibles', the sensible qualities of bodies. And these are very likely to give rise to error; for in their case our judgement has to adjust itself to differences of distance: things seen further away seem the smaller.

§ 664. Now[2] the movement of imagination, being derived from

[1] 428b 18.   [2] 428b 25.

the actuated senses, differs from these three types of actual sensation as an effect from its cause. Thus, just because effects, as such, are weaker than their causes, and the power and impress of an agent is less and less evident the further away are its effects, therefore imagination is even more liable than are the senses to fall into the error which arises from a dissimilarity between the sense and its object. For falsehood in the senses consists in receiving a sensible form as other than it is in the sensible object. I mean other in *kind*, not in point of materiality (for example, if a sweet savour is tasted on the tongue as bitter); for in point of materiality there is always a difference between the form as received in the sense and the form as existing in the object. It follows too, from what we have said, that imagination is generally truthful when it arises from the action of the 'proper sensibles'; I mean, at least so long as the sensible object is present and the image-movement is simultaneous with the sense-movement.[1]

§ 665. But when the image-movement occurs in the absence of the exterior sense-object we can be deceived, even with regard to proper sensibles. We may imagine *absent* black things as white. On the other hand, the image-movements arising from perception of objects *indirectly* sensed, or of the common-sensibles, are liable to go astray whether the exterior object be present or no; although they are the more liable to error in the object's absence.

§ 666. From this argument he then draws a conclusion[2] touching his main contention: namely, if the foregoing remarks are true of nothing but the imagination, and are certainly true of it, then imagination must be the movement proceeding from the actuated senses.

§ 667. Whether this movement also presupposes some potency other than the exterior senses, is a question which Aristotle leaves unanswered. Since, however, diverse acts imply diverse potencies, and diverse movements connote diverse receivers of movement (for the moving thing moves something other than itself), it seems necessary to posit an imaginative potency distinct from the exterior senses.

§ 668. (*b*) Next, at 'Since sight',[3] he explains the name *phantasia*. Note that *phos* is the Greek for light, whence comes *phanos*, i.e.

[1] *quando motus phantasiae est simul cum motu sensus.*   [2] 428ᵇ 30.
[3] 429ᵃ 2.

'appearance' or 'enlightening', and *phantasia*. He says, then, that, because sight is the principal sense, being more spiritual (as we have seen already)[1] and knowing a wider range of objects than any other, therefore imagination, which arises from actual sensation, gets its name from light, without which nothing can be seen.[2]

§ 669. (c) Then, at 'And since these images',[3] he explains why the actions and passions of animals are governed by imagination. Images, he says, 'dwell within' in the absence of sensible objects, as traces of actual sensations; therefore, just as sensations arouse appetitive impulses whilst the sensed objects are present, so do images when these are absent. And therefore images very largely determine the behaviour of animals. Nevertheless, this happens through their lack of intelligence; and where intelligence is present it is able, being a higher faculty, to make its own judgement prevail in practice.

§ 670. Hence, so long as the intellect is not in command animals are swayed by imagination; some animals because they simply lack intelligence (the beasts), and some in so far as their intellect is veiled (men). And men may be so swayed in three ways: (*a*) when they fall into some passion, such as anger, desire, fear etc.; (*b*) when they are of unsound mind, through delirium or insanity; and (*c*) when they are asleep and dreaming. In these cases the intellect ceases to control the imagination, with the result that men take their imaginary representations for the truth.

In conclusion, he says that he has now stated what the imagination is and whence it arises.

[1] §§ 417–18.   [2] cf. §§ 403–12.   [3] 429ᵃ 4.

BOOK III, CHAPTER IV

THE INTELLECT IN GENERAL

As to the part of the soul by which it knows and is wise (whether separate spatially or only in idea) we must consider how it is differentiated and, further, how the operation of understanding arises.

§§ 671–4

For if understanding is like sensing, it will be some kind of reception from an intelligible object, or some thing of that nature. It must then be impassible and yet receptive of a species, which it must already be potentially but not actually: and as the sense faculty stands to the sense-object, so will the intellective to the intelligible.

§§ 675–6

It is also necessary, since its understanding extends to everything, that, as Anaxagoras says, it be uncompounded with anything so that it may command, i.e. know. For what appeared inwardly would prevent and impede what was without. Hence it has no nature and is not one, except in being potential. What then is called the 'intellect' of the soul (I mean that mind by which the soul forms opinions and understands) is not, before it understands, in act of any reality.

§§ 677–83

Hence, it is a reasonable inference that it is not involved in the body. Were it so, it would also have some quality either hot or cold, and it would have an organ, like the sensitive faculties; but there is in fact none such.

§§ 684–5

And they spoke to the point who said that the soul was the place of forms—yet not the whole soul, but the intellectual part; nor actually, but only potentially, is it any form.

§ 686

That the impassibility of the sensitive faculty is not like that of the intellective faculty, is evident from the organs and from sensation itself. For the sense cannot receive an impression from too violent a sense-object—e.g. a sound from very great sounds, whilst from over-powerful odours there comes no smell, nor from over-strong colour any seeing. But when the intellect understands something highly intelligible, it does not understand what is inferior to these less than before, but more so. For whereas the sensitive faculty is not found apart from the body, the intellect is separate.   §§ 687–99

§ 671. Having treated of the sensitive part of the soul, and shown that to sense and to understand are quite distinct operations, the Philosopher now turns to the intellectual part. His treatment falls into two main divisions. First, he comes to certain conclusions on the intellectual part in general; after which, from what has been concluded about sense and intellect he deduces, at 'And now recapitulating',[1] some necessary consequences with regard to the soul as a whole. The former division falls into two sections: one on the intellect as such, and one comparing intellect with the senses. The latter begins at 'And it seems that the sense-object'.[2] The intellect as such is first treated in itself, and then, at 'Intelligence etc.',[3] in its activity. The former part then subdivides again into three parts: (a) on the potential intellect; (b) on the agent intellect;[4] and (c) on intellect as in act.[5] After defining the potential intellect,[6] he determines its object,[7] and then adduces an objection.[8] The definition of potential intellect involves explanations (i) of its nature, and (ii) of the way it proceeds into act.[9] And as to its nature, he first states the problems he is attempting to solve; after which, at 'For if understanding is like sensing',[10] he propounds his own view.

§ 672. So he says that, having dealt with the sensitive part of the soul, and shown that judgement and understanding differ from sensation, it is now time to discuss that part of the soul 'by which it knows', i.e. understands, and 'is wise'. We have already

---

[1] Lectio 13, § 787; 431[b] 20.
[2] Lectio 12, § 765; 431[a] 4.
[3] Lectio 11, § 746; 430[a] 28.
[4] Lectio 10, § 728; 430[a] 10.
[5] Lectio 10, § 740; 430[a] 20.
[6] *intellectus possibilis.*
[7] Lectio 8, § 705; 429[b] 10.
[8] Lectio 9, § 720; 429[b] 22.
[9] Lectio 8, § 700; 429[b] 5.
[10] § 675; 429[a] 12–13.

distinguished[1] between being wise and understanding;[2] to be wise pertains to intellectual *judgement*, to understand pertains to intellectual *apprehension*.

§ 673. At this point an old problem emerges (which Aristotle for the time being sets aside), namely whether this part of the soul is a really separate being, distinct from the other parts, or is merely separable in thought. He refers to the former alternative when he speaks of being 'spatially' separable, and he uses this expression because Plato, who thought of the soul's parts as really distinct entities, associated the latter with different organs of the body. This problem Aristotle sets aside.

§ 674. And he keeps two ends in view. One is to examine how this part of the soul differs from the others, if it can be separated from them in thought. And, as potencies are known from their acts, his second aim is to examine the act of understanding itself, i.e. how intellectual activity is completed.

§ 675. Next, at 'For if understanding',[3] he sets down his own view in three stages: (1) he suggests a similarity between intellect and sense; (2) whence he argues, at 'It is also necessary',[4] to a conclusion touching the nature of the potential intellect; (3) whence in turn he deduces a difference between intellect and sense, at 'That the impassibility'.[5]

First of all then, as a preliminary to the statement of his own theory, he suggests that the acts of understanding and of sensing are similar, in that, just as sensing is a kind of knowing, and as it may be either potential or actual, so understanding is a kind of knowing which may be either potential or actual. Whence it follows that, as sensing is a certain state of being passive to a sensible object (something like a passion in the strict sense of the term) so understanding is either a being passive to an intelligible object, or something else that resembles passion, in the strict sense.

§ 676. Of these alternatives the second is the more likely to be true. For even sensing, as we have seen,[6] is not strictly a being passive to anything—for this, strictly, involves an object of a nature contrary to the passive subject. Yet sensing resembles a passion inasmuch as the sense is potential with respect to its object; for it receives sensible impressions. So far then as understanding

---

[1] § 629.   [2] *sapere et intelligere.*   [3] 429ª 12–13.
[4] 429ª 18.   [5] 429ª 29.   [6] §§ 350–1; 393–4.

resembles sensation the intellect too will be impassible (taking passivity in the strict sense), yet will it show some likeness to what is passive, in its receptivity to intelligible ideas; for these it possesses only potentially, not actually. Thus, as sensitive life is to sensible objects, so is the intellect to intelligible objects, each being potential with respect to its object and able to receive that object.

§ 677. Then at 'It is also necessary'[1] he proceeds to deduce the nature of the potential intellect.[2] First he shows that this intellect is not a bodily thing nor compounded of bodily things; and then, at 'Hence it is a reasonable',[3] that it has no bodily organ. As to the first point, we should note that there used to be two opinions about the intellect. Some—and this, as we have seen, was the view of Empedocles[4]—thought that intellect was a composition of all the principles of things, and that this explained its universal knowledge. On the other hand Anaxagoras thought it was simple and pure and detached from all bodily things. And therefore, precisely because the intellect, as he has just said, is not in act of understanding, but in potency only, and in potency to know everything, Aristotle argues that it cannot be compounded of bodily things, as Empedocles thought, but must be separate from such things, as Anaxagoras thought.

§ 678. Now the reason why Anaxagoras thought this was that he regarded intellect as the principle that dominated and initiated all movement; which it could not be if it were either a composition of bodily things or identified with any one of such things; for in these cases it would be restricted to one course of action only. Hence Aristotle's observation that, in Anaxagoras' view, the intellect was detached 'so that it might command' and, commanding, initiate all movement.

§ 679. But, since we are not concerned at present with the all-moving Mind, but with the mind by which the soul understands, we require a different middle term to prove that the intellect is unmixed with bodily things; and this we find in its universal knowledge. That is why Aristotle adds 'That it might know', as if to say: as Anaxagoras maintained that intellect was unmixed because it commands, so we have to maintain that it is unmixed because it knows.

§ 680. The following argument may make this point clear. Any-

---

[1] 429[a] 18.   [2] *intellectus possibilis*.   [3] 429[a] 24.   [4] § 45.

thing that is in potency with respect to an object, and able to receive it into itself, is, as such, without that object; thus the pupil of the eye, being potential to colours and able to receive them, is itself colourless. But our intellect is so related to the objects it understands that it is in potency with respect to them, and capable of being affected by them (as sense is related to sensible objects). Therefore it must itself lack all those things which of its nature it understands. Since then it naturally understands all sensible and bodily things, it must be lacking in every bodily nature; just as the sense of sight, being able to know colour, lacks all colour. If sight itself had any particular colour, this colour would prevent it from seeing other colours, just as the tongue of a feverish man, being coated with a bitter moisture, cannot taste anything sweet. In the same way then, if the intellect were restricted to any particular nature, this connatural restriction would prevent it from knowing other natures. Hence he says: 'What appeared inwardly would prevent and impede' (its knowledge of) 'what was without'; i.e. it would get in the way of the intellect, and veil it so to say, and prevent it from inspecting other things. He calls 'the inwardly appearing' whatever might be supposed to be intrinsic and co-natural to the intellect and which, so long as it 'appeared' therein would necessarily prevent the understanding of anything else; rather as we might say that the bitter moisture was an 'inwardly appearing' factor in a fevered tongue.

§ 681. From this he concludes, not that in fact the nature of the intellect is 'not one', i.e. that it has no definite nature at all; but that its nature is simply to be open to all things; and that it is so inasmuch as it is capable of knowing, not (like sight or hearing) merely one particular class of sensible objects, nor even all sensible accidents and qualities (whether these be common or proper sense-objects) but quite generally the *whole* of sensible nature. Therefore, just as the faculty of sight is by nature free from *one* class of sensible objects, so must the intellect be entirely free from *all* sensible natures.

§ 682. He concludes further that what we call our intellect is not in act with respect to real beings until it actually understands. This is contrary to the early philosophers' principle that intellect must be compounded of all things if it can know all things. But if it knew all things, as containing them all in itself already, it would be an ever-actual intellect, and never merely in potency. In the same way he has remarked already of the senses,[1] that if they were intrinsically made up of the objects they perceive, their perceptions would not presuppose any exterior sensible objects.

§ 683. And lest anyone should suppose this to be true of any and every intellect, that it is in potency to its objects before it knows them, he adds[2] that he is speaking here of the intellect by which the soul understands and forms opinions. Thus he excludes from this context the Mind of God, which, far from being potential, is a certain actual understanding of all things, and of which Anaxagoras said that it could command all because it was perfectly unmixed.

§ 684. Next, at 'Hence it is a reasonable',[3] he shows that the intellect has no bodily organ; and then, at 'They spoke to the point', approves a saying of the early philosophers. First, then, he concludes from what has been said, that if the mind's universal capacity for knowledge implies its intrinsic distinction from all the corporeal natures that it knows, for the same reason it can be argued that the mind is not 'involved in the body', i.e. that it has no bodily organ, as the sensitive part of the soul has. For if the intellect had, like the sensitive part, a bodily organ, it would necessarily be just one particular sensible nature among many. Therefore he says 'some quality' etc., meaning that a nature of this kind would have some particular sensible quality such as actual heat or cold; for it is obvious that, if the soul acts through a bodily organ, the soul itself must correspond to that organ as being in potency to its act.

§ 685. It makes no difference to the act of the potency whether it is the potency itself that has a particular sensible quality or the organ, since the act is not of the potency alone but of potency and organ together. In the same way sight would be impeded if it were the visual potency, not the pupil of the eye,[4] that was coloured. So he says that it comes to the same to maintain that intellect has no bodily organ and that it has no particular bodily nature; and concludes that the intellectual part of the soul, unlike the sensitive, has no bodily organ.

§ 686. Next, where he says 'And they spoke to the point',[5] he

[1] §§ 352-5.   [2] 429ᵃ 23.   [3] 429ᵃ 24.
[4] Reading, with Pirotta's footnote, *sine*, not *sive*.   [5] 429ᵃ 27.

relates his view to an opinion of the early philosophers, saying that, granted intellect's lack of a bodily organ, we can see the point of the old saying that the soul is the 'place' of forms[1]—meaning that it receives these into itself. Now this saying would be false if every part of the soul had its bodily organ, for then the forms would be received into the composition of soul and body, not into the soul alone; for it is not *sight* that receives visible forms, but the eye. It follows that the soul as a whole is not the 'place' of forms, but only that part of it which lacks a bodily organ, i.e. the intellect; and even this part does not, as such, possess them actually, but potentially only.

§ 687. Then, at 'That the impassibility',[2] he shows how the intellect and the senses differ with respect to impassibility. He has already[3] observed that neither sensation nor understanding is a passion in the precise sense of a state of being passively affected; whence he had inferred that the intellect was impassible. But, lest it be supposed that sense and intellect were impassible in the same degree, he now distinguishes them in this respect. Though the senses as such are not, strictly speaking, passively affected by their objects, they are *indirectly* so affected, inasmuch as the equilibrium of the sense-organ is disturbed by any excess in its object. But the same is not true of the intellect, since it has no organ; it is therefore neither directly nor indirectly passible.

§ 688. This is what he means when he proceeds to say that the dissimilarity between sense and intellect in point of passibility appears 'from the organs and from sensation'. For a very strong sense-object can stun the faculty of sense. One can be deafened by great sounds, blinded by strong colours, made powerless to smell anything by over-powering odours; and this because the organ in each case is injured. But since the intellect has no organ that could be injured by an excess of its appropriate object, its activity is not, in fact, weakened by a great intelligibility in its object; indeed it is rather strengthened thereby; and the same would be true of the senses, if they could exist without bodily organs. All the same, an injury to an organ of the body may indirectly weaken the intellect, in so far as the latter's activity presupposes sensation. The cause, then, of the difference is that sensitivity acts in the body, but the intellect acts on its own.[4]

[1] *locus specierum.*   [2] 429[a] 29.   [3] § 676.   [4] *. . . est separatus.*

§ 689. All this goes to show the falsity of the opinion that intellect is the same as imagination, or as anything else in our nature that depends on the body's constitution. On the other hand, this same text has been, for some, an occasion of falling into the error of regarding the intellectual power as quite separated from the body, as a substance that *exists* on its own.[1] Which is an utterly indefensible position.

§ 690. For it is clear that the actually intelligent being is this particular man. Whoever denies this implies that he himself understands nothing; and therefore that one need pay no attention to what he says. But if he *does* understand anything he must do so in virtue of some principle in him of this particular activity of understanding; which is the intellectual power (as potential) to which the Philosopher refers when he says: 'I mean that mind by which the soul understands and forms opinions'. The potential intellect then is precisely that by which this particular man understands. Now that in virtue of which, as a principle of activity, an agent acts may certainly exist in separation from the agent; as e.g. a king and his bailiff have separate existence, though the latter acts only as moved by the king. But it is quite impossible for the agent to exist separately from that by which, formally and immediately, he is an agent; and this because action only proceeds from an agent in so far as the latter is in a state of actuality. It follows that the agent and the proper and immediate principle of his activity must exist together in one act; which could not be if they were separate beings. Hence the impossibility of a separation in being of an agent from its formal principle of activity.

§ 691. With this truth in mind, those who maintained the opinion to which I refer tried to think out some way of so linking up and uniting the separated substance, which for them was the intellectual potency, with ourselves, as to identify its act of understanding with our own. They said then that the form of the potential intellect, that by which it is brought into act, was the intelligible idea; and that the *subject* possessed of this idea was a kind of phantasm produced by ourselves. In this way, they said, the potential intellect is linked with us through its form.

§ 692. But this theory entirely fails to prove any continuity between the intellect and ourselves. For the intellectual power is only

[1] *sicut una de substantiis separatis.*

united with an intelligible object in the degree that it is in act; just as we have seen that the senses[1] cannot unite with their appropriate objects so long as these remain in potency. Therefore the intelligible idea cannot be the form of the intellectual power until it is actually understood; and this cannot happen until it is disengaged from phantasms by abstraction. Hence, precisely in the degree that it is joined to the intellect it is removed from phantasms. Not in this way therefore could an intellectual power be united with us.

§ 693. And obviously the upholder of this view was led astray by a *fallacia accidentis*. For his argument comes to this: phantasms are somehow united to intelligible ideas, and these to the potential intellect; and therefore the latter is united to the phantasms. But, as I say, it is clear that, in the degree that the intelligible idea is one with the intellectual power, it is abstracted from phantasms.

§ 694. But even granted that between the intellectual power and ourselves there existed some such union as this view supposes, it would not in fact cause us to understand, but rather to be understood. If the eye contains a likeness of a coloured wall, this does not cause the colour to see, but, on the contrary, to be seen. Therefore if the intelligible idea in the intellect is a sort of likeness of our phantasms, it does not follow that we perceive anything intellectually, but rather that we—or more precisely our phantasms—are understood by that separated intellectual substance.

§ 695. Many other criticisms might be urged, such as I have set out in more detail elsewhere.[2] Enough to note for the present that the theory in question is an implicit denial of the existence of thinking in the human individual.

§ 696. Furthermore, it is also clearly contrary to the teaching of Aristotle. First, because he has explicitly said (at the beginning of the treatise) that the subject matter of his enquiry is a *part of the soul*, not any separated substance.

§ 697. Moreover, he has set out to examine the intellect leaving aside the question whether it is a being distinct from the rest of the soul; so that even if it be not distinct in this way, that does not affect his argument.

[1] §§ 355–7; 382.
[2] Perhaps in the *De Unitate Intellectus contra Averroistas*. In any case there was the *Summa Contra Gentiles*, II, 59ss, composed 1258–64. *See* Introd., pp. 17–18.

§ 698. Again, Aristotle calls the intellect that *by which* the soul understands.

All these indications show that he did not assert that the intellect was a separate substance.

§ 699. Indeed it is astonishing how easily some have let themselves be deceived by his calling the intellect 'separate'; for the text itself makes it perfectly clear what he means,—namely that, unlike the senses, the intellect has no bodily organ. For the nobility of the human soul transcends the scope and limits of bodily matter. Hence it enjoys a certain activity in which bodily matter has no share; the potentiality to which activity is without a bodily organ; and in this sense only is it a 'separate' intellect.

BOOK III, CHAPTER IV, CONTINUED

INTELLECTUAL ABSTRACTION

BUT WHEN IT BECOMES[1] PARTICULAR OBJECTS, AS in a man of science, the intellect is said to be in act. (This comes about as soon as such a one is able to operate of himself.) It is, then, in a way still in potency, but not in the way it was before it learned or discovered. And then, too, it is able to think itself.   §§ 700–704

Now, as *dimension* is one thing and the *being of dimension* another, and as *water* is one thing and the *being water* another, and so with many other things (but not all things, for in certain things 'flesh' is the same as 'being flesh')[2] accordingly it discriminates either by some other [faculty] or by the same faculty differently disposed. For flesh is not separable from matter; it is like the snub of a nose, one [thing] existing in the other. There is discerned therefore by the sensitive faculty what is hot, what is cold, and anything else of which the flesh is a certain ratio. But either by another and separate

---

[1] 'once it has become . . . as a "man of science",—meaning by this phrase one who is actually so', 429^b 5. St. Thomas follows M. (as punctuated in Pirotta) in relating 'is said to be' to the intellect, not to 'the man of science', § 700.

[2] Pirotta's text runs '(*in quibusdam enim idem est esse carni et carnem esse*)' etc. Probably the bracket is misplaced: it should be closed after *idem est*; and *esse carni* etc. should be attached to the next sentence. One would then read, 'but not in all (for in certain things there is identity [of thing and its form]); the mind then distinguishes flesh and being flesh, either by some other faculty, or etc.' St. Thomas reads as in Pirotta's text, § 710.

faculty, or as if it were bent back upon itself (whereas it was previously straight), does it perceive the being of flesh.

§§ 705–13

Again, in the abstract sphere the straight line is as the snub-nose; for it goes with the continuum. But its essence, if being [straight] is other than a straight line, is different. Let it be, for instance, Duality. Then [the mind] discerns either by another faculty or by the same differently disposed. In general, then, as things are separable from matter, so are intellectual operations.   §§ 714–19

ST. THOMAS'S COMMENTARY
LECTIO EIGHT

§ 700. Having reached certain conclusions about the intellect as potential with respect to intelligible objects, the Philosopher now goes on to show how it is actualised. And first he shows that it is actualised *intermittently*; and then, at 'Now as dimension',[1] what is the precise *object* of its actualisation.

He explains how the intellect is actualised thus. The intellectual soul is, we have said,[2] only in potency to its ideas at first. 'But when it becomes particular objects',[3] i.e. when the mind reaches the degree of actual apprehension of intelligibles that is found in the knowledge habitually possessed by a man of science, then it can already be called an intellect in act; and that degree is reached as soon as one is capable of producing, on one's own initiative, the intellectual activity called understanding. For the actual possession of any form is coincident with the ability to act accordingly.

§ 701. Yet though a mind is already, in a way, in act when it has intelligible notions in the manner of one who possesses a science habitually, none the less the mind then is still, in a way, in potency; though not in the same way as it was before it acquired the science, either by being taught it or by its own unaided efforts. Before it acquired the habit of a science—which is its first state of actuality[4] —it could not actualise itself at will, it needed to be brought into act by the mind of another; but once such a habit is acquired, the intellect has the power to bring itself into action at will.

§ 702. What is said here disproves the un-aristotelian position of Avicenna touching intelligible ideas. Avicenna maintained that ideas are not *retained* by the potential intellect, but exist in it only so long as it is actually understanding. Whence it follows that, for this intellect to come to the act of understanding anything, it must

---

[1] 429^b 10.   [2] §§ 677–83.   [3] 429^b 5.   [4] *primus actus.*

413

have recourse to a *separated* active intellect, the source of intelligible ideas in the intellectual potency.

§ 703. But against this Aristotle is clearly saying that the manner in which the mind becomes actually possessed of ideas is that of one who, possessing a science habitually, is still in potency to a given act of understanding. Thus the mind actually understanding possesses its ideas in fullest actuality; and so long as it has the habit of a science, it possesses them in a manner half-way between mere potency and complete actuality.

§ 704. And having asserted that, once the mind has become partly actual with respect to certain ideas hitherto potentially apprehended, it is capable of understanding, whereas simply regarded in itself it lacks the capacity, because this might lead one to suppose that even as in act the mind never thinks of itself, Aristotle adds that, once in act, the mind is able to think not only of other things, but also of itself.

§ 705. Next at 'Now, as dimension is one',[1] Aristotle elucidates the object of the intellect. To understand him here we must recall the problem stated in Book VII of the *Metaphysics*,[2] namely whether the 'whatness' or quiddity or essence of a thing—whatever is signified by its definition—whether this is the same as the thing itself. And whilst Plato had separated the quiddities (called by him 'ideas' or 'species') of things from things in their singularity, Aristotle was concerned to show that quiddities are only accidentally distinct[3] from singular things. For example, a white man and his essence are distinct just in so far as the essence of man includes *only* what is specifically human, whereas the thing called one white man includes something else as well.

§ 706. And the same is true of anything whose form exists in matter; there is something in it besides its specific principle. The specific nature is individualised through matter; hence the individualising principles and individual accidents are not included in the essence as such. That is why there can be many individuals of the same specific nature—having this nature in common, whilst they differ in virtue of their individuating principles. Hence, in all such things, the thing and its essence are not quite identical. Socrates is not his humanity. But where the form does not exist

---

[1] 429[b] 10.   [2] VII, c.6; 1031[a] 15ss.

[3] *non sunt aliud a rebus nisi per accidens.*

in matter, where it exists simply in itself, there can be nothing except the essence; for then the form is the entire essence. And in such cases, of course, there cannot be a number of individuals sharing the same nature; nor can the individual and its nature be distinguished.

§ 707. This also should be considered, that things existing concretely in Nature—*physical* things—are not alone in having their essences in matter; the same is also true of *mathematical* entities. For there are two kinds of matter: sensible matter, which is intrinsic to physical things and from which the mathematician abstracts; and intelligible matter, intrinsic to mathematical entities. For it is clear that, whereas quantity pertains to a substance immediately, sensible qualities, like white and black or heat and cold, *presuppose* quantity. Now given two things of which one is prior to the other, if you remove the second, the first remains; hence if only its sensible qualities are removed from a substance by a mental abstraction, continuous quantity still remains, in the mind, after the abstraction.

§ 708. For there are some forms which can only exist in a matter which is possessed of certain definite sensible qualities; and such are the forms of physical things; and such things therefore always involve sensible matter. But there are other forms which do not call for matter possessed of definite sensible qualities, yet do require matter existing as quantity. These are the so-called mathematical objects such as triangles, squares and the like; they are abstracted from sensible matter, but not from intelligible matter; for the mind retains the notion of a quantitative continuum after abstracting from sensible quality. Clearly then, both physical and mathematical objects have their forms in matter, and in both there is a difference between a thing and its essence; which is why in both cases many individual things are found to share the same nature: e.g. men and triangles.

§ 709. If these points are understood, the text of Aristotle should present no difficulties. For he says 'dimension[1] and the being of dimension' differ, meaning a dimension and its essence—for by 'the being of dimension' he means its essence. So also 'water' and its 'being' are distinct; and similarly in the case of 'many other things', i.e. in all physical and mathematical objects. Hence his

[1] *magnitudo.*

415

choice of these two examples: for dimension is a mathematical object and water a physical one.

§ 710. But this distinction is not verified in 'all things'; for in perfectly immaterial substances the thing is identical with its essence. And as such substances are beyond the reach of the human mind, Aristotle could not assign proper names to them, as he could to physical and mathematical objects; so he describes them in terms drawn from physical objects. That is why he says that 'in certain things flesh' and 'its being' are identical.[1] He does not mean this literally, else he would not have said 'in certain things', but would have absolutely identified flesh and its being. He means that 'in certain things', i.e. immaterial substances, the two factors which we distinguish as the concrete thing and what is predicated of it—for instance flesh and its being—are identical.

§ 711. And since diversity in objects known implies diversity in the knowing faculties, he concludes by saying that either the soul knows a thing with one faculty and its essence with another, or both with the same faculty functioning in different ways. For it is obvious that flesh can only exist in matter; its form being in a certain definite and particular sensible matter. The being, too, which has flesh is a definite sensible thing, e.g. a nose. Now this sensitive nature[2] the soul knows through the senses; that is why he adds[3] that it is by the sense-faculty that the soul discerns the hot and the cold and so forth, of which flesh is a certain 'ratio', i.e. proportion. For the form of flesh requires a certain definite proportion of heat and cold and so forth.

§ 712. But the 'being of flesh', i.e. its essence, must be 'discerned' by some other faculty. But the functioning of two distinct 'faculties' takes place in two ways. In one way flesh and its essence can be discerned by powers in the soul which are completely distinct; the essence discerned by the intellect, the flesh by the senses; and this happens when we know the individual in itself and the specific nature in itself. But in another way the flesh and its essence may be discerned, not by two distinct faculties, but by one faculty knowing in two distinct ways—knowing in one way flesh, in another the essence of flesh; and this happens when the knowing soul cor-

---

[1] *See* note 2, p. 411.

[2] *naturam sensitivam* (Pirotta); apparently meaning *sensibilem*.

[3] 429[b] 14.

relates the universal and the individual. For, just as it would be impossible for us (as we have seen)[1] to distinguish sweetness from whiteness if we had not a common sense faculty which knew both at once, so also we could not make any comparison between the universal and the individual if we had not a faculty which perceived both at once. The intellect therefore knows both at once, but in different ways.

§ 713. It knows the specific nature or essence of an object by going out directly to that object; but it knows the individual thing indirectly or reflexively, by a return to the phantasms from which it abstracted what is intelligible. This Aristotle expresses[2] by saying that the intellectual soul either knows flesh sensitively and discerns the 'being of flesh' with 'another' and 'separate' potency,—i.e. other than sensitivity, in the sense that intellect is a power distinct from the senses; or it knows flesh and the 'being of flesh' by one and the same intellectual power functioning diversely; in so far as it can 'bend back', so to say, 'upon itself'. As 'stretched out straight', and apprehending directly, it 'discerns' the 'being' or essence of flesh; but by reflection it knows the flesh itself.

§ 714. Next, at 'Again, in the abstract sphere',[3] he applies what he had said of physical objects to mathematical objects, saying that 'in the abstract sphere', i.e. in mathematics, where we abstract from sensible matter, the straight line is like the snub-nosed in the sphere of sensible matter. For line is a mathematical object, as a snub-nose is a physical one; and line essentially involves a continuum, as what is snub-nosed a nose. But the continuum is intelligible matter, as what is snub-nosed is sensible matter. Therefore in mathematics also the thing and its essence, e.g. the straight line and its straightness, are different; hence too, even in mathematics, things and essences must be objects of different kinds of knowing.

§ 715. As an instance of this let us suppose for a moment, with Plato, that the essence of straight line is duality (for Plato identified the essences of mathematical objects with numbers, so that a line was unity, a straight line duality, and so on). The soul then must know mathematical objects and their essences in different ways. Hence, just as it can be shown, in the case of physical objects, that the intellect knowing their essences is other than the senses which

[1] §§ 601–4.   [2] 429^{b} 16.   [3] 429^{b} 17.

know them in their individuality, so too, in the case of mathematics, it can be shown that what knows the essences, i.e. the intellect, is distinct from what apprehends mathematical objects themselves, i.e. the imagination.

§ 716. And lest it be said that the mind works in the same way in mathematics and in natural science, he adds that the relation of things to the intellect corresponds to their separability from matter. What is separate *in being* from sensible matter can be discerned only by the intellect. What is not separate from sensible matter in being, but only *in thought*, can be perceived in abstraction from sensible matter, but not from *intelligible* matter. Physical objects, however, though they are intellectually discerned in abstraction from *individual* matter, cannot be completely abstracted from sensible matter; for 'man' is understood as *including* flesh and bones; though in abstraction from *this* flesh and *these* bones. But the singular individual is not directly known by the intellect, but by the senses or imagination.

§ 717. From this text of Aristotle one can go on to show that the intellect's proper object[1] is indeed the essence of things; but not the essence by itself, in separation from things, as the Platonists thought. Hence this 'proper object' of our intellect is not, as the Platonists held, something existing outside sensible things; it is something intrinsic to sensible things; and this, even though the mode in which essences are grasped by the mind differs from their mode of existence in sensible things; for the mind discerns them apart from the individuating conditions which belong to them in the order of sensible reality. Nor need this involve the mind in any falsehood; for there is no reason why, of two conjoined things, it should not discern one without discerning the other; just as sight perceives colour without perceiving odour, though not without perceiving colour's necessary ground which is spatial magnitude. In like manner, the intellect can perceive a form apart from its individuating principles, though not apart from the matter required by the nature of the form in question; thus it cannot understand the snub-nosed without thinking of nose, but it can understand a curve without thinking of nose. And it was just because the Platonists failed to draw this distinction that they thought that mathematical

---

[1] *proprium objectum.*

objects and the essences of things were as separate from matter in reality as they are in the mind.

§ 718. Furthermore, it is clear that the intelligible ideas by which the potential intellect is actualised are not in themselves the intellect's object: for they are not that which, but that *by* which it understands. For, as with sight the image in the eye is not what is seen, but what gives rise to the act of sight (for what is seen is colour which exists in an exterior body), so also what the intellect understands is the essence existing in things; it is not its own intelligible idea, except in so far as the intellect reflects upon itself. Because, obviously, it is what the mind understands that makes up the subject-matter of the sciences; and all these, apart from rational science,[1] have realities for their subject-matter, not ideas. Clearly then, the intellect's object is not the intelligible idea, but the essence of intelligible realities.

§ 719. From which we can infer the futility of an argument used by some to prove that all men have only one potential intellect[2] in common. They argue from the fact that all men can understand one and the same object; and say that if there were really many human intellects they would necessarily have many intelligible ideas. But these intelligible ideas are not precisely *what* the mind understands; they are only the latter's likeness present in the soul; hence it is quite possible for many intellects to possess likenesses of one and the same object, so that one thing is understood by all. Besides, the separated substances must know the essences of the physical things which we know; and clearly their intellects are distinct. Hence, if the above argument were valid, its conclusion—that all men have only one intellect—would still involve a difficulty; for one cannot reduce *all* intellects to one.

[1] *scientia rationalis*, i.e. logic.   [2] *intellectus possibilis.*

BOOK III, CHAPTER IV, CONTINUED

PROBLEMS ARISING
INTELLECT AS INTELLIGIBLE

ONE MIGHT WELL ENQUIRE (IF THE INTELLECT IS simple and impassible, having nothing in common with anything else, as Anaxagoras said) how it understands, if understanding is a receiving. For it seems that one thing acts and another is acted on, only in so far as there is a factor common to the two.   § 720

Again, if it is itself an intelligible: then either there is intellect in other intelligible things—(unless it is intelligible by virtue of some extrinsic principle) the intelligible being specifically one; or it will have, mixed with itself, something that makes it intelligible, as other things have.   §§ 721–2

Or what about the receptivity in a general sense,[1] already alluded to in making distinctions on this point? Before it makes an act of understanding, the intellect is its intelligible objects potentially, but not actually. It must be as with a tablet on which there is nothing actually written; and so indeed it is in the case of intellect.   §§ 722–3

---

[1] 'The receptivity (τὸ πάσχειν) involving a common element', i.e. common to agent and patient. But St. Thomas understands the phrase *secundum aliquid commune* in the sense of the translation given above. The allusion is to Bk. II, lectio 11, §§ 365–6.

And it is itself an intelligible like other intelligible objects. For in things separated from the material, intellect and what is understood by it are identical. Speculative knowledge is the same as what is knowable in this way.[1]   §§ 724–6

The reason why there is not always understanding must be considered.[2] In material things, each intelligible object exists only potentially. Hence in them is no intellect, for the mind that understands such things is an immaterial potency.[3] The intelligible exists, however [in them].[4]   § 727

[1] 'Speculative knowledge and its object are the same.' St. Thomas understands M.'s *sic scibile* as 'knowable in act', § 724.

[2] The modern translators—Hicks, Tricot, Smith—put this sentence in brackets and take it that Aristotle is proposing, for later consideration, the question why the intellect is not always actually understanding. St. Thomas, however, takes it as a question why anything intelligible is not also itself possessed of an intellect (§ 727). The sentence has been rendered here to suit this interpretation.

[3] 'mind can only become such as are freed from their matter', 430^a 7.

[4] According to the Greek, apparently, this 'intelligible', τὸ νοητὸν, is the mind itself. The translation given above is fixed by the Commentary.

§ 720. Having outlined the nature and object of the potential intellect, Aristotle now goes on to discuss some relevant difficulties; and this in two stages: first stating two problems and then, at 'Or what about the receptivity',[1] answering them. The first of the two problems might be stated thus: if intellect is, as Anaxagoras said, something simple and impassible and removed from all else, how can it actually understand? For to understand is a kind of receiving, and every receiver, as such, would seem to be affected by an agent; and it is precisely through having something in common that two things are related as agent and patient, this mutual relationship implying a material factor in common, as is shown in Book I of the *De Generatione*.[2]

§ 721. The second difficulty he states at 'Again, if it is'.[3] This difficulty is occasioned by his earlier statement that once the mind is in act it can understand itself.[4] Now if intellect itself is intelligible, it is so in either of two ways: either merely of itself, or by way of something else conjoined with it. If the first alternative be true, then, since the intelligible as such forms one species, and since *this* intelligible is an intellect, it seems to follow that other intelligibles are also intellects, and thus everything intelligible is also intelligent. Should we take the second alternative, however, it would follow that the mind was like other things that are understood in being conjoined with something which makes it intelligible,—with the result, it might seem, here also, that that which is understood is always possessed of understanding.

§ 722. Then at 'Or what about the receptivity', he removes these difficulties. As to the first, relying on his earlier analysis of

---

[1] § 722; 429^b 29.   [2] *De Gen. et Corr.*, I, c.7; 323^b 1ss.
[3] 429^b 26.   [4] cf. § 704.

passivity,[1] he reminds us that one can speak of passivity in a general
sense which is common to two different kinds of change: to the
mutual alteration of things which have their material factor in
common and mutually exclusive, alternating formal determina-
tions; and also to the change which implies nothing more than a
reception of forms from outside the changed thing. The mind,
then, is called passive just in so far as it is in potency, somehow,
to intelligible objects which are not actual in it until understood
by it. It is like a sheet of paper on which no word is yet written,
but many can be written. Such is the condition of the intellect
as a potency, so long as it lacks actual knowledge of intelligible
objects.

§ 723. This is against, not only the early natural philosophers'
view that the soul knows all things because it is composed of all
things, but also Plato's opinion that the human soul is by nature in
possession of a universal knowledge which only its union with the
body has caused it to forget. (This theory is implicit in Plato's
reduction of learning to remembering.)

§ 724. After this, at 'And it is itself',[2] he answers the second difficulty; and then, at 'The reason why there is not',[3] a fresh objection.
First, then, he says that the potential intellect is itself intelligible,
not indeed immediately, but like other intelligible things, through
a concept. To prove this he has recourse to the principle that the
actually understood object and the actually understanding subject
are one being—just as he said earlier in this book,[4] that the actually
sensed object and the actually sensing subject are one being. Now
the actually understood is so in virtue of an abstraction from
matter; for, as we have seen,[5] things become objects of the understanding just in the degree that they can be separated from matter.
So he says 'in things separated from the material'. So the understanding and the understood are one being, provided the latter is
actually understood; and the same is true of the object and subject
of sensation. Speculative knowledge and what is knowable 'in this
way' (i.e. in act) are identical. Therefore the concept of the actually understood thing is also a concept of the understanding,
through which the latter can understand itself. That is why all the
foregoing discussion of the potential intellect has been carried on

[1] §§ 365–6. [2] 430ᵃ 2. [3] 430ᵃ 5.
[4] §§ 590–3. [5] §§ 707–19.

in terms of the latter's act and object. For we only know the intellect through our knowledge that we are using it.

§ 725. The reason why the potential intellect cannot be known immediately, but only through a concept, is the fact that it is potential also as an intelligible object; for, as it is proved in Book IX of the *Metaphysics*,[1] intelligibility depends upon actuality. And there is a like dependence in the field of sensible realities too. In this field what is purely potential, i.e. bare matter,[2] cannot act of itself, but only through some form conjoined with it; whereas sensible substances, being compositions of potency and act, can act, to some extent, of themselves. So, too, the potential intellect,[3] being purely potential in the order of intelligible things, neither understands nor is understood except through its own concepts.

§ 726. But God who, among intelligible objects, is the one that is perfect actuality, and also the other immaterial substances midway between potency and act, know and are known simply of and in themselves.

§ 727. Next, at 'The reason why',[4] he answers an objection to the above solution. For if our mind, like other things, is rendered intelligible by union with some principle of intelligibility which is not precisely itself, why should not any intelligible object be itself a subject which understands;—or, as he says, we still have to enquire into 'the reason' for 'not always understanding'. Now the reason is that in any material thing the form is not actually intelligible; it is only potentially so; and only what is actually intelligible, not the merely potentially so, is identical with intellect; so that things whose form exists in matter are not themselves possessed of an intellect with which to understand. The 'mind that understands such things' (i.e. intelligible objects) is a certain immaterial potency. The material thing is indeed intelligible but only potentially, whereas what exists in an intellect is an actually intelligible form.

[1] IX, c.9; 1051ᵃ 30.　　[2] *materia prima*.　　[3] *intellectus possibilis*.
[4] 430ᵃ 5.

BOOK III, CHAPTER V

THE AGENT INTELLECT

NOW SINCE IN ALL NATURE THERE IS A FACTOR that is as matter in the genus, and is potentially all that is in the genus, and something else which is as cause and agent as making everything in it (thus art is related to its material): so there must be these differences in the soul. There is that intellect, which is such as being able to become everything; and there is that which acts upon everything, as a sort of state, like light; for light too, in a way, makes potential colours actual. §§ 728–31

And this is intellect separable, uncompounded and incapable of being acted on, a thing essentially in act. For the agent is always more excellent than the recipient, and the principle than its material. §§ 732–9

Knowledge in act is the same as the thing itself. But what is potential has temporal priority in the individual; yet this is not true universally, even with respect to time. Mind does not know at one time and not know at another time. §§ 740–1

Only separated, however, is it what it really is. And this alone is immortal and perpetual. §§ 742–3

It does not remember, because it is impassible; the passive

425

intellect is corruptible, and the soul understands nothing apart from this latter.[1]   §§ 744-5

[1] A much-disputed passage. A safe rendering of the Greek is: 'This alone is immortal and perpetual. We have however no memory of it because it is impassible, whereas the passive intellect (or, the mind that can be affected) is perishable; and without it nothing thinks'—taking 'it' to refer to the agent intellect. The Latin translation, however, followed by St. Thomas, takes this 'it' to mean the 'passive intellect' and inserts *anima*, 'the soul', as subject of 'thinks'. Hence St. Thomas takes the whole section to refer to the state of the intellect after death: it 'does not remember', etc., once the passive intellect has perished; the latter is only 'called' intellect and is really a *pars animae corporalis*. *See* Introd., pp. 34-7.

§ 728. Having examined the potential intellect, the Philosopher now turns his attention to the agent intellect.[1] He first shows by argument and illustration that there is such a thing as the agent intellect; and then, at 'And this is intellect',[2] he explains its nature. The argument he uses is this. In any nature which alternates between potency and actuality we must posit (1) a factor akin to the matter which, in any given class of things, is potentially all the particulars included in the class; and (2) another factor which operates as an active and productive cause, like art with respect to its material. Since then the intellectual part of the soul alternates between potency and act, it must include these two distinct principles: first, a potentiality within which all intelligible concepts can be actualised (this is the potential intellect already discussed);[3] and then, also, a principle whose function it is to actualise those concepts. And this latter is the agent intellect,—being 'a sort of state'.[4]

§ 729. This last phrase has led some to suppose that the agent intellect is one with the 'intellect' which is a habitual apprehension of first principles. But it is not so; for the latter 'intellect' *presupposes* the actual presence in the mind of certain intelligible and understood objects, which are the terms in understanding which we apprehend the truth of first principles. So the view in question would imply that the agent intellect was not, as Aristotle here maintains, the primary source, for us, of the actual intelligibility of anything. Therefore I hold that the term 'state' is used here in the sense in which Aristotle often calls any form or nature a 'state', to

---

[1] *intellectus agens.*   [2] § 732; 430ᵃ 17.   [3] *intellectus possibilis.*

[4] *sicut habitus quidam.* The Oxford translation: 'a sort of positive *state*'. This term seems less misleading than the transliteration, 'habit'.

distinguish it from a privation or a potency. In this case the agent intellect is called a state to distinguish it from the intellect in potency.

§ 730. So he calls it a state, and compares it to light which 'in a way' brings colours from potency to act;—'in a way' because, as we have seen, colour is visible of itself;[1] all that light does is to actualise a transparent medium which can then be modified by colour so that colour is seen. The agent intellect, on the other hand, actualises the intelligible notions themselves, abstracting them from matter, i.e. bringing them from potential to actual intelligibility.[2]

§ 731. The reason why Aristotle came to postulate an agent intellect was his rejection of Plato's theory that the essences of sensible things existed apart from matter, in a state of actual intelligibility. For Plato there was clearly no need to posit an agent intellect. But Aristotle, who regarded the essences of sensible things as existing in matter with only a potential intelligibility, had to invoke some abstractive principle in the mind itself to render these essences actually intelligible.

§ 732. Next, at 'And this etc.',[3] he states four qualities or conditions of the agent intellect: first, its separation from matter; second, its impassibility; third, its purity,[4] by which he means that it is neither made up of bodily natures nor conjoined with a bodily organ. Now these three qualities are also found in the potential intellect; but the fourth is proper to the agent intellect, and consists in its being essentially in act; whereas the potential intellect is essentially potential and comes to act only by receiving an intelligible object.

§ 733. To demonstrate these qualities he argues as follows. What acts is nobler than what is acted on, an active principle is nobler than its material. Now the agent intellect, as we have said,[5] is to the potential intellect as an active principle to its material; therefore it is the nobler of the two. If, then, the potential intellect be (as has been shown)[6] free from matter and impassible and pure, *a fortiori* the agent intellect. Consequently the agent intellect is also essentially actual, for only in virtue of its actuality is an active principle nobler than a passive one.

---

[1] § 400.   [2] cf. § 716.   [3] 430[a] 17.
[4] *quod sit immixtus.*   [5] § 728.   [6] §§ 677–83.

§ 734. Now what is said here has led some to conceive of the agent intellect as a separated substance, subsisting apart from the potential intellect. But this does not seem to be true; for human nature would be a deficient nature if it lacked any one of the principles that it needs for its naturally appropriate activity of understanding; and this requires both the potential and the agent intellects. Hence, complete human nature requires that both of these be intrinsic to man. Moreover, just as the potential intellect's function of receiving intelligible objects is attributed to the individual man as its subject, so also is the work of the agent intellect, the abstracting of such objects from matter. And this is only possible in so far as the formal principle of the latter activity is one in being with the individual man.

§ 735. Nor is it enough to say that the intelligible notions formed by the agent intellect subsist somehow in phantasms, which are certainly intrinsic to us; for as we have already[1] observed in treating of the potential intellect, objects only become actually intelligible when abstracted from phantasms; so that, merely by way of the phantasms, we cannot attribute the work of the agent intellect to ourselves. Besides, the agent intellect is to ideas in act in the mind as art is to the ideas it works by; and obviously the things on which art impresses such ideas do not themselves produce the art; hence, even granted that we were the subjects of ideas made actually intelligible in us, it would not follow that it is we who produce them by means of an agent intellect in ourselves.

§ 736. Nor does the above theory agree with Aristotle who expressly states that these two distinct powers, the agent and the potential intellects, are in the soul; thus making it quite clear that he takes them to be parts or potencies of the soul, not distinct substances.

§ 737. The chief difficulty arises from the fact that, while the potential intellect is in potency to intelligible objects, the agent intellect stands to the latter as a being already in act. And it would seem impossible that one and the same thing should be at once in act and in potency to the same object; and therefore that these two intellects should belong to the one substance of the soul.

§ 738. But there is really no difficulty in this if we understand

[1] § 692.

aright how the potential intellect is potential with respect to intelligible objects, and how the latter are potential with respect to the agent intellect. In the former case the potentiality is that of the indefinite to the definite; for the potential intellect is not, as such, endowed with any definite and particular sensible thing's nature. Yet only definite particular natures are, as such, intelligible—hence Aristotle's earlier comparison[1] of the intellectual power's relation to intelligible objects with that of a sheet of paper to particular definite pictures. And from this point of view the agent intellect is not in act.

§ 739. For if the agent intellect as such included the definite forms of all intelligible objects, the potential intellect would not depend upon phantasms; it would be actualised simply and solely by the agent intellect; and the latter's relation to intelligible objects would not be that of a maker to something made, as the Philosopher here says; for it would simply be identical with them. What makes it therefore in act with respect to intelligible objects is the fact that it is an active immaterial force able to assimilate other things to itself, i.e. to immaterialise them. In this way it renders the potentially intelligible actually so (like light which, without containing particular colours, actually brings colours into act). And because this active force is a certain participation in the intellectual light of separated substances, the Philosopher compares it to a state and to light; which would not be an appropriate way of describing it if it were itself a separate substance.

§ 740. Next, at 'Knowledge in act',[2] he states his conclusions concerning intellect as in act;[3] and first he states its properties; and then, at 'Only separated',[4] how the intellectual part of the soul in general differs from the rest of the soul. Regarding the former point, he states three properties of intellect in act. First, its actual knowledge is identical with the thing known; which is not true of intellect as potential. Secondly, though in one and the same thing potential knowledge is prior *in time* to actual knowledge, yet, speaking universally, potential knowledge is not prior either *in nature* or *in time*. In Book IX of the *Metaphysics*[5] Aristotle had said

---

[1] § 722.   [2] 430[a] 20. *See* Introd., pp. 34–7.

[3] *intellectus secundum actum*. This is not the same as *intellectus agens*. It is intellect as actually understanding (*ipsum intelligere*, cf. § 741).

[4] 430[a] 22–3.   [5] IX, c.8; 1049[b] 5–25.

that act is by nature prior to potency, but not in time in one and
the same thing; for a thing is first in potency and afterwards in act.
But universally speaking act takes priority even in time; because
no potency would ever be actualised unless something were already
in act. So, even in the case of potential knowledge, no one ever
comes to know anything actually, whether through his own effort
or another's teaching,[1] except in virtue of some pre-existing actual
knowledge, as it is said in Book I of the *Posterior Analytics*.[2]

§ 741. The third property of intellect as in act, differentiating it
from the potential intellect and from intellect in habitual possession of knowledge, is that it is always in act; for it simply is the act
of understanding. In the other cases intellect is sometimes in act
and sometimes in potency.

§ 742. Next, at 'Only separated',[3] he states the properties of the
intellect as a whole; first stating the truth, and then refuting an
objection. He says, then, that only the mind separated from matter
is that which really is mind; and he speaks here, not of the agent or
passive intellect in isolation, but of both together, since both have
been described as separated from matter. And the whole intellect
is so described because it operates without a bodily organ.

§ 743. And in line with what he said at the beginning[4] of this
book, that the soul might be separable from the body if any of its
activities were proper to itself, he now concludes that the soul's
intellectual part alone is immortal and perpetual. This is what he
has said in Book II, namely that this 'kind' of soul was separable
from others as the perpetual from the mortal,[5]—perpetual in the
sense that it survives for ever, not in the sense that it always *has*
existed; for as he shows in Book XII of the *Metaphysics*,[6] forms
cannot exist before their matter. The soul, then (not all of it, but
only its intellectual part) will survive its matter.

§ 744. Next, at 'It does not remember',[7] he meets an objection.
For we might suppose that knowledge would remain unchanged
in the intellectual part of the soul which survives. But already in
Book I he has disallowed this, where[8] he observed that the act of

---

[1] *non . . . inveniendo neque discendo.*   [2] *Anal. Post.*, I, c.1; 71ᵃ 1ss.

[3] 430ᵃ 22-3.   [4] § 21.   [5] § 268.

[6] XII, c.3; 1070ᵃ 20.   [7] 430ᵃ 23-4. *See* note 1, p. 426.

[8] §§ 163-7.

the intellect must cease when something else dies; and that after death the soul remembers and loves no more.

§ 745. So now he adds that what we have known in life is not recalled after death; because 'it is impassible', i.e. that part of the intellectual soul of which he speaks; which, therefore, is unaffected by passions such as love and hatred and reminiscence and so forth, which all depend on modifications of the body. For the 'passive intellect'—a part of the soul which depends on the aforesaid passions—is certainly mortal; for it belongs to our sensitive nature. Nevertheless, it is called 'intellect' and 'rational' because it has a certain share in reason: it obeys and is governed by reason (see Book I of the *Ethics*).[1] And without the co-operation of this embodied part of the soul there is no understanding anything; for the intellect always requires phantasms, as we shall see.[2] Hence, after the body's death the soul no longer knows anything in the same way as before. But how it does know anything then is not part of our present enquiry.

[1] E.N., I, c.13; 1102^{b} 10ss.   [2] § 772.

BOOK III, CHAPTER VI

INTELLECTUAL OPERATIONS
SIMPLE AND COMPLEX 'INTELLIGIBLES'

INTELLIGENCE OF WHAT IS NOT COMPLEX IS IN A sphere where there can be no deception. But in matters where there is false or true, there is also some composition of things understood as of many brought to a unity. As Empedocles said, 'The heads of many grew with no neck',[1] [but] concord afterwards brought them to unity; so in the same way these disjunct terms are combined, like 'the diagonal' and 'the incommensurate'. If the composition be of things done, or of future events, time also is taken into the reckoning, as one of the component elements. Falsity is always in a combination, as for instance when one brings together 'white' and a not-white object, or 'not-white' with a white one. All these statements can also be divisions. It is not only, then, false or true that Cleon is white, but that this fact was true or will be true. It is the intellect which imposes a unity in each case.   §§ 746–51

As the indivisible is twofold, the actual and the potential, there is nothing to prevent the intellect from apprehending an indivisible when it apprehends an extended length.

For this length is actually undivided, and is [understood] in an undivided space of time: for time is divided or undivided like the length. It is not right to say that [the mind]

---

[1] 'Where the heads, etc.', 430^a 29.

understands both by halving both;[1] There is no half, save potentially, unless an actual division has been made. However, in apprehending separately each of the halves, it divides the time also, which is then [divided] like the length. But if this is considered as a whole made up of two halves, then there is something corresponding to each in the time also.

§§ 752–4

But whatever is not indivisible quantitatively, but specifically, the mind apprehends both in an instant of time and by a single act of the soul; incidentally, however, [it apprehends division] not in so far as what the mind understands and the time in which it understands are divisible, but as they are indivisible;[2] for there is in these something indivisible, but perhaps not separable, which gives unity to time and extension; and this holds of all that is continuous, whether by time or extension.

§§ 755–6

A point, and anything separated out and thus incapable of further analysis, is shown as a privation. A similar principle holds in other matters, as in the way we know air or blackness. For in some way the knowledge is by contrariety; but the knowing faculty must be in potency, and one [of the contraries] be in it. But if there is some cause that includes no contrary, it is self-knowing, and in act, and separate.

§§ 757–9

Now every utterance, e.g. an affirmation, is of something, about some subject; and is always either true or false. Yet not all understanding is thus; understanding is true about what anything is, in the sense of the quiddity of it; not as to every fact about a subject, but, as sight is always true about

---

[1] 'One cannot tell what the mind thought in each half' (i.e. of the time). With this M.'s version would seem to agree: . . . *quod in utroque dimidio intelligat.* However, St. Thomas takes the phrase in the sense of the translation given above, *intelligatur sec. medium utriusque* (§ 754).

[2] A disputed passage both as to text and interpretation. The text of M. can yield our rendering; which suits the Commentary.

its proper object, yet it is not always true about a white thing being a man or not. So it stands with whatever is immaterial.   §§ 760–3

CHAPTER VII

Knowledge in act is identical with the thing. But what is potential is prior in time in the individual; though universally it is not prior, even in time; for all that comes into existence comes from an actual existent.   § 764

§ 746. Having come to conclusions about the intellect the Philosopher now examines its activity; and this in two parts; first distinguishing two such activities, and then reaching conclusions about each of these. First, then, he says that the intellect, by one of its activities, understands things simply; understanding, for instance, man or ox, or any such thing, simply in itself. And this operation involves no falsehood, both because objects considered simply in themselves are neither true nor false, and also because, as we shall see later on,[1] the mind is infallible with respect to what things are in themselves.

§ 747. On the other hand, where truth and falsehood are found in the intelligible objects themselves, there must have been already a certain composition of these objects, i.e. of the things understood, joining several such objects together. He gives as an example the theory of Empedocles that all things originated by chance, not design; by merely following a process of division and conjunction through strife and love respectively. Thus Empedocles said that in the beginning many heads 'grew' without necks; and similarly that many other parts of animals grew up in separation from other parts; and he says 'grew' as though these things sprang from the elements, not from the seed of animals, as grass grows from the earth. Only afterwards did these parts, thus differentiated, come together in harmony and make up the single animal with its various parts—head, hands, feet and so on. And if all the parts necessary for the animal's existence were present it could go on living and would beget its own kind; but not if any were lacking. So then, just as love (according to Empedocles) brought together the

[1] §§ 761–3.

different parts of animals and formed of them one animal, so too the intellect is able to combine many simple and separate objects and make one intelligible object of them. And such combinations are sometimes true and sometimes false.

§ 748. They are true when they put together what are combined and united in reality, e.g. the diagonal and incommensurability—for the diagonal of a square is incommensurable with its sides. And they are false when they put together what are not combined in reality, saying, e.g. that the diagonal of a square *is* commensurable with its sides.

§ 749. Now commensurability and the diagonal are sometimes understood separately, making two distinct intelligible objects; but when combined they make one object which the mind understands all together. But again, since the objects so combined are sometimes things past or future, not present, he adds that when the mind combines things 'done'—i.e. past—or things to come, it should include the notion of time past or future; and in this way its combination will refer to past or future.

§ 750. And he proves this by saying that combinations concerning past or future may be false, and that the falsehood is always in the combination itself. Again, there is falsehood if the not-white is combined with what is white, as when swans are said to be not white; or if white is combined with the not-white, as when crows are said to be white. And because all that can be affirmed can also be denied, he adds that all these combinations might also have been divisions.

§ 751. For the mind can always separate things, whether in the present, or past or future; and it can do this both truly and falsely. Clearly then, since combinations can be made with reference to time past and future as well as present, and since truth and falsehood are found precisely in combinations and separations (or divisions), it follows that not only are propositions about the present true or false—e.g. that Cleon is white—but also propositions about the past or future—e.g. that Cleon was or shall be white. Since, however, the combination that makes a proposition is a work of reason and understanding, not of nature, he subjoins that the agent of such propositions, composed of intelligible objects, is the mind. And since it is in combinations that truth and falsehood are

437

found, he can say, in Book VI of the *Metaphysics*,[1] that truth and falsehood are not in things but in the mind.

§ 752. Next, at 'As the indivisible is twofold',[2] he comes to conclusions on both the aforesaid intellectual activities: (1) on the understanding of objects simply in themselves; (2) at 'Now every utterance',[3] on the intellect's combinations and divisions; after which (3) he states something common to both. Section (1) divides into three parts according to three ways of considering indivisibility—that is to say, unity which consists in indivision.

First of all, a thing may be one by continuity;[4] hence the continuum is called an indivisible because it is actually undivided, though it is potentially divisible. So he says that, since anything may be divisible either potentially or actually, there is nothing to prevent the mind thinking of a continuum or length as indivisible actually. And, so doing, its thought will also occur in an undivided time.

§ 753. This is against the view of Plato,[5] that the understanding of things in space involved a sort of continuous movement. In fact spatial things can be understood in two ways: either as potentially divisible—and thus the mind considers one section of a line after another, and so understands the whole in a period of time; or as actually indivisible—and thus the whole line is considered as a unity made up of parts and understood simultaneously. He adds therefore that, in the act of understanding, either both time and length are divided, or both are not divided.

§ 754. Consequently it cannot be said that the understanding involves dividing both by half, i.e. that half a line is understood in half the given time it takes to understand a whole one. This would be the case if the line were actually divided; but a line, as such, is only potentially divisible. If each of its halves, however, is understood separately, then the whole is actually divided mentally; and the time is divided also. But if the line is understood as a unity made up of two parts, the time also will be undivided or instantaneous—the instant being that which persists in every part of time. And if the mind's consideration is prolonged in time, the instants will not be separated with respect to distinct parts of the line

[1] VI, c.4; 1027^b 20–25.   [2] 430^b 6.   [3] 430^b 26.

[4] 430^b 6–14.   [5] cf. §§ 107–31.

understood one after another; but the whole line will be understood at every instant.

§ 755. Next, at 'But whatever',[1] he mentions another kind of
unity, namely that which comes of a thing being one in kind,
though made up of discontinuous parts, e.g. the unity of a man, or
a house, or even of an army. This is a *specific*, not a *quantitative* indivision; and the soul, he says, understands it by what is undivided
in the soul and in an indivisible point of time—not, as Plato
thought, by anything quantitative in the intellect. And though
division may be contained *in* such unities, the divided parts are not
understood—so far as the object and time of the understanding are
concerned—*as* divided, but as united; for even though there be an
actual division into parts, the species itself, as such, is indivisible;
and this it is that is indivisibly understood. But if the parts are
understood separately—e.g. the flesh and bones and so forth—the
whole is not understood in an undivided time.

§ 756. Then he points out wherein this second kind of unity
seems to resemble the former kind. For as the species is something
indivisible unifying the parts of a whole, so perhaps there may be
something indivisible in any period of time or spatial length,—the
point perhaps or the instant, or perhaps the species itself of length
and of time. But there is this difference that, while the indivisible
in the continuum is one and the same in every continuum, whether
temporal or spatial, the unity of species differs from one thing to
another; for some things are made up of homogeneous and some
of heterogeneous parts.

§ 757. Then at 'A point etc.',[2] he goes on to show how the third
sort of indivisibility, i.e. whatever seems to be entirely one, such as
a point or unit, is understood. A point, he says, is a sort of sign of
division between sections of a line, as an instant between periods
of time; and all such—being, like the point, both actually and
potentially indivisible,—are 'shown' to the mind 'as privation', i.e.
as privations of the divisible continuum.

§ 758. The reason being that our mind has to start from sense-
data. Sensibles therefore are the first things intellectually apprehended; and these all have some magnitude; hence the point and
the unit can be only negatively defined. For the same reason whatever transcends the sensibles which we apprehend is known by us

[1] 430^b 14.   [2] 430^b 20.

only negatively. Of 'separated' substances we only know that they are *im*material and *in*corporeal and so forth.

§ 759. It is the same[1] with things known by opposition, such as evil or black, which are privations of their opposites; for of two contraries one is always a lack or privation of the other. So he adds that the mind somehow knows each of these by its contrary: evil by good and black by white. Now if our mind thus knows one contrary by means of another, it must do so by moving from potency into act, and also by receiving into itself the likeness of one contrary, e.g. of white, and only after and in virtue of this, the likeness of the other, e.g. of black. But if there exists a mind that does not have to move from one contrary to another, it must have itself for its primary and immediate object; and it must know all other things in knowing itself; and be always in act and entirely immaterial—even in its being; and such is the Divine Mind according to the teaching of Book XII of the *Metaphysics*.[2]

§ 760. Then at 'Now every utterance',[3] he states a conclusion about the mind's second activity of combining and distinguishing. He says that whenever a statement is made about anything—as when a mind affirms anything—the statement must be either true or false. Understanding as such, however, need not be true or false; its proper object is a simple one, and therefore, as bearing on this object, the act of understanding is neither true nor false. For truth and falsehood consist in a certain adequation or comparison of one thing to another, as when the mind combines or distinguishes; but not in the intelligible object taken by itself.

§ 761. Yet though this latter object as such is neither true nor false, the mind understanding it is true in so far as it is conformed to a reality understood. So he adds that just so far as the mind bears on an essence,[4] i.e. understands *what* anything is, it is always true; but not just in so far as it relates one thing to another.

§ 762. The reason for this is that, as he says, essence[5] is what the intellect first knows; hence, just as sight is infallible with respect to its proper object, so is the intellect with respect to essence. It cannot, for instance, be mistaken when it simply knows *what* man is;

---

[1] 430^b 22.   [2] XII, c.7; 1072^b 10–25.   [3] 430^b 26.

[4] *intellectus qui est ipsius quid est secundum hoc quod aliquid erat esse . . . verus est semper.*   [5] *quod quid est.*

on the other hand, just as sight can be deceived in respect of what is joined with its proper object, e.g. in discerning that some white object is a man, so too the intellect sometimes goes astray in relating one object to another. But the totally immaterial substances understand in a manner corresponding to our human apprehension of essences; so that they are infallible.

§ 763. But note that even in knowing essences deception can occur indirectly, in two ways: (*a*) inasmuch as one thing's definition becomes false when applied to another thing; e.g. the definition of a circle applied to a triangle; and (*b*) inasmuch as the parts of a definition do not agree together, in which case the definition is simply false; e.g. if one were to include 'lacking sense-perception' in one's definition of 'animal'. Whence it follows that deception absolutely cannot occur where the definition involves no combining of parts; in this case one either understands truly or not at all (see Book IX of the *Metaphysics*).[1]

§ 764. Finally, at 'Knowledge in act', he repeats what he has said of intellect in act, that actual knowledge is one with its actual object; and that in one and the same thing potential knowledge precedes actual knowledge in time; but that this is not true universally; for all actualities derive from one Actual Being, as was explained above.[2]

[1] IX, c.10; 1051^b 15–30.   [2] §§ 740–1.

BOOK III, CHAPTER VII, CONTINUED

SENSE AND INTELLECT COMPARED
THE PRACTICAL INTELLECT
ABSTRACTION AGAIN

AND IT SEEMS THAT THE SENSE-OBJECT [SIMPLY] brings the sense-faculty from a state of potency to one of act; for [the latter] is not affected or altered. Hence it is a specifically distinct kind of movement. For movement is the actuality of the incomplete; whereas in its plain meaning act is different, as being of the thing completed.

§§ 765–6

Sensation therefore is like mere uttering and understanding; but, given a pleasant or painful object, the soul pursues or avoids with, so to say, affirmation or negation. To be 'pleased' or to feel pain is to act in the sensitive mean in relation to the good or the bad as such; and pursuit or avoidance are this operation in act. And the faculties of desire and avoidance are not distinct,—nor distinct from the sensitive faculty; though in essence they differ.   §§ 767–9

Imaginative phantasms are to the intellective soul as sense-objects. But when it affirms or denies good or evil it pursues or avoids. Hence the soul never understands apart from phantasms.   §§ 770–2

This is comparable to the way that air affects the pupil with such and such a quality, and this in turn affects another part with the same quality: and the hearing operates likewise. The ultimate is one, a single common mean whose essence, however, is various. With what it discerns how the sweet differs from the hot has been stated already and must be re-affirmed here.

For it is a unity in the sense of a terminus; and this unity—according to analogy and number—is related to distinct objects as they to one another. (What difference indeed does it make whether the comparison be of qualities not homogeneous, or of contraries, like black and white?) Thus, as A (white) is to B (black) so is C to D; hence therefore, also, alternating the proportions. If then C and D pertain to one unifying principle,[1] they are to each other as A and B: identical though distinct in essence; so too is the aforesaid [principle].[2] The same relation holds if A be the sweet and B the white.   §§ 773–6

The intellectual faculty therefore understands forms in phantasms. And as in these [forms] what is to be pursued by it, or avoided, is marked out for it, so too when these are in the imagination apart from sensation, is it moved. [For instance] when one sees something fearful [e.g. fire,] seeing the fire move one knows in general that someone is fighting.[3] Sometimes, however, it is by means of the phantasms or concepts in the soul that one calculates as if seeing, and that one deliberates on future or present matters;[4] and when one has said that the pleasing or the disagreeable is present, then one pursues or avoids.   §§ 777–8

---

[1] Perhaps 'to one subject', 431ᵃ 27. But St. Thomas: 'one intellect' (§ 776).

[2] The Greek of this clause allows more than one rendering; ours is fixed by the Commentary, § 776.

[3] 'perceiving that the beacon is fire one knows by the common sense, on seeing the fire moving, that an enemy is approaching'. M. has mistranslated τὸν φρυκτὸν, the fire-brand or beacon, as *fugibile*, τὸν φυκτὸν, 431ᵇ 5.

[4] 'on future in relation to present matters', 431ᵇ 8.

And generally in practical affairs[1] and apart from action, true and false are in the same category, whether good or evil. But they differ in being absolute and relative.   §§ 779–80

The mind understands by abstraction, so called, as one might understand a snub-nose: as snub-*nose*, not in separation; but as *curved*, then, if the understanding be actual, the mind thinks of the curve apart from the flesh in which it exists. Thus, understanding mathematical objects, the mind understands things not separated *as* separated. And in general, the mind in the act of understanding is the thing itself.

§§ 781–4

Whether it is possible for a mind that is not itself separated from extension to understand anything separated or no, is to be considered later.   §§ 785–6

---

[1] 'And so generally in practical matters.' This phrase ought to close the preceding paragraph. The rest of the sentence is translated to suit St. Thomas' reading of it (§ 779). Hence the comma after 'category', and the omission of any rendering of *cum* in *in eodem genere est cum bono et malo*.

ST. THOMAS'S COMMENTARY

LECTIO TWELVE

§ 765. Here[1] the Philosopher turns to consider the intellect as compared with the senses; first explaining the kind of movement that sensation involves; and secondly,[2] showing how this movement resembles that of the intellect.

On the former point he observes that the sense-object appears to play an active part in sensation, in so far as sensitivity as a whole is, to start with, in potency. For the sense-object and the sense-faculty are not mutually exclusive things, as though, when one acted on the other it had to transform and alter the latter by destroying something within it. In fact, all that the object does to the faculty is to actualise it; so he adds that sensitivity is not passive to the change-producing activity of the sense-object in the ordinary sense of the terms 'passivity' and 'change', which generally connote the substitution of one of two mutually exclusive qualities for the other.

§ 766. Since, as he shows in the *Physics*,[3] changes of bodies are of this latter kind, it is clear that if we call sensation a change we mean a different sort of change. Movement from one mutually exclusive quality to another is the actuality of a thing in potency; for while the thing is losing one quality, and so long as it still has not the other, its movement is still incomplete and it is in potency. And because the potential as such is imperfect, this kind of movement is an actuality of the imperfect;[4] whereas the kind we are concerned with here is an actuality of what is perfect,[5]—the response of a sense-faculty already actualised by its object. Only the senses in act can have sensations. So their movement is quite different from physical movement. It is this movement also which, together

---

[1] 431ª 4.   [2] 431ª 5.   [3] *Phys.*, V, c.5.
[4] *actus imperfecti.*   [5] *actus perfecti.*

445

with understanding and willing, is properly called an 'operation';[1] and this also is what Plato referred to when he said that the soul moves itself through knowing and loving itself.

§ 767. Next, at 'Sensation therefore',[2] he likens the intellect's movement to that of the senses;—first showing how the senses move, and then,[3] at 'Imaginative phantasms', how a similar movement takes place in the intellect. As regards the former point he says that, since the sensible object actualises our sensitivity without any accompanying passion (properly so called) or alteration, and the like also happens in intellection, as we have already seen,[4] therefore sensation resembles the act of the intellect—that is to say, mere sensation, with its sensuous apprehension and judgement, resembles mere intellection, with its intellectual apprehension and judgement.[5] Pure sensuous apprehension and discernment resemble intellectual understanding and discernment. But when the senses affirm (so to say) pleasure or pain in their act of perceiving, then appetite comes into play, i.e. a desire or avoidance of the object perceived. And note the phrase 'so to say'; for properly speaking affirmation and denial are acts of the intellect;[6] but something like them occurs when pleasure or pain is experienced sensuously.

§ 768. And to show what pleasure and pain are, he observes further that the act of perceiving pleasure and pain takes place in the 'sensitive mean'; that is to say, it is the act of a certain midway faculty of sense—so called because the common sense is a sort of medium between the particular senses, like the centre of a circle in relation to lines drawn from the circumference. But not every act of the sensitive part is a sense of pleasure or pain. This perception relates precisely to the good and the bad as such. For the good of the senses—i.e. what suits them—gives pleasure; while what is bad, i.e. repugnant and harmful to them, causes pain. And pain and pleasure are followed, respectively, by avoidance and appetite (or desire); and these are a sort of activity.

§ 769. Thus the movement from sense-object to sense passes through three stages, as it were. There is first an awareness of the object as being in harmony or out of harmony with the sense: then

---

[1] operatio.   [2] 431[a] 8.   [3] 431[a] 14.

[4] §§ 722; 738-9.   [5] 'judgement' renders dicere; 'apprehension', intelligere.

[6] cf. §§ 746-51.

a feeling of pleasure or pain; and then desire or avoidance. And although desiring, avoiding and mere sensing are different acts, still they are all acts of identically the same subject, though they can be distinguished in thought. This is what he means by adding that the 'desiring and avoiding'—i.e. that part of the soul which desires or avoids, is not divided in being nor distinct from the sensitivity; although in 'essence' they 'differ', i.e. are represented by different concepts. He says this against Plato in particular, who maintained that desire and sensation had distinct organs in different parts of the body.

§ 770. Next, at 'Imaginative phantasms',[1] he compares the mind's movement to the process of sense-knowledge as he has described it. And he does two things here: he shows how the mind is related (a) to sense-objects, and (b) at 'The mind understands by abstraction',[2] to objects beyond the range of sense. (a) divides into (i) an explanation of the way the mind is related to sense-objects in practical activity; and (ii) at 'And generally in practical affairs',[3] a comparison of the practical and speculative intellects. And with regard to the former point, he first states and then, at 'This is comparable to the way',[4] illustrates the resemblance between the mind's activity and that of the senses.

First, then, he observes[5] that phantasms are to the intellectual part of the soul as sense-objects to the senses; as these last are affected by their objects, so is the intellect by phantasms. And as sensation of the pleasant or painful is succeeded by desire or avoidance, so also the intellect, when it affirms or desires goodness or badness in an object it apprehends, tends either towards or away from that object.

§ 771. But note that Aristotle's use of terms here suggests a twofold difference between intellect and senses. For in the first place, when the senses apprehend *their* good and evil, this awareness is not immediately succeeded by pursuit or avoidance, but by pleasure and pain,—after which the sensing subject pursues or withdraws. The reason is that as the senses are not aware of goodness in general, so sense-appetition is not swayed by the good or the bad in general, but only by this or that particular good, pleasant to sense, or, by this or that particular evil, unpleasant to sense. The soul's

[1] 431ᵃ 14.   [2] § 781; 431ᵇ 12.   [3] § 779; 431ᵇ 10.
[4] 431ᵃ 17.   [5] 431ᵃ 14.

447

intellectual part, on the contrary, is aware of goodness and badness in general; hence its appetition at once and immediately responds to this apprehension.

§ 772. The other difference appears in Aristotle's observing, unconditionally, that the intellect affirms or denies, whereas of the senses he only says that they affirm 'so to say'. The reason for this has already been given. And from what has been said he draws the further conclusion that if intellect is related to phantasms as the senses to their object, then just as the senses cannot sense without an object, so the soul cannot understand without phantasms.

§ 773. Then, where he says 'This is comparable',[1] he explains the resemblance still further: (a) as regards the likeness between phantasms and sense-objects in relation to the intellectual soul; and (b) —at 'The intellectual faculty therefore'[2]—as regards the avoidance or pursuit that follows the affirmation or denial of goodness or badness.

First, then, he remarks that colour-affected air itself modifies the pupil of the eye in a particular way, i.e. it imprints on it a likeness of some colour, and that then the pupil, so modified, acts upon the common sense. Similarly our hearing, itself affected by the air, acts upon the common sense. And though there are several exterior senses, their reactions all come back to one point, which is a certain common medium between all the senses, like a centre upon which lines from a circumference all converge.

§ 774. And while this mid-point is a unity as a subject, its 'essence' is manifold, that is to say, the idea of it varies according as we relate it to the different senses. It is the faculty by which the soul sees the difference between the sweet and the hot, as we saw when we were considering it in itself;[3] and now, relating it to the intellect, we may say that, as all sensible objects find a common terminus in the common sense, so do all phantasms in the intellect. And as in the one case many objects were said to be judged by a single principle, so in the other case also in a like proportion. Again, as to the number of objects judged: the intellect is related to both objects whose distinction it perceives as 'they' to one another, i.e. as the single common sense to the different sensibles whose differences it discerns.

§ 775. It makes no difference whether we speak of the non-

[1] 431ᵃ 17.   [2] 431ᵇ 2.   [3] §§ 609–10.

homogeneous, i.e. of different sensibles differing in genus, for instance of white which is a colour, and sweet which is a savour; or of contrary qualities of the same genus, like black and white. For the common sense discriminates between both kinds of difference.

§ 776. For white, then, let us put A, and for black, B; so that, as A is to B, so is C to D; the latter standing for the phantasms of white and black respectively. Then, varying the proportions, A is to C as B to D: i.e., white is to the phantasm of white as black to the phantasm of black; and as the intellect is to C and D, so is the sense in question to A and B. If therefore C and D, the phantasms of white and black, are related to a unity in so far as they are judged by one intellect, they resemble in this A and B, namely white and black, which are judged by one sense; so that, just as the sense which discriminates these two is in itself one, but twofold in thought, so also is the intellect. And the same reasoning is valid if we take non-homogeneous objects—taking, for instance, A for sweet and B for white.

§ 777. Next, at 'The intellectual faculty',[1] he explains what he said above,[2] that in affirming or denying good or evil the mind either avoids or pursues; and so concludes that the intellectual part of the soul understands intelligible forms abstracted from phantasms. And just as, when sensible objects are actually present, the mind is impressed by whatever is congenial or abhorrent in them, so too, in the absence of such objects externally, the mind is induced to desire them or fly from them by their representations present in the imagination.

§ 778. And he gives examples. First, of the process that is started by sense-objects actually present—as when a man sees something fearful, for instance the confusion caused by a fire in a city; seeing the flames leaping he knows 'in general'—i.e. by some common faculty of judging, or perhaps according to what commonly happens—that a conflict is raging; and thus the mind is moved to pursue or flee by objects present exteriorly. But sometimes phantasms or ideas presented inwardly cause the soul to deliberate about things future or present, reckoning them to be desirable or horrible,—as though they were actually seen here and now.

§ 779. Next at 'And generally',[3] he compares speculative with

[1] 431^b 2.   [2] § 767.   [3] 431^b 10.

practical knowledge. Truth and falsehood, he says, i.e. true and false knowing, both in the sphere of action (the practical intellect) and outside that sphere (the speculative intellect), belong to the same category, whether good or evil.[1] This can be taken in two ways: (1) That the thing understood, either speculatively or practically, may be either good or bad, and that it remains such from the point of view of either mode of understanding; or (2) that the knowing itself is, if true, a good for the intellect, whether it be speculative or practical; whereas if false, it is an evil for the intellect, again in both cases.

§ 780. Thus he is not reducing truth and falsehood to a common genus with good and evil, but truth and falsehood in action to a common genus with truth and falsehood in speculation. This is clear from his distinguishing 'in-action' and 'not-in-action' as 'absolute' and 'relative'. For the speculative intellect considers a thing as true or false universally or 'absolutely', whereas the practical intellect relates its apprehensions to particular things to be done; for doing is always in the particular.

§ 781. Then, at 'The mind understands',[2] having already said that there is no act of the intellect without a phantasm, and that phantasms derive from sensation, the Philosopher begins to explain how we understand things that are outside the range of sensation. Here he proceeds in two stages: (1) he explains how we understand mathematical objects abstracted from sensible matter; and (2) he enquires whether we understand anything that is immaterial *in being* at 'Whether it is possible'.[3] As regards the first point, note that of things joined in reality the mind may think, and think truly, of one without the other, provided that the concept of the one is not included in that of the other. If Socrates is both white and musical his whiteness can be understood without regard to his musical character; but I cannot understand 'man' if I do not understand 'animal', for the concept of man includes animal. Thus it is possible to distinguish mentally things conjoined in reality, and yet not fall into error.

§ 782. But if the conjoined things were understood as *separate* things the mind would err,—as, to take our former example, if it judged that the musical person was not white. Certain aspects, however, of sense-objects the mind simply considers in separation

[1] *See* note 5, p. 444　　　　[2] 431[b] 12.　　　　[3] 431[b] 17.

or distinctly, without judging them to exist separately. This is what he means by saying that what the mind understands by abstraction (even mathematical objects) it understands in the same way as, e.g., a snub-nose; understanding it precisely as a snub-nose, yet not in separation from sensible matter; for sensible matter, the nose, is included in the definition of a snub-nose.

§ 783. When, however, the mind understands actually anything precisely as *curved*, it abstracts from flesh; not that it judges the curved thing to be *not* flesh, but it understands 'curved' without regard to flesh; because flesh does not enter into the definition of a curve. And it is thus that we understand all mathematical objects, —as though they were separated from sensible matter, whilst in reality they are not so.

§ 784. But we do not so understand physical things; for in *their* definition (unlike mathematical objects) sensible matter is included. Yet in understanding them we still abstract a universal from particulars, in so far as the specific nature is understood apart from the individuating principles; for these do not enter into the definition. And the mind in act is its object; for precisely in the degree that the object is or is not material, it is or is not perceived by the mind. And just because Plato overlooked this process of abstraction he was forced to conceive of mathematical objects and specific natures as existing in separation from matter; whereas Aristotle was able to explain that process by the agent intellect.

§ 785. Next, at 'Whether it is possible',[1] he puts a question about things that *exist* immaterially: whether, that is, our intellect, though conjoined with spatial magnitude (i.e. the body), can understand 'anything separated', i.e. any substance separated from matter. He undertakes to pursue this enquiry later,—not at present, because it is not yet evident that any such substances exist nor, if they do, what sort of thing they are. It is a problem for metaphysics. In fact, we do not know Aristotle's solution of this problem, for we have not the whole of his *Metaphysics*; either because it is not yet all translated, or possibly because he died before he could complete it.

§ 786. We should note, however, that when he speaks of the

[1] 431^b 17.

intellect here as not 'separated' from the body he refers to the fact that it is one of the powers of the soul, which is the actuality of the body; whereas speaking, at an earlier stage,[1] of the intellect as 'separated' he was referring to its non-organic mode of activity.

[1] §§ 688, 699.

BOOK III, CHAPTER VIII

RECAPITULATION

INTELLECT. SENSE. IMAGINATION

Now, RECAPITULATING WHAT WE HAVE SAID about the soul, let us repeat that the soul is somehow all that exists; for things are either sensible or intelligible; and knowledge is in some way the knowable, and sensation is the sense object. But how this is so we must enquire. For knowledge and sensation are divided into realities: the potential answers to things that are really in potency, the actual to things really in act. In the soul the sensitive faculty and that which can know are these [things] in potency; the latter [faculty] the understandable, the former the sensible. §§ 787–8

Now they must be the things themselves or their forms. But they are certainly not the things themselves: no stone is in the soul, but only its form. Thus the soul is like a hand: the hand is the instrument that includes other instruments, and the intellect is the form that includes other forms, and sense the form that includes sensible things. §§ 789–90

But since there are no real things apart from things sensible and extended (so it would seem), then in the sensible species are the intelligible, both what are predicated as a result of abstraction and whatever qualities and habits are found in sensible things. And on this account, what does not perceive

453

by sensation acquires no knowledge or understanding at all; and when thinking occurs there must be at the same time a phantasm as its object; for phantasms are as sense objects save that they are without matter. §§ 791–2

Imagination is other than affirmation and negation: for the true and the false are a combining of intellectual concepts.

§ 793

What difference have the primary concepts that they should not be phantasms? But neither are the others[1] phantasms, though they do not exist apart from phantasms. § 794

[1] M. has *aliis* when he should have *alia*. It is the other than primary concepts that are referred to.

ST. THOMAS'S COMMENTARY
LECTIO THIRTEEN

§ 787. After treating of its powers of sense and intellect the Philosopher goes on now to draw conclusions about the nature of the soul: showing first that the early philosophers were partly right and partly wrong about the soul; and then explaining how the intellect depends on the senses. As to the former point, he first explains how the soul, as the early philosophers said, is in a way all things; and then how it is not all things in the way they supposed. He says then, recapitulating,[1] that one can admit that the soul is in a way all things; for everything is either sensible or intelligible, and sense and intellect (or science) are in the soul, sense being somehow the sensible, and intellect, or science, the intelligible or the scientifically knowable.

§ 788. But we must ask how this is so. For sense and intellectual knowledge are divided 'into realities', that is, their division into act and potency corresponds to a like division in reality; but in such a way that while potential intellectual or sensuous knowledge answers to things potentially understood or sensed, and actual intellectual or sensuous knowledge answers to things actually understood or sensed, there is a difference between the two relationships. For the sense in act and the intellect in act are the objects they actually sense or understand; but neither the sensitive nor the intellectual potency is actually its object; it is only so potentially. And that is how the soul is 'somehow' everything.

§ 789. Next, at 'Now they must be',[2] he shows how the ancients misapplied this formula. He says that if the soul is indeed all things, it must be either simply identical with all things or a formal likeness[3] of all things. The former view was that of Empedocles who made out that we, being earth, know earth, and being water we

<hr>

[1] 431[b] 20.   [2] 431[b] 28.   [3] *species*.

know water, and so on. But obviously the soul is not simply identical with the things it knows; for not stone itself, but its formal likeness exists in the soul. And this enables us to see how intellect in act *is* what it understands; the form[1] of the object is the form of the mind in act.

§ 790. Thus the soul resembles the hand. The hand is the most perfect of organs, for it takes the place in man of all the organs given to other animals for purposes of defence or attack or covering. Man can provide all these needs for himself with his hands. And in the same way the soul in man takes the place of all the forms of being, so that through his soul a man is, in a way, all being or everything; his soul being able to assimilate all the forms of being—the intellect intelligible forms and the senses sensible forms.

§ 791. Next, at 'But since there are':[2] the doctrine just stated, namely that intellect is, in a way, the intelligible object as sense is the sensible object, might lead one to suppose that the intellect did not depend on the senses; as would be the case indeed if the intelligible objects attained by our mind had their existence apart from sensible things, as the Platonists thought. So he now shows the intellect's dependence on the senses; and then goes on (at 'Imagination is other')[3] to show that it differs, none the less, from imagination which also depends on the senses. First, then, he observes that, since all the objects of our understanding are included within the range of sensible things existing in space, that is to say, that none seems to have that sort of distinct existence apart from things of sense which particular things of sense have apart from one another, it follows that all these intelligible objects have their beings *in* the objects of sense; this being true not only of the objects studied by natural science, the properties and modifications of things of sense, but even of mathematical abstractions. It follows then that without some use of the senses we can neither learn anything new, as it were for the first time; nor bring before our understanding any intellectual knowledge already possessed. Whenever the intellect actually regards anything there must at the same time be formed in us a phantasm, that is, a likeness of something sensible.

§ 792. Phantasms, however, differ from things of sense by their

---

[1] *species.*   [2] 432ᵃ 2.   [3] 432ᵃ 9.

immateriality. For as we have shown,[1] the senses receive the forms of things immaterially; and phantasms are nothing but movements started by actual sensation.

It will be clear now that Avicenna erred in saying that once the mind had acquired knowledge it no longer needed the senses. For we know by experience that in order to reflect on knowledge already gained we have to make use of phantasms; and that any injury to the physical apparatus underlying these will tend to prevent our using the knowledge we already have.

§ 793. Then at 'Imagination is other'[2] he distinguishes between intellect and imagination. (1) With respect to the normal activity[3] of the intellect, which is by composing and dividing, he says that imagining is neither intellectual affirmation nor intellectual denial; for these immediately involve truth and falsehood; which is not the case with imagining. Only the intellect knows truth and falsehood.

§ 794. (2) He asks (at 'What difference etc.')[4] how the primary intellectual notions, the understanding of indivisible objects, differ from phantasms; and he replies that while these are always attended by phantasms, they differ from phantasms by their universality: they are abstracted from individuating conditions, whereas phantasms are always of particulars. Phantasms in fact are not actually, but only potentially, indivisible.

[1] §§ 284, 551.
[2] 432ᵃ 9.
[3] *quantum ad operationem communem intellectus.*
[4] 432ᵃ 12.

BOOK III, CHAPTER IX

THE PRINCIPLE OF MOVEMENT
IN LIVING BEINGS
WHAT IT IS NOT

S INCE THE SOUL IS DEFINED BY TWO POWERS FOUND
in animate beings, the one, discernment, the work of
intellect and sensation, the other, movement by local
motion; and as a certain amount has been decided about
sensation and understanding, we must now consider what
can be the moving factor in the soul: whether this is a single
part of it, separate either spatially or by definition, or the
whole soul; and, if it is a part of the soul, whether it is a
special part other than those generally acknowledged and
already dealt with, or some one among these. § 795

A difficulty at once arises as to how it is possible to speak
at all of parts of the soul, or to say how many they are. For
in one way their number seems to be infinite and not merely,
as some say, the reasoning, the irascible and the concupiscible
[parts]; or as others say, the rational and irrational.

§§ 796–7

For according to the differences by which these are distinguished, other parts seem to show greater diversity than
[we see] in those just mentioned. In particular: the vegetative
part, which is in plants and all living things; and the sensitive,
which one cannot easily place among either the irrational or
the rational elements. §§ 798–800

Further, there is the imaginative power, which seems in essence to be quite different from any other. With which of these others it is identical, or from which it differs, are difficult problems: if one is to suppose that parts of the soul *are* separate.   § 801

Furthermore, there is the appetitive faculty, which, both by its notion and as a capacity, seems to be diverse from all others; and it would be unreasonable to split this up. For will operates in the rational part, desire and anger in the irrational; and if the soul is in three parts, appetition will be in each.   §§ 802–6

But to come to the matter that is now before us: what is it that moves the animal by local motion? For the movement which is in all animals, by which they grow and decay, would certainly seem to be due to the principle of generation and nutrition. Of respiration and exhalation, sleep and waking, we must treat later on: these also raise many difficulties.   § 807

But of local motion: what, we must consider, is it that moves an animal from place to place? It is obviously not the vegetative power. For a movement of this sort is always directed towards an end, and is accompanied by phantasm or desire. For nothing moves unless with desire or dislike, except under compulsion.   § 808

Further: plants would also move about, and would possess some organic part suitable for such movement.   § 809

Likewise, it is not the sensitive power. Many animals endowed with sensation are fixed and motionless all their lives. Yet if Nature does nothing in vain and is never deficient in what is necessary (save in imperfect or injured specimens; but such animals are complete and not defective, and there is proof of this in that they reproduce, grow and decay), it follows that they should also have the parts requisite for moving about.   §§ 810–11

Nor is the reasoning faculty or what is called intellect the moving power; for the speculative function does not consider in view of action, and has nothing to say about the avoidable or the desirable. But movement is always the avoidance or the pursuit of something. Nor, even when it does consider something of this kind, does it at once command pursuit or avoidance—for instance, it often thinks about some object of terror or delight, but without enjoining fear; though the heart moves, or, in the case of something pleasant, some other part.   §§ 812–15

Further; when the mind and the understanding do command avoidance or pursuit, the soul does not move [accordingly] but acts according to desire, as in the case of the incontinent. And in general we observe that one who knows the art of medicine does not [necessarily] heal,—as though it were the function of some power other than science to act according to science.   § 816

But not even appetition imperates such movement as this. For the self-restrained do not act according to their desires even while they are actually wanting and desiring; instead they obey reason.   § 817

ST. THOMAS'S COMMENTARY
LECTIO FOURTEEN

§ 795. Having studied the soul in its vegetative, sensitive and intellectual parts, the Philosopher now considers it as a subject of movement. Introducing the problem, he observes first of all that the old philosophers defined the life-principle of animals in terms of two capacities: the capacity to discern or know, which is the function of intellect and sense; and the capacity to move from place to place. It is the latter capacity that we are concerned with now. We want to understand the principle of movement in relation to the soul: whether, if it is a part of the soul, it is really spatially separate from the other parts, so that it is located in a special part of the body, as the Platonists supposed; or, on the contrary, separable only in thought; whether perhaps it is not a part at all, but the entire soul; and whether, granted that it is only a part, it is or is not distinct from the parts usually enumerated, and distinct from those already studied in this treatise.

§ 796. Next, at 'A difficulty etc.',[1] he begins a controversial section, which itself leads him, at 'It seems that there are two',[2] to certain conclusions. This section contains two parts: (1) an argument against a certain division of the powers of the soul; and (2) an argument, at 'But of local motion',[3] concerning especially the motive-principle as a part of the soul. As regards (1) he first states a division of the powers of the soul made by some philosophers, and then, at 'For according to',[4] disputes it.

He begins then[5] by saying that we are met at the outset of our enquiry by the problem of dividing the soul's powers. What should be the principle of this division, and how many powers are there? It has seemed to some that the number of these powers was

[1] 432ᵃ 22.   [2] Lectio 15, § 818; 433ᵃ 9.   [3] § 808; 432ᵇ 13.
[4] 432ᵃ 26.   [5] 432ᵃ 22.

461

infinite, i.e. quite indeterminable; and this would indeed be the truth if every act or movement in the soul had to be assigned to its own distinct part. Thus it would seem inadequate to divide the soul, as some do, into a rational part, an irascible part, and an appetitive (i.e. concupiscible) part; for these include only the motive powers of the soul.

§ 797. And if others make the dividing line fall between the powers that share in reason and those that do not, this division, though comprehensive enough in a sense, is not exactly relevant to the parts of the soul *as such*, but only to the parts of the *rational* soul; and so Aristotle uses it in the *Ethics*.[1]

§ 798. Next, at 'For according to the differences',[2] he brings several objections against these divisions. (1) Granted that the differences just mentioned between the various parts of the soul are truly differences, they are not the only ones; the soul has other parts, already mentioned in this Treatise,[3] which differ even more from one another. For instance, in all plants and animals (and thus in all living things) exists the vegetative part; and in all animals the sensitive part; and these two obviously differ from each other, and also from the rational, irascible and concupiscible parts, more than these last two parts from each other. Yet neither is included in the divisions given above.

§ 799. Not, it is clear, in the first division: for neither vegetability nor sensitivity can be called either rational, irascible or concupiscible. Again, passing to the second division, Aristotle shows that neither vegetativity nor sensitivity are envisaged thereby. It is difficult, he says, to identify either with what shares or does not share in reason.

§ 800. That neither is rational in nature is obvious; but we can also show that neither is irrational. For the irrational means what is either anti-rational or lacking a rationality that it ought to possess; and neither of the aforesaid parts is such. Whereas if one were simply to call them *non*-rational they would not constitute, properly speaking, a classification of the soul's powers. Clearly, then, the aforesaid divisions are inadequate.

§ 801. (2) Then, at 'Further, there is',[4] he observes that it is very

---

[1] E.N., I, c.13; 1102ᵃ 25ss.   [2] 432ᵃ 26.
[3] §§ 199–210.   [4] 432ᵃ 31.

hard to decide whether imagination, which can certainly be distinguished in thought from the rest of the soul, is or is not really the same thing as any one of the powers already mentioned; especially if we were to follow those who say that the parts of the soul are really separate beings.[1]

§ 802. (3) Then again, at 'Furthermore, there is',[2] he remarks that the appetitive capacity seems distinct, both in thought and as a real potency, from other parts of the soul. Now, assuming that the soul was so divided into a rational and an irrational part that each was a *thing* distinct from the other, one would have to 'split up', i.e. to divide the appetitive capacity in the same way—a very questionable procedure; and yet this capacity is certainly in part rational or volitional, and in part irrational (the irascible and concupiscible parts). Similarly, if we add the irascible part as a distinct *thing* to the rational and irrational parts of the soul, we should have to posit a different appetitive force in each: in one a volitional force, in another an irascible force, and in the third a concupiscible force; making three distinct things of this kind.

§ 803. But the question now arises why the sensitive part of the soul has two appetitive capacities, the irascible and the concupiscible, whereas there is only one rational appetitive force, the will. I answer that potencies differ according to the objective terms of their acts; and the objective term of appetite is the good as apprehended.

§ 804. Now the intellect and the senses apprehend the good differently: the intellect apprehends it under a general idea of goodness; but the senses in this or that particular determination.[3] And this is why there is only one kind of appetite following intellectual apprehension, whereas the desire arising from sensuous apprehension divides according to diverse kinds of apprehended good. For some things seem good to the senses simply as affording pleasure; and this kind of goodness is answered by the concupiscible appetite. But other things seem good and desirable as terminating in pleasure in so far as by means of them one is enabled freely to enjoy pleasant things; and to this good corresponds the irascible appetite; which fights, as it were, on behalf of the concupiscible. Thus animals only get angry and fight for things that will afford

[1] *separatas subjecto.*   [2] 432[b] 3–4.   [3] cf. § 771.

them pleasure, that is to say, when they are hunting or mating, as it says in Book VI of the *Historia Animalium*.[1]

§ 805. Therefore every movement of the irascible appetite starts from and ends in a movement of the concupiscible appetite. Anger springs from a sadness and ceases in a pleasure; for the angry find their satisfaction in punishing. Hence some say that to overcome obstacles is the precise object of the irascible appetite.

§ 806. But it is quite unreasonable to say, as some do, that the specific function of this appetite is to avoid evils. For one and the same potency bears upon contraries—as sight upon both black and white; hence good and evil cannot by themselves differentiate the appetitive potency. Hence, just as loving some good pertains to the concupiscible appetite, so does hating an evil (as Aristotle says in Book IX of the *Ethics*);[2] and similarly both the hope of good and the fear of evil pertain to the irascible appetite.

§ 807. Then, at 'But to come',[3] he observes that what we are at present concerned to elucidate (the principle of local movement in animals) does not seem to be accounted for by the aforesaid divisions; and that this is a further point against the latter. Now clearly the movements of growth and decline, common to all living things, spring from some common generative and vegetative principle; whereas certain other mutations, such as breathing in and out, or sleeping and waking, are not at all easy to explain and require to be treated of separately later.

§ 808. Then, at 'But of local motion',[4] he asks what is the principle of local movement in animals. And he shows first that it is not the vegetative principle; secondly, at 'Likewise',[5] that it is not sensitivity; thirdly, at 'Nor is the reasoning faculty',[6] that it is not the intellect; and fourthly, at 'But not even appetition',[7] that it is not the appetitive power.

That it is not the vegetative principle he proves by two arguments. The first is as follows. Local movement from place to place is always occasioned by something the animal imagines and desires; no animal moves (except under compulsion) unless it wants, or withdraws from, something. But since the vegetative principle

[1] Apparently a general reference to *Hist. Animal.*, VI, c.18.
[2] Perhaps the text referred to is in Bk. II, chap. 5; 1105^b 20.
[3] 432^b 7.   [4] 432^b 13.   [5] 432^b 19.   [6] 432^b 26.
[7] 433^a 6.

is without imagination and desire, it cannot be the principle of this kind of local movement.

§ 809. The second argument at 'Further: plants',[1] runs thus. If the vegetative part were this principle, all plants would move about in this way, and be equipped with the necessary organs for doing so: which they obviously do not and are not. Therefore . . .

§ 810. Next, at 'Likewise',[2] he shows that sensitivity is not the principle we are seeking. For if it were, every animal would have the power to move from place to place. But many animals, though capable of sensation, are fixed in one place and motionless so long as they live.

§ 811. And to meet the objection that perhaps the reason why such animals are immobile is that they lack, not the *principle*, but the *organs* of movement, he adds that Nature is never purposeless: it never fails to provide what is necessary for a given animal, unless this animal is deformed or a monster; and such monsters are exceptions to the normal course of nature, being caused by some defect or other in the parental seed. Now these immobile animals are perfect in their own way, not deformed like monsters: they generate offspring in their own likeness and grow and decline quite normally. In them, therefore, Nature does not act without purpose or fail in what is necessary for life. If then they were endowed with a motive-principle they would also have organs of motion; otherwise this principle would be useless, being unequipped with the necessary instruments. Note that this reasoning implies that wherever a vital principle exists there also will be found a corresponding organic apparatus; and that the parts of a living body subserve the powers of its soul.

§ 812. Next, where he says 'Nor is the reasoning faculty',[3] he shows that not even mind is the motive-principle we seek. His words, 'nor is the reasoning faculty . . . called intellect', indicate, by the way, that reason and intellect are not distinct parts of the soul. The intellect is called 'reason' in so far as it comes to intelligible truths by a process of enquiry.

§ 813. That intellect is not the principle of movement he first proves with regard to the speculative intellect. So far as the mind merely considers things which are simply objects of speculation,

[1] 432[b] 17.   [2] 432[b] 19.   [3] 432[b] 26.

not things to be done (e.g. that a triangle has three angles equal to two right angles) it is obviously not concerned with action and makes no judgement as to what should be avoided or pursued. In this state therefore the mind initiates no movement; for all movement is a pursuit of, or withdrawal from, something, by way of appetition.

§ 814. Again, the mind sometimes considers something to be done, yet not in a practical or effective way, but only speculatively,—considering it universally, not in view of an action in the particular. So he says that so far as the 'speculative' mind considers 'something of this kind', i.e. as the intellect regards even a practical affair in a merely speculative way, it makes no decision as yet about decision or flight. Thus we can often think of terrible or desirable things without commanding ourselves to fear or desire them; even if, for example, our hearts are moved by fear. And if, he adds, it is a desirable thing that moves us, it does so through some other organ than the heart.

§ 815. (This he adds with Plato in mind, who located the parts of the soul in different parts of the body, the irascible part, whence fear arises, in the heart; and the concupiscible in some other organ such as the liver.) Clearly then a merely speculative consideration, even of something practical, does not of itself move to action. As such the speculative intellect is in no way a motive power.

§ 816. Next at 'Further, when',[1] he shows that not even the practical intellect moves to action. For when a man, he says, comes to a decision, understanding that something should be avoided or pursued, he may nevertheless fail to follow this intellectual decision and follow his feelings instead,—as incontinent people do, who know what ought to be done but fail to carry it out. It would seem therefore that mere intellect does not suffice to move us. Similarly, doctors may know quite well how to recover health, yet not recover it, because they fail to put into practice their own prescriptions. Apparently then, to act according to knowledge involves something else besides even practical knowledge.

§ 817. Lastly, with 'But not even appetition',[2] he shows that the appetitive part itself does not simply command our movements; for we may see continent people in a state of want and desire yet

[1] 433ᵃ 1.   [2] 433ᵃ 6.

refusing to act according to their desires. And the converse is true of the incontinent, as he explains more clearly in the *Ethics*, Book VII.[1] So it seems that neither is appetition the cause of movement.

[1] E.N., VII, c.3; 1146^b 20.

BOOK III, CHAPTER X

THE PRINCIPLES OF MOVEMENT
IN LIVING BEINGS CONTINUED
WHAT THEY ARE

IT SEEMS THAT THERE ARE TWO MOTIVE-FORCES, MIND
and appetency (if one is to account imagination a sort
of mind. For many follow the imagination instead of
intellectual knowledge, while in other animals there is no intellect or reason at all, but only imagination). Both of these
effect movement in place then,—intellect and appetency.

§§ 818–19

Now, the intellectual power which reasons to some purpose in view, and is practical, differs in its end from the
speculative. Appetition also is always for a purpose; for that
of which there is desire is the principle of the practical intellect. The last end is the first principle of action. Hence, it
seems reasonable to take these two as the motive forces,
appetition, and the practical reason. For the object of appetite
causes motion; and it is for this that reason also initiates movement, the desirable being its principle. And when imagination moves, it only does so with appetition. Therefore there
is one single mover,—the object desired. For if there were
two movers, intellect and appetition, they would move in
virtue of some common principle.[1] Now reason does not
appear to cause movement apart from appetency; for will is

---

[1] 'in virtue etc.' is not in Pirotta's text of M., but seems to be supposed by
St. Thomas (§ 824).

an appetency. When there is movement by reason there is also movement by will. But appetition moves apart from reason, for concupiscence is a sort of appetition.   §§ 820–5

All intellect, then, is right, but imagination and appetition may be right or not right. Hence, while the object of appetite is always what motivates, this can be either a good or only a seeming good. Not, however, every good, but the practical good. Now a practical object is that which is able to be other than it is. It is therefore evident that what moves the soul is a power of this kind called appetite.   §§ 826–7

For those who divide the soul into parts, if they split it up by distinguishing its powers, a great many parts result: the vegetative, the sensitive, the intellective, the deliberative, and lastly the appetitive. These differ from one another much more than do the concupiscible and irascible.   § 828

Since appetites may run counter to one another, this occurs when reason and desire are contrary (and only in beings possessing a time-sense. Reason commands restraint for the sake of some future thing, but desire is for what is now present. For what appears desirable at any given instant appears desirable without qualification and good without qualification; because the future is not apparent).   § 829

The motive-force will therefore be specifically one,—the desirable, or the appetite itself; and first of all the desirable, for this is what causes motion without itself being moved, simply through being understood or imagined,—but numerically there are several moving factors.   § 830

Since there are these three: the mover; secondly, that by which it moves; thirdly, that which is moved; and since the mover is double (the immobile one, and the mover that is also moved) the immobile mover is, accordingly, the practical good, whereas that which both moves and is moved is the appetite. For the subject desiring is moved in so far as it desires, and its desire is an act or movement of a certain kind. What receives the motion is the animal. But that by which it moves is an organ, already something corporeal. Hence, what pertains to it must be studied along with activities common to body and soul. · §831

Now, in short, organic movement arises where the principle and term are the same: as in the joint of a hinge are the convex and the concave,—the latter being the end, the former the beginning.[1] Hence one is at rest while the other moves. They are distinct in idea, but inseparable spatially. All things move by pushing and pulling. Hence there must, as in a circle, be something that stays still; from which [point] movement begins. §§832-5

[1] 'The former the end, the latter the beginning', 433^{b} 23.

ST. THOMAS'S COMMENTARY
LECTIO FIFTEEN

§ 818. So far the Philosopher has pursued his enquiry into the principle of local movement in animals by the method of refuting unsatisfactory solutions; but now he states the positive truth on the matter: first, showing in general what that principle is;[1] and secondly, at 'Generally then',[1] how it varies in different subjects. The first point again divides into (a) a statement of the motive-principle in animals; and (b), at 'The motive-force will therefore',[2] an analysis of the factors at work when this principle is in action. Again (a) subdivides into three points: (1) That there are two motive-principles; which (2) he reduces to one, at 'Now the intellectual power',[3] while with (3) he answers an objection (at 'Since appetites . . .')[4] already raised.

First, then, he says that the foregoing examination makes it clear that neither the vegetative nor the sensitive part is the motive-principle, since they are found in things that do not move. So it would seem that the moving principles are two: intellect and appetency. Note, however, that he includes imagination under intellect; for it resembles intellect in that it impels to action in the absence of sense-objects.

§ 819. For in their actions many people follow the changes in their imaginations rather than rational knowledge; for instance, those who act impulsively without reflection. Besides, other animals are obviously only impelled to action through imagination, not through intellect or reason; but men through both intellect and imagination. Clearly, then, both these are motive-principles: intellect (including imagination) and appetition.

§ 820. Then at 'Now the intellectual,'[5] he reduces the two to

---

[1] Lectio 16, § 836; 433^b 27. [2] § 830; 433^b 10.
[3] § 820; 433^a 13. [4] § 829; 433^b 5. [5] 433^a 13.

one; and this in three stages: (1) justifying the reduction; (2), at 'All intellect, then, is right,'[1] using it to show the cause of a particular accidental factor in animal movements; and (3) refuting, at 'For those who divide',[2] an early division of the powers of the soul.

First, then, he says that the mind as a motive-principle is the mind in so far as it reasons for some purpose other than mere reasoning; in other words, it is the practical reason, which differs from the speculative by a different finality; for while the latter regards truth for its own sake and nothing else, the practical reason relates its knowledge of truth to some deed to be done.

§ 821. Now obviously every appetition is for some end beyond itself. It is absurd to say that desire is for the sake of desiring; desire is essentially a tendency to 'the other'. Moreover, an object of desire is always the practical reason's starting point; what is first desired provides the end whence its deliberations begin. If we wish to weigh a course of action we first lay down some end and then deliberate about the means, moving back, so to say, from what is to come later on to what is immediately to be done at the beginning. So he adds that the last thing that the practical reason considers is the first thing that has to be done—i.e. the starting point of the whole action. This is why it is reasonable to assert that both appetition and the practical reason are motive-principles; for the object desired certainly incites to action, and it is also what the practical reason first considers; so that the latter is said to impel to action because the starting point of its deliberations, the object desired, does so.

§ 822. And what is said of the intellect may be applied to the imagination; if it moves it does so only in virtue of an object desired: of which it contains, like the intellect, a representation.

§ 823. So it is clear that there is ultimately one mover, the object desired. For this both moves appetition and affords a starting point for the practical intellect—the two motive-principles which have been assumed.

§ 824. And it is reasonable that these two principles should be reduced to unity in the object of desire; for if both intellect and appetition are principles with respect to one and the same movement they must, as such, share the same specific nature; since a single effect implies always a single cause of precisely that one

[1] 433ᵃ 26.   [2] 433ᵇ 1.

effect. Now it cannot be said that appetite is a moving principle through sharing the specific nature of intellect, but rather *e converso*; for intellect only moves anything in virtue of appetition. It moves by means of the will, which is a sort of appetition.

§ 825. The explanation of this (given in Book IX of the *Metaphysics*)[1] is that the practical reason is essentially balanced between alternatives; nor can it initiate movement unless appetition fixes it exclusively upon one alternative. Appetition, on the other hand, can move to action independently of reason, as we see in the case of the concupiscible desire which is a sort of appetite. He mentions this desire rather than the irascible because, unlike the irascible, it has no admixture of rationality (as he shows in Book VII of the *Ethics*).[2] Clearly, then, the motive-principles are reducible to the one object of appetition.

§ 826. Next at 'All intellect then',[3] he applies what has been said to a particular accidental factor in movement or action, explaining why we go amiss in our actions. 'All intellect', he says, 'is right', by which he means that we never err about the first principles of action, about such truths as 'it is wrong to do harm to anyone', or 'injustice is never right', and so on. Those principles correspond to the equally infallible first principles of the speculative reason. But as for the consequences of these first principles, if we apprehend them aright it is because our thought is consistent with our grasp of the principles, whereas if we deviate from the truth the fault lies in our reasoning. Appetition and imagination (motive-principles likewise) may be, on the other hand, either right or wrong. Hence if we act amiss it is, in the last analysis, because we fall short of what we intellectually know; and our previous conclusion stands, that the final motive-impulse comes from the object of desire.

§ 827. Now this object is either a real good or a seeming good: it is a real good if the mind's original correct judgement is maintained; it is only a seeming good if appetite or imagination cause a deflection from that judgement. Yet not every good is desirable as a cause of action, but only the good-as-term-of-action, i.e. a good that is actually related to our actions.[4] And precisely as such no such good is always good in the same way; for it must vary in relation to ourselves. That is why the ultimate and absolute good,

[1] IX, c.5; 1048ª 5ss.   [2] E.N., VII, c.6; 1149ª 25ss.
[3] 433ª 26.   [4] *bonum applicatum ad operationem* . . .

regarded in its universality, does not, as such, move us to act. Clearly, then, the final motive force derives from the soul itself acting through the appetitive power.

§ 828. Then at 'For those who divide',[1] he rejects an old division of the motive parts of the soul into the rational, irascible and concupiscible potencies. If, he says, the intention was to enumerate the potencies which are really distinct from each other, others should have been included, namely the vegetative, sensitive, intellectual, deliberative and appetitive powers. These last two are distinguished in the same way and for the same reason as, in the *Ethics*,[2] Book VI, Aristotle distinguishes the ratiocinative faculty, which has to do with contingent matters, from the scientific faculty which has to do with necessary objects. All these parts of the soul differ more than the irascible and concupiscible, which are both included in the sensitive appetite. Hence that old division was incomplete.

§ 829. Next, at 'Since appetites may'[3] he meets an objection already touched upon,[4] namely that if desire were a motive force, nobody would be continent; the continent, by definition, do *not* follow their desires. But this difficulty vanishes if we consider that in man there are contrary appetites, of which the continent follow one and reject the rest.[5] Contrariety of desires springs out of an opposition between reason and the concupiscible appetite; and this happens 'in beings possessing a time-sense', i.e. that are aware, not of the present moment only, but of past and future as well. For sometimes the mind forbids a man to indulge a desire in view of what will happen in the future if it is indulged: thus a man in a state of fever sees with his mind that he ought to abstain from drinking wine. But desire prompts one to take things for the sake of 'what is now', i.e. in the present moment. For what is here and now pleasant seems absolutely pleasant and good if it is not related to the future.

§ 830. Then at 'The motive-force'[6] he analyses the process of the movements in question; and this in three stages. First, he shows how the factors in movement are at once many and one. Next, at 'Since there are these three',[7] he explains how they are interrelated. Finally, at 'Now, in short . . .'[8] he briefly defines each of the factors

[1] 433[b] 1.   [2] E.N., VI, cc.3–5.   [3] 433[b] 5.   [4] § 817.
[5] Reading *alii* as *alios*.   [6] 433[b] 10.   [7] 433[b] 13.   [8] 433[b] 21.

on which movement depends. First, then, he observes that if the moving principles are considered formally and specifically they are reducible to one, to the object of desire or appetite; for this is the absolute starting point of movement, inasmuch as, being itself unmoved, it initiates movement through the mind or the imagination. And because the secondary motive-principles only move in virtue of their share in the primary one, therefore they all as such partake of the nature of this primary one. And yet, though specifically one, they are numerically many.

§ 831. Then at 'Since there are these three',[1] he interrelates three factors in movement: (1) the mover, (2) the organ by which it moves, and (3) the thing moved. Now the mover is twofold: an unmoved mover, and a mover that moves through being moved itself. In the case of animals, the unmoved mover is some actual good influencing desire through the intellect or imagination. The mover moved is the desire itself; for whatever desires is moved inasmuch as it desires, desire itself being a certain act or movement in the sense that we give to the term 'movement' when we apply it to activities that are *consequent* upon actuality,[2] such as sensing and understanding. Then the thing moved is the animal itself. And the organ by means of which desire issues into movement is a part of the body; it is the primary motor-organ; hence it has to be treated along with the activities common to body and soul (and is, in fact, examined in the *De Causa Motus Animalium*).[3] But here and now we are concerned particularly with the soul.

§ 832. Next, at 'Now, in short . . .',[4] he briefly states his view on the organ of local motion. He says that the primary organic motive-principle must be such that the movement starts and finishes in the same point, proceeding in a circle, as it were, and having a swelling out at the starting point and a concavity at the end. For the contractual movement draws the organ into concavity, while the expansive impulse, whence movement begins, follows a swelling out of the organ.

§ 833. Now, granted that this primary organ is both the starting point and term of movement, it must, as starting point, be motionless, and, as term, in movement; and both these at once. For in any movement the starting point itself does not move, all movement

---

[1] 433^b 13.   [2] *prout motus est actus perfecti.*

[3] *De Motu Animalium*, c.6; 706^b 15ss.   [4] 433^b 21.

must proceed from the motionless,—as, for instance, while the hand is moving the arm is still, and while the arm moves the shoulder is still. However, these two factors in the organ, the motionless and the moved, though distinct in thought, are substantially and spatially inseparable.

§ 834. And that the organ is both starting point and term (and therefore both motionless and moved) is clear from the fact that all animal movements consist of impulsions and retractions. In impulsion the motive force comes from the *starting point*, for the impelling agent thrusts itself *forward* against what is impelled. But in retraction the motive force comes from the *term*, for the drawing power draws something *back* to itself. Thus the first organ of local motion in animals must be at once both a starting point and a term.

§ 835. So then there must be in it something that stays still and yet initiates motion. And in this it resembles circular movement: for a body revolving in a circle is kept *as a whole* in the same place by the immobility of the centre and the poles. In thought it may move as a whole, but not in reality. In reality it keeps to one place. But its parts are changing their places really, and not only in thought. And so it is with the heart: it remains fixed in the same part of the body while it dilates and contracts and so gives rise to movements of impulsion and retraction. Thus it is, in a sense, both motionless and moving.

BOOK III, CHAPTER X, CONTINUED

THE PRINCIPLES OF MOVEMENT
IN LIVING BEINGS, CONTINUED

GENERALLY, THEN, AN ANIMAL IS SELF-MOVING IN-asmuch as it is appetitive, as we have said. But there is never appetition apart from imagination; and all imagination is either rational or sensitive. It is in the latter, then, that other animals also participate. §§ 836–7

CHAPTER XI

Now we must consider the motive force in those imperfect animals in which there exists no sense but touch; and whether or no they have imagination and desire. Pain and pleasure do seem to be present in them; and if these, then, necessarily, desire as well. But how can there be imagination in them? It may be that as they are moved indeterminately, so these qualities are present indeed in them, but only indeterminately. §§ 838–9

Sensitive imagination, then, is found in other animals, as we have said; but the deliberative only in rational beings. For [to deliberate] whether to do this or that is the work of reason, and there must be a single standard to measure by; for the agent follows the more excellent. Hence [reason] is able to make one phantasm out of several. And this is why the [irrational animals] are thought not to have opinion; they lack that which derives from reasoning; which, indeed, involves opinion. For this reason [the lower] appetite is without deliberation.　　　　　　§§ 840-2

Appetite sometimes overcomes and moves deliberation. But sometimes the latter moves the former, like a heavenly sphere; one appetition governing another, as in continence.[1] Naturally the higher principle always holds priority, and originates motion, so that movement occurs on three[2] courses.　　　　　　§§ 843-4

The cognitive faculty does not move, but remains at rest. But since one judgement or conception is universal, while the other is particular, it is the former that dictates that such and such a man should perform such and such an action; whilst the latter says that *this* is such an action and I am such and such a man. It is *this* opinion, not the universal, that causes movement; or both together; but the one as being more at rest, the other less so.　　　　　　§§ 845-6

[1] The Greek is doubtful here; possibly three states are being contrasted: (1) irrational desire overcoming deliberation; (2) *vice versa*; (3) one irrational desire overcoming another. St. Thomas—and perhaps M.—combines (2) and (3), or rather absorbs (3) in (2). 'Continence', *continentia*, should be 'incontinence', ἀκρασία: Aristotle's name for state (1). State (2) is ἐγκράτεια, which St. Thomas calls *continentia* (§ 843, and *see* footnote *in loco*).

[2] St. Thomas takes this last clause as part of the sentence beginning 'Naturally'. But 'Naturally . . . motion' is a parenthesis. 'So that' should refer back to the sentence preceding the parenthesis.

ST. THOMAS'S COMMENTARY
LECTIO SIXTEEN

§ 836. The Philosopher now passes from a general consideration of the principle of local movement in itself to viewing it in relation to different types of animal. And he does three things here. First, he states what is common to all animals that move; then, at 'Now we must consider',[1] he discusses the motive-principle of imperfect animals; and thirdly, at 'Sensitive imagination', that of the most perfect animal, man, in whom this principle exists in a unique way.

First, then, he observes that all animals have the power of self-movement inasmuch as they have appetition; for appetition is precisely the cause of movement. Now appetition connotes imagination, either rational or merely sensuous; and while the latter is found in other animals, the former is proper to man alone.

§ 837. Note, however, that, just as Aristotle has included imagination under the term 'intellect',[2] so now he extends the term 'imagination' to denote something intellectual; and in this he is guided by the meaning of the term itself. For imagination[3] is a sort of appearance;[4] and things 'appear' to both sense and intellect. Besides, imagination can function, like reason or intellect, in the absence of exterior sense-objects.

§ 838. Then, at 'Now we must consider',[5] he points to the motive-principle in imperfect animals, that is, in those which have no sense but touch. We must ask, he says, what it is that moves these animals: can it be imagination and desire? They seem indeed to have desires, for they seem to feel joy and displeasure: they shrink back when touched by things that trouble them, but open out and extend themselves towards things that suit them,

---

[1] 433[b] 31.   [2] §§ 818–19.   [3] *phantasia*.

[4] *apparitio*.   [5] 433[b] 31.

which implies a sense of pain and pleasure. And this in turn implies desire. And since desire springs from a sense of pleasure it must involve some kind of image-representation.

§ 839. But of what kind is this? An answer, he says, may be gleaned from considering the movements of these animals. They do not move as with a definite end in view, as if intending to arrive at any particular spot, as do the animals that move from one place to another and that form an inward image of things at a distance, and so desire these things and move towards them. The imperfect animals form images only of objects actually present to their exterior sense—not of things at a distance. When they are hurt the image which they form conveys to them the exterior object as harmful, and thus they shrink from it. And as soon as anything affords them pleasure they reach out to it and cling to it. Thus both imagination and desire in them are *indefinite*, in the sense that they form images which warn or attract them without being images of any distinct thing in this or that definite place. They have a *confused* imagination and desire.

§ 840. Next, at 'Sensitive imagination',[1] he points out the motive-principle in man; and this in three stages. He shows first how this principle is the deliberative reason; next, at 'Appetite sometimes overcomes',[2] how it is sometimes overcome by desire; and thirdly, at 'The cognitive faculty',[3] of what 'reason' he is speaking here. First, then, he says that while sensuous imagination exists also in other animals,[4] deliberative imagination is proper to rational ones; to deliberate, that is to weigh alternatives, is a function of reason.

§ 841. And this deliberation requires some sort of rule or end by which to reckon what most needs to be done. Clearly, a man will 'follow', i.e. seek for, the better and more suitable alternative: which is always measured by some standard. We need therefore a measure for our actions, a criterion for discerning what is most worth doing. And this will be the middle term of the syllogism of the practical reason issuing in a choice. It follows that reason, deliberating, can form several images into a unity—three, to be precise; for one object is preferred to another, and a third gives the standard of preference.

[1] 434[a] 5.   [2] 434[a] 12.
[3] 434[a] 16.   [4] cf. §§ 657, 838.

§ 842. We can see now why animals form no opinions, though they have images. They cannot prefer one thing to another by any process of reasoning. Rational deliberation, however, issues in opinion—else it would not unify a number of phantasms. Similarly, the lower appetite springing from imagination is non-deliberate: it moves at once into desire or repulsion following the sensuous imagination.

§ 843. Next, at 'Appetite sometimes',[1] he explains how rational deliberation may yield to the lower desire, may be overcome by it and drawn away from its own decision. Again, conversely, the superior appetite that follows rational deliberation sometimes sways the lower one that follows sensuous images (as a higher heavenly body may impel a lower). This happens in the case of 'continence'; for the continent are those in whom deliberation gets the better of passion.[2]

§ 844. Note that it is according to nature that the higher appetite should sway the lower. We see this in the heavenly bodies; the higher sphere gives the first impetus, moving the lower which, in turn, has a three-fold local movement. For the sphere, e.g., of Saturn moves first in diurnal motion, turning about the poles of the Universe; then in the contrary zodiacal motion; and thirdly, in its own proper motion. Likewise, the lower appetite, retaining something of its own proper movement, is also moved by another, and this naturally, following the impulse of the higher appetite and of rational deliberation. If the converse takes place, and the higher is in fact moved by the lower, this is contrary to the natural order of things.

§ 845. Then, at 'the cognitive faculty',[3] he explains which 'reason' it is that initiates movement. It is not the speculative reason (here called 'cognitive'); for this remains quiet and still and makes no decisions about tending to or away from anything, as we have seen.[4] And as for the practical reason, it is either universal or particular. By the universal practical reason we judge that such and such ought to be done, e.g. that children ought to

---

[1] 434ᵃ 12.

[2] *Continentia* is present when rational deliberation governs the sense-appetite, but with the latter still in revolt. It is therefore an imperfect state compared with the full virtue of *temperantia* (S.T., II–II, 155, 1). *See* note 1, p. 478.

[3] 434ᵃ 16.   [4] § 813.

honour their parents. By the particular practical reason we judge
that this particular subject *is* such and such, e.g. that I am a son
and I ought here and now to honour my parents.

§ 846. Now it is this latter judgement that moves to action, not
the other universal one;—or, if both move, the universal moves as
a first and motionless cause of movement, the particular as a
proximate cause already, to a certain extent, applied to the movement itself. For deeds and movements are in the particular, and
if any movement is actually to take place, the universal opinion
must be particularised. In the same way the commission of any
sinful action implies that one's good judgement as to what should
be done in the particular is neutralised by a pleasure or emotion
of some kind; one's universal opinion remaining, however,
unaltered.

BOOK III, CHAPTER XII

SENSITIVITY AND LIFE
TOUCH IS THE FUNDAMENTAL SENSE

ALL LIVING THINGS HAVE THE VEGETATIVE SOUL; and this from generation to corruption. For every thing generated must grow, maintain itself and then decay; and this is impossible without nutriment. Of necessity, then, a vegetative power is found in all that is born and dies.

§§ 847–8

Sensation, however, is not necessarily found in everything that lives. Beings whose bodies are uncompounded even lack touch, without which no animal can exist at all; nor can those be animals which are unable to receive forms without matter.

§§ 849–50

But if Nature does nothing in vain, animals must have sensation. For all things in Nature exist for a purpose, or accompany that which exists for a purpose. Every body that is able to move about, if it lacked sensation, would soon be destroyed, and would never attain its end, which is the purpose of Nature. For how would it be nourished? Immobile animals indeed find nourishment in that out of which they are produced.[1]

§§ 851–3

But a body, generated, not stationary, cannot possess a soul and intellectual discernment and yet not have sensation,

[1] 'have grown', 434^b 2.

(nor indeed can an ungenerated one). For why should it not have it? For the good [presumably] of either the soul or the body. But neither, surely. The soul would not think better nor the body benefit on that account. No animal then, whose body is mobile, lacks sensation.   §§ 854–7

But having sensation, a body must needs be either simple or compound. It cannot, however, be simple; for then it would lack touch, and it must have this sense.   § 858

Which is evident from these considerations. Since an animal is an animate body, and every body is tangible, and the tangible is what is perceptible by touch, the animal's body must be able to touch if it is to survive. For the other senses perceive through an extraneous medium; e.g. smell, sight, hearing. But if the animal that comes into contact [with other things] had no sense of touch it could not avoid certain things and seize upon others; and thus it could not preserve its existence.   §§ 859–60

This is why taste is a kind of touch; for food is a tangible body. But sound and colour and smell do not nourish, or contribute to growth or decay. Taste must then be a kind of touch, being a sense of the tangible and the nutritive. These senses then are necessary to the animal. Hence it is plain that no animal can exist without touch.   § 861

The others exist for its greater good; and then not in every kind of animal, but in some, namely in those that need to move from place to place. For if [such] an animal is to survive it must perceive not only what is in contact with it, but also what is afar; and this will happen, if it perceives through a medium, this being affected and moved by the sense object, and the animal itself by the medium.   § 862

It is [as when] a thing is moving locally: it operates till it affects a change and, impelling something else, causes another impulsion, so that movement traverses a medium. The first mover causes motion and is unmoved: the last is moved, moving nothing else; but the intermediary is both; or the many intermediaries. So it is with the alteration in question, except that what is changed remains in the same place. If one dips an object into wax, the wax moves to the extent that the object enters it; whereas a stone is not moved at all; but water a long way, and air most of all, giving and receiving motion, so long as it remains a unity. Hence, as regards reflection, it is better to say that the air is affected by shape and colour, so long as it retains unity, than to say that the sight proceeds out and is reflected back. On a smooth surface [air] has unity, and so in turn, moves the sight; as if a seal were to sink into and right through wax. §§ 863–4

§ 847. After taking the various parts of the soul in turn, and discussing each one separately, the Philosopher now shows how they are interrelated: explaining, first, that the vegetative part is common to all animate beings, and then, at 'Sensation is not necessarily found',[1] that the sphere of sensitivity is more limited.

In the light, then, of his previous conclusions[2] he observes, first, that all beings that participate in any way in soul must, from the first moment of their generation until their final corruption, have some share in the vegetative principle; indicating by these terms that he speaks especially of animate beings which come to being through generation and cease through corruption.

§ 848. And he proves the point thus. No animate and generated being can exist without passing through the stages of growth, maturity and decline. And these all presuppose food. Growth implies that more food is being absorbed by a subject than is needed to maintain its existing bulk. Maturity implies à balance of food and bulk; whilst in decline less food is being absorbed than suffices to maintain the subject's bulk. And as it pertains to the vegetative principle to make use of food, this principle must be common to everything that is born and that dies; and must be related to the other parts of soul as the foundation they all presuppose.

§ 849. Then, at 'Sensation etc.',[3] he shows how sensitivity is related to living things: and first, that it is not found in all of them; secondly, at 'But if Nature'. . . ,[4] where it is found. First, then, he remarks that touch (the sense presupposed by all the other senses, and therefore by all animal life as such) need not exist

[1] 434ᵃ 27.   [2] §§ 262–846.
[3] 434ᵃ 27.   [4] 434ᵃ 31.

wherever life exists. The organ of touch requires (as we have seen)[1] a sort of balance of contrary qualities; hence it cannot exist in *simple* bodies, which are characterised by the predominance of some one particular sensible quality—as heat in fire or cold in water.

§ 850. Similarly, whatever is unable to receive into itself forms free from matter cannot sense; for this way of receiving forms is, as we have seen,[2] essential to sensitivity. Now plants, because in them the earthy element predominates, so that they are near neighbours to the simple bodies, are unable to receive forms from outside, except with a material alteration. Not all living things, therefore, are sensitive.

§ 851. Then, at 'But if Nature',[3] he shows that all animals are sensitive. He does this (1) with regard to animals that can move from place to place; and (2) with regard to all animals without exception, at 'But having sensation'.[4] As regards (1) he first proves his point; and then, at 'But a body . . .'[5] refutes a possible objection. To prove that all animals are sensitive he assumes as a principle that Nature does nothing in a purposeless way. Everything in Nature has a reason, exists to supply the needs of purposeful being. Thus in order that certain activities may be carried out, things have a natural equipment of suitable organs. These organs, it is true, being composed in this or that way, have certain accidental qualities or adjuncts, e.g. hairs or colours, not to mention innate weaknesses, which are due rather to the matter of which they are composed than to the ends which they subserve. But since Nature always does act for an end, whatever natural thing simply could *not* reach a natural end would be quite out of place in Nature.

§ 852. Now Nature has adapted the bodies of mobile animals for movement; and they move for the sake of obtaining the food which keeps them alive. And to this end they require sense-awareness; otherwise they would not perceive the noxious things to which their movement sometimes brings them, and thus they would die and the very purpose of their movements would be frustrated. For they move about in order to get food, and could not get it otherwise.

[1] §§ 521-4.   [2] §§ 284, 551, 792.   [3] 434ᵃ 31.
[4] 434ᵇ 9.   [5] 434ᵇ 2.

§ 853. (The case of immobile animals is not relevant here, for the food they naturally require is joined to their substance; they do not have to seek it at a distance.) Clearly then, if mobile animal bodies lacked sense-awareness they could not reach the end for which Nature designs them. They would be futile; which is an unacceptable conclusion.

§ 854. Next, at 'But a body etc.',[1] he removes a possible objection. It might be suggested that some moving animal bodies could reach their natural end through an intellectual awareness of things that would do them harm, even though they lacked sense-awareness. But Aristotle rejects this hypothesis with respect to mobile animals, whether these come into existence by generation or no. The point has been proved with regard to generated animals; for the only animate things that come into being by generation and are endowed with intellect are human beings, and the human mind presupposes sensation, as we have seen.[2]

§ 855. But his rejection of the suggestion that intellect might exist without sensitivity in non-generated living things may seem at variance with Aristotle's own opinion. For it was his view that the heavenly bodies are both animate and intelligent, and yet lack sensitivity because their bodies are not organised into the distinct parts which alone make sensation possible. Hence some commentators make the sentence end at 'yet not have sensation'; and its meaning they take to be that no mobile body can be intelligent, lacking sensitivity, provided that it is a *generated* body. And what follows—'nor indeed etc.'—they take as the beginning of a new sentence, meaning that the case of non-generated bodies is different.

§ 856. Hence, according to their view, what follows, namely 'Why should they not etc.', must not be understood as an interrogation, but as a relative clause inserted to explain why non-generated bodies, i.e. the heavenly bodies, lack a sense-apparatus even while they *have* intelligence: Aristotle's argument (they say) being that neither the body nor the soul of a heavenly body would get any benefit from its having senses;—not the soul, because it would not understand any better thereby, since its understanding, like that of spiritual substances, bears upon the purely intelligible; nor yet the body, because, being essentially

[1] 434^b 2.   [2] §§ 772; 791.

incorruptible anyhow, its senses would play no part in maintaining its existence.

However, this interpretation hardly squares with the conclusion which follows, namely that no animate body which has the power to move from place to place lacks sensitivity (unless we choose to relate this conclusion to the previous statement;[1] not to the immediately preceding one).

§ 857. Since, then, this seems a forced interpretation, it is better to understand by 'non-generated body', not any heavenly body, but the bodies of certain airy animate beings called by the Platonists *demons*. Apuleius, for instance, defined them as airbodied animate beings, rational, passive,[2] eternal. And it would be concerning these beings, then, that the Philosopher seeks to prove that the Platonists were wrong in allowing them intelligence without senses. So the 'Why should they not' ought to be taken interrogatively, as meaning 'why should such bodies as these lack senses?' For, if they *do* lack them, this must be for the good either of their soul or their body; and neither reason is valid; for without senses their souls would understand no better, nor would their bodies be any the less corruptible. And the conclusion immediately follows, as given above, namely that no living bodies that are able to move about in space lack sensation. That this is indeed Aristotle's meaning appears from his immediately adding that no simple body can possibly be the body of an animal.

§ 858. Then at 'But having'[3] he proves the absolute necessity, for all animals, of sensitivity; first proving the point, then at 'It is then evident',[4] drawing a conclusion. The proof subdivides. Thus: (1) he puts forward his own view; (2) he proves it, at 'Which is evident from these considerations'.[5] His own view contains two points, of which the first is that whatever body has sensation must be either simple or mixed. But it cannot be simple; for if it were it would lack the sense of touch; which he has already shown to be necessary for all animals, not only the mobile but also the immobile.[6]

§ 859. Then, at 'Which is evident',[7] he proceeds to show (1)

---

[1] Presumably to § 854.   [2] *animo passiva.*   [3] 434[b] 9.

[4] Lectio 18, § 869; 435[b] 4.   [5] 434[b] 11.

[6] § 849; cf. §§ 260, 266, 288, 300, 484, 602.   [7] 434[b] 11.

that touch is found in all animals; (2) at 'It is clearly impossible',[1] that no animal body can be a simple body. With regard to (1) he first shows the necessity of touch for all animals; and then, at 'The others exist',[2] that the other senses are not found in all. As to this necessity, however, having shown it in the case of touch, he then, at 'This is why taste'[3] proves that it belongs also to taste.

First, then, he observes that the necessary universality of touch in the animal world can be clearly shown. For every animal is a living body; and every body is tangible or sensible to touch. By 'body' is here meant exclusively the generable and corruptible sort of body, not the non-generated, incorruptible heavenly bodies. These latter are not tangible; being outside the sphere of the elements they lack the elemental qualities which alone are tangible. But all corruptible bodies, being either simple elements or compounds of elements, are necessarily tangible.

§ 860. Whence he concludes to the necessity, for the preservation of the bodies of animals, that they be endowed with touch. For they are tangible, i.e. made up of tangible qualities; and so are the other bodies which actually touch them; and in the course of nature the animal's body might well be so affected by these latter bodies as to be destroyed by them. It is not the same with those senses whose medium of contact with their objects is not by touch, i.e. smell, sight and hearing; for their objects, being at a distance, do not actually touch the animal's body; they cannot therefore be a danger to its life, as tangible objects may be. Hence, unless the animal were able to touch, and touching to discriminate between, objects harmful and congenial to it, it could not avoid the former and accept the latter, and so preserve its existence. Touch, then, is a necessity for animals.

§ 861. Then, at 'This is why taste',[4] he shows that the same is true of taste. For taste is a kind of touch, discriminating, as it does, between the goodness or harmfulness of different foods. Now food is essentially tangible and bodily; it nourishes the body just because it has the bodily qualities of being hot, moist, cold, dry. Bodies are nourished by bodies,—not by sounds or colours or scents; for sounds, colours and scents have nothing to do with growth or decay. Savour, however, is connected with nourishment by way of the body's natural disposition. Since then taste

---

[1] Lectio 18, § 865; 435ᵃ 11.   [2] 434ᵇ 24.   [3] 434ᵇ 18.   [4] 434ᵇ 18.

perceives food, and food is something tangible in the vegetative or nutritive order, taste is a kind of touch. Both these senses then are necessary; from which it is all the more evident that animals could not exist without touch.

§ 862. Next, at 'The others exist',[1] he explains why the other senses are not found in all animals, but only in some; after which, at 'It is as when',[2] he explains one of his own expressions. First, then, he observes that the other senses, sight, hearing and smell, are required for the well-being of certain animals, but not for their bare existence. Yet for some animals (not all), these senses *are* absolutely necessary—for those, namely that can move from place to place; for these need to be able to perceive objects at a distance as well as what immediately touches them. Now to sense things at a distance is only possible though a medium; the medium being affected and altered by the object, and the sense by the medium.

§ 863. And at 'It is as when'[3] he proceeds to show this by a simile from local motion. Anything moving from place to place will cause a succession of changes which terminate at its destination; for what is first propelled forward is itself the cause of something else being propelled; so that the first agent disturbs a third thing through a medium—the first thing being a disturber itself undisturbed; the last, where the movement terminates, being disturbed but not itself a disturber; whilst the medium is both disturber and disturbed; and there may be many such media. And this order in local motion is observable also in changes by alteration: where there is a primary agent of change, a final recipient of change, and a medium both changing and changed.

§ 864. But with this difference, that, in the case of alteration, the agent of change is not moving from place to place as it changes, unlike the agent of propulsion. And he gives an example. If you touch soft wax it will be moved just so far as the warmth that accompanies your action makes the wax move. The hardness of stone would make it impervious to this kind of action; but water would be affected in this way, and still more air which is extremely mobile and has the maximum mobility at a distance from the moving agent. Air especially, then, is able to move and be moved as a medium, provided of course that it be continuous,

[1] 434[b] 24.　　　[2] 434[b] 30.　　　[3] 434[b] 30.

i.e. not interrupted by any obstacle. With regard then to the impact of an object upon the senses, it is reasonable to hold (against the Platonists who said that sight emitted rays which the visible object reflected) that the intervening air is affected by the shape and colour of an object all the way between this object and the eye; provided of course that the air be uniform and continuous and smooth. Air, on this view, itself affected by shape and colour, affects sight; so that it is the visible object which modifies all the air between itself and the eye. It is as though the shape of a seal were to modify a piece of wax right through from one side to the other.

BOOK III, CHAPTER XIII

TOUCH, THE FUNDAMENTAL SENSE

IT IS CLEARLY IMPOSSIBLE FOR THE BODY OF AN animal to be a simple element: to be, I mean, fire or air. For no other sense can exist without touch; since every animate body, as we have seen, is tactual. The sense organs, indeed, can be constituted of other elements (except earth) for they effect sensation by perceiving through some other thing, i.e. through a medium. But touch occurs by immediate contact with things; that is why it has this name. Other senses no doubt also perceive by contact, but through something else; touch alone, it would seem, through itself. Hence the body of an animal will not be of such elements as these; nor yet be earthy. For touch is a kind of mean between all tangible objects, and is receptive, not only of all the differences that characterise earth[1] but also heat and cold and all other tangible qualities. This is why we do not feel with the bones or hair or other such parts,—because they are earthy. Plants, too, have no sensation, for the same reason,—they are of earth; and without touch there can be no other sense; and this sense does not consist either of earth or of any other [single] element.   §§ 865–8

It is then evident that animals must perish if they are deprived of this sense alone. For it is neither possible for what is not an animal to possess this, nor, to be an animal, is any

---

[1] 'that characterise earth' is lacking from Pirotta's M. St. Thomas supposes it, § 867.

other necessary. And this again is why no other sense-object (e.g. colour, smell and sound) will destroy the animal by excessive intensity, but only the [corresponding] faculty of sense;—except incidentally, as when, for example, together with a sound, a thrust and a blow take place; or when other [things] are set in motion, by objects seen or smelled, which destroy by contact; and flavour too, in so far as it happens also to be tangible, may destroy thus. But an excess of tangible qualities, of heat or cold or hardness, destroys the animal itself. For as every excess in a sense-object is destructive of the sense, so may the tangible destroy touch; and by touch life itself is defined. For it has been shown that without touch no animal can exist. Hence an excess in the tangible destroys not the sense only, but the whole animal; for only this one sense is necessary to animals.　　　§§ 869–71

As we have said, the animal has other senses, not for being, but for well-being. Thus [it has] sight so that [living] in air, water, or generally in what is transparent, it may see. Taste it has on account of the pleasant or unpleasant, that it may perceive what it desires in food, and be moved towards it. Hearing it has that it may receive signs, and a tongue to signify something to another.　　　§§ 872–4

§ 865. After proving that touch must exist in all animals, the Philosopher now sets out to show that no animate body can be made up of one simple element:[1] of fire, for instance, or air,—as certain Platonists thought when they imagined animals made of air. He argues this from the fact that the other senses all presuppose touch and that therefore, as he has said already,[2] no animal can be without this sense. Every body that is both animate and sensitive must be such as is able to sense by touching. Now all the elements, except earth, can be organs of, or the medium for, the other senses: air and water for instance are adapted to sensation at a distance, which takes place through something other than the sensitive body itself, namely the medium. But touch involves no medium, it occurs by direct contact with its object. That is why it is so named: it is 'contact' *par excellence*, whereas the other senses perceive by a sort of contact, indeed, with their objects, but through a medium, not immediately. Only touch perceives of and by itself, and with no medium.

§ 866. From which it is clear that the animal body must be, of and by itself, capable of touching. This necessity is not found in the case of sight or hearing; for these senses work through an extrinsic medium. That is why the animal body cannot be made of any one single element,—not of earth alone, for earth in any case is not sensitive; nor of any of those other elements presupposed by the other senses.

§ 867. The reason is that the organ of touch must be balanced midway between the various tangible qualities; otherwise it could not receive their impressions. For as we have seen[3] already, touch is in potency to these qualities. And this is true with respect to all

[1] 435ᵃ 11.   [2] § 858, etc.   [3] §§ 521–4, 849.

tangible qualities, not to those of earth alone. Now simple bodies cannot be thus balanced half-way; they have one or other of opposed qualities to an extreme degree. Hence no simple body, nor any body approximating to simplicity, can touch. This is why we do not feel with such parts of our bodies as bones and hair, and so on, in which the element of earth so predominates that there is no balance of tangible qualities such as the sense of touch requires.

§ 868. It is for the same reason that plants lack sensitivity. They contain too much earth for touch, and without touch no other sense can exist. No simple body, then, can be animated by the sensitive soul.

§ 869. Then, at 'It is then evident',[1] as a conclusion from what has been said, he shows how all the senses are related to animals; first the sense of touch; then, at 'As we have said, the animal',[2] the other senses. First, then, he observes that, touch being necessary for all animals,[3] they would die if deprived of it alone. It is indeed convertible with animality: only the animal has touch, and all animals have it.

§ 870. And he goes on to say that, while excess in the object of the other senses can destroy these senses one by one (as excessive brightness is blinding, and excessive noise deafening) yet, because the animal can survive the loss of these senses, such excess in their objects only *indirectly* endangers its life—inasmuch, that is, as destructive *tangible* objects are brought into play, as when blasts and blows accompany noise, as in thunderstorms for instance. So also, if things seen endanger life it is not precisely as seen, but as somehow infecting the air with some poison or other. So also smells might affect the air. Similarly, a savour might harm an animal, not precisely *as* a savour, but as accompanied by some tangible quality in excess, for example heat or cold.

§ 871. On the other hand, tangible qualities can *directly* endanger an animal's life. For as any excess in the sense-object may injure the corresponding sense, an excess in the object of touch may destroy this sense; and it is on this sense that the animal's life depends. It survives just so long as it can touch. Only this sense is strictly necessary to animal life; hence its destruction involves the death of the whole animal.

[1] 435^b 4.   [2] 435^b 19.   [3] §§ 859, 865.

§ 872. Then at 'As we have said, the animal',[1] he relates the other senses to the animal as a whole; they pertain, he says, to its greater perfection; they are not sheer necessities. Thus animals that live[2] in air or water have sight in order that they may see things at a distance through air or water,—or indeed through any transparent medium, including the heavenly bodies. Similarly, animals have the sense of touch that they may find pleasure, or its contrary, in their food; and thus, taking pleasure in eating, may desire to eat, and so to look for the food they need.

§ 873. Notice that here Aristotle places taste among the senses which are not strictly necessary, whereas he had previously[3] said that it was necessary for animals; but then he was considering taste as a kind of touch—the touch of nourishment—whereas now he is considering it as a discrimination between the savours which make nourishment agreeable or disagreeable, and thus the more readily taken or rejected. And the same applies to the sense of smell; its function is to draw the animal to its food from a distance,—though indeed in man, as Aristotle explains in the *De Sensu et Sensato*,[4] smell has a different nature and utility.

§ 874. The purpose, too, of hearing is to provide communication between animals. It is necessary that animals transmit their experiences to one another; for they help one another to live; as is especially evident in the gregarious animals whose young are reared by the parent. Hence, too, the tongue is necessary that one animal may communicate, by sound, its feelings to another.

Let this suffice for the present concerning the soul.

[1] 435^b 19.
[2] Altering *qui videt* (Pirotta) to *qui vivit*.
[3] § 861.
[4] c.5; 444^a 3-20.

FINIS

INDEX TO COMMENTARY

(The numbers refer to sections)

498